PERCEPTION, MOTIVES, AND PERSONALITY

GEORGE S. KLEIN
New York University

PERCEPTION,
MOTIVES,
AND
PERSONALITY

ALFRED A. KNOPF / NEW YORK

ACKNOWLEDGMENTS

Permission to use the following selections is gratefully acknowledged.

Chapter 3, "Motives and the Perception of Objects," an extensive revision of "Perception, Motives, and Personality: A Clinical Perspective." In *Psychology of Personality*, editor, J. L. McCary. New York: Logos Press, 1956, pages 121–199. Permission granted by Leonard Small, for both Leonard Small and Leopold Bellak.

Chapter 4, "A Clinical Perspective for Personality Research," first published in *The Journal of Abnormal and Social Psychology*, 44: 42–49, 1949. Reprinted by permission of The American Psychological Association.

Chapter 5, "The Personal World through Perception," first published in *Perception: An Approach to Personality*, editors, R. R. Blake and G. V. Ramsey. New York: Ronald Press, 1951, pages 328–355. Reprinted by permission.

Chapter 6, "Need and Regulation," first published in *Nebraska Symposium on Motivation: 1954*, editor, M. R. Jones. Lincoln: University of Nebraska Press, 1954, pages 224–274. Copyright of article assigned to George S. Klein by the University of Nebraska Press.

Chapter 7, "Cognitive Control and Motivation," first published in *Assessment of Human Motives*, editor, G. Lindzey. New York: Holt, Rinehart and Winston, 1958, pages 87–118. Reprinted by permission of the editor and the publisher.

Chapter 8, "Consciousness in Psychoanalytic Theory: Some Implications for Current Research in Perception," first published in *Journal of the American Psychoanalytic Association*, 7: 5–34, 1959. Reprinted by permission.

Chapter 9, "On Subliminal Activation," first published in *The Journal of Nervous and Mental Disease*, 128: 293–301. Copyright © 1959, The Williams & Wilkins Company, Baltimore, Maryland, 21202, U.S.A. Reprinting permission. Alfred A. Knopf.

Chapter 10, "On Inhibition, Disinhibition and 'Primary Process' in Thinking," first published in *Proceedings of the XIV International Congress of Applied Psychology*, Vol. 4, *Clinical Psychology*, editor, G. Nielson. Copenhagen: Munksgaard, 1961, pages 179–198. Also in *Psychoanalysis in America: Historical Perspectives*, editor, M. H. Sherman, 1966, pages 456–473. Courtesy of Charles C Thomas, Publisher. Permission also granted by Murray H. Sherman and Munksgaard; International Booksellers and Publishers, Ltd.

Chapter 11, "The Several Grades of Memory," first published in *Psychoanalysis—A General Psychology: Essays in Honor of Heinz Hartmann*, editors, R. M. Loewenstein, L. M. Newman, M. Schur, and A. J. Solnit. New York: International Universities Press, 1966, pages 377–389. Reprinted by permission.

Chapter 12, "Blindness and Isolation," first published in *The Psychoanalytic Study of the Child*, 17: 82–93. New York: International Universities Press, 1962. Reprinted by permission.

Chapter 13, "On Hearing One's Own Voice: An Aspect of Cognitive Control in Spoken Thought," first published in *Psychoanalysis and Current Biological Thought*, editors, N. S. Greenfield and W. C. Lewis. Madison: University of Wisconsin Press, 1965, pages 245–273. Reprinted with permission of the copyright owners, the Regents of the University of Wisconsin. Also (revised) in *Drives, Affects, Behavior*, Vol. 2, editor, M. Schur. New York: International Universities Press, 1965, pages 87–117. Reprinted by permission of the publisher.

Chapter 14, "Peremptory Ideation: Structure and Force in Motivated Ideas," first published in *Motives and Thought: Psychoanalytic Essays in Honor of David Rapaport*, editor, R. R. Holt. *Psychological Issues*, Monograph 18/19: 80–128, 1967. Also in *Cognition, Personality, and Clinical Psychology*, editors, R. Jessor and S. Feshbach. San Francisco: Jossey-Bass, Inc., 1967, pages 1–61.

Chapter 15, "Credo for a 'Clinical Psychologist': A Personal Reflection," first published in *Bulletin of the Menninger Clinic*, 27: 61–73, 1963. Copyright of article assigned to George S. Klein by The Menninger Foundation.

In memory of David Rapaport

Preface

The essays in this volume speak for a particular point of view in the study of perception and cognition and reflect several interlocking themes within a continuing program generated by this point of view. The unifying theme is motivated cognition. The book deals with the interplay between a person's simultaneously active motives and the conditions that support or undermine effective perceiving.

The work reported here began in the decade following World War II, when issues of motivation and perception became ascendant in American psychology. Two essays are previously unpublished, three have appeared only in rather inaccessible sources, and Chapter 3, which sets the stage for the parts that follow it, is completely rewritten from its original version and has been given a new title. All the essays have been reedited. Within each part, representing a major theme, the essays are arranged so that the reader can follow the development of the central idea.

My indebtedness to many people, in the various places and settings in which the work described in this book was carried out, is great. I cannot easily name them all without danger of significant omission, and I shall limit mention to particular friends whose presence in my professional and personal life during these years and afterward has been continuously important: Merton M. Gill, Harry Rand, Philip S. Holzman, Herbert J. Schlesinger, Riley Gardner, Jan Frank, Robert R. Holt, Margaret Brenman, Leo Garel, Gardner Murphy, Fritz Heider, David Krech, Gardner Lindzey, and Lester Luborsky. My colleague, David L. Wolitzky, contributed valuable help in updating references and footnotes.

I must single out for special mention my colleague Leo Goldberger who encouraged me in the thought that the collective appearance of these essays would add to their usefulness, and patiently assisted in making selections for this volume.

Suzette H. Annin's help has been indispensable. More than an editor, she has been alter ego and superego. She pondered the logic and expression of every thought in the book; not a phrase or reference escaped her critical eye. If the essays have virtues of clarity beyond their original form, the reader owes it to her. I regret only that my own limitations have brought the result short of the standards of precision and directness that she unrelentingly held up to me.

I wish to record my grateful acknowledgment of the grants that made possible the work and the writing time. To The Menninger Foundation I am indebted for happy and productive years; there I was given funds to develop a laboratory for studying individual differences in perception. Grants from the National Institutes of Health and The Ford Foundation have been crucial over the years. The Foundations' Fund for Research in Psychiatry made possible an especially productive sabbatical year, and more recently a Research Career Award from the National Institute of Mental Health has had immeasurable importance. I must mention too that a good many of the undertakings that appear here came to fruition in summers at the Austen Riggs Center in the lovely Berkshire hills, first through the kindness of its late director, Dr. Robert P. Knight, who extended all kinds of help and above all friendship, and more recently through the warmth and generosity of its present director, Dr. Otto H. Will, in extending my welcome in the Riggs community.

All the wifely virtues traditionally extolled by authors for their excessive claims upon a family's forbearance, my wife, Bessie Boris Klein, has more than amply demonstrated. But most of all, the work in this book indirectly benefited from her introducing me to the world of art and from the opportunities I have had over the years to observe her artist's sensibility at work.

My lasting indebtedness to David Rapaport is expressed in the dedication of this volume. Much of the work reported here germinated in years of close collaboration with him, and from his encouragement as a teacher and friend. My knowledge of the psychoanalytic outlook I owe mostly to him. But another part of Rapaport's teaching is also vitally important: He taught an eclectic, nondoctrinaire psychoanalysis guided by the belief that it must link itself to the traditions of psychology, of which it is a part but by no means the culmination. This anchor in an integrative yet freely ranging perspective made it possible for me to draw undiminishing profit from the work of two other great teachers, R. S. Woodworth and Gardner Murphy, and later on from Henry A. Murray and Gordon W. Allport, despite the latter's own grave reservations about psychoanalysis.

I wish to thank the following editors and publishers who granted me permission to include materials that originally appeared in their publications: Dr. Leopold Bellak, Dr. Eugene L. Hartley, Dr. Gardner Lindzey, Dr. John G. Peatman, Dr. Murray H. Sherman, Dr. Leonard Small, The American Psychological Association, Inc., The American Psychoanalytic Association, International Universities Press, Inc., Jossey-Bass, Inc., The Menninger Foundation, Munksgaard Publishers, Ltd., The Ronald Press Company, Charles C Thomas, Publisher, The University of Nebraska Press, The Regents of the University of Wisconsin, and The Williams & Wilkins Company.

New York   G. S. K.
May, 1970

Contents

PART ONE

MOTIVATION IN COGNITION

Chapter 1

The Problem Stated

In different ways the essays of this book confront the dilemma posed by two contrasting approaches in psychology during the last thirty years. On the one hand is the psychophysical program epitomized in James Gibson's work; it starts from the premise that the most impressive fact about perception is its built-in means of effective coordination with the environment. On the other hand there is the person-centered point of view that sees perception as reflecting intention; aim, self-interest, and individual differences are its prominent concerns. In the psychophysicist's program for the study of perception, motivation is subordinated to the theme of how the perceptual system is equipped from the start and how it becomes ever more capable of acquiring and processing information. He searches for and accounts for this efficiency solely on the basis of properties specific to the perceptual system. The psychophysicist heckles the motivationist, "If motives are as pervasive in perceiving as you say they are, how come we perceive as effectively as we do?" The motivationist has his own challenge: "If perception is always as closely attuned to the environment as you claim it is, how come people differ in what they see? Considering that perception does its job remarkably well most of the time, how are individual differences to be explained?"

Gibson's approach and his program of "global psychophysics" have the great virtue of eliminating once and for all the notion of perception as a still camera that gives us an accurate transcription of reality. Effectiveness and accuracy are not synonymous. Gibson has focused on the informational achievements of perceiving and in that sense his is a functionalist point of view. He has, however, considered it enough to view these achievements as outcomes of "local" properties of the perceptual system, conceived as information-gathering "organs," and because of this conviction he tends to play down the vital fact that perception is not an end in itself and that it occurs in the context of *action*. Action is different from mere movement because it embodies intentions; it reflects aims and purposes. A purely perceptual psychology can thus ignore motives only by limiting itself to a narrowly tailored experimental strategy that screens out such considerations of action.

The search for a common ground between the two approaches brings certain questions to the forefront: Why and how is certain stimulus-information emphasized of the options that are potentially available, and how do we select the motivations upon which we can potentially act? By what means is responsiveness to relevant stimulation and relevant motive safeguarded? What course does behavior take when the processes that ordinarily guarantee such effective selection are in abeyance? These themes are explicit and implicit throughout this book.

The position I take is that perception is an adaptive cognitive act, always rooted in the intentional life of the person, in his motives and aims vis-à-vis the environment. Behavior answers to multiple motives yet can at the same time be effectively responsive to environmental probabilities and events. But the criteria of effective encounter are not the same for all people; perception is adaptively effective in different ways in different people. My emphasis is upon the *person*—meaning his intentionality, of which perception is a function—rather than upon perception itself as a self-contained system. This approach tries to avoid the solipsistic notion that motives distort perception; instead, the organizing properties of a class of motives that we call "executive intending"—reality-oriented motives—are an important emphasis. The studies of cognitive style described in Part Two deal with structures that develop out of the necessity for the cognitive process to achieve an adequate fit between perception and reality.

I do not want to mislead the reader by implying that a clear and certain reconciliation of points of view is provided here. I am convinced that the two approaches must converge and that each must be responsive to the other. My own interest has been to highlight aspects of the total cognitive process that a functional-motivational approach to perception brings into the foreground. Let me give an example. Current information-processing models tend to speak of perception as "essentially" a matter of "discrimination" and of "matching" and propose automaton models that reflect such input-output relationships; it is then presumed that perception is accounted for. Leaving aside the oft-made observation that such attempts stumble over issues of motivation and action, we may note an even more serious failing: They neglect the fact that, certainly in humans, perception is a distinctive kind of *experience*, different from experiences of remembering and imagery. The experiencing of information in one of these qualities rather than in another—not simply the information alone—determines how the information itself is dealt with. We try to eat not an imaged hamburger but a perceived one. In a perceptual psychology oriented toward intentionality, it is hard to ignore qualities of experienced contact, for such a psychology assumes that all aspects of experience have functional significance and that the quality, as well as the substantive contents, of an experience contributes to the adaptive effectiveness of motives and action. Viewing perception in the context of person-centered activity at least draws attention to phenomenological events that are otherwise overlooked.

In this book, the approach to motivational issues in perceiving is informed by contemporary psychoanalytic theory, particularly its conception of ego structure. The point of view of ego psychology recommends itself, first of all, by providing a broader basis for motivation than simply the derivatives of libidinal and aggressive wishes, as earlier psychoanalytic theory had it; it gives prominence to efforts at adequacy and control in the environment. At the same time, it recommends itself by its regard for issues of conflict, defensive control, and the tendency of both motives and controls to manifest themselves through perception and cognition. Furthermore, its emphasis upon the differing roles of consciousness and unconsciousness in relation to motivational effects provides still another helpful conceptual anchorage for investigation. Finally, in its concept of primary process it offers a means of ordering the twists and turns of thinking under conditions of adaptive stress and in circumstances in which the usual pragmatic concerns of everyday adaptive perceiving are in abeyance.

Some of the papers, particularly those in Part Two, originated in the unprecedented revival of interest in perception during the years immediately following World War II, the movement that David Krech dubbed the "New Look." An evaluation of this movement, in a thirteen-year hindsight, was given by Jerome Bruner and me (1960). It was a time of restless philosophical readjustments created by the war, of "New Looks" everywhere. Perhaps this climate contributed to the zeal, enthusiasm, and overstatement that characterized the New Look in psychology. For psychology in particular the war was a great turning point, for it brought psychology into direct touch with a range and depth of human potentiality that experiments with college sophomores had never allowed. Psychology proved its usefulness and won unprecedented respect as a profession. It came at last into the marketplace, where passion is only tempered by reason—and all too difficult to ignore. The scholarly concerns of academic psychology were irreversibly altered. It was in this climate that the New Look was born. It is easy now to dismiss its enthusiasms, its overstatements, and the impetuosities of its conclusions, but the issues that inspired it and its perspectives were not trivial then, nor are they now.

The essential spirit of the New Look was antiseparatism, an effort to combine long-existing strands of American functionalism, given added encouragement by Egon Brunswik's presence on the American scene, as well as by the dynamic theories of Freud, McDougall, and Lewin and the organismic points of view of Kurt Goldstein, Heinz Werner, and Gardner Murphy. These trends within the movement converged upon an interest in perception looked at anew as an expression of organismic direction, purpose, and motives, and took the premise that perception is guided by processes that answer to laws beyond those of the characteristics of perceptual mechanisms themselves. Although the focus was at first on showing the operation of such transformative processes in perception, it quickly turned into a New Look at *cognition* generally and into an approach in which all behavior is seen in its relation to processes of knowing, knowledge finding, and knowledge making.

Actually, the New Look comprised several different ways of looking at perception. Three approaches were discernible, not altogether consistent among themselves. Our zeal in a common attack on old dragons obscured these disparities. We were more gentle with one another than with our elders, and in some ways it seems now, from a backward look, that we had less in common with one another than we acknowledged at the time.

One form of the New Look, its earliest and most ephemeral version, viewed perception as expressing solely wish or need fulfillment (a view once summarized in the crude formula "that which looms large in motive looms large perceptually"). This guideline was based on a vulgarized version of Freud's message and had a solipsistic bent. It seemed to imply that motivation was essentially *distorting* in its effects (most of the studies used perceptual "errors" as indicators of motivational effect); perception has a built-in tendency to distortion caused by its primary wish-fulfilling function. This approach foundered on a paradox in its premise: If perception is motivated (and therefore distorted), why is it as effective as it is much of the time? On the positive side, it cannot be denied that this point of view brought a new vitality to laboratory studies of perception and cognition and had much to do with enlarging the scope of academic tolerance. Previously, motivation had been regarded rather like the lady of easy virtue—valued and even indispensable in private but an embarrassment in public. Out of the extreme motivationist version of the New Look developed a concern for the varieties of motives that play into perception and into cognitive processes generally. It carried questions about perception far beyond what had been possible within the Gestalt and other frameworks that preceded it.

A second version of the New Look was epitomized in the work of Adelbert Ames and his collaborators at Princeton. It was an extreme functionalism that elevated "past experience" to the status of both a necessary and a sufficient "cause" of perceptual experience, in a radical reaction to the Gestalt thesis of inherent organizational givens. Ames' functionalism was more in conflict with the wish-fulfillment notion than met the eye. As Krech and I put it, "Ames, perhaps the most thoroughgoing contemporary functionalist, speaks of the 'purpose of a percept' as if this were intrinsic in the perceptual process itself and were invariant from person to person" (Klein & Krech, 1951, p. 3n). Concern for individual differences was not part of this functionalist program.

The third version of the New Look regarded the study of perceptual achievement not as an end in itself but as a medium, in Fritz Heider's terms, through which experimenters might glean *personality constants*. Perception was treated as one of a number of cognitive functions that must be studied in relation to one another to discern organismic rules of regulation. At the Menninger Clinic we were wary of the first two versions. Neither seemed to fit our developing enthusiasm for the ego psychology that was then being vigorously formulated by Heinz Hartmann and David Rapaport. Of the work then going on, Herman Witkin's and Louis L. Thurstone's seemed most congenial.

From the ego-psychological approach came our own New Look at perception in the shape of the concept of *cognitive style*. This conception of motivated perception was influenced by Hartmann's notion of conflict-free functions, a notion out of keeping with the view that motivated perception is simply "need reducing." In Hartmann's view, the environmental adequacy of perception is safeguarded by an autonomous development, each stage of which readies the organism for responsiveness to an "average expectable environment." At the same time, and at each developmental stage, perceptual functioning is responsive to and molded by organismic aims as well as by temporary need states. Perceptual experience and its contents reflect stabilized rules of control operating *through* the perceptual system; the achievements of perception and its motivated selectivity cannot be understood simply as a response to temporary need states. In this view, the organismic controls are not ad hoc constructions but workable strategies that have proved themselves in countless environmental encounters. We referred to them at different times as "perceptual attitudes," "style," and, finally, "cognitive controls." To say, then, that perception is motivated and individualized is not to assume that it is always serving the discharge of needs; individual differences in perception are not always the products of projective distortions determined by need states. An important influence on this conception was Rapaport's pioneering work in diagnostic testing, which demonstrated that a person's characteristic modes of adjustment—not merely his "intelligence"—are reflected by the shape of his thinking, his ways of perceiving, remembering, conceptualizing. Furthermore, Rapaport's work demonstrated that hysteric, obsessive-compulsive, schizoid, and other clinical syndromes can be distinguished according to variations in cognitive functioning.

One explicit goal of our work was the reassessment of the concept of personality itself. Instead of a language that would convey no immediate implications of cognitive processes, we tried to develop concepts that could imply both the constant or stable aspect of personality and its specific manner of appearance in the workings of thought and action. It was a general point of view that Krech and I found compatible, and it was shared by Thurstone and Witkin as well.

Chapters 2 and 3, completing Part One, describe the orientation and programmatic context of the studies that make up the succeeding Parts of the book. The cast of this orientation, described in Chapter 2, is contemporary psychoanalytic theory, in its emphasis upon the simultaneous play of conscious and unconscious aims, and upon the interactions between ad hoc motivations aroused in particular adaptive situations and stabilized organizational trends of the organism.

Chapter 3 is particularly vital in bringing this orientation directly to bear on the relationship between perception and motivation. Perception is seen as part of a functional cognitive effort, never to be studied for itself but always as a distinctive *class* of experienced information that occurs within a more comprehensive train of cognitive events. We also see that motivated perceiving is not simply need-reducing, nor is it necessarily distorting; the rules of perceptual selectivity are much of the time highly stable across changes in need states, and even when perception is responsive to specific needs it is usually effectively coordinated with environmental structures and conditions. A functionalist and motivationist perspective is thus maintained without by-passing the issues of effective coordination stressed by psychophysicists.

Each of the remaining sections takes up a different aspect of the comprehensive sketch of Chapter 3. Part Two develops the particular theme that people differ in self-consistent modes of effective environmental encounter. Individual differences are treated as arising in part from different, developmentally molded cognitive styles. Each in its own way has proven itself effective in the person's history yet none is more or less effective than the others by any absolute criterion of "perceptual truth." Several dimensions of cognitive style that seem to be relatively invariant across changes in need state are hypothesized. The conception of cognitive style proposed in these papers implies a view of the nature of personality structure itself: that it is misleading to separate cognitive events from those that reflect "personality" and to speak of their "interaction." Rather, personality embodies stabilized dispositions of perception and cognition—or what we refer to as "cognitive style." Stable modes of cognitive control are thus presumed to reflect basic personality invariants.

Part Three deals with the theme, relatively neglected in psychology, of the relation of focus and periphery in motivational activity and informational inputs. Selectivity, said William James, is the keel of thought. But, because what we perceive is so much of the time tied in with intention, there is clearly a problem of potential intrusion from multiple intentions that are simultaneously active. The problem of focus and periphery exists also in relation to environmental input—potential information. Selectivity operates here too, for much more input plays upon sensory surfaces than is representable in behavior or thinking. The two essays in this Part consider different facets of the influence of peripheral motives and stimuli. In this connection the functional importance of *awareness* of stimulus input is considered in relation to stimulus effectiveness and impact. The studies upon which these papers draw employ the experimental strategy of subliminal and marginal stimuli. We are interested in the subliminal and the peripheral, however, not in order to demonstrate "discrimination without awareness"—the traditional mold in which such studies were cast—or to demonstrate a "supersensitive discriminatory mechanism," but in order to explore the functional importance of awareness itself. We are interested in how the processing and impact of stimulus input differ when one is explicitly aware of the input from when one is only peripherally aware or even completely unaware of it.

The considerations of Parts Two and Three lead to the view that reality-oriented cognition includes processes of active inhibition guaranteeing that perception is kept effectively "on track" and coordinated with environmental fact and preventing intrusions from peripheral trains of thought. Processes of *attentional focus*, responsiveness to *informative feedback*, and the *stabilized cognitive controls* described in Chapter 3 all help to ensure or support intentional, reality-oriented behavior. How man keeps on a reality-centered track in the face of multiple motivated trains of thought is one of the neglected issues in the study of perception. The essays of Part Four explore the importance of such supports as revealed in experimental and clinical studies involving radical alterations of attentional focus and reduction in informational feedback. This importance is highlighted by studying the consequences of removing them, as in experimental situations which make them temporarily nonfunctional.

The "disorders" produced by such removal have in the past been regarded simply as "disorganization." The psychoanalytic conception of primary process provides a helpful framework for understanding such changes. Thinking does preserve a kind of order in such circumstances, but an order determined by peripheral trains of thought that are now able to preempt attention and action channels. The result is to encourage modes of thinking of the kind described as "primary-process."

Some years ago I had an experience under mescaline that had bearing on my thinking about these issues. I had been under the drug for some five hours in the continuous presence of friends who were observing me. At lunch we separated, they in normal hunger, I in abnormal unappetite. I was already a bit fatigued by the whirlwind quality and intensity of my experiences up to that point, and in the quiet room in which they left me I lay down on a couch hoping for a moment's respite. All at once a vivid train of images appeared in vivid color on the prefrontal cinema screen of my mind—strange images of castles and battlements with knights in armor, crests and armored mounts, vivid banners flying from turrets. Unbeckoned and uncontrollable, the images frightened me. I leaped up, and immediately the images clicked off, like the whir of a camera suddenly disconnected by a break in current. And then, in the curious detachment that seems to remain intact through all the labyrinthine twists and turns of the drug experience, I made a mental note: "I must remember this; posture and the upright are important for secondary-process thinking."

The experience seemed to indicate two things (I shall omit the less obvious emotional meanings): First, that latent trains of thought are inhibited by a system of supports enlisted in the course of executive thinking; second, that the effectiveness of perceiving derives not simply from those peripheral mechanisms in the perceptual system itself that ensure veridicality, but also from organismic orientations that implement purposeful action and thought: attitude and postural set, responsiveness to informative feedback, constancies of cognitive style. Correspondingly, disinhibition leading to primary-process thinking is encouraged by removing such supports.

Finally, Part Five, the most recent, returns to issues raised in Part One, in particular Chapter 3. It brings into sharper focus the nature of a motivated train of thought, considering motivation more closely as a cognitive structure. In developing this model we turn away from the notion of motivation as a state of tension, which is prominent in the essays of the earlier Parts.

The book closes with a personal addendum that could as easily have been a prologue. It reaffirms the clinician's orientation to cognition not only as appropriate to his practical concerns but as an invaluable orientation for experimentation on cognitive processes.

The book, then, deals with motivated cognition, with the interplay of simultaneously active motives and their effects on action, with the conditions in which reality-effective perceiving is supported, and with the conditions in which it is undermined. It emphasizes tendencies of thought that, in Lewin's words, "speak out for reality" while expressing a person's motivational life—and the means which guarantee the adequacy of this contact.

Chapter 2

Orientations from Psychoanalysis

A growing self-consciousness about the conventions and objectives of theorizing and about ways of systematizing evidence for psychoanalytic concepts is discernible within the psychoanalytic community. Major parts of the psychoanalytic framework are coming under skeptical scrutiny, not with the objective of showing how Freud was "wrong," but with the constructive aim of assessing their fruitfulness for clinical work. In particular the utility of "metapsychology"—that inelegant label for such speculative attempts as the "structural point of view" and the energy model to stake out a general theory that would account for clinical observations through hypothetical structures and processes—is being questioned (for example, Home, 1966; Rycroft, 1966). In view of this restiveness about the theory among psychoanalysts themselves, it seems paradoxical to say that psychoanalysis continues to provide vital nutriment for research in nontherapy settings. In this period of stocktaking, of concern with both indispensable and expendable concepts in the psychoanalytic enterprise, it is appropriate to examine some of the guidelines afforded by the psychoanalytic theory to researchers in such *nontherapeutic* investigative contexts as the university laboratory.

I hesitated over the word "theory" and was tempted to say "framework" instead. The hesitation was partly occasioned by my own uncertainty about what a theory is, an uncertainty that reading various philosophers of science has intensified rather than diminished. It is probably correct to say that psychoanalysis is not really a theory by any standard put forth by the philosophers of science. Certainly it is not a theory in the sense of being a clear organization of diverse facts according to a few basic principles. It is probably more accurate to describe psychoanalysis as an assemblage of propositions within two classes of theory. On the one hand are what Rapaport (1959a) called the "clinical" principles, those for classifying the meanings of, or "reasons" for, behavior viewed as expressing conflict and defense, sexual and aggressive wishes, conscious and unconscious events, substitution of aims, and so on. On the other hand is metapsychology, which consists of Freud's attempts to account for clinical meanings or principles in the impersonal causal terms of an energic system. The situation is further complicated by the fact that Freud's own thinking underwent radical shifts and variations; later revisions stand awkwardly beside earlier conceptions. To give but one example, Freud's conception (1900, Chapter 7) of two modes of thinking—primary- and secondary-process—was formulated long before he evolved his conceptions of ego, id, and superego. Yet he never revised his ideas of these different cognitive processes in the light of the later, so-called "structural," theory. It could be demonstrated that a consistent theory demands such a reconciliation. (Even without it, however, I believe that the conceptions of primary and secondary process have investigative utility.) Altogether—and to summarize—psychoanalysis is by no means the monolithic orthodoxy that inspires so much awe and contempt, no tightly developed and unshakable structure deviations from which can be easily recognized and denounced as heresy. Its concepts span an extraordinary range of human complexity, linked by a language that only loosely coordinates one part with another, a situation that moved Rapaport to say, "The general theory, far from being well-ingrained dogma, is a waif unknown to many, noticed by some, and closely familiar to few" (1959a, p. 140).

In examining the body of psychoanalytic thought it is important to appreciate that many of its fundamental concepts are anchored in a distinctive data-gathering, clinical situation. It is distinguished by certain relatively invariant physical and temporal conditions, by a code of responsibility between observer and observed, by a method of eliciting verbalizations, and perhaps most important by a distinctive, deliberately fostered type of relationship between two people—a therapeutic alliance, as Karl Menninger aptly called it (1958)—that is surely one of the most extraordinary forms of long-term interpersonal commitment ever concocted by man. Freud envisioned the psychoanalytic situation as a relatively stable setting for therapeutic effort and—I emphasize—for systematic study of the lawfulness of behavior. Never did he waver in his belief that the therapeutic situation was primarily an *investigative* opportunity and the method of free association its instrument. I think this investigative orientation may be one reason why Freud steadfastly insisted on keeping the psychoanalytic method free from domination by the medical-therapist community, a matter in which he was overruled—to the melancholy detriment of both psychology and psychoanalysis.[1]

In contrast to the observational conditions to which psychologists are accustomed, the psychoanalytic situation is most certainly unique in that the *therapeutic pact* and the *interpersonal relationship* are the indispensable—or at least the most likely—bases for observing many of the dramatic phenomena that constitute its legacy of discovery for psychological science. As a method and setting for observation the psychoanalytic session

---

[1] He wrote in a letter to Paul Federn (March 27, 1926), "As long as I live I shall resist that psychoanalysis be swallowed up by medicine" (E. Federn, 1967, p. 270).

undoubtedly elicits and highlights a broad range of conflict-determined phenomena—transference, regression, eruption of unconscious fantasies and the like—that are still unmatched by and largely unrepresented even in those bold and imaginative experiments of recent years that involve observations of behavior in stressful environments. How many laboratory scientists can (or would dare) set up a situation in which a subject dissolves into tearful helplessness and permits us to watch him in the tyrannical grip of a peremptory unconscious fantasy—even assuming that it were possible to circumvent the ethical issues?

But the very conditions that contribute to the uniqueness of psychoanalytic observations are at the heart of the difficulties in bringing psychoanalysis into the "mainstream of psychology." For the kinds of data and the observational situation of the psychoanalytic hour present challenges to the systematizing of observations and the inferring of lawfulness that are different from those encountered in the more common experimental models to which twentieth-century psychology has so far anchored its fate.

This consideration throws light on existing dissatisfactions with psychoanalytic theory among nonpsychoanalytic psychologists. I doubt that the distaste among university and laboratory psychologists for psychoanalysis is altogether attributable to the fact of its being "poor" theory. Psychology has always had "poor" theories, and we can even make a case that it has had *only* "poor" theories, which nonetheless have been recognized as useful, even welcome, soil for exploration. Undoubtedly the gamey taste of psychoanalysis is partly the result of its unpalatable conceptual novelties, partly of crudities in the manner of theorizing. To my mind, however, the single most important basis of the experimentally minded psychologist's discontent with the theory is the circumstances of data gathering from which psychoanalytic concepts have emerged and the rules of inference by which the analyst arrives at statements of lawfulness. Even were there none of the complications that arise from the fact that therapeutic rather than investigative interest must prevail in the gathering of data, the therapeutic nature of the situation makes direct access to the data impossible for nonpsychoanalysts. The fact that the data depend upon a therapeutic context makes them a pretty exclusive sort of data, accessible to only a few. It is easy to see why this inaccessibility would alienate laboratory and university psychology from psychoanalysis. Moreover, the phenomena are not easily replicable in the university laboratory, and, worst of all, the published glimpses of data show that the application of rigorous criteria for stable evidence and rules of inference is long overdue.

From its beginnings, psychoanalytic investigation has been faced with the dilemma of how to coordinate investigative intentions with therapeutic considerations. Working with a therapeutic context as a source of data presents a persistent and unresolved difficulty: Although the "classical," long-term treatment situation is uniquely valuable from an investigative standpoint for eliciting unusual phenomena, we do not really know if it is uniquely valuable therapeutically. Psychoanalysis has always had faith that the two orientations are harmoniously served; we still do not know whether this faith is justified. If the classical context and procedure are an incomparable source of researchable phenomena but of uncertain therapeutic effectiveness compared with competing strategies, then a dilemma confronts us: how far to modify, or to resist modifying, the clinical situation in the interest of one or the other. Shall we retain the classical therapeutic context and its procedural conventions for their investigative utility, or shall we change therapeutic strategy, even though this change may narrow the range of potentially observable phenomena? Freud chose the former course, possibly because of the investigative richness he observed in the "classical" analytic procedure; he regarded with distrust all attempts to manipulate the psychoanalytic situation for purposes of therapeutic advantage alone. For example, he wrote: "It would be desirable to obtain practical results in a shorter period and with less trouble. But at the present time theoretical knowledge is still far more important to all of us than therapeutic success . . ." (1919b, p. 183).

Another source of difficulty deserves mention. Freud worked in the manner we have come to call "clinical," meaning that a concept is developed through repeated observations under relatively standard conditions in which the determining conditions of a phenomenon are not under tight manipulation or control. This is the time-honored method of clinical medicine. It has been a productive source of physiological discoveries, but it is not an adequate basis for a science of controlled manipulation of variables—experimental science. A vital accompaniment to clinical *medicine* was therefore the physiological laboratory. A hypothesis based on clinical observation can hope for testing, sometimes quickly, in the controlled conditions of the laboratory. But this opportunity is precisely what psychoanalysis does not have, despite repeated valiant efforts to provide it. For, in the attempted translation from consulting room to laboratory, something happens that happens less readily in physiology: either the phenomenon itself changes, or the new interactions created by the altered conditions of observation and method present complications in extracting the phenomenon.

I emphasize the clinical psychoanalytic context of observation not only because it is the key to psychologists' dissatisfaction with the theory but also because it calls into question the view that psychoanalytic concepts can become more useful only if first the logic of the metapsychological theory is cleaned up and tightened and its concepts tested in experimental contexts. The intimate links between psychoanalytic clinical theory and the clinical situation, the difficulties of testing the concepts of the clinical theory outside this situation, suggest that any attempt at propositional rigor and validations begin with *the data of the psychoanalytic situation, not* with those of the experimental laboratory, that such attempts concentrate upon the concepts of the *clinical* theory of psychoanalysis, *not* its metapsychology. The clinical concepts derived from the psychoanalytic data-gathering situation have not yet been cast in a form that is easily translatable to other contexts. The phase of accommodating psychoanalytic *clinical* theory more systematically to the data of the psychoanalytic situation is still ahead of us; it is a phase that would greatly ease the way of translations to nontherapeutic contexts. Those who are primarily interested in achieving formal elegance in the theory must first apply to the original context improved strategies of systematizing observations and inferences (see, for example, Luborsky, 1967). A number of investigators are in fact currently occupied in this fashion (Luborsky, 1967; B. B. Rubinstein, 1965, 1967; Sandler *et al.*, 1962; Sandler & Rosenblatt, 1962; Shakow, 1960; Knapp, 1963, Gill *et al.*, 1968).

But for the *non*psychoanalyst to get observational mileage out of psychoanalytic concepts does not require a formally pure theory. Rigor of this kind is necessary mainly when the central objective is to assess the *predictive power* of concepts and their generality; it is *not* a requirement for other productive, if less systematic, uses of the theory, which I shall summarize. These uses are strictly empirical; they are not geared to improving or "purifying" the theory as a whole. In view of the fact that many of the concepts are still inextricably linked with the data of the psychoanalytic situation and because it is doubtful that experiments can successfully simulate many of the phenomena of the clinical situation, the psychologist who works with psychoanalytic concepts is well advised to take an informal, flexible approach to exploring their surplus meanings and implications. He can hold a concept lightly, ready to modify it radically or discard it entirely according to the vicissitudes of experimental necessity and measurement conditions. Of course, it is incumbent upon him to state as rigorously as possible the distinction between his use of a concept and its application in the clinical situation. And, to be sure, he cannot feel free to claim either proof or disproof of a psychoanalytic proposition; the new context, new methods, new situations may have produced new phenomena and interactions as well.

So then, if he acknowledges difficulties with psychoanalytic theory qua theory and concedes that he can hope to contribute little to the formal elegance of the theory, what nutriment does the body of psychoanalytic concepts hold for the investigator who relies upon experimentation, who is not a psychoanalyst, and whose main concern is not with preserving psychoanalytic theory as such or with the aesthetic appeal of its structure? Those who use psychoanalysis in experimental work can still obtain vital nourishment even though they have only a spectator's interest in the quest for theoretical clarification. I shall try to specify how.

Ultimately, whatever attractions psychoanalysis holds for the nonpsychoanalytic investigator are traceable to Freud's seminal ideas about the dynamics of purposeful behavior, ideas that have implications for virtually every major segment of man's behavior, emotional life, and development—from love to grief, normality to psychosis, infancy to old age. These core ideas have withstood the many vicissitudes of theorizing and controversies among psychoanalysts. They are perhaps the sole bases for accusations of orthodoxy in psychoanalysis. Recalcitrance will be most visible in an analyst's countenance if the three following precepts are challenged.

1. *The central, most pervasive condition for the development of motives and of psychopathology is conflict.* The usage of many psychoanalytic concepts hinges upon this pivotal interest in conflict. For example, for many analysts the main use even of the concept of ego lies in its relation to conflict rather than in its more popular contemporary meaning as an "adaptive system." Waelder comments, for instance, that to look for ego, superego, and id in the fact that John Doe wants to eat breakfast and enjoys it would not be regarded by psychoanalysts generally as a very valuable enterprise, but that the "situation changes if, e.g., John Doe has been put on a diet by his doctor; in this case, his hunger and his oral desire may be opposed by concern for his health and by conscience reminding him of his responsibilities" (1960, p. 84). In this situation of conflict we see the ego and superego represented, each with its own claims, in his behavior.

Conceptions of the component forces of conflict (for example, sexual and aggressive wishes) and of the forms of their resolution make up a large and incomplete theme in psychoanalytic theory and are at the heart of many changes that have been occurring in the theory. A large body of concepts is ultimately traceable to this emphasis on conflict and its varieties and levels. The concepts of drive and defense are, of course, rooted in it, having evolved from early notions simply of conflict among ideas, to a conception of the stages and crises in psychosexual development that contribute to conflict, to various conceptions of drives, restraints, and controls—all proposals to deal with issues of genesis, forms, intensity, and resolution of conflicts.

In recent years this concern with conflict has been revised and expanded, but it is still central. It is from this anchorage in the importance of conflict that ego theory has come to include the conflict-*free* functions and to ponder the distinction between the conflicted and the conflict-free functions. The conditions under which conflict-free functions become involved in conflict and the manner in which conflict stimulates regressive tendencies in certain functions while others are unaffected—such contemporary concerns arise from traditional psychoanalytic concern with conflict.

2. A second seminal idea, stated in its most general form, is that *a person may respond knowledgefully to internal and external stimulation, but be unaware of the meaning that informs his response and even of the response itself.* Here we have the principle of motivated thought, which includes forceful ideation unaccompanied by conscious experience, the critical principle of *repressed* yet *active* ideation. This precept differs from pre-Freudian psychology and even from many theories that followed it; they simply assumed that most memories are silent and uninfluential until activated and that if one motive is active other potential motives are meanwhile inactive. Freud brought to light a kind of "dynamic knowledge" beyond awareness, showing that it is powerful and capable of exercising a decisive influence on our behavior. The revolutionary principle in this discovery was that an ideational system can exercise motivational force without being introspectively accessible, that such ideas in a state of imbalance can affect action.

Rather than being simply a basis for redefining mental concepts, the discovery of unconscious motivating and symbol-inducing processes was the discovery of a new range of facts. With it came the implication that we are less free because we are less fully self-conscious than we had previously believed. The discovery of unconscious purposes implied "that the occasions on which we have, to a greater or lesser degree, misrepresented to ourselves what we are trying to do is much more common than we had previously believed" (Hampshire, 1959, p. 180). To this core idea are linked the great distinctions among conscious, preconscious, and unconscious modes of thought, repression, and repression-instigated unconscious fantasies, which underlie a good many psychoanalytic conceptions.

Testimony to the fertility of this assumption comes from none other than B. F. Skinner, not the gentlest critic of psychoanalysis, who credits Freud with having assisted the behaviorist movement through this idea. In Skinner's view the principle of unconscious activity had much to do with moving psychology away from a nonbehavioristic emphasis upon conscious mental events, which had been expressed in the approach of the introspectionists.

Curiously enough, part of the answer was supplied by the psychoanalysts, who insisted that although a man might be able to see some of his mental life, he could not see all of it. The kind of thoughts Freud called unconscious took place without the knowledge of the thinker. From an association, verbal slip, or dream it could be shown that a person must have responded to a passing stimulus although he could not tell you that he had done so. More complex thought processes, including problem solving and verbal play, could also go on without the thinker's knowledge. Freud had devised, and he never abandoned faith in, one of the most elaborate mental apparatuses of all time. He nevertheless contributed to the behavioristic argument by showing that mental activity did not, at least, *require* consciousness. His proofs that thinking had occurred without introspective recognition were, indeed, clearly in the spirit of Lloyd Morgan. They were operational analyses of mental life—even though, for Freud, only the unconscious part of it. Experimental evidence pointing in the same direction soon began to accumulate. (Skinner, 1963, p. 952)

3. A third basic idea, related to the other two but independent, is Freud's emphasis *upon the preemptive power of ideation, especially the repetitive hold of unconscious fantasy upon thought and behavior.* It is an interesting historical fact that psychoanaly-

sis did not at first begin with a drive theory but with the notion that *ideas* themselves have a force component that affects behavior (Rapaport, 1958). The first and central elements of the theory in accounting for neuroses were the facts of psychic trauma and conflict among ideas, and the consequences of repetitively insistent, conflicting ideas for behavior. In Freud's early statements of the theory (Breuer & Freud, 1893; Freud, 1894; see also Strachey *et al.*, 1962) the critical force in conflict involved a repressed meaning—the meaning of a real event that was incompatible with the main body of a patient's socially and consciously acceptable ideas. That unacceptable, repressed ideas owed their unique power to sexual involvement contributed, of course, to Freud's eventual emphasis upon drives as the motive power of conflict and unconscious ideation. The core idea that dissociated or unconscious fantasies exert a preemptive hold upon behavior led to tremendous advances in observation, culminating in the theory of dreams; in the conception of two classes of ideation, primary- and secondary-process; in the theory of drive itself; and, of course, in the special theory of the restraining forces of defense.

The theoretical and empirical exploration of these three seminal ideas has been the main objective of the enormous proliferation of concepts and shifts of emphases among psychoanalytic workers ever since. No psychoanalyst would claim that the conceptual links within and among these central themes exist in any acceptable final form or that the parts of the total conception are commensurate either in theoretical origin, observational specificity, or validity. But one need not swallow the theory whole in order to digest some of its parts, nor is there any formal barrier in the theory itself to reflection on different parts with varying degrees of skepticism and acceptance. On the other hand, awareness of the many ramifications of these ideas in all sectors of the theory can very possibly add to the generative implications of a particular part of a theory. For this reason, study of the theory should attempt to embrace as much of it as possible, even if one's central interest is in one of its parts.

I pause at this point to remark on the accusation of orthodoxy that is often thrown at those who refuse to be drawn into the game of showing how Freud was "wrong." I believe that it is not worshipful respect for Freud's genius that keeps one within the so-called "orthodoxy" of working within the framework of these seminal themes of psychoanalysis but rather the still unexplored implications that lead from them. More often than not, attempts to redress imbalances in psychoanalytic theory have only produced new, often worse, ones. On close inspection, such corrective efforts require retreat from Freud's basic respect for the complexities of man's personality. As far as developing a theoretically sounder personology is concerned, Freud's perspectives are still an important safeguard against superficiality.

If this area is ultimately the lifeline from which nonpsychoanalyst students of the theory are to derive nutriment, there is still the matter of how to go about using it. I shall ignore the crucial nonexperimental alternative that would confine investigation to data of the psychoanalytic situation per se. I shall also by-pass efforts directed primarily at the theory's structure. I am concerned here with research objectives whose method is primarily experimental, but even here I am not concerned with research that aims specifically to validate or invalidate psychoanalytic propositions. My view is that the *usefulness* of the theory in expanding discovery and in illuminating phenomena deserves precedence *over considerations of improving the formal rigor of the theory itself*.

I am expressing here a bias about the objectives of science and what is useful in theory for attaining them. I may as well own up to a certain skepticism about whether a full-scale effort to achieve "formal elegance" in the theory as a whole will significantly increase its investigative potential. Emphasis on theoretical rigor can distract attention from a fundamental aim of science, the discovery of *phenomena*—progress in *perception*, if you will—and expansion of the range of the observable in order to help determine the contingent and sufficient conditions of phenomena. Theory helps, but only if *conception* aids *perception*, as when, after the conceptualization of the chromosome, it became possible to *see* chromosomes under the microscope. A good concept or proposition, then, is in the category of an observational instrument. But the perceptual process can be advanced in other ways too; for instance, the development of observational hardware like the microscope may also help—a process of "deanthropomorphizing" observation, as Bertalanffy (1955) calls the development of artificial aids to man's sensory equipment. A beautiful instance of the confluence of concept and instrumental advance is seen in the current research on dreams. Here, Freud's conception of the functions and contingencies of dreams has obvious utility, but it took the almost accidental discovery of the relation of eye movements to dreaming to produce a significant breakthrough in this area.

In the process of uncovering the heretofore unperceived and unperceivable, a theory that is formally inelegant in the lexicons of philosophers of science may serve all the same. Not logic alone but improvements of observation as well unmask a theory as poor, or help to reveal its mettle; formally elegant as well as inelegant theories may suffer either fate. I do not know a psychologist who would not happily exchange all of Hull's rigorously developed propositions for the discovery of the relation between eye movements and dreaming, or the Olds-Milner discovery of positive and negative reinforcement centers, which was, by the way, wholly accidental. *The heart of Freud's success was in refocusing the observational intentions of twentieth-century psychologists* on, for example, the vicissitudes of sexuality and aggression in behavior and development, unconscious determinants of behavior, varieties of conflict, and motivational complexity generally. For an allegedly "inferior" theoretician he did not do badly.

It may seem that I am downgrading theory, but I am not; I am merely putting it in the proper perspective of the aims of science as I see them. We cannot *avoid* theory if only because words always have surplus meanings that must be controlled and accounted for when we plan to *use* our descriptions for purposes of experimental control. But words, concepts, propositions are in the service of observation. They are mediations of the perceptual process, not the perception itself or the regularity observed.

People who do not distinguish concept from perceivable regularity are making an error that is well known in the perceptual laboratory: confusing mediation with that which is mediated, the ruler with the object it is measuring. I take issue with the view that reality is itself only a conceptual matter, a view that equates the perceptual regularities observed with the words used to describe them, thus elevating theory to being the objective of research itself.

So—the various strategies for working with psychoanalytic concepts that I am about to mention all have a frankly empirical and rather informal theoretical focus. Two are perhaps even atheoretical; the other two start from the theory only with a view to what it can do in generating new observations.

There are four such strategies: *exploring the theory for descriptive concepts that may have utility in specifying and classifying observed regularities; scanning the theory for propositions that may direct a search for new phenomena; conceptual gap filling;* and *searching for small-scale explanatory models within the body of the theory.* I shall take them up in order.

A first important source of investigative usefulness of psychoanalytic theory is its wealth of descriptive concepts that are relatively independent of the psychoanalytic situation and can be used to specify behavioral units observed under conditions of experimentation. Although many psychoanalytic concepts are too much contingent upon the psychoanalytic situation to be of much descriptive value in other contexts, many *are* capable of such use. For example, the conception of defenses such as "isolation," "denial," and so forth, does have a descriptive utility in bringing order to behavior observed in contexts other than the clinical situation.

I draw attention to one such conception that is virtually untapped for its promise in sensitizing descriptions of thought processes—that of *primary-* and *secondary-process* modes of thinking. Freud's idea of two modes of thought organization was most fully developed in his attempts to understand dreams (1900, Chapter 7). In Ernest Jones' view, Freud's description of the altogether different logic of the dream and its similarities to psychotic thinking was at least as monumental a contribution as his demonstration of unconscious wish-fulfilling contents (1953, p. 397). Though basically linked to the data of dreams, the concepts have descriptive utility for classifying behavior in a variety of environments that tend to undermine the kinds of realistic thinking more familiar to psychologists. It ought to be mentioned that Freud's account of primary- and secondary-process modes of thought also implies controversial assumptions of mechanism as well. Nevertheless, I do not think that their descriptive value is vitiated by the questionable notions of mechanism in which they are encased.

Experiments at the New York University Research Center for Mental Health and elsewhere furnish examples of how cognitive products induced under stress exemplify primary-process thinking. Behaviors that psychology has previously been able to designate only as "disorganized" acquire, through this concept, significance as uncommon forms of organization. The concept is proving useful in distinguishing the complex behavioral effects of such drugs as LSD-25 according to how much the drug diminishes secondary-process thinking (Linton & Langs, 1962, 1964). The concept of primary process has given a fresh slant on the effects of perceptual isolation (Goldberger, 1961; Goldberger & Holt, 1961a). It has also been helpful in describing the kind of thinking that develops when informational feedback from action and perception is disrupted, as, for instance, when a person is deprived of the feedback from his own voice while talking (Holmes & Holzman, 1966; Holzman & Rousey, 1966; Klein & Wolitzky, 1970).

A second way of working with psychoanalytic concepts is to search the theory for concepts and propositions that promise novel behavioral observations. (I distinguish propositions generating predictions of behavior from weaker ones that, though not lending themselves to rigorous predictive inference, nonetheless suggest new regions of observation.) I think it is fair to say that at the present time not much should be expected from psychoanalytic concepts in respect to generating genuinely predictive statements *outside* the psychoanalytic situation. The main exception may be in developmental studies, but as far as *laboratory* simulation of psychoanalytically observed phenomena is concerned, few, if any, significant discoveries have thus far originated as deductions from a psychoanalytic proposition. Perhaps existing psychoanalytic propositions will in time acquire this power after their predictive capability has been more systematically explored *within* the psychoanalytic situation itself. I do not think that we shall know until such an effort is seriously made. For the present, the difficulty of transferring the concepts to other contexts and across differences in observational technique, situation, and behavioral indicators should make us less sanguine about expecting them in their present form to generate specific predictions in experimental contexts. I take comfort, however, in the fact that prediction is *not* the only goal of the scientist nor the only productive use of theory. A proposition that only *raises a question* is no less useful than one that can generate a specific prediction. Psychoanalytic theory *does* contain many assumptions capable of generating questions about possible mining sites for observational ore.

In this strategy the aim is to find leads to possible conditions determining a phenomenon. Interest in the phenomenon may have developed from outside of the theory, not from the psychoanalytic proposition itself, and may even have been an accidental yield of observations produced by a new laboratory technique. The investigator looks to psychoanalysis for propositions that seem to imply, directly or by analogy, phenomena within his range of observational possibility. He does not, or should not, delude himself that he is thus validating psychoanalytic theory; he is simply exploring a perceived similarity between his data and those *implied* by a psychoanalytic proposition.

I would like to give a recent example of such a use of psychoanalytic concepts, one designed not to validate theory but to flesh out discovery with understanding. Dement and Kleitman (1957a, 1957b) and others have found that dreaming is associated with bursts of rapid eye movements (REMs) and that they occur only during periods of emergent stage 1 sleep, which, in terms of EEGs, are periods of low voltage, relatively rapid brain-wave activity, absence of spindles, low or absent muscular tonus, and respiratory irregularity. An entire night's sleep may yield three to six such dream periods. There is ample reason to think that dreaming sleep differs from other stages of sleep and is triggered and regulated by a different physiological mechanism. Discoveries have, of course, a way of generating further questions, regardless of whether or not theory is present to help the process along, and this area of work has been no exception. The dazzling questions that have been opened up by the discovery of this basic phenomenon are infinitely more varied than could have been provided by deductions from any theory alone, which at best would be only a gap-filling substitute in advance of actual opportunity for observation.

Still, there are points at which psychoanalytic propositions about dreaming *can* raise fruitful questions. For example, Freud's theory holds that the main function of dreaming is to provide an opportunity for the "discharge" of instinctual drives, drives that are endogenously generated from birth on through unknown neurohumoral mechanisms. Second, by virtue of the distorting and disguising effects of the "dream work" (for example, condensation, displacement, and so on), dreams have the function of preserving sleep. Third, although there is a relative deactivation of mental functions during sleep, repressed ideas and ordinarily preconscious ones, called "day residues," remain active. There is plenty to criticize and to clarify in the terms—"discharge," "drive," and so on—of these propositions. But the propositions are nonetheless useful in the laboratory context. In light of the drive conception, the stage 1 REM phase of sleep may be viewed as the periodically insistent physiological concomitant of drive arousal and the accompanying dreams as the cognitive activity motored by the drive process. The main elements of dream cognition would be infantile as well as later concepts and memories that are especially active when the neurohumoral drive structure is in a high state of arousal.

One question that this presumed relationship between dream cognition and drive brings into focus is, How necessary is it to dream? Here psychoanalytic theory, in my opinion, does not offer clear guidelines but does provide launching points for fresh questions. If dreaming is *discharge*, then clearly no good can come from the *suppression* of dreaming, from closing the safety valve. If we accept these assumptions, we would expect *inhibition* of drive discharge to be synchronously associated with intensified pressure *toward* such discharge. If the dream actually has a discharge function, a highly active need state that persists into the dreaming phase of sleep should receive some relief through hallucinated gratification in the dream. For instance, in our laboratory Bokert (1967) found encouragement for the proposition that dream content may actually have a "discharge" effect. Intensity of thirst following a night's sleep seemed to be significantly reduced if gratification themes were preeminent in the dream content. There is a second alternative, however. The importance of the dream may lie less in "discharge" than in an effort to synthesize or integrate an unassimilated emotional experience; perhaps, to use Erikson's term (1954), a "restitutive" effort (see also Breger, 1967). Possibly dream suppression is harmful from this point of view too, although I believe that different observational leads proceed from it than from the discharge theory. (The notion of "discharge" is critically assessed in Chapter 14.)

Be that as it may, the discharge conception has raised interesting possibilities. Experiments by Dement (1960) have shown that increased compensatory dreaming occurs after a period of dream deficit produced by the constant interruption of dreams. On each succeeding night, subjects increasingly attempt to dream. Dement favors the conclusion that dreaming is a necessary psychobiological function and that "more or less complete suppression of it might have serious psychic consequences" in waking day thought and behavior. It is, of course, too early to say what modifications will be required in this generalization.

It is possible, too, that the drive-dream connection proposed by psychoanalytic theory may prove useful in assessing the psychological importance of recent findings about physiological concomitants of dreaming. Jouvet (1961) has discovered that discharges in the caudal pontine nucleus of the reticular formation are closely coordinated with the occurrence of stage 1 REM sleep. This discovery points to a mechanism of dream sleep that is consistent, at least superficially, with the kind of drive activation that psychoanalytic theory says is connected with dreaming. In the end, of course, this hypothesis may turn out to be as mistaken as Columbus' belief that he had found India when he encountered our primitive shores, but the theory of drives will at least have served as a useful starting point for selective empirical inquiry.

The uses of psychoanalytic concepts so far described really proceed less from an interest in psychoanalytic theory as such than from efforts to understand *particular* phenomena. The next two uses I shall describe are also linked with empirical intent, but theory itself is a more explicit objective.

The first approaches the theory with a kind of hypersensitivity to its *gaps*—asking what segments of behavior seem not to be provided for in the theory. Then, by developing conceptual terms coordinate with other terms of the theory, it attempts to enlarge the scope of the theory. Some useful additions to psychoanalytic theory and, I might add, observational incentives have come from this bone-graft type of theoretical surgery. In one example, proceeding from the theory's central emphasis upon *conflict*, Hartmann (1950), Kris (1950), and later Rapaport (1951c, 1957b) and others (Gill & Brenman, 1959, Chapter 4; Holt, 1965a; S. C. Miller, 1962; White, 1963) have raised questions about the conditions and forms in which behavior may be conflict-*free*, questions that have produced far-reaching changes of orientation in psychoanalytic therapy and theorizing. In another example, proceeding from the assumption that drives are pervasively involved in the development of thought functions, Hartmann (1952), Erikson (1951), and recently White (1963) have tried to bring into the theory provision for nondrive determinants of motivation. In still a third example, the dynamic consideration of forces and conflicts, which so long held the center of the psychoanalytic stage, logically demands a concern with the structures that determine the vectors of force. This demand has led to a broadened conception of control and restraint beyond the theory's earlier preoccupation with defense alone (see Rapaport, 1959a).

Attempts to map dimensions of cognitive style, with which I have been associated, are anchored in this interest in ego controls as a way of tackling the age-old enigma of personality constancy (this volume, Chapters 5, 6, and 7; Klein, Barr & Wolitzky, 1967; Gardner *et al.*, 1959; Gardner & Moriarty, 1968). But the notion of cognitive style also aims at bringing psychoanalytic theory into more direct confrontation with the problem of generalized personality dispositions, which it has long handled in a desultory way as "character defenses." We have viewed personality constants as stable strategies of control that channel drives into adaptively attuned activities, organizing cognitive and affective processes in ways that have little to do with conflict but that give personality much of its individual flavor. This effort at defining general forms of integrative control seeks their manifestations in the various sectors of a person's cognitive behavior. Because this empirical effort to describe cognitive styles requires a detailed regard for cognitive processes, it always has one foot, and sometimes seven others as well, outside psychoanalytic theory, for psychoanalysis has had little to say about the details of cognitive processes. Although psychoanalysis is the most ambitious attempt yet made to describe the pushes and pulls of organismic functioning, it is virtually silent on the details of perception, learning, concept formation, and the like. At the same time, work on cognitive controls and dimensions of cognitive style tries to link them to the larger family of psychoanalytic concepts through terms that are at least commensurate with it. The notion of control implied in the concept of cognitive style seems related to but not synonymous with the notion of defense that has been virtually the only means by which psychoanalysis has dealt with the issue of regulatory constants in personality. The concept of defense, even of "autonomous character defenses," does not seem wholly adequate to describe the behaviors that we have called "leveling" and "sharpening," "focusing" and "scanning," "tolerance for unrealistic experiences," and so on.

The underlying theme of this work has been that those aspects of perception and cognition that analysts currently regard as autonomous secondary-process functions are themselves idiosyncratically organized within individuals. Of course, a personality theory that attempts to define personality dimensions within the psychoanalytic framework but at the same time bases itself on cognitive and perceptual theory must inevitably force revision of, or at least more detailed specification of, segments of psychoanalytic theory.

Another approach to developing psychoanalytic theory for purposes of generating investigation outside the treatment situation—and the final one that I shall mention here—concentrates on extracting from the theory, or applying to portions of its concepts, *models of behavior processes.* The term "models" has no single meaning for all psychologists. What I have in mind is a conception of a phenomenon stated in such a way as to offer clues to the variables to be investigated in seeking to understand contingencies of the phenomenon. Models from one area in psychology may be applied to another, as, for example, when a model of the perceptual process is applied to an understanding of personality. Or they may be derived from another discipline, as when the phenomena of thinking are conceptualized in terms of information theory. Ideally, a properly developed explanatory model is not simply a metaphor or an analogy; its power is demonstrated by showing that the terms of relationship holding true within it also hold true of relationships in the sector of behavior under investigation.

Parts of the body of psychoanalytic thought suggest models in this sense; others lend themselves to the application of outside models in an effort to systematize the clinical theory. In bringing the matter of models to the foreground my intention is only to underscore the possibility that parts of psychoanalytic clinical theory may be carried beyond the functional statements in which most of the theory's concepts are cast. Frankly, I am not sure that such attempts will be a fruitful source of new *clinical principles* of meaning that will enlarge the scope of a therapist's interpretive insights. But those who favor this direction have a point in insisting that psychoanalysis will not have maximal usefulness for *experimental* application unless and until it can proceed from models that are able simultaneously to account for both the adaptational or *functional* aspects and the *process* or mechanismlike aspects of a phenomenon. That is a tall order, and, as I say, its feasibility is open to doubt, but it is perhaps achievable for modest segments of the theory in which the model starts with a clearly specified phenomenon to explain.

One such attempt involves a conception of attention cathexis and its deployment developed by Rapaport (1959b) and his colleagues, Schwartz and Rouse, at the Austen Riggs Center, which in recent years has generated interesting experiments in learning and attention (Schwartz & Rouse, 1961; Schwartz & Schiller, 1967, in press). Another example is Engel's attempt (1962) to explicate the psychoanalytic conception of affect in terms of specific discharge and signal aspects of affect.

A third example is a neuropsychological conception developed by Freud (1895) himself almost seventy-five years ago, posthumously published some sixty years later and until recently completely neglected. This early model has intrigued neuropsychologists because it is an attempt to embrace in neurostructural terms basic *functional* trends of psychic behavior that made up the main body of his later work. There are many aspects that have a contemporary flavor: First, it specifies a neurophysiological structure with power and signal capacities; second, the basic systemic principle is not tension reduction but homeostasis, in which neurological structures tend toward the maintenance of optimal rather than zero levels of excitation—in keeping with contemporary notions of open systems; third, it contains a neurone conception capable of accommodating excitation in electrical terms; and, fourth, it involves a system of ascending and descending corticosensorimotor feedback loops. Karl Pribram (1965) points out that an especially interesting feature of Freud's model was his conception of the neurone as a capacitor, capable of graded changes of potential; the nervous system is not simply a conductor but also a means of retaining and building up potential, and neurone activity is interpretable as changes in capacitance of conduction units. It would be fascinating and possibly profitable to study in detail the respects in which Freud's neurological assumptions, freshened by the dramatic changes currently taking place in neurophysiological theory, can convert the functional statements of psychoanalytic theory into process terms.

The virtue of such an attempt, again, is not simply worshipful obeisance to Freud but that this model encompasses so much of the scope of his later formulations about the dialectics of conflict and unconscious events.

If, through such investigative application of its terms, psychoanalytic theory as we know it in its therapeutic context takes on a different look, we can draw solace from the thought that, after all, in psychological science the main objective is not theory as an end in itself but theory as a tool for the best accounting of *observed phenomena* and for the discovery of hitherto *unobserved* ones. If the terms of the theory change beyond recognition from their original form, we have lost only a theory—only words and symbols—but we may have gained thereby a means to greater understanding of nature's regularities.

Chapter 3

Motives and the Perception of Objects

ISSUES AND PARADOXES IN PERCEPTION-MOTIVATION RESEARCH

Issues of motivated perception have probably attracted more man-hours of study in recent years than have most other segments of psychology. This momentum has been generated mainly by the clinician and personality theorist, on the one hand, and the social psychologist, on the other. Proclaiming the vulnerability of perception to sets, expectancies, needs, values, and social norms, these interlopers have invaded perceptual theories comfortably settled in a tradition of psychophysical correlation, a tradition that cushioned even the earlier impact of Gestalt theory's broader emphasis upon field events and context. With or without Gestalt theory, perceptual theory remained relatively unmoved by the parallel activities of personologists and motivation theorists.

To a great extent the invasion was inspired by the organismic emphases of Murphy (1947), Goldstein (1939), Allport (1937), and Brunswik (1947) and by the pioneering studies of Murphy and his students (Levine, Chein & Murphy, 1942; Proshansky & Murphy, 1942; Schafer & Murphy, 1943). But it also drew encouragement

from the revelations of the psychoanalytic hour about the penetration of drive into all levels of behavior. The perceptual function
seemed to be a crucial point of contact between the world and
personal strivings. Here the major pulls and pushes of living
might be observable under controlled conditions.

From the point of view of personality theory, perceptual
responses seemed to be the long-needed measurable events for
testing typological theories and conceptions of alleged organismic
adjustive strategies. The pioneering use of so-called "intelligence"
tests in clinical diagnosis by Rapaport (Rapaport, Gill & Schafer,
1945–1946) and Schafer (1954) gave impetus to this trend by
piercing the wall that had cut psychometrics and "differential
psychology" off from theories of cognitive processes and personality structure. By tracing the outlines of character integration
through responses on purely cognitive tasks, Rapaport and
Schafer encouraged the belief that thought functions in general—
and therefore why not perception in particular?—could clarify
the personal nexus of integrated activity that had previously been
discussed largely outside the traditions of experimental psychology. Proponents of the more avowed "projective tests" had, of
course, long proclaimed such links, but in the main they had
developed their procedures with a "service" outlook and with a
cavalier disregard for theory that isolated them from the main
currents of experimental activity. Personality investigations now
became focused not merely on contents (attitudes, values, and so
on) but on the *formal qualities of thought* as well.

It will be important, as this discussion develops, to bear in
mind a distinction between two trends in this convergence upon
the perception laboratory: One approach, the motivational, was
based on drive theory (a conception of drive tension discharging
itself on particular objects and relationships); another approach
emphasized adaptive style or forms of adjustment (Witkin *et al.*,
1954; this volume, Chapter 5). These approaches pose different
problems and call for different types of evidence, though the
emphasis in both is generally upon function and direction in
behavior.

From social psychology the migration to the perception laboratory started with Bartlett's studies (1932) and gathered momentum with Sherif's studies (1936) of social norms, which suggested that the genesis and impact of values and social frameworks could be traced through such (allegedly) simple phenomena as the autokinetic response. One can imagine the hopes that this idea produced in social psychologists bogged down in the jungle of complicated social events and casting an envious eye at the simplified (if, from the social point of view, trivial) world of their experimental colleagues! Not only did the perception laboratory seem to promise controllable methods, controllable variables, and altogether an emotionally less hectic setting; more than this, perceptual phenomena seemed to be *the* crucial factors to demonstrate how major social forces obtain *psychological* status and exert their impact. Perception promised to reveal the grooves into which socialization guides behavior—and to show how they are learned and unlearned. It promised also to elevate the status of social psychology by suggesting that the study of social influences would provide the basis for a sound individual psychology. The controlled setting of the perceptual laboratory seemed to offer an equally effective—perhaps more effective—strategy for studying the social.

Within perceptual theory itself there were faint stirrings of support for the possibility of linking perception and other regions of a person's activity; for example, there were psychophysiological findings that indicated hypothalamic innervations even of peripheral sensory structures, evidence of tonic components in perceptual response (Werner & Wapner, 1949), and dramatic demonstrations by Ames that suggested a priority of *achievement* over "stimulus properties" in perceptual organization (1946–1947). There were thus a number of workers—though a minority—within the specialized camp of perceptual research who were ready to greet the newcomers.

Where did matters stand in the mid-fifties? The cumulative impact of all those studies and theories of the New Look movement in perception had been great enough to occasion a major stocktaking effort in perceptual theorizing (F. H. Allport, 1955). The personologists and motivation theorists undoubtedly energized perceptual research with novel questions. Their experimental work was and remains even now hardly decisive, however. For the most part it has been demonstrational; it limits itself to experimental conditions that are most conducive to the influence of motivational variables, for example, impoverished stimuli like ambiguous pictures or affectively loaded symbols. To accommodate their convictions, investigators of the New Look persuasion have broadened and loosened the definition of perception to allow room for "verifying" the primacy of motive in perceptual response. From the first enthusiasm for these demonstrations emerged the well-known generalization that what looms large in value looms large perceptually. In this view, hypothesis, need, value (the terms for the directing agents vary but share the same premise) are allegedly involved in all perceptions in the very processes that mediate experiences of shape, size, distance, and so on. Closer inspection, however, shows that the evidence itself is less clear-cut than the claims: Perceptual activity, judgment, apperceptive elaboration, memory all seem hopelessly enmeshed with the phenomena studied, defying a probe of *where* precisely in the cognitive act the alleged forces exert their alleged effects.

On their face these studies brought current thinking to a point far removed from the concept of perception as a still camera or fact-registering mechanism and even advanced it beyond the Gestalt emphasis on the coerciveness of configurations in the physical environment in isomorphic correspondence with patterned brain fields. But in much of this work of the early 1940s there was a disconcerting solipsism that went unnoticed in the first burst of enthusiasm. The drift of the work would lead one to believe that perception is the most labile of functions, at the mercy of wish and need. Not much attention was given to the *limits* of this malleability. When noted at all they were given an embarrassed nod and relegated to secondary importance, as in Bruner and Goodman's early distinction (1947) between "autochthonous" and "behavioral" determinants of perception, according to which the organism is apparently more likely to misperceive than to perceive. The projective hypothesis seemed to have carried the day.

Some important voices protested. Wallach (1949) doubted that purported distortions by motive were *perceptual* effects in the strict sense. If need or value has a distorting effect, this effect is on something already formed; *something*, some stimulus, must be in *some* stage of organization, must have *some* form, for a selective force to operate on it. The effects must thus actually be *post*perceptual elaborations, rather than indications of influences upon percept formation itself. Indeed, as Wallach pointed out, veridicality would seem to be a necessity, as it is hardly conceivable that the organism could survive unless perception had some means of taking into account the actual structures of environment—the physical field.

Perhaps the most effective blast at the projective hypothesis in perception theory was offered by Gibson (1951, 1953). He pointed out that the experiments of the motivation theorists aim to demonstrate the impact of meanings and values upon response and perhaps also individual differences and consistencies in these respects. Such experiments deliberately maximize the *noncorrespondence* of perception to stimulation in order to highlight motives. They do so either through the use of impoverished stimuli (like inkblots) backed up by instructions that encourage the subject to take associative flight, or through selectively treating responses to highly evocative stimuli (like a swastika or a dollar bill), so that only the stimuli's emotive impact is measured, without regard to the organizing effect of their nonemotive attributes. What these experiments completely by-pass therefore are questions about *efficiency and "correctness" of perception*, which are and always have been the central concern of the psychophysical experiment. The psychophysical experiment, conversely, is designed to maximize the *correspondence* of perception to stimulation; it too is subject to limitations of generalization. It is thus treacherous to generalize to all perception from either of these types of study—a point emphasized in Brunswik's plea (1947) for a representative design in experimentation on perception.

But the crucial matter, in Gibson's view, is not overgeneralization from a restricted experimental inquiry. He insists that an adequate understanding of the projective aspects of experience must be founded on a theory of *effective* perceptions; the first problem in perception is not its errors but its success. It is only from such a theory that we can evolve a systematic view of the processes contributing to error and distortion.

> We know that patterns, pictures, and symbols may be conceptualized, stereotyped, and distorted by perceptual customs . . . What we do not sufficiently understand is, for instance, how a face is perceived as such, or is perceived as the face of an acquaintance, or is perceived as the face of a hostile man. . . . In other words, what do we discriminate and identify in these complex stimulus-situations which, when conditions are favorable, yields a correct perception? This ought to be the primary line of inquiry, but instead it is almost completely neglected. (1951, pp. 95–96)

This point applies even to a full understanding of specific "projective tests."

This very important matter of strategy will be discussed further later. It is worth noting in passing, however, that Gibson's criticism of the stacked deck in motivational studies of perception applies only to studies that overgeneralize in the manner he describes, like those that do indeed confine themselves to impoverished stimuli ("ambiguous" stimuli, brief exposures, "open-ended tasks"). It does not touch those studies that have yielded evidence of stylistic consistency in perceptual response (Witkin et al., 1954; this volume, Chapter 6) or such studies as those by Pötzl (1917) and Fisher (1954) showing that even a motivational setting that favors highly efficient discriminations is not free of "unadaptive" drive influences. The main lesson of the latter studies is that distortion and autism are *not* the only marks of motivational influence in perception.

In order to prepare the ground for a survey of some of the critical variables in motivation-perception relationships, it is necessary to examine the polar points of view in the controversy. It is not possible to examine all variations in these points of view, but a schematized review will highlight the critical issues and is worth the risk of oversimplified amalgams of disparate perspectives.

Motivation-Centered Approaches

Most motivation-centered studies address themselves to the "interaction" of motive and perceptual processes. Examples include demonstrations of "autistic" distortion, elaborations, and selective sensitivity, as in "perceptual defense." This literature has been critically reviewed by a number of investigators from the point of view of perceptual theory (Helson, 1953; M. B. Smith, 1952; Luchins, 1951), and there is little point in repeating their work. As observed earlier, criticisms have revealed the ambiguity of such studies as to the locus of the alleged interaction—whether it involves process formation (in the Gestalt sense) or merely preperceptual or postperceptual processes. On the other hand, the inadequacy of such studies from the standpoint of motivation theory itself has escaped notice, and a few remarks on this matter are appropriate.

Many of these studies assume a linear relation between intensity of motive and perceptual effect, that is, the more intense the motive the greater the perceptual distortion, an assumption both unlikely in theory and inefficient in predictive power. In part the fault has lain in a basic lack of clarity about the motives at work in the experimental situation. Little attention is paid to the complexity and range of motives that converge upon response in a situation—motives other than the immediate, specific one induced by an experimental instruction. I have in mind dispositions ranging from more or less conscious motives concerned with self-esteem, achievement, and failure, to silent, "unadaptive," but nonetheless potent erotic and aggression-tinged motives that may also be triggered in an experimental situation. Few if any studies have taken into account the entire motivational field or tried to link experimental effects to *levels* of participating motives. It has even been rare for experimenters to evaluate the relevance or irrelevance of a task to the motives favored by an experimental instruction or a consciously self-imposed task. It seems naïve to assume that a given perceptual outcome represents the workings of a *single* motive or that all tasks are equally subject to influence by the same motive. Pötzl's pioneer studies (1917) and more recently those of Fisher clearly show that the motivational aura of an experiment ranges far beyond the seemingly explicit experimental instructions or even the motivational components of the subject's "ego investment"—his incentive to do well, to avoid failure, and so on. Fisher (1954) found that the experimental occasion itself—in his study, attending to tachistoscopic exposures —had profound personal significance. For instance, peering through the darkness to glimpse the momentary stimulus had, for one subject, a voyeuristic meaning. To most subjects the experimenter himself took on important symbolic significance.[1]

Studies of the effects of specific motivational states have not only oversimplified the motivational context but until recently have also neglected the importance of stabilized personality dispositions. Perception can be motivated without necessarily being in the grip of immediate need gratification. Besides temporary need states, two other classes of motives should be distinguished: defenses and those related to styles of cognitive behavior. Temporary need states include such conditions as hunger and thirst; transitory intentions or sets; and aims triggered by momentary arousals of anger, admiration, jealousy, or ambition. Motivational studies have dealt mostly with the effects of temporary need arousal; for example, thirst may create a readiness to perceive water and may inhibit responsiveness to other stimuli. The activities involved in the other types of motive need not entail projected gratifications, yet they are no less personal. Not only defenses but also cognitive styles or attitudes seem to reflect stabilized organizing principles that are brought into play in a wide variety of circumstances. The role of such enduring "motive structures" as cognitive styles has proved an especially important

---

[1] [There is also the impressive evidence in Rosenthal's studies (1966) of subtle and unwitting experimenter-subject interactions that extend beyond the compass of experimental manipulations and affect outcome.]

consideration in determining the limits of certain perceptual "distortions." (See especially this volume, Chapter 6.)

Another flaw of motivation-centered studies of perception has been their narrow view of the "effects" or "influences" exerted by a motive. Usually the issue of effects has been squeezed through the eyelet of measurements of perceptual "error" and verbalized communications and limited to conditions in which the subject carries out a purposeful adaptive task in conformity with the experimenter's instruction. But such purposeful perceiving is not the prototype of all states of consciousness in which a person perceives and in which motive-organized percepts guide behavior. Motivationally colored percepts may appear in the convolutions of a dream, in reverie states, in daydreams, and in "twilight" states, and the intrusion of ordinarily alien motives upon percepts seems to be more profound in these states than in adaptive discriminative behavior. Most studies have been confined to situations in which a *central* consciously acceptable motive steers the subject toward a disciplined adaptive response, usually a discrimination. But, if we recognize that an experimental situation includes a fringe of subsidiary, if irrelevant, motives; if we further conceive of occasions and states of consciousness ranging along a continuum from purposeful perceiving to dreams; and, finally, if we take into account that responses can occur on various levels from conscious communications to nonverbal interoceptive events, then the search for the "effects of motive on percept" is broadened to its proper scope.

Evaluations of effects have usually been based upon single-level responses that are often trivial in relation to the motive concerned. For instance, in perceptual-defense studies *absence* of response is the exclusive indicator of effect; evidence of the impact of the motive has rarely been sought on response levels that may become simultaneously and substitutively active.

Perhaps the grossest oversight in motivation-centered studies is their failure to resolve a paradox created by their own demonstrations: In view of distortion, perceptual defense, and other testimony to the corruptibility of perception, how is it possible that perception is as effective as it *can* be and usually is? Even in the Bruner-Goodman study (1947), the distortions were actually quite small, though the subjects were children, and one wonders if they would have any *practical* significance in the adaptive circumstances of everyday life. A simple motivational hypothesis is insufficient. Perception seems to be at the mercy of *every* motive; at most it is amenable only to particular motives in special circumstances of stimulation, according to Bruner and Rodrigues' rather watered-down version of earlier claims (1953). A host of qualifying conditions *in the stimulus situation* must be stated. It is easy to see why Gibson could conclude that it takes impoverishment in the stimulus situation to highlight such "autistic" influences of motives. Under conditions in which a subject is oriented to make a purposeful, adaptive discrimination, motives dominate response only when instructions are ambiguous or the subject is otherwise handicapped by inadequate cues: A motive exercises influence on what is perceptually experienced only when there is little to go by in the information provided.

There is in fact impressive evidence that actions based on perception are efficiently coordinated with the attributes of objects toward which action is directed. Perception can do its job of discrimination remarkably well. It creates workable notions of what things are in accord with what one wants, of where things are to be seen when one wants them.

Michotte's ingenious and systematic studies (1946, 1950, 1951) have demonstrated that even such higher-order experiences as impressions of *causality, permanence*, and *transience* of an object, of surfaces as "picture" or "real" are difficult to explain as secondary projections of ideas or as interpretations conditioned by experience. They seem to be direct outcomes of complicated arrangements of movements, events, and object surfaces in the physical field; experiences in response to such configurations have the same directness and immediate "sensory quality" that characterize the phi-phenomenon.

For instance, kinetic configurations of objects yield definite and unequivocal impressions of *leading and following, pursuit, propulsion*, and other features of mechanical causality. Perceptual coordination with the properties of surfaces, events, and movements in the world of things apparently can thus reach remarkably high levels of intricacy. This possibility had been obscured by a philosophical assumption derived from Hume that emphasizes associative learning as the only basis for complex experiences and that de-emphasizes direct correlations between environmental regularities and the patterning of the perceptual process itself. Heider (Heider & Simmel, 1944) has shown that the structure of events, definable solely in terms of temporal sequences and movements, calls forth highly uniform percepts of predictable cause, attribution, and effect. Two geometric figures that move in a certain relation to each other will thus invariably call forth a causal attribution of "A is hitting B." A may be variously termed a "cruel father," a "bully," and so on, and B "a helpless son," a "weakling," and the like, but the perceived actions of the figures are themselves quite stable. "Projection" is quite definitely confined to symbolic embellishments of perceptually apprehended coordinations. A study of the perception of emotion by Michotte (1950) impressively makes the same point, the more so as the projective hypothesis is all too easily assumed by clinicians to account for how emotion is recognized. Impressions of loving, fear, hostility, and so on are often *direct* outcomes of kinetic invariants in movement patterns. Quite clearly, the Michotte and Heider investigations demonstrate the remarkable adjustive capacity of perception to convey intricate and definable qualities of objects and events.

Finally, the important studies of Ivo Kohler (1951, 1953) further highlight the remarkable capacity of the perceptual apparatus to achieve complex coordinations with invariant properties of the "real" object world. Extending Stratton's earlier studies of reversals of the visual field (1897), Kohler investigated the effects of wearing distorting lenses for prolonged periods—days and weeks—upon spatial orientation. He systematically biased visual stimulation in several ways. Wearing lenses that produced an upside-down reversal, his subjects soon achieved high motor facility. But far more significant was his finding that, in time, phenomenal reversal developed—the world "looked" right side up. Kohler has shown, in short, "that a persistent abnormality of optical stimulation leads in the end to a reduction of the phenomenal abnormality of the world, and that a return to normal optical stimulation then yields a new phenomenal abnormality of the world of exactly the opposite sort" (Gibson, 1959, p. 491).

"The habituation that results is not simply a matter of appropriate motor response, of manipulation, and locomotion; the actual *appearance* of the world changes in time, and then it changes all over again in the opposite direction when the optical device is removed from in front of the eyes" (Gibson, 1954). Perception thus seems to be modifiable, but, more crucial, the modification is very much a matter of coordination with a field of *invariants* in the real world, which it eventually "reproduces" in experience, regardless of the initial "distortions" of proximal stimulation.[2]

A crucial lesson in the Kohler experiment is the implied distinction between *medium* and *thing* (see Heider, 1926)—that, despite changes in the medium (proximal stimulation), repeated contact with the real world of invariants results in effective coordination of action, perceptual experience, and the structures of objects. Sharply altered optical stimulation does change perception for a time, but it does not lead to a permanent disruption of coordination. Optical distortion induces a *shift* in the correspondence between stimulation and experience, not a disruption of the correspondence itself. The learning that occurs does not alter the ultimate *appearance* of the real world; it involves a shift in the correspondence between stimulus and experience. The proof is the shift to a world that appears upside down again when the lenses to which the subject has become adapted are removed. In short, the studies prove the modifiability of the *medium* but not of the *distal invariants* with which experience is coordinated.

Kohler's work poses difficulties for the thoroughgoing "functionalist" position of Ames (1946–1947) and his students. Their view is that what one sees and experiences perceptually is the

---

[2] [The reader will find especially valuable Gibson's more recent assessment (1964) of Kohler's studies in his introduction to the English translation of Kohler's work.]

product of the purposeful transactions that have developed between person and objects. *Where* something is depends entirely upon *what* it is and the purposeful relationship that exists between it and the subject. The meaningful world is built from transactions—a learning theory of perception. On the face of it the Kohler results seem to encourage this point of view, but the essential point of coordination with distal invariances *despite a labile medium* finds no place in the Ames theory. Actually, a perceptual system that undeviatingly followed the trajectory of purpose should produce uniqueness rather than generality of experience, because of the variety of "transactions" and the individuality of purposes that occur in different personalities. Such an unbending functional theory is unsatisfactory because it does not accord any determining role to object organization independent of the experiencing subject.

The Psychophysical Solution

In the light of these and other considerations, the emphasis given by Gibson (1950a, 1954) and Hochberg (1954) to psychophysical coordinations seems at first glance to be a necessary counterweight to what has sometimes been called "motivational imperialism." According to Gibson, the essential tie between real world and experience is a

correspondence between certain mathematical properties of the retinal image and certain phenomenal variables of the visual world—not only the qualities of color and so-called location but also qualities of the curvature and density and proportions and motions of things. These mathematical properties of the stimulus, if they can be specified, are the key to the deepest problems of perception. (1954)

The chief novelty in this point of view is the conviction that behind every quality of experience is a specific discoverable stimulation.

This means not only that the sensory qualities, so called, have stimuli, but that all the qualities of surfaces, edges, slopes, and shapes have stimuli, and that all the qualities of motion, action, and causality have stimuli, and that all the qualities of persons, groups, institutions, words, and symbols have stimuli. (Gibson, 1951, pp. 104–105)

The main problem in analyzing a perception is therefore to discover the stimulus, rather than merely to measure the response, and the failure to keep this problem in focus has led to an overemphasis on *response* in motivational studies.

This approach is fundamental, says Gibson, even to the understanding of the perceptual bases of projective-test responses. Even the Rorschach is determined by stimulation—of a special sort—that involves, in Gibson's view, "a game of controlled misperception."

The Rorschach inkblots contain gradients of texture, shading, and color, including moderate gradients of varying definition, and steep or sharp gradients, the latter tending to produce margins. In this respect it is like an ordinary photograph, but the essential characteristic of the inkblots is that these are *not* the specific gradients and margins which yield the surfaces and edges of objects in a photograph. The edges and surfaces which emerge in experience are ambiguous or equivocal. There are stimuli for corners, curves, indentations, protuberances, and interspaces in the inkblots, but these stimuli are mutually discrepant or conflicting. Since the spatial properties are not consistent, the objects are not consistent and what is seen can be almost anything. The orthodox description of the inkblots is to say that they are "unstructured," borrowing a term from Gestalt theory, but this is a poor word since it has never been clear whether the physical stimulation lacks structure or whether it is only the perception which is unstructured or, for that matter, exactly what the term structure means. (1951, p. 97)

The relevant stimulus variables may be complex (ratios, patterns, reciprocals), but they are no less measurable than are variations of intensity in a single dimension (for example, brightness). Indeed Gibson (1954) and Hochberg (1954) have proposed a program of "global psychophysics" to discover such "higher-order" variables through an entirely different strategy of psychophysical measurement than usual. An example of this approach is Gibson's explanation of size and shape constancy in stimulus terms. In general, the psychophysics of space perception would come down to a search for *invariants* on both the distal and proximal (retinal) sides. Invariants of three-dimensional experience are present in retinal images as "specific high-order variables of stimulation." The "adequate" stimulus for an experience of the constancy of size or of shape is an invariant—a reciprocal relation among proximal conditions on the retina, as between the retinal stimuli for size and distance.

Although granting priority to the problem of discrimination and its bases in stimulation, Gibson interprets the findings of motivation-inspired studies and projective tests, typically obtained in settings that encourage a wide latitude of "acceptable" responses, as reflecting a loose schematic attitude and the standards that ordinarily govern normal "looking" behavior. Only rarely are the stringent demands of the psychophysical laboratory for discriminative efficiency met in real life. Adequate behavior does not usually require precise discrimination. Behavior can be effective enough within a wide range of departures from the stimuli, for example, conforming to "schemata" or stereotypes. When in addition the central portions of a field of stimulation are unclear, then and only then, according to Gibson, does projection work. To provide for both "tendencies" in behavior—actions based on precise discriminations and actions based on schemata—he defines two kinds of perception: schematic and literal. Both, it should be added, are consistent with his point of view that stimulation precedes meaning, for stimuli are involved even in schematic perception. But the "effective" stimuli in schematic perception are representations (memories and concepts) of objects, whereas in "literal" perception experience is directly coordinated with measurable relations—invariants—in the stimulus field.

At this point Gibson's corrective emphasis becomes overemphasis. Upon closer inspection, the phenomena involved in Gibson's two types of perception seem more alike than different.

When Gibson acknowledges that perception does not often occur under "optimal conditions" of discrimination, he must mean in part optimal conditions of *motivation*. But, even when stimulation is not impoverished, literal perception is the product of a certain *intentional* state; all perceptions, schematic or literal, occur in a context of motives and intentions. Second, both "kinds" of percepts require a sorting out of *relevant* and *irrelevant* stimulus aspects.

Wallach's demonstration of memory effects in perception (Wallach & Austin, 1954; Wallach, 1955) offers an excellent illustration of how closely geared the stability of Gibson's psychophysical correlations is to an *appropriate motivational setting*— one might say a stacked motivational deck—containing built-in guarantees of the correlation that he is positing.

Proceeding from Gibson's finding about the importance of textural gradients for perceived slant and three-dimensional perception, Wallach has shown that, in order for a textural gradient to become an *effective* stimulus for perceived slant, a particular set must be induced. The effective operation of a textural gradient requires that the subject recognize the object and appreciate its meaning. Once a meaningful context is given, then a textural gradient can indeed be an effective indicator of slant, whereas in the absence of the set it was not. When the gradient appears without a context that gives it pertinence, it is much less effective as a basis for perceiving slant.

A profoundly important lesson to be read in Wallach's experiment is that the "stimulus" is very much entwined with the internal organization of motives that are active in the situation. The conditions that convert an event into a stimulus include whatever it is that makes it *worth* discriminating—the purposes it serves in the situation—as well as the conditions of mediation. To carry the point a bit further, one can even say that what Gibson calls an "effective stimulus" is also a *response*. His critical stimulus for slant, a textural gradient, is a *discriminable aspect* in a total field of stimulation. But that this rather than another quality of an object field becomes the *focus* for perception is partly a matter of expectancy or set—the product of an intention created by instruction and adopted by the subject. The *effective* "stimulus" of the selectively focal percept thus also includes an intention.

It is more precise to say that what Gibson calls a "schematic impression"—an evaluative experience of things—occurs not only when stimulation is impoverished but also whenever certain properties of objects become *significant* for a person. Not that physical stimuli per se are any less important than he suggests; there is simply more than one invariant in any object or event manifold that is *potentially* perceivable. Different *intentions* in relation to an object make certain properties of the object more or less relevant and therefore perceptually more or less salient. Gibson also fails to take into account that, if one changes a person's state of awareness from that common to the antiseptic psychophysical experiment to that induced, for instance, by LSD-25, the neat psychophysical correlations are undone—but the person still perceives. Under such "nonoptimal" conditions the result is not nonresponse to stimuli but *novel stimulus organizations* (from the standpoint of the person's previous perceptual experience) emerging to participate in the percept.

Gibson's point of view makes no provision for the *selection* of what will be responded to in the stimulus. As his own experiments are uniformly tailored to only one condition of motivation, his answers apply only to that condition. When several motives are simultaneously active, one can doubt that analysis of the "distribution of energies on sensory surfaces" will suffice to explain perceptual selection. In criticizing the motivation-centered theorists for their seeming assumption that the stimulus is a matter of accidental occurrence, he overlooks the part played by motives in disposing discrimination to favor one or another attribute of the stimulus.

The heart of the difficulties in Gibson's point of view appears to be, then, the slight regard given to intention in *literal* perception. This oversight causes him to distinguish literal from schematic perception when the issue may really be one of determining what motives are dominant—nonveridical or counterveridical motives. In my view, schematic and literal perceptions are not essentially different but define the ends of a continuum characterized by changes in the *motivational context* of perceiving, rather than by different sets of perceptual processes.

It is possible that two of Gibson's assumptions stand in the way of his recognizing the problem of what governs selection in perception. First, he seems to take it for granted that the "gradients" formed on sensory surfaces are identical with the *object* qualities that one is trying to perceive. But one does not discriminate *gradients;* one discriminates *size* and *shape*. The gradients are only cues or mediators for the actual qualities and are not identical with them. There are instances, as Heider (1926) points out, in which medial qualities themselves can become the *objects* of perception; for example, movements mediate perceived actions between objects, but under other conditions the movements themselves can be the "objects" of perception. The distinction between thing and medium inevitably raises the question of what perception owes to intention or focus; the *relevance* of a stimulus, its role either as mediator or as object property aimed for, is not given in the stimulus arrangement.

Gibson seems also to take for granted that the psychophysical correspondences he obtains are not only the necessary but also the sufficient conditions for a given perceptual experience. He seems to reason that, if a proximal invariant like a textural gradient is highly specific to an experience of slant, this correlation exhausts the means of experiencing depth. But a variety of proximal conditions may serve interchangeably as media for the representation of the distal invariants or object qualities (Boring, 1952; Brunswik, 1947; Heider, 1926). The very distinction between the qualities of *things*, to use Heider's term, and the *medium* (carrier) of qualities in perceptual experience, the possibility also that things may be interchangeably mediated by a variety of mediating patterns ("ordinal stimuli," in Gibson's term)—these two aspects of perception alone offer the potentiality for more flexibility in perception than Gibson allows for.

It is thus easy for experimenters who seek to emphasize the importance of external stimulus order to go too far in ignoring motivational context by restricting experiment to conditions that exaggerate the role of correlated sensory order in shaping perceptual experience. Their studies invariably construct a *motivational reduction screen* in which a single motivational condition —to discriminate correctly—is given maximal opportunity to work effectively; the experimenters trust their data only when they can safely assume this "optimal condition." Gibson has demonstrated correlations between object and proximal invariants *under such conditions* and no more. He has not provided a basis for determining what aspect of an object will dominate experience. To account for the coordination between experience and the object properties and different options of mediation that occur in any situation requires respect for the active, selective participation of the organism in the perceptual process. The essence of this activity, as I shall try to show in more detail later, is the coordination of *intentions*—whether conscious or not—with properties of things that are functionally relevant. To make any headway with this problem, the experimenter must appreciate the range of motives in a situation. Krech's reminder is apt:

. . . motivation is neither superimposed from above nor injected from below, but is an attribute of the total field situation. (1951, p. 121) . . . . . . instead of giving a *partial* description of the experimental situation, we must seek for as *complete a description as feasible.* No matter what experiment we are doing, we must seek to describe the so-called "internal" *and* external stimuli, or the so-called physical *and* social. And this holds, I repeat, whether we are doing a rat experiment, a perception experiment in the dark room, or a Rorschach study. (p. 136)

In what follows I shall consider, first, the variety of motivated trains of thought—the field of intentions—that play into behavior, both those central and those irrelevant or peripheral to immediate intent, and, second, the relations of these trains of thought to centrality and peripherality in the environment. My concern includes motivational activity irrelevant to purposeful intentions of the moment, and the problem created by its relation to peripheral environmental events for maintaining the *effective-*

ness of the dominantly intended train of thought. My aim is largely descriptive, to examine the play of ideas in the focus and periphery of behavior when a person is engaged in purposeful adaptive effort.

The discussion will center upon an experimental situation that requires the subject to make a particular *discrimination*. This situation is not, of course, typical of all situations in which perception occurs or even of all experimental situations. It is extremely common, however, and indeed the paradigm for most experiments that have sought to demonstrate motivational distortions of perception.

THE FIELD OF INTENTIONS: EXECUTIVE AND PERIPHERAL MOTIVES

Executive Intentions

In a typical experiment, the experimenter asks the subject's cooperation in an enterprise important to the experimenter: trying to discriminate some part of the stimulus array, say its hue, by adjusting the saturation of a comparison color wheel. Instructions to the subject orient him to particular qualities in the objects or events to which he is exposed. The subject's response, his "discrimination," is the terminal event, presumably "satisfying" both the experimenter and the subject ("he is doing his job"). Whatever the subject does subsequent to the instruction is focused on this end. The experimenter has evoked an orientation to a class of qualities in relation to which some communicative act (in this case a verbal response) terminates the intention. The instruction presumably activates in the subject color categories and color connotations; the verbal response particularizes the match he experiences between such categories and the perceived color events.

This situation is not, of course, very representative of real life. Much of the time perception is enmeshed in *action*, providing a basis for doing or not doing something about the events perceived, and guiding us to next steps in relation to these events and objects. The typical laboratory experiment aborts this process: the subject usually does not do something about the stimulus, he only *tells* something about the stimulus, reporting his perception. He must frame his experience in a communication to someone else, most of the time in a verbal report or a restricted action like pressing a lever or adjusting a color wheel. Furthermore, the subject is often barred from knowing how effective his answers are. He is thus denied the trial and check so critical in real life when he needs to make precise discriminations to ensure the effectiveness of certain actions. Yet the laboratory task emphasizes accuracy as an aim in itself and requires the subject to maintain an analytic attitude, to be immune to distraction and preoccupation, to operate solely on the level defined by the experimenter's instructions. The subject is not supposed to wonder what it is all about; he is to pay attention only to what the experimenter directs him ("No tricks, please") and not to become bored ("Only a few minutes more"). In short, he must perceive on the experimenter's terms, which exclude private motives and wishes.

On the face of it, the task sets a problem in "reality testing." For example, the subject searches available cues that will lead him to a response (about the object's color in this example) that is adequate by some internal standard. But the reality testing is to be performed for its own sake and is justified on no other grounds than the instruction to be as accurate and as precise as possible. (Perhaps he is encouraged by being paid.)

Considering the restrictions that they must accept, it is remarkable how accurate subjects can be under such conditions. This accuracy testifies to the kind and intensity of motivation that the experimenter is able to induce. It is a type of reality-oriented, "conflict-free" motivation that is evoked in real life when a person has designs of mastery, domination, and control over objects. It may be called an *executive intention*.

In order to appreciate more fully the nature of executive intentions, which are elicited in the laboratory by winning the subject's cooperation, it is useful to explore the role they usually play in real life. Executive intentions turn one toward an object, in order to discriminate a particular quality in preparation for effective action upon it. When I look at a chair, I am usually drawn to some aspect of it. I can concentrate on its texture, its style, its promise of comfort or discomfort. It may be important for me to know that the edges are sharp rather than curved so that I will not catch my trousers as I walk past it. What I see of the chair is usually tied up with what I want to do about it or am required to do about it within the intentional context of behavior at the moment. Discriminations of this kind are adaptive in the sense that they influence action toward the chair itself. In short, an executive intention establishes a focus: One does not pay attention to all qualities of an object at any one time but to a particular aspect of it, some perceivable *sub*unit of it. Another way of expressing this point is to say that an executive intention brings an object property into the center of awareness for purposes of effective prediction and action upon it. In an executively intended behavioral sequence, effectiveness of selection is revealed by the control exercised in the succeeding action, or in predictability. Executive intentions may also involve delays in action for purposes of efficient discrimination, of control in preparation for action.

The main effect brought about in perception by this class of motives is efficient coordination of perceptual experience with discriminable properties of an object field—efficient coordination in the sense that what we perceive is in harmony with our behavior toward the object field. Knowledge of the object is a basis for developing a policy toward it (evaluation), communication with it, and control of it. These three objectives of executive intention may, of course, vary in importance in any single situation, but together they constitute the positive aims of executive cognition.

Although we can therefore say that such executive intentions influence perception, it is clear that, to the extent that they are successful, they promote *efficiency* rather than autism or distortion. It is too often assumed that motives are necessarily distorting in their effects.

The Peripheral Motivational Field

But the executive intention is not the whole motivational field of perception. The stake that a subject feels in any experiment may extend beyond the immediately relevant instructions. Certainly the executive intention alone does not account for the subject's attitude and is not the only condition of his feeling "involved." He may feel challenged; he may want to do as well as possible; he may be hostile to the examiner or react to the examiner's manner in some way that colors his cooperation generally or specifically. The picture of motivation that develops from a central concern with reality testing is bound to lead to a limited description of what is moving the subject in the situation. Without denigrating the priority of the executive intention in the subject's behavior, we can note that the care with which an experimenter frames instructions and his assiduous efforts to discipline subjects to respond solely in terms of the single executive intention are a respectful nod to the possibility that other motivational factors might acquire precedence. Even with such precautions, an executive intention preempts channels of action against a background of other, less relevant, and even (for the immediate purpose) unadaptive intentions.

Few studies have actually tried to assess the relative contributions of the various motives operative in a laboratory situation —motives other than the immediate and specific one induced by an experimental instruction.[3] Wallach's investigations, mentioned earlier, are suggestive, however; they indicate that perceptual registration can elicit what he calls "perceptual memories," which in turn can affect the continuing process of perception. This finding at least suggests that perceptual activity may activate traces (meanings, connotations) on a much wider scale than is immediately relevant to a particular act of discrimination.

More direct evidence comes from Fisher's studies (1954),

---

[3] [Rosenthal's recent systematic studies (1966) are a notable exception. See also Friedman (1967).]

which show that even in an experimental situation an aura of "transference motives" envelops a subject's participation and is not easily dissipated by the experimenter's explicit instructions. These motives can insidiously set up "claims," counterintentions, and competing intentions toward thing qualities of the object field. In Fisher's experimental session subjects were instructed to describe and draw what they saw following brief exposures (.005 second). That night one woman subject, a psychotherapy patient, had a dream in which the experimenter appeared as one who could rectify a fantasied mutilation of her body. Numerous elements of the stimulus shown during the day, as well as allusions to the experimenter himself, appeared in the dream fabric, taking on special meanings that conformed to the underlying contents of the dream. One of the stimulus slides showed three tall pieces of sandstone eroded into kinglike forms. The same subject, whose other clinical protocols revealed a fantasied castration, reported only the *upper* portions of the slide. It is likely, says Fisher, that the experimental instructions (to look and describe) stirred up exhibitionistic wishes. In his immediate response to the slide, one male subject, also a patient, drew three girls, clad in shorts and bras, taking a picture. From knowledge of the major conflicts of the patient gleaned from his clinical history, Fisher had good reason to conclude that the similarity of the projector to a camera aroused exhibitionistic wishes in the experimental setting. This subject's dream following the experimental session was also concerned with watching and exposure, and elements of the stimulus slides contributed concrete details to the development of this theme in the dream.

From these observations it is possible to say that, although executive intentions direct the subject toward certain and not other attributes of the field, other intentions created by "silent" motives (wishes) compete for the total field of perceptual registrations. Nonadaptive and irrelevant meanings are potentially arousable by the experimental situation, the apparatus, the subject's conception of the manner and importance of the experimenter himself—all beyond the adaptive intentions of control and mastery required by the task instructions. The motivational aura of an experiment ranges far beyond the seemingly controlled and explicit experimental instructions, even beyond the motivational components of the subject's wish to do well, to avoid failure. It seems useful to visualize the motivational field as having a center and a periphery determined by the adaptive relevance of component motives, the peripheral ones including not only those irrelevant to the specific adaptive purpose but also repressed motives. The simultaneous arousal of more conflict-related, incompatible tendencies to action may result in their selective coordination with functionally relevant properties of the stimulus situation, often without focal awareness. These possibilities of peripheral activation make up the motivational context in which the properties of objects lose their neutrality for the organism.

It is perhaps not surprising that the fringe of irrelevant motives has only rarely elicited experimental interest, for they are silent participants whereas executive intentions are more easily accessible to introspection and report. More important, however, is the fact that in order to specify the nonadaptive peripheral components of the motivational field one must have an understanding of the *individual* subject, to see the particular interplay of motives that makes the situation significant for him. The experimenter must broaden his interest to include consideration of personality organization. Perceptual theory alone cannot provide such a perspective, which is why theories predicated on what perception *can* accomplish in discrimination tasks result in biased views of what is *possible* in any single occasion of perceiving. A complete theory of perception must entail an awareness of what the perceptual process is able to do and at the same time an appreciation of the cognitive strategies of the total organism reflecting motivational aims.

In what ways do peripheral motives affect perceptual selection and the shaping of a train of thought and behavior? If the active motivational field is as diverse as we have pictured it, what safeguards veridicality? Or, what supports ensure the effectiveness of an executive intention? We shall have more to say on these matters after considering the structure of the stimulus field toward which executive intentions and peripheral motivations are geared.

COORDINATION WITH THE STIMULUS OBJECT

The activity of executive and peripheral motives is coupled to relevant events of the environment—surfaces, relations, and movements—for completion. In relation to motive, an "object" is an objective. Far from freeing inquiry from concern with the nature of "objects," the conception of motivated perception requires attention to this very matter.

Oddly, it is not only motivational theorists who have shown no particular interest in the distinction between objects as *physical units* and as *perceived order*. Even behaviorists, presumably interested only in stimuli and responses, often give only rudimentary descriptions of the "stimulus object" and even less attention to what is stimulating about an object. Usually what is described as the stimulus is only a limited, measurable physical attribute of an event—luminosity, contour, wave frequency—exposed to a sensory surface. But such a limited account leaves unclear what the *effective* stimulus in action is—the *perceived* attribute or the physical property itself? Other theories, particularly those concerned with personality organization, show even less concern for the properties of perceived objects. They concentrate almost invariably upon stable properties of *responses* following exposure to physical events, tending to ignore distinctions among perceptual experiences and to blur the relation of perception to physical events on the one side and action on the other. Understanding the coupling of the physical event with its perceived aspect may provide clues to the directional role of motives in selective perceptual experience.

Unit Property and Thing Quality

The word "object" is commonly taken to designate an aggregate of physical properties. It usually refers to surfaces and volumes. But when we perceive it is with some regularity, some patterned arrangement that we make contact. Such potentially perceivable regularities are often called "invariants." The term "object" is less usually applied to regularities of movement, relationships, and temporal order. Kinetically and temporally constituted regularities are also, however, very much part of the domain of potential information over which perception ranges.

Regularities in the physical domain presume what Heider (1926) has called a "*macro*physics" of organization, a realm of organization "beyond perception" or indifferent to perception, so to speak. We may call such regularities *whole properties*, implying that each such invariant is itself constituted of physical components. For our purpose of distinguishing macrostructures from perceived structures, we shall use the term "unit property" to cover any stable physical unit without regard to the complexity of its component organization. A unit property refers to *any* organized arrangement in and among physical events to which perception is potentially responsive.

Presumably a physics of "whole structures" would be capable of describing physical units independently of their status as percepts. Such a systematic macrophysics does not exist, unfortunately, and our terminology for describing macrostructures is woefully deficient. For instance, we may presume that unit properties and arrangements of unit properties are loose or rigid, or in varying dependence upon one another, but we lack the terms to distinguish, in their strictly physical aspect, units built into other units and into whole structures. The assumption that there *is*, however, such a realm of macrostructures will affect our discussion of perceived structure. It gives us a starting point for analyzing issues of perceptual *selection;* it suggests that the realm of unit properties is more extensive than the scope of perceptual capability. It is a useful reminder not to equate the *perceptually* salient with what is salient in macrophysical actuality.[4]

---

[4] ["... optical motion ... [is] clearly distinguished from material motion ... A perspective transformation is unlike a rotation and a magnification is unlike an approach, but each *corresponds* nevertheless to its objective event" (Gibson, 1966, p. 145).]

That there is a *correlation* rather than a point-for-point identity of unit property and perceived order helps to remind us that perceptual salience and perceptual selection involve more than physical structure alone and that motivational considerations, as well as physical structure, are to be considered in accounting for them.

Unit properties refer, then, to those organized arrangements of a macrophysical realm that are presumably describable along such dimensions as stability, hierarchical dependence, strength, tautness, and the like. Unit properties are superordinate and subordinate to one another, dependent and independent of one another in their composition, and more or less necessary in the formation of a particular physical invariant or regularity. There is a dependence, for instance, among the component properties of what we call a "book," and they are in a loose relation to units around them. If one pulls the corner of a book, the rest of the book comes with it but not necessarily also an adjoining book on the shelf.

Unit properties are potential information—potentially perceivable regularities. When they are actually *perceived*, we call them *thing qualities*. Thing qualities include not only perceived properties of surfaces (such unit properties as colors, shapes, textures) but also perceived relations among objects and even temporal patterns of events (like movements). Perceived properties of surfaces may themselves be components of a more complex thing quality that we can call a *contingent relation*. That A is to the *left* of B is obviously not a thing quality in the same sense that perceived A and B are thing qualities, but it is certainly an aspect of the experienced world that can become the focus of selective action. The components of contingent relations may also be either surface properties or movements. For example, the perceived quality of "pliability" of an object is given by the component perception that the object's shape is determined by its support. The perceived pinkness of a face is different from the pinkness of a mere circular shape that reflects the same spectral frequency; the quality of the pink is conditional on perception of the context "face." Physiognomic and expressive qualities fall into the category of such perceived contingent relations (see Werner, 1940; Werner & Kaplan, 1957; Scheerer & Lyons, 1957; Rosett, Robbins & Watson, 1967). In this class are those aspects of objects perceived as emotionally significant without being subjective in character. That is, they are not delusive projections but features *of* things, and an aspect of knowledge of physical events. Such a thing quality is implied by the term "oppressive heat" or "angry storm." We need not feel or actually be in the state of the ascribed emotion. The properties are perceived as *of* the *object*, not of ourselves. Something may be perceived as *pitiable* by a person in complete coolness.

Perceptions of *causality* are another example of such contingent relations. A perception of causality involves attributions of antecedent and consequent in a temporal sequence. Something is seen as *belonging* to something else or as an *agent* that causes something else. In the causal impression "A is hitting B" or "A is leading B," attributions of agency and consequence are applied to kinetic arrangements, as in the phenomena studied by Michotte (1946). Such sequences of events, having definable structures, are just as independently perceivable as the surface properties of objects. Perceivable properties of objects and events are thus roughly classifiable into varieties of thing qualities: *surface properties, movements, actions, contingent relations*, and *causal relations*. This classification is not by any means hard and fast, however.

Just as we included temporal order in the unit properties of the macrophysical realm, so we strain terminology a bit more and include contingent relations and causal units in the perceptual realm as thing qualities. Given this extended meaning of "thing" as a perceived unit or relationship existing within and between events, it is possible to speak even of personalities as perceivable (the perceivable qualities are "traits"), but this line of thought cannot be pursued further here. Similarly, a person's intention, or "purpose," can be construed as a structured "stimulus" to someone else, as a fact of the environment or a unit property, and thus potentially perceivable (not merely inferable). Heider has been the outstanding pioneer in this conception of "persons" as "perceivable units."

The difference between unit property and thing quality is illustrated by a pattern of temporal order in which B follows A. An objective sequence or order itself has no "past" and "future," just as a physical event has no "right" and "left" side. "Earlier" or "later" is a *perceived* quality of physical events in a temporal arrangement. As a thing quality, this order is perceived as B being "later" than A.

Mediating Events

Perception is paradoxical in that, although *directness* of contact is its most striking quality, distinguishing it from such other modes of experience as imagining and remembering, it is also the outcome of a constructive process. It is contact at a distance *experienced* as direct contact. Actually, unit properties are conveyed by carrier waves. One sees and hears things through air, through empty space, through smoke. In visual perception, unit properties are available to the organism through a physical medium of air, mist, or dust, and under various conditions of illumination. It is therefore through physical events that unit properties are formed in the environment and mediated to sensory surfaces. There is no direct contact in perception; it is actually only in the *experience* of the contact, rather than in the process of perceptual structuring itself, that the directness exists. As a thing quality, the event elicits a conscious quality of direct contact.[5]

---

[5] [Gibson writes:

The act of drawing a visual pattern, or matching it to a sample, may be taken either as form-perception or as memory for form. The objective operations do not distinguish memory from perception. Only our subjective feeling about them separates the two kinds of activity. We have the feeling that perception is confined to the present, whereas memory refers to the past. But this distinction, be it noted, is wholly introspective. (1966, p. 142)

That the quality of direct contact of perception is the mark of a kind of

It is through still another stage of mediating events that a structure must pass to emerge in experience. They consist of receptor-cortical activity that separates the systematically related excitations from transient unstable ones and positions these regularities in a cognitive context. Just as a unit property is composed of subsidiary unit properties, a thing quality is composed of subsidiary events of mediation within the organism. At this stage, a physically mediated regularity or unit property undergoes further ordering in two main phases, one of primary and one of secondary mediation.

The phase of primary mediation consists of patterning at the sensory surface, organization in which facts of "nonchange" are separated out and registered.[6] These registrations include figure-ground distinctions, gradients, contour formation, temporal units, color variations.

Primary and secondary mediational coding differ in one important respect: The primary coding registers a regularity or

---

knowing distinct from various forms of intellection can be readily demonstrated by asking a subject to stand on a low stool and look at the floor through aniseikonic lenses, which produce a powerful illusion of a precipitous slant in the floor. When asked to jump, he will almost invariably hesitate embarrassedly before the jump while he reminds himself, in spite of the cogent *perceptual* experience, that the floor "really isn't that way." Here perceptual *experience* momentarily took precedence over knowledge; this rule of thumb is usually, but not always, a reliable guide to action.]

[6] We found that continuous optical transformations can yield quite simple perceptions, but that they yield two kinds of perception at the same time, one of *change* and one of *nonchange* . . . The perspective transformation of a rectangle, for example, was always perceived as both something rotating and something rectangular. This suggests that the transformation as such is one kind of stimulus information, for motion, and that the invariants under transformation are another kind of stimulus information, for the constant properties of the object. . . . This hypothesis of a persisting stimulus underlying a flux of changing stimuli, of invariant variables accompanying the variant variables, is a very powerful one. (Gibson, 1966, p. 145, italics added)

See also Klein (1949), and Bruner and Klein (1960).]

stability in the flux; it separates what is stable from what is changing in the array. Secondary coding is the positioning of the registered stability in a connotative and denotative organization; its outcome is a coded regularity perceived as a thing quality. A thing quality does not exist before coding but is a *product* of coding. Registrations at the level of primary mediation are a kind of raw material that can thereafter contribute to any number of possible thing qualities, depending in part on the intentions and motivations of the moment.

Which properties of a scene are registered at the primary level is limited by the capabilities of primary organization. There is evidence that not all stimulus units achieve structuring in primary mediation. For example, Granit and Hartline speak of inhibitory mechanisms at the retina that mute transmission (Granit, 1955; Hartline & Ratliff, 1956).

Structural anomalies would, of course, change the character of primary mediation. When mediational capacities are absent, limited, or impaired, certain unit properties may not be registerable, or may be registered ineffectively. For example, a person whose effective range of hearing extends to only 6,000 cycles a second will not hear many of the overtones in the music he listens to. Astigmatism becomes an aspect of primary mediation, just as dust on glass or smoke filling a room become aspects of physical mediation. Each impedes the process of separating a relatively stable form from a relatively changing flux of events. Klein and Krech (1952) found qualitatively distinct features of perceptual experience in brain-injured and nonbrain-injured subjects, which they attributed to varying efficiency in transcortical conduction. To the extent that a mediating process is limited in its capacity to serve as such, it is important to recognize this inadequacy in accounting for perceptual anomalies.

The restructuring of unit properties must go beyond the primary coding so far described to the secondary step of placing such coded properties in a context of meaning. In secondary mediation they are positioned in a field of connotations and denotations. The unit property, having been coded through the structuring processes of primary and secondary mediation, is now a perceived thing quality of which the person is either focally or marginally aware. It is in this sense that a unit property becomes a thing quality—a perceptual outcome. A drawing of a house can, for instance, be considered as lines, contours, and surfaces projected on the plane of a sheet of paper. These elements give enough information to the retinas so that the units coded in primary intraorganismic mediation can be secondarily coded as "house," or rather as a *picture* of a house; the recognition that the object is in fact a *picture* is also a product of the secondary coding. In short, the mediational coding of the primary and secondary phases is a kind of "language" of the perceptual system upon which an *experienced* regularity is predicated. Without such coding, there is no perception—inchoate sensation perhaps, but not perception.

When a unit property has achieved the stage of primary mediation within an organism, we may say that it has "registered"; when it has reached the stage of secondary mediation, we may say that it is nearer actualization as a perceived thing quality.[7] Physical impingements thus become subjective structures through mediational processes; from the latter develops the terminal or represented thing quality.[8]

Some theorists—Gibson is their most persuasive spokesman

---

[7] ["Nearer actualization" hedges the crucial issue of whether our formulation of a thing quality properly includes the processes that make one *aware* of a registered event—either focally or marginally, and with the *quality of direct contact* that distinguishes perceptual from other modes of experience. These issues of consciousness—*intensity* and *quality* of awareness —imply a level of excitation different from that at which "meanings" are coded in secondary mediation. Whether it is necessary to regard them as an aspect of secondary mediation or as still a third phase in the formation of a thing quality must be left to that future time when we shall have penetrated the complete ignorance that still shrouds the bases of perceptual consciousness.]

[8] In distinguishing two main aspects of an object's organization we have

—view the structuring that occurs in primary mediation to be the essential aspect of perception, as when sensory surfaces "compute" the stable ratios of an incoming flow of light. The coding of denotation and connotation is said to be *post*perceptual, cognitive elaboration. Gibson considers his program for a "global psychophysics" to be all that is needed for a full account of perception. For example, in Gibson's view, experiences of constancy do not require us to assume what I have called "secondary mediation"; he believes that constancy is determined by stabilities of the surrounding world represented as (correlated with) gradients of texture and other "ratios" given by the computational capacities of sensory surfaces. This approach runs into difficulty with the problem of perceptual *selectivity*, the relative salience of one or another registered unit in perceptual experience. As Brunswik

---

followed Heider's model. He pictures the arrangement as in the following diagram.

Environment	Perceptual System
Th *M*	*M'* *Th'*

Th: The vitally relevant environment (we often call it "the world of things" but people, events, etc., also belong to it).

M: The mediating events, the stimuli which directly impinge on the organism.

M': The processes in the organism correlated to the stimuli; they can be experienced under certain conditions, e.g., as reduction color.

Th': Experiences which refer to things. (Heider, 1930, p. 43)

For what Heider calls "thing" (*Th*) we have used the term "unit property" to emphasize its distinctiveness from thing quality. Furthermore, in his section *M'*, Heider does not distinguish "primary" and "secondary" intraorganismic mediation.

Brunswik (1952) used an essentially similar model to define perception as "a relatively stabilized connection between focal variables," that is, a link between an initial focus—an "object," "situation," "event," or the like—and a terminal focus, the representation of this object in the life space.

and Boring first pointed out,[9] there are other ways, besides gradients of texture, of producing depth experiences. In our terms, the registered qualities in primary intraorganismic mediation can *interchangeably* represent the unit property that they jointly or separately convey. What then determines selection, their respective impacts on a perceptual outcome? Some central "decision," or coding in a context of motivated activity, seems to be inescapable.

The units formed in primary mediation seem, then, to be subject to a further integrative step, the referral of such units to relevant classes of meaning. Tajfel (1957) has convincingly shown that the person judges an object's physical dimensions of size, texture, color, and so forth, not according to absolute units of reference, but by reference to appropriate categories or classes. The perceptual experience of size, of color, of texture that emerges reflects the relationship of the dimension of the stimulus to class. Take size, for example: if for a person all Swedes are tall and all Frenchmen are short, a 5′8″ man identified as a Swede might *look* taller than a 5′8″ Frenchman.

Moreover, others (Holzman & Klein, 1956; this volume, Chapter 6) have shown that the interaction between a series of magnitudes and a scale of value may also depend upon the "general flexibility" or "constrictedness" of the perceiver, and upon variations in need states.

Differences among people in such tacit encoding make for individual differences in perceptual experience. It would be wrong to regard individual differences in, say, perceiving size as *mis*perceptions or distortions from some absolute veridical standard that exists within the subject. The tendency to consider such differences as indicative of "distortion" hobbles understanding that a perceptual experience entails a relational act—encoding—in which some registered physical dimension of input is brought into relationship with a value or class, in interaction with the perceiver's more general cognitive characteristics. Subjects thus perceive not the primary unit of mediation (size, texture, and

---

[9] [And more recently Gregory (1963, 1966).]

so on), but the unit tacitly classified and scaled. The encoding of units formed in primary mediation is an essential step in the coordination of a thing quality." [10]

We speak, then, of the coding that helps accomplish a perception as intraorganismic mediation divided into two phases—the primary level of reception and the secondary level of denotation and connotation. The experienced event, the thing quality, is the experienced consequence of these processes. The conceptualization of primary and secondary coding activities is meant to convey something of the active nature of perceptual construction. Rather than being simply a passive record on a receptive surface, perception is more akin to an act of scanning. This observation is true of all the sensory avenues of perception. In touch, movements of the skin surface over an object, rather than a single contact, produce perception. Intraorganismic mediation is a constructive rather than a duplicative process. Reception, even at the level of primary mediation, is more an arranging process, radically different from the operation of a still camera. In reception, mediation is bound to be determined by the physiological nature of the organ itself. For instance, the fovea of the eye is pointed to a scene by successive scanning movements (pursuit, head motion).

The range of the potentially perceivable is restricted by the capabilities of primary mediation and by the limitations and biases of secondary mediation. The realm of unit properties is much more extensive than is the scope of perceptual capability; many units go unperceived. Even when a variety of unit properties have achieved primary mediation, not all of them achieve secondary mediation. Furthermore, not all properties that reach the latter stage of construction are equally prominent in perceptual experience. The distinction between unit property and

---

[10] [In this classification of events, incidentally, we are by-passing the problem of reconstruction through mediation. Bruner and Klein (1960), discussing "selectivity" versus "stimulus dominance," review some possibilities. My present purpose is simply to inventory the variables that we must assume in an experiment on perceptual discrimination.]

thing quality helps also to remind us that perception is a selectively emphatic experience. In hearing a piece of music, a listener may be very much aware of the melody; the harmony may also register but not as the dominant thing quality.

To summarize the central and peripheral coordinations of intraorganismic events: First, a thing quality is made up of primary registrations coded within the activity of a motivational train of thought. Second, in respect to motives, primary registrations may be focal or subsidiary to executive intentions, or focal or subsidiary to peripheral motives. Third, primary registrations that are irrelevant to an executive intention may be elevated to thing qualities within a peripherally active motivation. Fourth, a primary registration may be *simultaneously* a thing quality for one motive *and* a subsidiary component of another thing quality in another motivational train of thought. (For instance, a quality of texture that subsidiarily cues the perception of slant in an executive train of thought may be coded within a peripheral train of thought in an erotic meaning.)

In the present viewpoint the formation of a focal thing quality is inextricably linked with motivational activity. A thing quality is a product of coding, and coding is an inevitable part of the events of a motivational train of thought. That several trains of thought may be active simultaneously means, in turn, that multiple codings are possible; the *same* primary registrations can be coded into *different* thing qualities by several activated motives.

Perceptual Salience

Our consideration of unit properties and thing qualities brings us to the problem of *selectivity* in perceptual *experience*. Units perceived with differing salience also differ in their stimulus effects on action. What, then, determines *focal* and *subsidiary* status in perceptual experience, and what makes one perceived thing quality predominant over another as a goad to action?

"Objects" have so far been pictured as seemingly unitary but actually comprising multiple, potentially informative unit properties. Clearly it would be erroneous to infer that what is salient perceptually is the sole defining property of the object's *macro-physical* structure. The apparent unity of an "object" in perception is very much a matter of *experienced* unity, reflecting that it is a thing quality—a coded event rather than a unit property—that is experienced. This experienced unity should not, however, obscure the fact, stressed earlier, that a thing quality is composed of subsidiary registrations—the events of primary mediation. A perceived object is an arrangement of registered qualities experienced in a *particular* aspect of meaning. A chair, for example, is a particular organization of form, softness, color, texture, slant. But dominating the perceptual experience is a meaningful aspect of "chair." If executive and peripheral motivational activity has an important role in secondary mediation, it also has a role in whether one thing quality is more dominant than another in awareness. In general, experiential emphasis can be expected to fall on the coded properties that are relevant to an executively intended line of action. To account for what is perceptually salient, it is necessary to consider whether a registered event is an aimed-for property or a structural medium of another aimed-for property.

Before turning to motivational activity as a factor in perceptual salience, it is important to acknowledge the influence of the physical macrostructure itself upon this salience. The unit properties constituting a solid object or the component movements that make up a sequence of events are not of equal macrophysical rank; some may be components of a superordinate structure. This macrophysical fact may affect *perceptual* selectivity—that is, which unity property is more prominent in awareness. The basis of this influence may be that what is physically salient in object organization is likely to bias organization at the level of primary mediation. Such properties may receive preferred treatment, as it were, in primary coding. This physical salience may coincide with the coding requirements of an executive intention, but even if irrelevant, a physically salient unit may come to be coded in secondary mediation as well and rival the more relevant units of the executive intention in perceptual experience. Recognizing the macrostructural principle prepares us to expect that what is perceptually salient will at times be determined by the physical hierarchy, even though another unit property is more relevant to the executive intention. For example, in Figure 1, the physical structure reflects some degree of hierarchy, in that the central circular area receives special emphasis. The *Gestaltdrang* makes it hard to focus on the little gap at 10:00 in the outer ring.

Particularly important in experienced salience is looseness or firmness in the part-to-whole relations within a patterned physical arrangement. This factor seems to be highly correlated with looseness and firmness in the field of perceived thing qualities. The unit properties of a loose arrangement can be easily perceived as different thing qualities. On the first Rorschach card,

Figure 1

for example, the properties that make up the percept "bat"—the side projections and the center—may just as well make up the percept "two witches dancing around a Maypole." The properties of a statue seen through a heavy mist would be in a loose arrangement too, but the physical medium of the mist is not intrinsic to the organization of the object. On the other hand, a macrostructure in which the function of a part is unambiguous could be regarded as a firmly organized unit. For example, the perception of a real face depends upon the unit property corresponding to contour; without contour we cannot see a face. This distinction between loose and firm arrangements is an important one in determining the range of perceptual flexibility in particular circumstances. It determines the relative potential of perceivable information in the scanning operations of perception.

The character of the physical *medium* itself is also a factor

affecting this range. For instance, an illusion need not necessarily reflect an inefficiency in the coding processes of intraorganismic mediation: It can be occasioned by qualities of the physical
medium, as when a man looking through a fine haze rubs his eyes
under the misapprehension that the blurring is taking place *here*,
not there, or when a person in a dark room who has been handed
a flashlight with a red filter concludes that the *room* is red when
he flashes the light.

Nevertheless, the physical macrostructure alone cannot tell
us which of its properties will be focal—perceptually salient—for
perceptual salience is geared to the relevance of coded unit properties to intentions and actions.

In perception, such relevance is achieved through a process
of *attribution* described by Heider (1944). A man looks through
the window at the buildings beyond. The glass is dirty; if he says
that the building he sees has a fuzzy outline, he has wrongly attributed a quality of the medium to the relevant unit property.
Through attribution, components of the registered unit properties acquire the status either of *focal* or *leading* thing quality, or
of *subsidiary* thing quality jointly carrying or mediating the focal
quality.[11] In the *phenomenal* organization of a chair, certain qualities are important indicators or carriers of—and in that sense
components of—the focal thing quality; their function as mediating qualities also renders them subsidiary in the field of experience. Registered qualities having medial status will be in
subsidiary awareness; the thing quality they indicate or "carry"
will be dominant or focal in awareness. We do not ordinarily perceive an object's surface features of softness, texture, form, or
figure and ground separately, although the registration of these
qualities is an important contingency of what we do experience
focally. In Polanyi's words (1966), it is as if we see *through* these
properties to some aspect of denotation or connotation beyond—
to use, cause, expressiveness, and the like. We see, as it were,
through subsidiary events to the *particular* thing quality they
jointly convey.

---

[11] [The terms "focal" and "subsidiary" are Polanyi's (see Polanyi, 1966).]

Attribution is particularly important in perceptions of causal and contingent relations (perceptions which involve such impressions as that one unit "belongs to" another, or that A is the "origin" of an effect upon B, or that A is "pushed" by B). Through the ordering process of attribution, various components of the temporal array are assigned medial or focal status related to origin and consequence, agent and recipient. It is only when movements of objects are specifiable in such respects that they jointly acquire meaning as a perceived *action*. As Heider (1930) points out, the same pattern of objective sequence can be seen as A chasing B or as B leading A, two events of entirely different social meaning.

Although attribution is more easily seen in the perception of actions and of temporal sequences than in the perception of surfaces, it does play a role in the latter too. For instance, we do not confuse a picture of a cube on a page with an actual solid cube. The experience of *picture* involves attributing the locus of its contour to the page, not to the cube. It is possible, of course, to manipulate conditions so as to reduce this perceived adherence to a surface, that is, to present the lines of a cube so as to produce a phenomenal separation of the lines from a page—the experience of a three-dimensional cube. Similarly, colors take on different meanings according to the surfaces on which they appear. The same pink color has a different quality of "pinkness" when it is seen as a "face" than as an oval patch of color.

Attributions are also important in perceived *persistence* and *stability* of objects, and constancies generally. In such instances, the observer is called upon to discriminate between qualities originating in the conditions of his observation and those inherent in the object. For example, to see an object not as "defective" but as intact though viewed under unfavorable conditions depends on a perceived contingency. The "gaps" are attributed not to the object itself but to the process of observation. When a person's view of an object is cut off, his awareness of his temporal and spatial limits (his "personal space") makes it possible for him to attribute the interruption to *his* participation and not to the object itself. "X hides Y" is viewed as *my* experience, not as Y vanishing permanently. An object appears "dim" as a result of *my* limitation—restrictions in my field of vision. Some "overconstancy" experiences in children's perceptions result perhaps from the fact that this distinction is not yet highly developed. For instance, a four-year-old child will at first have trouble in distinguishing a capital Z from a capital N, for the Z and the N differ only in that the one is "turned on the side." Attribution may produce *variation* in constancy. Piaget (1941) describes how a child perceives a fixed amount of fluid as varying in amount according to the circumference and height of tumblers into which it is poured.

Another good example of the effects of attribution is offered by art historians who describe the emotional jolt that perspective must have given viewers when it first appeared in the work of Renaissance painters—for instance, the impact of Mantegna's painting, *The Dead Christ*. Mantegna painted the slain Jesus from a position at the corpse's feet. If the viewer does not attribute perspective to the picture plane, the foreshortened impression can be of a very deformed, even "mutilated," Christ; the *novelty* of perspective in the fifteenth century made just this "interpretation" possible, and the picture had a striking emotional force. By now, of course, people automatically appreciate perspective as a "contingent cue" that helps to preserve object constancy for the viewer of a picture; we simply see the dead Christ "in perspective," from a particular angle of the *observer*. Such conscious manipulation of forms to upset the usual formulas of causal attribution is a device often used in painting.

It is in biasing the attribution process that motives have their major effect upon perceptual experience. Perceptual relevance is relevance to *aim*; attribution creates order in terms of intention. Through attribution, intentions participate in perceptual structure—a reflection of the intimate tie between perception and pragmatic concerns and of the larger principle that motive is a process biasing the events of cognitive-motor activity. The influence of executive intention consists essentially of biasing relationships among registered thing qualities and thus affecting experienced perceptual salience.

The potential of registered qualities for functioning in perceptual experience interchangeably, either as mediating substructure or as focal thing quality, is a particularly important consideration in understanding perceptual selectivity.

The link between motive and attribution makes it possible for an intention that is invested with emotion to promote arbitrary causal relationships. Such arbitrary biasing of perceptual salience is likely to occur particularly with loosely organized arrays under conditions of ineffectual physical mediation (for example, an object seen through fog), but even perceptions of firmly organized objects are affected by biases of attribution created by motives, to the extent that the relative perceptual salience of thing qualities is influenced. For instance, in Michotte's experiments (1946) on "causal perceptions," attributions of origin and direction are highly correlated with particular kinetic patterns under ordinary conditions of "objective" viewing; a particular rate of movement of A in relation to B gives an impression of "A leading B." However, a strong attitude can upset the perception which is given in the more "usual" interpretation by biasing attribution (for example, "B chasing A"). Because attribution is so much a part of the very structuring of contingent relations, it is to be expected that in this class of perceived thing qualities especially, as in the perception of causation, the effects of motives will be particularly evident.

Utility and Novelty in Perceptual Experience

If the executive intention focuses perception, we would expect the codings most likely to be activated in perceiving to be those that have had, and continue to have, the greatest utility. The codings of secondary mediation reflect the history and emphases of executive intentions in the person's everyday living. The interactions of executive intending and coding in time produce biases in secondary coding that are highly stable across many need states. Indeed, what Hochberg (1957) describes as "economy" in perception reflects the workings of such generally effective rules of transformation. At any given moment what is perceptually dominant within a train of thought is more likely to reflect a highly practiced coding of proven utility than any other.

An example of the emergence of such structural biases from constant use is given in Brunswik and Kamiya's highly informative experiment (1953). The well-known principle of proximity in grouping was their subject of study. According to this principle, the closer parallel lines are to each other in the visual field, the greater will be the tendency to perceive them as a single perceptual figure. According to Gestalt theory, perceptual organization of this sort is controlled by an inherent property of the brain rather than by a functional principle based on experience (the level of secondary coding). Brunswik and Kamiya, however, suggested that organization by proximity has an adaptational utility. We tend to *see* unjoined but adjacent parallels as perceptual *units* because we make an assumption that is reliably based on environmental fact: that closely spaced parallels *do* usually form the sides of the same single object, whereas distantly separated parallels do not. Brunswik and Kamiya demonstrated their hypothesis by measuring distances between parallels among objects appearing in randomly selected frames from a movie. Each pair of parallels was classified according to whether it formed the joint contour of a unitary object or was in some other, incidental relationship. Closely spaced parallels constituted unitary objects far more frequently than did more distantly separated ones. One need not go so far as to say flatly that such a principle as proximity is "learned"—an issue whose complexities need not concern us here. It is enough to say that there is a strong disposition to favor codes that have been pragmatically useful over a wide variety of intentions. In this respect perception is conservative.

If the intimate interplay of executive intending and secondary coding fosters a conformist tendency in perception, a disposition to resort to codings of proven reliability for the pragmatic concerns of living, what makes for *novel* or fresh perceptions? In one view, perceptual novelty simply amounts to experiences that are the opposite of recognition, the detection of something different. According to Gibson (1966), for instance, recognition is the detection of *same-as-before*; novelty is essentially the primitive converse of recognition, an experience of *different-from-before*. But novel impressions of this kind would be experienced as essentially meaningless, and such experiences are surely a limited and trivial sample of novel experiences.

Our discussion of the interplay of motive and secondary coding suggests one possible origin of the experience of meaningful novelty. When a new *concept* arises from the gropings of motivational activity, it involves a new basis of *secondary coding*: Inputs so coded will be experienced not simply as something different from before but also as new and different in meaning. In this view, fresh perceptions would come from novel *con*ceptions that had become part of the repertoire of secondary coding. Such novel concepts may have differing motivational origins. They may have developed, for example, as aspects of the ordering activity of a motive that is rarely ascendant in executive behavior. Though inappropriate under ordinary conditions, they may surface to prominence in secondary coding in unique organismic states conducive to the activation of the exceptional motive. At such times a perceived quality that ordinarily has only subsidiary status may become perceptually salient as a focally intended quality relevant to the unusual concept. In this view, perceptual discovery would require, then, an ascendant, active, and novel conception. (It should be added that such conceptions need not be verbalizable, nor need they necessarily be linguistic conceptions.)

We have an example in one painter's description of an instance of "inspiration":

I am looking out of a window, a long window with a number of sections opening outwards onto a balcony; through and beyond the balcony is St. Ives Harbour and beyond that, the spaces of the Bay. Horizontal strips of various blues, from indigo to peacock blue. Suddenly I find I am no longer looking at all this with the practical eye of one wondering whether the boat is coming in to anchor. Suddenly I'm only conscious of a dark blue horizontal slab sitting on top of a pale blue-green strip which, in turn, rests apparently on a much larger oblong of color—a roundish oblong of incredibly light, almost dazzling

Naples yellow. Across these abstract, horizontal, rectangular slabs of color (which, you will have guessed, are simply the strips of sea, harbour water and, under those, the yellow of a near sandbar)—across these cut the verticals of the very near window frames and the balcony rails. Horizontal strips of color cut up by verticals; result, a check; a pattern of square patches—but squares which each sink back into space—creating the intense illusion of pictorial space.

Now the 'inspiration' for this was not St. Ives Bay seen through a window, merely; even though that particular window, that special framelike aperture, happened greatly to enhance the sense of recessive depth in the Bay outside. No. The picture suggested itself equally because it was constructed in terms of a rectilinear framework of a certain kind; and *intersecting rectilinear lines were an abstract preoccupation of mine at that moment.* So two sources of inspiration happened to merge; two spheres of experience happened to coexist at the moment of vision. One, the view through the balcony window, might be called the objective stimulant. The other, the urge, within myself, to weave a rectilinear structure of lines: this was the subjective stimulant. Suddenly, the possibility seemed to exist of translating one's objective vision of the bay into terms of a strong, subjectively felt rhythm. Suddenly one saw in the scene before one the design which the very muscles of one's arm wished to make, but saw it superimposed on the sea, the harbour, the window. (Heron, 1955, italics added)

Here a motivated but uncommon visual conception became salient and resonated with a formal, not usually perceived aspect of the visual world. Heron's description illustrates how a novel conception of things must push aside a conventional one in order for fresh percepts to develop. A conventional regularity is experienced in a fresh meaning. We are given no hint of the motivations for the geometric focus that sought perceptual specification. We cannot assume that this quickly triggered and intense preoccupation with geometric arrangements had no deeper motivational significance; whatever the motivation was, however, it required the conceptual perspective described by the artist, which in turn led to his scanning the environment for perceptual confirmation. It should be mentioned that a possible condition for such perceptual resonances of a novel conception with an environmental datum may be an altered state of consciousness—one in which conventional coding rules are overruled by others expressing motives that are ordinarily peripheral. Such an altered state produces only the possibility of novel perceptual experience: An appropriate *conceptual* activation is still required.

Artists exemplify the capacity for bringing into focus what is ordinarily subsidiary. They characteristically explore and register unit properties that are rarely the *direct* aims of conscious, purposeful vision in everyday life. This exploration seems, indeed, to be the main reason for the oft-noted liberation of the artist from common object constancies. The artist, in his search for forms that are expressively relevant, characteristically learns to perceive *against* the normal biasing codes that determine perceptual salience. Tried-and-true ordering and grouping principles that usually govern realistic perceiving are necessarily pushed aside in this creative enterprise. He breaks through constancies in order to focus on component units hidden in the apparently unitary, ordinarily perceptually salient object. Out of this activity unit properties acquire new "meanings" and novel concepts are perceptually actualized. It is in this sense that an artist makes a "discovery." Although our considerations of perceptual novelty have centered on the artist's experience, they apply to that of the scientist as well. But we must leave these considerations of creative discovery for another time.

CODING IN CENTRAL AND PERIPHERAL TRAINS OF THOUGHT

The multiplicity of motivations—both focal and peripheral—described here reminds us that for an adequate appraisal of motivational effects in an experimental situation we must recognize activity outside the influence of an executive intention. Not only the executive intention but also *several other motivational trains of thought* are concurrently active. Furthermore, we have seen that the field of objects, as well as of motives, has both focal and peripheral organization; its components extend beyond the consciously apprehended thing qualities. These two considerations converge in the assumption that physical arrangements comprise multiply layered organizations that may be simultaneously relevant to diverse, peripherally active intentions.

We have noted an intriguing possibility: that coding in the activity of an executive intention does not preclude codings within other, simultaneously active motivational trains of thought. Given that various such trains of thought are active, a subsidiary component of a salient thing quality in one may itself be the relevant focus in another. Shape and color qualities that mediate a perceived "cigar" may thus have meaning as thing qualities within a quite unrelated, but simultaneously active, peripheral erotic fantasy. In this view, perceptual registration can be said to occur in depth, ranging from thing qualities immediately relevant to the dominant intention to peripheral thing qualities having no or only tangential relevance or having relevance only to peripheral motives in the motivational field. The idea that qualities can be registered without being in focal awareness does not find easy acceptance in current theories of perception, yet that is where our considerations of central and peripheral motives and central and peripherally perceived thing qualities lead us. This idea implies that the actual range of perceptual registrations that occurs in an experiment is much broader than is necessary to meet the explicit requirements of the instructions.

To take a step forward in understanding the multiple coordinations that may occur between intentions and thing qualities in an experiment, we must consider the nature of the organizing activity of motives, both executive and peripheral, and their role in what we have called the "registration of thing qualities."

An executive intention is an example of what Hebb (1954) has pictured as a train of thought—a semiautonomous sequence of excitations dependent upon stimulation but in critical respects disengaged from internal and external promptings. Its relatively autonomous components include ideoaffective-motor events corresponding to concepts, expectations of future outcomes, attentive "holding" of stimulations without necessarily acting upon them, decision, choice, and confirming actions. Actually, a more appropriate image of the course of excitations is a loop rather than a linear sequence, for intentional activity is best considered as a self-completing cycle in which the terminal events fulfilling the intention critically affect the initiating conditions of activation (see Chapter 14 for a fuller account of this model of a train of thought).

An essential selective function of an ongoing train of thought is to code stimulus inputs. In a condition of activation the ideomotor components of a motivational train of thought potentiate certain codings; they may be said to create a readiness for certain thing qualities. Their effect is to code appropriate unit properties. The input thus coded becomes part of the excitatory pattern of the intention. Such intentional coding activity increases the probability that the registered events will prevail in perceptual experience and become the foci of action. In this way do intentions predispose thought and behavior toward particular objects and events. When we say that an intention is in a state of *partial* activation we mean that excitations among components have not actually preempted motor channels. In such a condition a cognitive segment can be said to be *primed*; it is in a state of readiness sufficient for coding and classifying registered units but not sufficient for releasing motor consequences. This type of coordination is what develops between activated trains of thought and registrations (at the level of primary mediation) in any instance of environmental contact. It is what we mean by saying that motives program environmental regularity into personal reality.

Such coding is implied when it is said that a subject's preoccupation with the texture of a Rorschach blot signifies the presence of anxiety or even a phobic tendency; or that his responsiveness to the color of the card has some particular meaning in relation to his handling of affect. A physical property of the card's structure fits in with, is coordinate with, a motive—an activated structure of conceptual and affective-motor components. The second Rorschach example is a good one because it suggests that the coding motive that "captured" the color aspect was one of which

the subject was not explicitly aware, reminding us that peripheral motives as well as executive intentions may be simultaneously active.

In addition to the central train of thought, then, we must consider the possibility of simultaneously active motives—partially
activated ideomotor units—that are wholly irrelevant to executive
objectives. The existence of active peripheral motives raises the
possibility that recruitment through coding is going on at the
margins, as well as at the principal focus, of action. Thing qualities relevant to these peripheral motives may be formed even as a
focal train of thought is being acted upon consciously and intentionally.

Peripheral motives have the same coding capacities as does
an executive intention, except that their motor facilitations are in
a much reduced state of activation (they may indeed be subject
to special inhibitory excitations). Active peripheral motives may
thus be called "primed cognitive fields"—partial states of readiness for coding or classifying receptor events. They involve orientations toward and actions related to objects. Also in this category are repressed but active tendencies (see Chapter 14 for a
fuller account of the activity of repressed trains of thought). They
become foci of relevant *stimulation.* The peripherally active
field of motives has additional importance as a potential acti-
vator of motor channels; under appropriate conditions that we
shall describe later, they can put an executive intention under
competitive strain, adversely affect it, and even preempt conscious
experience and motor behavior.

To summarize our conception of focal and peripheral motives: They are structural representations of events—meanings—
that in partial activation create a readiness for certain thing
qualities and actions; their effect is to code the presence of
appropriate stimuli.

The dominance of executive intentions in an experimental
situation (preemption of channels of action) occurs against a
background of such partially activated irrelevant, even nonadaptive, motives. Coding by peripheral motives is not precluded by

the activations and codings of an executive intention. In this view, an object field and even a single thing quality may be coded by activated ideomotor units of not only one but several motives. It seems at least possible that different peripheral motives can be represented in a response, even while one in particular dominates action.

We are led to the possibility also that thing qualities that are relevant only to *peripheral* motives and not in the focus of awareness may affect action even within the train of *executively intended* thought. Such peripherally coded thing qualities may seem to have little relevance to what the subject is *directly*, or focally, aware of and acting upon. It is possible, however, that the peripheral qualities have *subsidiary effects* in immediate experience, as well as in other phases of a person's thought and behavior. For instance, when a perceived quality has only subsidiary status within one train of thought but is coded emotively in a peripheral train of thought, the latter coding may be reflected in a subjective experience of intensity or uniqueness—a generalized feeling of inchoate complexity and ambiguity of the kind that Freud reported when he first viewed the Acropolis. We may experience the focal as something both familiar and strange.

Questions about central and peripheral registrations might be phrased according to the distinction between figure and ground: Are background forms perceived, and are they structurally independent of figural forms? What are the necessary conditions for the persistence of such registered forms? How do they affect thinking and behavior related to executive intention?

The most explicit recognition of peripheral or background-stimulus registration came from Gestalt psychology in its recognition that unperceived context is a critical aspect of perceived wholes. As Asch put it, "We may in fact observe changes and disturbances in the part while remaining unaware of the change of framework which is the responsible factor. (1952, p. 58) . . . Many internal processes that influence action are not all represented in awareness" (p. 69).

Even though Gestalt psychology does have much to say about

the relation between figure and ground, it actually leaves little room for the assumptions made here. There is a crucial sense in which peripheral events as we have posited them have no place in Gestalt theory, despite its concern with contextual background. This lack of recognition stems from its tenet that perceptual organization is guided by "whole properties" that create single perceptual experiences graded between foreground and background. In this view, there is no sense in which it can be said that background is perceived *independently* of foreground.

To illustrate the nonindependence of background, Köhler (1947) offers the example of the contours of land and sea on a map. Customarily, land areas are shown in vivid colors, water in blue. The Italian "boot," for example, stands forth as figure. But, if the color values of water and land are reversed, surprising new forms emerge. They are definitely unfamiliar, indicating that they had not previously been "perceived." Köhler draws the conclusion that background as such has no form and therefore no psychological existence in itself, as figure is form that is in awareness. Forms may provoke retinal excitations, he asserts, but if they are not included in the perceived gestalt (figure) they have no independent behavioral effect; they are not separately registered. Background and foreground are integral to a single organization characterized by "whole properties." If background forms have any effect it is not as independent structures but only as parts of a single organization intensifying the figural center of the whole. The classical Gestalt laws of figure and form apply to formations that are perceptually *central*. Although the theory does thus provide for what Köhler has called "silent organizations" (as in frames of reference that govern figure formation), it does not support the idea of independent registration of forms that are not actually perceptually experienced in central focus.[12]

We may sharpen the contrast between Gestalt assumptions and the assumption of simultaneous multiple coding with an

---

[12] The interesting suggestion offered by Klüver (1930) that "whole organizations" mask what he called "gestalt quanta" has been neglected by perceptual theorists generally and Gestaltists in particular.

example, given by Wertheimer (1923), of whole properties in perception. In Figure 2 the components M and W lose their identities in the perceived whole property. The "good continuation" of contour produced by their physical juxtaposition prevails in perception. Gestalt theory would claim that these components no longer exist psychologically, that they have no independent status as registrations. The assumptions of this chapter, on the other hand, do not rule out this possibility, on the principle that the organizing of consciously perceived forms does not preclude other independently coded, though not actually experienced, units. If asked what he sees in Figure 2, the subject might say, "The outline of a butterfly." He does not report the component M or W; his response seems to be entirely at one with the contour defined by good continuation. Let us suppose, however, that we have primed a motive through an experimental conditioning procedure so that it is specifically responsive to an affect-laden

Figure 2

idea to which either M or W is symbolically keyed. Such a primed train of thought may create a higher sensitivity to parts of the contour that most readily resonate with it; the priming may show its effect, requiring a kind of splitting of the figure, although conscious experience is dominated by the "common fate" principle of contour. On this assumption, while the subject is responding with a verbal account of the abstract pattern that he is perceiving, he would unknowingly release a highly specific recognitive response (for example, a conditioned eyeblink).[13] The

---

[13] [An experiment modeled on this example has in fact been carried out; see Eagle, Wolitzky, and Klein (1966).]

singly perceived form is thus multiply registered in different neural firing patterns.

Ehrenzweig has pointed out (1953) that assumptions made by painters contrast with Köhler's and Wertheimer's conclusions. Artists often count on the principle that forms are capable of independently registering even when they are irrelevant to the central form of the picture and not directly experienced. By manipulating such elements as movement, texture, and shading in the *background* of his picture, an artist tries to bring about distinctive effects through the *interactive* impact of peripheral upon centrally dominant forms in a picture. When, in addition, such background forms symbolically convey (we might say are coded by) an emotion, the effects are intensified. Such coordinations between medial and background forms with peripherally active meanings are meant to lend an aura of richness and controlled complexity to the picture.

Quite commonly in artistic productions the hidden form combinations are superimposed on readily recognizable objects; for example, the human figures in a painting by Poussin may describe a rectangle, or the light masses may describe a definable shape. But, if the spectator does not consciously see them and they have no visual existence, why bother with them? The artist assumes that they *do* make a difference. When he takes pains to keep these forms in the background, he assumes that they may gain in emotional impact by that very fact, that the peripheral status of a form gives it certain *positive* properties that might be lost if it were in focal awareness. If "background" forms are influential in this manner, they must have visual existence, at least potentially, even though they are registered outside awareness.

The painter's assumptions, indeed, go even further: The emotional impact exerted by a peripheral or background form may actually be lost if the form is brought into focal awareness. This proposition is intriguing. It suggests that peripheral (background) forms in a painting may often be important because of what they symbolize, and they may become effective in their symbolic use precisely because they are not bound up in the particular meanings of executive intentions.

Clinical observation discloses many instances of preconscious perception, and the assumption of preconscious registrations has indeed achieved almost axiomatic status in psychoanalytic theory. The theory has, however, dealt with the distinction between central and peripheral activity almost solely in terms of repression of ideas. This assumption is too narrow to cover all the factors determining periphery and center in a field of stimulation. Obviously there are processes other than "repression" (in the psychoanalytic sense) that help to relegate contents to peripheral status. But what is their relation to such repression?

What has escaped study in the psychoanalytic framework is the range and content of registrations of preconscious forms, the conditions under which they persist, and their impact (in their peripherally active state) on the *continuing activity of thought*. The problem has been touched on only in connection with the presence of day residues in dreams. It has been assumed that such "peripheral" registrations, resonating with motives and wishes, initiate the process that results in a dream. But why certain day residues and not others, and how does the preconscious percept acquire permanence and persistence? Freud pointed out that certain preconscious perceptions have an advantage in this respect: Recent ones are unencumbered by associations; brief ones are not cathected and therefore do not have the *single* concrete meaning of an adaptive, focal percept (1900, Chapter 7). When we also consider the fluidity and interchangeability of medial forms, we can further appreciate the unique value of peripheral forms in representing latent wishes in perceptual experience.

In this section we have proposed that unit properties may be multiply registered and acquire the status of thing qualities in different motivated trains of thought, that the parts of an apparently singly perceived form may be independently coded by activated motives responsive to them. Admittedly, exploration of this point of view has hardly begun. The conditions that facilitate and inhibit simultaneous, multiple coding remain to be determined, as do those related to the excitatory effects of such coded, peripheral inputs.

A MODEL OF CENTRAL AND PERIPHERAL INTERACTIONS IN AN EXPERIMENTAL SITUATION

A conception of motivated perception has to envisage how perception is responsive both to the inherent organization of objects and to directive forces seeking expression in behavior, that is, how behavior is subject to focal and peripheral directives and is coordinated with focus and periphery in the structure of objects. This question has been the major theme of this chapter. The effects of these interactions must be sought both in focal and peripheral experience and in focal and peripheral regions of motor behavior and action. Any complete inventory of the effects of motives in an experimental situation must take into account these multiple coordinations among the centers and peripheries of these main regions.

Such a model is pictured in Figure 3 (see following pages 94 and 95). It is probably not quite correct to speak of its components as variables in the strict sense; rather they are classes of phenomena. Some have received only limited attention in laboratory studies and will probably require more definition before they can be elevated to the status of variables.

The model shows several trains of thought simultaneously active in an experiment. Figure 3 pictures these events as sequences extending from preperceptual or preparatory processes to behavioral outcomes. These trains of thought comprise the subject's *intentional field*, his motivational context. This context is conceptualized as a hierarchy, at the center of which is an intention—induced by an instruction—to single out a particular quality (in this case hue). When a subject "intends," he develops an orientation, an expectancy or anticipation, toward a particular property of the object field. In daily life such discriminations are usually part of a more inclusive behavioral intention to do something to or about an object, to control it in some respect; hence the term *"executive* intention."

Other motives are also active. They vary in their accessibility to the subject's conscious experience, but their coding activity can go on independently. Motives range from those consonant with the effort to focus on the relevant quality (wanting to cooperate or to make a good showing, or curiosity about the proceedings, for instance) to those pictured on the outermost fringes, which are for various reasons either nonadaptive or irrelevant to the executive intention (sexual interest in the experimenter, aggressive intentions, and the like). The latter motives may be provoked by the setting, the apparatus, the experimenter, or any other element. Their peripherality is determined by inattention or repression. Their *activity*, despite this peripherality, may be guaranteed by associative overlap with the dominant train of thought or by the affect they arouse.

In Figure 3, the active motive field is shown by concentric rings, to indicate central and peripheral motives and their accessibility to awareness. The executive intention is that part of the field of potentially greatest clarity (both in dominating motor channels and in the subject's awareness of its relevant thing quality), whereas other purposes shade off into the shadows of semiconsciousness, to preconscious and unconscious motives. The diagram thus pictures a more complex array of motives activated in an experiment than is usually implied by the experimenter's instruction.

We take it for granted that motives on the fringes vary in their consonance with the executive intention and with its outcome. Those at the farthest periphery are generally least relevant to the adaptive concerns of the executive intention. Whether an activated peripheral intention is related to the executive motive is not, however, a simple yes-or-no matter. For example, curiosity about the proceedings and a desire to cooperate are supplemental aims wholly in keeping with the executive intention. But at a deeper level they may involve various sexual and aggression-tinged aims (like an unconscious voyeuristic wish) that, in the circumstances, are adaptively irrelevant. Of course, these deeper-lying motive systems are presumably of lower intensity than, say, the nagging of a sore tooth, and are effectively kept in abeyance.

Efficient implementation of the executive intention requires

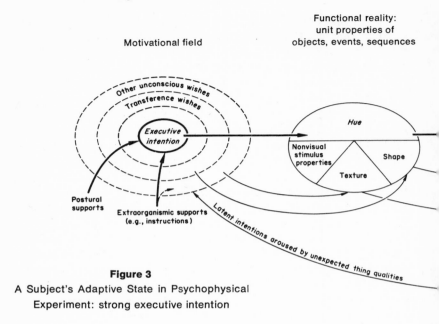

Figure 3
A Subject's Adaptive State in Psychophysical
Experiment: strong executive intention

that behavior channels be responsive primarily to that intention
and to no others. There must be means of guarding experience
and response channels against preemptions by peripheral motivations, thus preserving the dominance of the executive intention.
The experimenter's usually careful instructions, his efforts to
reduce or forestall anxiety, reinforce this focus. Also of likely
importance are postural states—muscular orientations that accompany the activation of an executive intention—whose role in
preserving such an intention has often been overlooked and about
which we shall say more in the next section. They include the
favored upright position and the preferred foveal (rather than
peripheral) fixation in vision, tonic distributions over the body,
and informational feedbacks from action.

Although executive aims are pictured as prevailing in Figure
3, there is no implied claim that peripheral motives are thus
rendered inactive. Like the executive intention, activated periph-

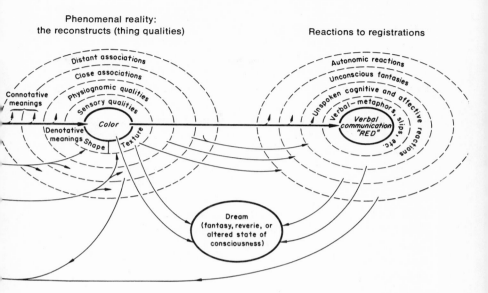

eral dispositions also establish claims upon objects and events exposed to the subject. Activation implies responsiveness, on some level, to appropriate unit properties; the activity of all motives, central or peripheral, consists of efforts directed at certain kinds of objects and relationships. Motives are particularized through the unit properties that achieve perceptual representation.

All intentions, then—even repressed but active peripheral wishes—create preperceptual anticipations toward a range of object properties. Earlier we saw that an "object" is not a single entity but a hierarchy of structural units, independently definable in a physical macrostructure, quite apart from the phenomenal (subjective) field of "appearances." A particular experimental setup has shapes, surfaces, volumes, colors, tactile qualities, forms, and so on. There may also be movement at various speeds. All are potential thing qualities.

The structural property of an "object" that is particularly relevant to the executive intention is positioned within a macro-physical organization that includes various other properties. This position is determined by the physics of the object's structure as a "whole." The physical patterning of unit properties makes certain discriminations much easier than others. It is easier, for example, to see the shapes of objects than the shapes of the empty spaces between them. In the experiment schematized in Figure 3 the task might call for responding to hue in the picture of a face. Hue may not, however, be as vital to the definition of a "face" as is shape; the salience of hue in the *physical* hierarchy would then be relatively low. In this instance, a physical event is *phenomenally* salient because it is relevant to an executive intention, despite the fact that it is not *physically* salient. An adequate description of a "stimulus object" includes, then, not only its *phenomenal* reconstruction but also its part-whole relations in the macrophysical structure, quite independent of their phenomenal representation. The second part of Figure 3 pictures this hypothetical physical hierarchy, in which the intentionally salient property, hue, has less prominence than in the physical object. Such inherent physical arrangements make a difference in the arrangements that can develop in the phenomenal field.

The relation of macrostructure to phenomenal representation presumes another set of events, not pictured in the diagram: events of the physical medium, whose adequacy affects the fidelity of patterned units upon the sensory surfaces. In addition, as we saw earlier, the sensory surfaces themselves involve another set of mediating processes, those responsible for primary unit formation and transmission within the perceptual system. Again mediation limits representability of thing qualities. In this schema any physical invariant, given appropriate mediation, is potentially a thing quality. These events of primary mediation are the necessary basic units in the construction of the phenomenal field of thing qualities. Some of the more commonly subsidiary structural events are figure-ground relations, contours, gradients of texture—units formed from primary mediational structuring and corresponding generally to what Gibson has termed "ordinal stimuli." They have acquired registration, reflecting the coding of some degree of structural stability and making further structuring at the secondary mediational level possible.

To the extent that a unit property has achieved at least primary structuring, it is registered information; to some degree it represents an invariant or stability and is thus potentially capable of being experienced. The number of primary registrations increases the number of *potentially* perceivable phenomenal qualities for incorporation in motivational trains of thought.

The third portion of the diagram shows the *reconstructed* object, the subjective reality of an object. The diagram labels the field of thing qualities—the registered unit properties—as "phenomenal reality." This field consists of the structures formed from the registrations of primary mediation, but the apparent immediacy of perception obscures this reconstructive process. In this schema meaning is depicted as belonging not in external reality but in this phenomenal (personal) reality. The term "phenomenal" connotes the personal aspect of object representation; it is not used here in its perhaps more usual connotation of availability to conscious introspection. A repressed wish may find an apt representation in peripheral thing qualities; the latter would then have phenomenal reality but would not be directly experienced, for they are subject to the inhibitory excitations characteristic of an executive train of thought that control access to awareness (see Chapter 14). The model does assume, however, a positive correlation of the center-to-periphery arrangement of the phenomenal structure is highly correlated with phenomenological *accessibility*, that is, reportability. Presumably the registered qualities that are most central to the executive intention are generally most easily available to conscious report, whereas on the outer fringes are coordinations wholly unavailable to direct conscious communication.

The distinction between registrations one is and is not aware of is an important one in the scheme. Not all units of an object's physical structure that are registered, coded, and active within a motivational train of thought are necessarily accessible to conscious report, especially those formations that become linked with repressed wishes.

In the segment of Figure 3 picturing "phenomenal reality," the first ring around the center indicates a composite of registered sensory qualities (form, texture, physiognomic); peripheral rings represent denotations and connotations mediated by these sensory qualities—information conveyed. The arrows show some hypothetical coordinations that may develop among peripheral intentions, the macrophysical structure, and the field of reconstructs. They are meant to illustrate the point that the motivational fringe resonates as much with associative aspects (connotations) that are deliberately set aside by the executive intention as with other disregarded sensory qualities like texture. For instance, "hue," the focal thing quality, also has physiognomic qualities, although they are irrelevant to the intent of the experiment. Figure 3 shows the possibility that hue can give rise to at least three properties of the reconstruct—the *sensory experience* on which the subject's adaptive intention focuses, *physiognomic reverberations* (like "color shock," or rather the emotive aspects of the colors), and *meanings* (associations both close and distant).

The phenomenal hierarchy in part parallels the strata of the *intentional* field, but only in part, for the physical organization of the field limits the transpositions of attentional emphasis and also the coordinations among specific registered properties. Furthermore, not all properties of the physical field or of mediation achieve registration. For instance, nystagmoid movements of the eye, which are necessary to preserve continuity in perception, do not themselves have phenomenal significance as registered events, although they contribute to the formation of thing qualities.

The central point about motivated perception in this schema is that it involves *simultaneous coordinations in depth between* intentions and unit properties, the organization in the phenomenal field being defined in part by what is central and peripheral in the intentional field. In this model, perceptions affect behavior only within a motivational context; to the extent that perceptions owe their coding to a motivational schema, they are the product of motives. In this sense, motives play a central role in perception even in the "purest" psychophysical experiment.

The expression "coordination" can be understood only with proper regard for two parameters: first, the central and peripheral foci produced by the multiple intentions composing the motivational aura of the experimental situation and, second, the hierarchically organized physical manifold of properties and relationships within and among objects. The coordination of a particular unit property with an executive intention does not exhaust the possible coordinations that can develop in an experiment. The model allows for the possibility that precisely those unit properties that are relevant to active peripheral motives have the better chance of registering and that thing qualities coded by an executive intention are likely to be the more perceptually *salient*. If a tachistoscopic experiment emphasizes color, color will prevail in perceptual experience. However, the blackness of a light-tight compartment in a tachistoscope, though totally irrelevant to an executive intention, may be relevant to a peripherally active wish and gain registration within its connotative realm.

Moreover, a registered unit that in one motivational context is experienced as a subsidiary structure can on another occasion and with another executive intention be the focal thing quality. We pointed out earlier that we do not ordinarily look *for* a "gradient" or a figure-ground differential. Although such primary registrations are essential "raw material" for secondary coding, they are rarely themselves perceptual *objectives*. Usually they are used in the formation of various thing qualities depending on motivations. Awareness of most such events is only fleeting at best, because most of the time they serve solely as mediational data for the process of secondary coding. But events that are mediational and subsidiary in one perceived arrangement *can* become the foci of discrimination in another context—that is, they can become objectives—the aimed-for thing qualities—of an executive intention. In a psychophysical experiment in which threshold sensitivities are measured, for example, an executive intention can single out a textural gradient or a figure-ground difference as such. In this instance, the influence of the executive intention is to raise the ordinarily subsidiary event to the status of a thing quality.

We come now to behavioral manifestations of the coordinations that have occurred in the phenomenal field. A critical consideration is the various ways in which these coordinations are translated to different *levels of action*—active communication, conscious fantasy or imagery, manipulations, and the like. Figure 3 reflects the fact that reactions to percepts in behavior can occur on a *variety of levels* and that the penetrations of a motive into cognitive activity can occur at all or some of these levels. In the usual experimental situation the discrimination is *communicated*, either verbally or through some other motor response. In either case the response is a communication to the experimenter. But such communications do not exhaust the behavioral reactions to coordinations of motives and primary registrations. For instance, autonomic reactions may result from certain coordinations between *peripheral motives* and *peripherally registered qualities* (that is, a person's verbalization may give little hint of an emotional reverberation in the autonomic system). It is also possible that some of the coordinations among the peripheral participants in the perceptual registrations will actually penetrate to conscious experience, either in fleeting, unspoken impressions or in certain emphases and affective intensity in verbal reports.

The fourth segment of Figure 3 pictures various ways in which a perception may terminate in several such levels of action *simultaneously*. It also shows the possibility that the activity of the phenomenal field and behavioral reverberations in varieties of action may in turn excite new intentions, different trains of thought that were not at first present. These intentions would in turn participate in subsequent perceptual selection and further ordering of the phenomenal field.

Figure 3 thus shows the possibility that a relationship of center to periphery is also characteristic of reactivity. Behavior and action can occur on various levels, and the penetration of a motive into cognitive activity can potentially occur on all or any of these levels.

Finally, the possibility of *delayed behavioral manifestations* of motive-percept coordination is acknowledged in the descriptive scheme. The "effects" of the interactions may not be exhausted in the immediate behavioral reactions observed in the experimental situation. The multiple codings of motives in the experiment proper may be revealed later in a dream, in a fantasy, or in some other state of consciousness in which executive intentions related to the object field no longer dominate, thus allowing the emergence of peripheral coordinations into awareness.

POSTURAL SUPPORTS OF EXECUTIVE INTENTIONS

Considerations of peripheral reactivity and action bring us back to the question, How is it possible, in the face of multiple influences from within and stimulation from without, for an executive intention to fulfill its objectives effectively? How are irrelevant motives and stimulation relegated to the background? If the motivational aura is as pervasive as has been suggested, what ensures the dominance of an executive intention over other claims?

In the single-motive orientation of classical experimentation, this question did not arise. An experimenter simply assumed that the subject's intention to make effective contact with reality was the only operative motive, and that what preserves the central focus required for discrimination is the instruction, buttressed by the subject's cooperation.

It must be that intentional thinking has built-in guarantees to keep it on course, preventing it from being deflected from its aim, confining response to relevant information, and holding open appropriate motor channels while inhibiting others. What are these guarantees?

A clue is given in the way a person "prepares" himself for a stimulus when he is aiming for an accurate or efficient discrimination. Observe him as he "sets" himself. His body orients itself in a particular manner toward the object field. He braces himself (the most congenial position for discrimination is evidently the upright position); he looks directly at the object; he tries to focus on the relevant field. Subtler measurements might show that a pattern of muscle tensions is involved in this attitude of "alertness." Eye movements are rapid when accurate discrimination is the aim. Saccadic eye movement, without loss of the object, is perhaps an evolutionary achievement aiding detailed discrimination. The eye, even in focused attention, is never still: Its activity prevents quick fatigue and ensures more prolonged scrutiny of an object than would otherwise be possible. The significance of the upright posture and associated postural components in aiding efficient discrimination has often been overlooked (see, however, the work of Witkin, 1949; Werner & Wapner, 1949).

"Preferences" for the vertical over the supine position, the foveal over the peripheral focus, and bodily "sets" generally are not to be taken for granted; they seem to be important bases or "supports" of effective discrimination. Sensitivity to object qualities, to gradients, to cues of perspective and figure-ground distinctions may be crucially supported by such preparatory activity of the musculature. Malmo and his associates (1951) have succeeded in recording patterns of tension distribution over the body in acts of attention and focused discriminative effort. Recent studies by Soviet investigators within the Pavlovian framework (Zaporozhets, 1954) also suggest the critical involvement of preperceptual muscular "sets" in discriminative behavior. In short, active discrimination seems to involve both large-scale and local muscular supports, properties of a postural state associated with executive perceiving. Whether such "muscular sets" are themselves the manifestation of the discriminative act, and whether perception is itself a "tonic state" as Werner's theory holds, are issues that need not be argued here. It is enough to suggest their importance as conditions for implementing an executive intention.[14]

-----

[14] The value of distinguishing executive intention from postural supports (rather than simply treating the latter as an aspect of the former) is in accounting for circumstances in which one's firm intention to make a particular discrimination cannot be realized because postural supports are lacking (in conditions of fatigue, enforced restraints, and so on).

It should then be possible experimentally to reduce the dominance of executive intentions by upsetting the efficacy of such postural supports. This should be favorable to the freer play of nonadaptive intentions in cognitive behavior and to intrusions at various response levels of peripheral wishes activated in the experimental situation. Projective perception should thus be much more evident when the postural supports for executive intentions are either absent or difficult.[15]

That discriminations required by an executive intention may become more difficult in the absence of postural supports is illustrated by the importance of the couch in the associative process of a psychoanalytic therapy hour. There is a tendency nowadays to consider the use of the couch in therapy as simply a ritual or convention, not crucial to the analytic process. This attitude overlooks one of Freud's great intuitive insights: that the supine position is conducive to a nonlogical wandering of thought and associations and the emergence of drive-organized contents in awareness, and, conversely, that the upright position is very important for logically ordered thought and for inhibiting precisely such tendencies. Of course, the supine position does not inevitably produce associative fluidity. Such fluidity is intolerable to some people, and they react defensively to the first premonitions of it. For them, inhibition increases on the couch. Muscular tension is, however, very much in evidence in such instances, consistent with tightness, constriction, and withholding of communications.[16]

Man's evolution to the upright position probably had enormous consequences for his perceptual potentialities and his capacity to discriminate objects around him. It may well be that spatial perception was much affected by the vertical orientation. In making possible new discriminative sets it perhaps also made possible many more intentions and claims upon objects than man would have developed without it.

---

[15] [For some recent experimental explorations of this proposition see Paul and Fisher (1959), Fisher and Paul (1959), Segal and Glicksman (1967).]

[16] [See Berdach and Bakan (1967).]

In a significant paper Erwin Straus (1952) speculates about these possibilities:

In getting up, in reaching the upright posture, man must oppose the forces of gravity. It seems to be his nature to oppose, with natural means, nature in its impersonal, fundamental aspects. However, gravity is never fully overcome; upright posture always maintains its character of counteraction. It calls for our activity and attention. . . . Awakeness and the force of gravity are mutually interdependent. While awakeness is necessary for upright posture, that is, for counteracting gravity, gravity determines waking experiencing. (p. 535)

[Upright posture] lifts us from the ground, puts us opposite to things, and confronts us with each other. . . . It is true that sleep and rest, lying down and lying with someone, are essential functions; it is no less true that man is built for upright posture and gait, that upright posture, which is as original as any drive, determines his mode of being-in-the-world. (pp. 559–560)

Wilhelm Reich proposed some years ago that the "defensive armor" of hysterical, compulsive, narcissistic, and other character structures manifests itself in stabilized forms of muscular tensions (1949). He suggested not only that *specific* discriminative acts are accompanied by muscular orientations, but also that such orientations may become structured, affecting reactions to situations and cushioning stimulus input. Such differences in muscular orientation may affect how an intention unfolds even in a laboratory task. For instance, perhaps the hysteric's "muscular armor" produces a special kind of selective reactivity to stimuli that affects discriminative perception. To pursue Reich's thought a step further, the postural processes serving *defense* might promote delays and detours of thought that channel discriminative responses in different ways. There are hysterics whose repressive tendency prevents detailed perceptual registrations, so that they do not see what they consciously fear to see. Muscular orientations could well serve such an orientation of "not letting reality penetrate." On the other hand, repression may work, not through such preparatory avoidance, but rather *post*perceptually in the form of developed sensitivity that is actually overly vigilant to a stimulus field in order the more efficiently to repress any noxious connotation that is signalized. The relationship of postural states to defensive and control functions is a problem that promises considerable yields to empirical study.

The thesis is, then, that peripheral coding and motivation are more likely to exert direct influence upon perception in the absence of those postural states that ordinarily supplement executive perceiving. The absence of postural support for an executive intention could conceivably cause inefficient registration of appropriate unit properties in the phenomenal field, allow preemptions of response channels by peripheral coordinations, and increase the potential impact of peripheral coordinations upon the perceptual experience of relevant thing qualities.

THE MOTIVATIONALLY CAPTURED OBJECT: SELECTIVE INFLUENCES OF MOTIVATION

We have seen that not even a laboratory experiment can escape the multiplicity of intentions that are active in waking life. These intentions shift in their relative importance, imparting relevance and irrelevance to unit properties. Motivational participation cannot be reduced to the activity of a single level of intention but is rather to be construed as a field ranging from relatively central to peripheral. Even while executive intending is mobilizing perception to its full discriminative potential, unadaptive wishes and dispositions can be activated by peripheral conditions of the experiment, by the apparatus, and by the manner and conceived importance (perhaps as an authoritative figure) of the experimenter himself. Each activated motive constitutes an attraction field of ideas that code and thereby recruit unit properties that have attained primary mediation. Intentions on different levels may *simultaneously* share a unit property. Or, to put it differently, the same unit property may acquire thing-quality status in different motivational trains of thought. Its meaning as thing quality would differ accordingly. An elongated brown object may be coded as a cigar and simultaneously as a symbolized penis; it is possible for an object to gratify a routine hunger and also an unconscious fellatio fantasy. Furthermore, a good portion of this coordinating activity of intentions with unit properties may occur outside awareness.

Clearly, there is also little basis for expecting all activity of the intentional field to be embodied in a single effect. There are more possibilities of reaction than the apparent cohesiveness of a single executively intended response suggests at first glance. Although adaptive response may emphasize a particular form and level of reaction, this level is not to be identified with the full scope of possible reactivity. Taking the gamut of the total cognitive act as the field of possible effects, it may be, for example, that peripherally active motives have more impact on *pre*perceptual events (for example, in reducing the strength of an executive intention) and on various *reactions* to the percept than on perception itself. Thus, other cognitive events, as well as perception, should be separately assessed for their responsiveness to motives. They include the events involved in translating a peripheral experience into acts of *communication* (that is, in fantasy or imagery) or into a *manipulative* action upon the object field. In fact, report itself probably reflects several levels of reaction. Furthermore, as indicated earlier, the possibility of *delayed* behavioral effects of peripheral recruitment must be taken into account. The effects of peripheral motives may be evident not only at various levels of response during the laboratory situation, but later and in altered states of awareness, as in dreams, daydreams, reverie states, and so on (see Rapaport, 1957a). Such altered states are important in two respects: first, as conditions in which executive intending is weak or absent and the impact of certain motive-unit property coordinations upon trains of thought may therefore become particularly evident,[17] and second,

---

[17] [In the present schema, the distinction between experienced phenomenal structure and behavioral effects is important as a corrective to the common tendency in need-perception studies to take "distortions" in *response* to represent the full range of a perceptual experience. *Phenomenal organization* of the percept includes much more than the recordable or

as conditions which improve the chances that coordinations that had developed peripherally between certain motives and the phenomenal field in another situation will now become focal and preempt consciousness.

In short, the interplay of the variety of intentions and cognition can be investigated in the different phases of organization pictured in Figure 3: in the preperceptual expectations and dispositions, in the organization of primary mediation, in the arrangement of reconstructs (the phenomenal field), in the actions and communications that follow, and in the observable behaviors in altered states of awareness. The organizing effects of peripheral motives must be assessed in relation to the influence of executive intending at these loci.

In general, the central considerations in assessing motivational influences are whether or not conditions favor coding of unit properties by intentions and whether or not conditions favor

---

observable response. Although we may be emotionally moved by the color and structure of a Turner landscape, we will hardly be tempted to take a walk through it. The perception here includes the experience that it is a *picture* we are viewing, not the "real thing," though this aspect of the total experience goes unremarked. (It is possible to fool an observer with viewing conditions that eliminate cues of the picture plane.) When a subject gives a "movement" response on the Rorschach, we would not necessarily assume a kinetic experience. To distinguish the kinetic from associative components of the percept, one would have to know whether the *phenomenal* formations involved are similar to those that would develop if the eye confronted the distal invariants of an *actually* moving object.

It is, therefore, not certain how percept formation itself was affected under the conditions of the need-perception studies. We can be certain only that these studies directly demonstrated selectivity in *report* or, more generally, behavioral reactions to percepts (as in the fourth segment of Figure 3). The effects of an emotional stimulus in the alleged phenomenon of "perceptual defense" serve as an example (Lazarus & McCleary, 1951). "Recognition failure" may mean either that phenomenal organization itself has been modified or that some level of communication with the experimenter has been affected, or both.]

manifestations of peripheral coordinations in phenomenal experience and action. It is possible to manipulate experimentally the conditions so far described in a number of ways that would enhance or reduce the organizational influence of a motivated train of thought at different phases of cognitive organization. These imbalances in an experimental situation can be expected to have consequences either in the perceptual appearance of object properties, in behavioral reactions associated with them, or in both. I turn now to a few such imbalances that may exist among the principal classes of events shown in Figure 3 and to the effects that may result.

The strength of an executive intention is an important consideration. A strong executive intention is one whose coordination with appropriate unit properties is relatively unhindered by peripheral codings of fringe intentions and the subject's verbal communications correspondingly unaffected. If the intention is clear-cut and well-implemented in the experimental situation itself and if no obstacles develop in actualizing it, peripheral coding will not be very apparent. The response to a Rorschach blot, for example, would change considerably if, instead of an equivocal intention, a strong one were induced—for instance, if one were to ask the subject to look *only* for particular shapes or forms, or to see only animals, or to "try to be accurate." Compared to results under the usual condition of an equivocal executive intention (promoted by an ambiguous instruction), coordinations of fringe wishes with unit properties would then not be as strikingly visible in conscious reports.

Even in such narrowly restricted response situations, however, evidence of peripheral coordinations of motive and unit properties may appear at peripheral reaction levels, and even in conscious report if the unit properties coded by a peripheral motive are also physically prominent in the object's macrostructure. Furthermore, it is not impossible that they will appear in other cognitive states—dreams, daydreams, reveries—when the executive intention of the earlier setting is no longer active to inhibit them. The previously peripheral train of thought may now frame experiences during such states. States of consciousness differ according to the relations of inhibition and disinhibition among simultaneously ongoing trains of thought in preempting the phenomenal field and action. An adequate accounting of the ways in which experienced encounters with unit properties reflect different levels of meaning and their influence upon thought and action must therefore take into account this structured context of "state of awareness."

But an executive intention can be undermined in a variety of ways conducive to more immediately evident influences of extraneous motives, to nonveridical representations and "perceptual distortions." For instance, an executive intention may be affected by reducing orienting supports or by deliberately complicating a subject's objectives. The schema of Figure 3 allows for the possibility that reduced postural supports can make it difficult to carry through an executive intention. Reducing the efficiency of an executive intention through procedures like diffusion of focus, elimination of postural supports for discrimination, prolonged fixations, drugs, and the like should increase preemption of response channels by peripheral activity and nonadaptive wishes. When a person is, for example, geared toward making "accurate" discriminations but lacks the postural and informational feedbacks that implement it, his verbally communicated discrimination may become inaccurate. Meanwhile, the absence of these discriminative supports may encourage the emergence of peripherally active coordinations at other levels of thought and action. Peripheral registrations may even become consciously accessible through alterations of consciousness produced by such means, and peripheral coordinations influential in how the centrally relevant unit property is itself experienced. For example, a drug like LSD-25 greatly diminishes the capacity for executive intending and increases the experiencing of registrations that are peripheral in the person's normal experience. It is also possible to weaken executive intention by equivocation, as, for instance, in the typical Rorschach instruction. The open-ended instruction and loose macrostructure are meant to encourage peripherally active motives to intrude upon the phenomenal field in the responses to the cards.

It is possible to conceive of a circumstance in which the subject's executive intention is strong but the stimulus field impoverished, because of either a weakly unified object array or inadequate mediation. These conditions, too, may be conducive to the impact of peripheral codings upon various levels of thought and action. Such circumstances would favor the appearance, in the verbal report, of responses that resemble projections. In general, then, the distortion of executively intended discriminations may be considerable when events supporting an executive intention are relaxed.

In all the events pictured in Figure 3, little mention was made of *personality constants* in cognitive functioning, those components variously called "cognitive style," "stabilized regulative mechanisms," "character defenses," and the like—forms of control that have been hypothesized to account for the integration and consistency of a person's behavior. The importance for cognition of such quasi-stable structures, or system principles, as Angyal (1941) has termed them, has been treated in detail elsewhere (Klein & Schlesinger, 1949; Holzman & Klein, 1954; this volume, Chapter 5). A number of studies have attempted to define personality constants in cognitive terms, for example, "cognitive attitudes" of leveling and sharpening, focusing, tolerance and intolerance for instability, broad and narrow equivalence-range tendencies, flexible and constricted control (Gardner, 1953; Holzman, 1954; Schlesinger, 1954; this volume, Chapter 6). Witkin (Witkin *et al.*, 1954) has demonstrated a cognitive-control dimension that he terms "field dependence-field independence," and Frenkel-Brunswik has proposed another basis of consistency in cognitive behavior in her distinction between tolerance and intolerance for ambiguity (1951). Various other studies have demonstrated that these dimensions must be taken into account in explaining individual differences in cognitive behavior.

There is evidence suggesting that such regulatory constants, or cognitive attitudes, influence the level of primary mediation itself, determining the potential for registration of certain and not other properties, thus making it easy or not for different types of discrimination to occur. Studies by Holzman (1954), G. J. W. Smith (1952), Johansson and his associates (1955), and others reveal reliable individual differences on conventional psychophysical measures of primary organization and show that higher-order regulatory principles account for some of this variation.

It seems likely that the controls involved in these individual differences are different from "defenses." Experimenters have attempted to show how processes of "repression," "isolation," and the like affect cognitive performance. It is possible, however, that defenses are specifically associated with the control of particular drives and drive derivatives, for example, "reaction formation" with aggression. Their regulatory function may, therefore, be quite different from those modes of cognitive control whose directive influence is independent of particular needs and need gratification.

This distinction between defenses and other regulatory constants of personality is discussed in Chapter 6.[18] It must suffice here to suggest that these two classes of regulatory constants may be effective at different points in the cognitive process. Certain principles of control may directly influence phenomenal organization, affecting the primary mediation of unit properties, whereas other regulatory constants may exert influence on formations at the level of secondary mediation and motor response. For instance, defensive regulations may influence associative processes, judgment, and motor behavior, that is, processes that are instrumental in delaying action and controlling approaches to objects through actual motor coordinations.

Much remains to be clarified, in both theory and experiment, about the nature and properties of regulatory constants. Systematic investigation of their influence is still in an early stage and does not yet allow firm conclusions about whether their effect is most telling upon preperceptual events, upon the phenomenal field, or upon processes of communication and action. The point of view outlined in this chapter allows for the possibility that not

---

[18] [See also Gardner et al. (1959), Chapter 1.]

all phases of a train of perceptual-cognitive activity will necessarily reveal equally the workings of a defense or a "cognitive attitude." For present purposes, the complexities of personality constants in cognitive behavior have been by-passed in favor of a general discussion of the phases of percept formation and their behavioral effects, to which an eventual theory of personality constants in cognition must accommodate itself.

The preceding account of center and periphery in cognitive activity is an attempt to bring together two main currents of cognitive psychology that have sometimes seemed incompatible: on the one hand, that of the psychophysicist, who stresses reliable correspondences between features of the stimulus field and responses to it and, on the other hand, that of the functional theorist, who emphasizes the responsiveness of all levels of behavior to motive, purpose, and intention. This survey has highlighted some dilemmas and oversights that hamper each approach when it ignores the other. Abetted by the methodological artifice I have labeled a "motivational reduction screen," the psychophysicist overlooks the fact that a variety of registrations at the level of primary mediation may interchangeably mediate thing qualities; he thus eliminates from his experimental program the issue of perceptual selection. On this point, drawing attention to the range of motives in a given situation seems timely. At the same time I have tried to provide for structures that guarantee effective coordination with external regularities, those processes that promote executive intention and are often ignored in the near solipsism of dealing with perception exclusively in functional-motivational terms. Perception seems not to be at the mercy of every activated motive. A variety of qualifying conditions in the components of stimulus structure and its mediation must be specified, as must the motives peripheral to the one emphasized in a particular research design.

I have tried to provide for both approaches to perception by assuming that the extent of central transmission and registration of physical invariants exceeds the momentary requirements of executive intention, and by proposing that the range of what a person does respond to through a given channel is much more restricted than the range of thing-quality formations that occur.

A final word about the "stimulus" and about "objects" as stimuli is in order. The common conception of a stimulus as an *external* object or event that provokes the organism to action is clearly untenable. It tends to ignore even the distinction between unit property and physical mediation, a distinction that alone complicates the notion of "an external stimulus." But the equation of "stimulus" and "external" event becomes hopelessly unwieldy when we recognize that a perception is also "stimulated" by (is an outcome of) a variety of "internal" events. The stimulus includes not only the unit property and its physical mediation, but also, strictly speaking, the carrier events or mediation within the perceptual system. Furthermore, we have seen that considerations of *relevance within the motivational field* may also be fairly included among the events making for perceptual *dominance*. When we go further and attempt to specify the stimulus of *actions* occurring in relation to perceptually dominant thing qualities, emphasis must shift even more to activity of the intraorganismic field.

The difficulty in applying "internal" and "external" illustrates the ambiguities and difficulties of a Cartesian dualism that still paralyzes psychological analysis. Perhaps the key point in steering a clear course is to remember that a unit property is a "stimulus" only in the sense of being *potential* information—a *possible* focus of an act of perceiving. Even then we must say, however, that it must share status as a "stimulus" with *motives* that establish the direction of—the "reason" for—perception. Such reasons for perceiving are not easily accounted for simply by "exposure" to a unit property. It is the difference between saying that we "react" to a unit property and saying that we are *drawn* to a unit property in the context of an active motivational field. Clearly it is not the unit property but the *thing quality* that is the critical stimulus; we respond not to a unit property but to its meaningful aspect as a thing quality. And, as we have seen, this quality of thing that we call the "perceived event" is already an elaborated or constructed event—reconstructed in the sense that it is brought into some schema of meaning and the percept carries these implicit meanings.

Some of the misunderstanding of perception as "stimulus" or "response" results from conventional laboratory ways of experimenting with perception. In the laboratory a *report* of a perceptual experience is usually the experimenter's only concern; he then comes to think of perception solely as a *response*. Usually, however, in a context of action, perception is both a condition for changing behavior (a "stimulus") and a response. We act *in terms of* the meaning and quality of a percept. It is tied up with intention and with consequences in action, producing a change in one's relations in the environment.

Some essential components of a more precise understanding of the selective effects of motives in the cognitive process have been surveyed in this chapter. The intention was primarily descriptive and classificatory: to arrange in proper juxtaposition classes of phenomena, some commonly overlooked, that are critically involved in responses people give when they are asked to discriminate effectively, as in a psychophysical experiment. Some of the variables treated as especially important here require more detailed definition and systematic investigation to clarify their predictive capabilities. Nevertheless, the inescapable conclusion is that any assessment of the extent and nature of motivational control of perception must take into account the relationships of central and peripheral events both in the structures of objects and in motivational activity.

PART TWO

COGNITIVE CONTROLS AND PERSONALITY

Chapter 4

A Clinical Perspective for Personality Research

It used to be common practice to draw invidious distinctions between the words "academic" and "clinical," "applied" and "pure." This attitude is becoming less and less fashionable as the intersections among "academic" investigations and those of clinical psychology and psychiatry become more visible and the dependence of one upon the other recognized. For years all three paths of study shared the common goal of personality analysis but pursued it independently, even to the point of developing relatively self-contained literatures.

To an extent this separation has been fortunate. The different approaches to the same goal have ensured explorations on different levels and in many directions. But isolation has fostered weaknesses as well as strengths. Academic theorists are subject to a twofold danger. Insofar as they work within the confines of traditional methodologies, the "laws" that they develop may be highly specific, restricted, and unsuitable to predicting the complexities of the clinician's world. Furthermore, because of their limited contacts with subjects, they tend to deal with only a *single* level of personality expression. On the other hand, the preoccupation of the clinician with individual patients tends to

117

divert him from systematization; the result is that he suffers from weak underpinnings for his unintegrated observations and must often resort to poorly justified "shotgun" techniques in practice.

There is much to be gained from a joining of efforts. But if there is to be rapprochement each discipline must take full stock of the others' assumptions about personality. If the practicing clinician is to rely on the personality theorist for useful constructs, he must be sure that they refer to those qualities of behavior and response that clinical experience has taught him are fundamental; they must also have been achieved by methods that do not do violence to those qualities. Systematic theorists will require similar assurances that the personality constructs used in the laboratory have the same meanings in clinical practice and vice versa.

In the present paper I approach the possible meeting ground of these disciplines via the clinical path. I shall deal with those salient attitudes that identify the clinician, the assumptions that color his thinking. They are rarely stated explicitly, but they are inevitable implications of the clinical method. In the clinical framework with which I am most familiar, they have become the *sine qua non* for directing his efforts to improve individual adjustment. I shall try to demonstrate their importance by applying them to the problem of experimental design in a clinical setting, in order to examine how they relate to principles underlying the conventional experimental approach. Further, let us see what implications may be derived from them that will help us to develop a *clinical* experimental design.

ASSUMPTIONS IMPLICIT IN THE "CLINICAL ATTITUDE"

Four assumptions in particular are implicit in the "clinical frame of mind."

The first assumption is of *the uniqueness of the individual.* The clinician's routine problem is always an individual. How well he understands and ministers to his patient is the yardstick of his success. His frustrations on this account have led him to a deep respect for the intricacy of personality. He takes for granted that a pathological process will show itself in singular forms. He does not find it sufficient to define general patterns but is continuously alert to the *special* properties of the *particular* personality pattern confronting him.

At first glance, the clinician's interest in diagnosis and classification seems to contradict his concern for the uniqueness of the individual. Actually, classification is no more than an economical device for bringing appropriate clinical experience to bear quickly upon a single case. Properly used, it is merely a starting point from which to deal with the special properties of the individual's adjustment. It makes possible the rapid elimination of those considerations that will be least useful for understanding and aiding the patient and a focus upon those more likely to be relevant. In practice, then, the clinician is interested in the general, but only as a guide to the particular, the more effectively to cope with it.

The clinician in his research orientation will, therefore, be especially attuned to the *individual differences* that emerge from his study of patterns of covarying personality factors. Again, this emphasis does not minimize the importance of the generic for the clinician, but it does imply another way of developing general laws. The latter point we shall consider later.

The second assumption of the clinical frame of mind is expressed in William Stern's dictum *Keine Gestalt ohne Gestalter*. In principle, this phrase means that everything a person does and the means by which he does it express his individuality. The usefulness of this idea, of course, extends only so far as we have clinical knowledge of what this "individuality" is and how it manifests itself. One clinical formulation of this assumption is that the organism forms a quasi-stable but dynamic system whose relations with the outside world will be in part functions of its own organization. Psychoanalysis has taught us that some of the unifying principles in such a system are to be sought in the modes of delay and control of impulses. Through these delaying and controlling processes, compromise between the pressure of needs and the exigencies of the outside world is achieved. Such mechanisms of delay influence the formal characteristics as well as the contents of cognition, perception, and learning. When the clinician speaks of an obsessive-compulsive or schizoid ego structure, he refers to a typical pattern of impulse control.

In research these principles encourage us to seek adaptive connotations in all behavior and response processes and to ask how and to what extent they express individual modes of stabilization.

The third assumption is that *interactions are themselves units of behavior analysis.* In clinical practice it is a commonplace that similar symptoms may arise from quite different sources or even that the same cause can give rise to very different symptoms. This observation is crucial for the clinician. It tells him that the most basic attribute of an interacting set of variables is not the component variables but the *interaction* itself.

There are several main ways in which this all-important principle of interaction affects our notions of causation. We shall state them as corollaries. First, when a group of factors operate together, the ensemble determines how freely any one of them can influence a response. To what *degree* a single factor will *determine* a phenomenon can be predicted only from the pattern of interrelationships in which it appears. Second, causes are interchangeable; among a set of factors that can precipitate an event, for example a symptom, the appearance of one as the focal cause will depend upon the limiting influence of simultaneously covarying factors. The way in which a personality feature will show itself in behavior will thus depend upon its interaction with other features. The mode of appearance of such a personality feature as anxiety will vary depending upon the total personality make-up. In interpretation of psychological tests this principle is expressed in the dictum that test scores do not have rigidly fixed interpretations apart from the contexts in which they appear.

As we shall see, the clinician's emphasis on interaction and its corollaries has far-reaching implications for developing clinically oriented research methods.

A fourth assumption of the "clinical frame of mind" stresses the *continuity of abnormal and normal* in personality variables.

Abnormality does not require the positing of new personality dimensions. They are presumed to be the same for all persons; abnormal developments reflect extreme variations along one or several dimensions. Clinical observation tells us, too, that there is no general pattern of adaptation that can unequivocally be called "normal." In the course of reconciling intraorganismic with extraorganismic demands, the individual develops modal or "normal" variations in some respects only at the cost of extreme, often called "abnormal," variations in other dimensions. The term "normal" can be useful only when it indicates "normal in a certain dimension."

In research this principle may often be misconstrued to mean continuity of such artificial groupings as "normals" and "schizophrenics." The fallacy is in assuming that such categories themselves represent personality axes along which continuous variation could occur. Categories like schizophrenia and hysteria are abstractions. They summarize *patternings* of extreme variations in a set of personality dimensions. The indicators or diagnostic signs of these categories are interchangeable in individual cases and no single one is special to the grouping itself. The principle of continuity directs us toward research in which the subjects are chosen for personality variables rather than according to nosological groupings. We shall explore shortly the methodological implications of this principle for clinical experimentation, especially for that type called "experiments in nature."

We can now ask what implications these assumptions have for methodology in clinically oriented research: Can we use the traditional laboratory method, or must we derive an experimental method that is consonant with these assumptions?

CLASSICAL EXPERIMENTAL DESIGN FROM THE POINT OF VIEW OF THE "CLINICAL ATTITUDE"

Were we to follow the traditional procedure in research, we would systematically vary a single factor, or independent variable, holding all other relevant factors constant. We would then take variations in the dependent variable as indicators of the relationship in question. We would follow the same procedure with other single variables, and in this way we would establish relationships. Though difficult to achieve in practice, this procedure has remained the shining ideal; many personality investigators feel guilty or apologize when they must compromise with it in practice.

This path of investigation involves presumptions about personality that are untenable from a clinical standpoint. It implies the existence of discrete, functionally autonomous systems and truly independent variables; perhaps in the past this assumption was useful. If it were possible to assume that the perceptual apparatus, for instance, is a mere tool of the person but no more reflects him as a person than a hammer reflects the carpenter who uses it, then it would also be feasible to exclude central personality variables from experimental consideration. If we could also assume that a variable acts independently as a causal agent, unaffected by its neighbors, it would be obvious that we should demonstrate its variability "uncontaminated" by other factors present, which would have to be kept constant. If it were possible to make these assumptions, it would then seem proper for us to generalize the relationships observed in such "controlled" situations to all circumstances in which the specific variables are operative.

But it is clear that such assumptions clash with our clinical principle of interaction. In fact, an experimental situation that holds neighboring variables constant effectively suppresses their "natural" covariations. It is therefore a special interaction situation, artificially created; it produces only one type of interaction pattern within which the variable in question *may* operate causally. The relationship found pertains only to the situation in which it is obtained. Clinicians can justifiably reject many experimentally derived "laws" of learning, perception, and other functioning on the basis of neglect of this principle.

A converse of this point is frequently overlooked: that such suppression often *prevents* the appearance of significant relationships. A negative result may reflect circumstances in which covariance is suppressed. Under conditions of free variation, the expected relationships may appear. Brunswik (1947) has made this point in connection with perception of size-constancy cues: Distance operates as a contributory cue to size constancy under certain conditions but not under others. If size-constancy laws had been evolved only in situations in which distance was not operative, the causal efficacy of this cue would have been unrecognized. In an important study of indicators of hypnotizability in psychological tests, Schafer (1949) also showed how significant relationships are obscured when the principle of interchangeability of indicators is violated.

To investigate the causal significance of a factor requires that it be permitted to vary as it does in its usual relationships with other factors. In this respect the classical design loses in the validity of its results what it gains in the precision of its controls. If classical design were studiously applied to personality research it would require even greater elaboration, rigor, and ingenuity in developing controls because of the complexity of the material and the profusion of relevant variables. If the diligent investigator were to achieve this Herculean feat, he would lose his single most relevant datum.

AN EXPERIMENTAL METHODOLOGY CONSISTENT WITH THE "CLINICAL ATTITUDE"

It is possible to retain the notions of controlled variation and manipulation of variables that are the heart of the experimental method without violating clinical conceptions of personality. The solution lies in applying two principles that follow from the conceptions we have described: systematic use of individual differences to derive hypotheses about general relationships, and use of "experiments in nature." Combined, they provide a framework for personality investigation. We shall deal with each briefly.

The analysis of individual differences is the stage of the experimental process that is especially productive of hypotheses. It seems paradoxical to think of studies of individual differences as useful and even necessary in the derivation of general laws. In the past the occurrence of individual differences was considered "disturbing" and often attributed to "experimental error." The aim of rigorous controls was frequently to suppress or eliminate such differences. When they were systematically considered at all, it was as a *special* problem of interest only to applied psychologists, as a side issue to the more basic quest for general laws.

Clinical research must depart radically from this point of view. We consider the analysis of individual differences an integral phase of systematic investigation, often to be invoked deliberately as a searchlight for possible relationships. This view recognizes an important attribute of individual differences that is too often overlooked—that distributions of such differences express *general* relationships among the relevant operating variables. For example, a psychological-test score is the product of at least two factors—the task posed by the test and the subject's mode of resolving the task. The meaning of the score is defined by the relationship between these factors, which is in turn the relationship tapped by the particular test item. Were this general relationship known and mathematically definable, each person could, through his score, be placed on the general curve of the function. To restate this point, every obtained score in a distribution is attributable to, and potentially understandable in terms of, the functional relationship of which it is an expression.

When we know the functional relationships that underlie a test score, we say that the test is "valid" and that it has an unambiguous "rationale." Its scores are correctly interpretable. But when the relationships are unknown or poorly defined, the appearance of individual differences sets a task for analysis: to discover the sources of the variations, the relevant intervening variables upon which response variation depends. The inability of the investigator to account for them or to manipulate them stimulates him to invoke new hypotheses. The continued persistence of individual differences in the experimental situation will ultimately bring into consideration all levels on which relationships may exist. Hypotheses are successively tried, and retained or eliminated until one or more are found that significantly relate to the phenomenon in question and therefore account for the individual differences. We can see that the analysis of a distribution of individual differences can be an important way station to a set of functional relations or general laws. The search for personality generalizations originates in problems of individual differences.

We can now better express the consequence of ignoring individual differences: obscuring of principles that govern behavior. Yet this practice has been traditional in research on perception, for example, and has resulted in the focusing of attention on only a very limited number of functional relationships. Central determinants or personality factors could not be investigated because they were never *permitted* to enter into the experiment as sources of variation. Had they been allowed to appear, attempts to explain them would have laid bare far earlier the limitations of contemporary explanatory concepts and would perhaps have prompted more fruitful hypotheses involving personality variables.

Used in the manner described, studies of individual differences could contribute to exploring the limits of Stern's organismic principle cited earlier and make of it something more than a declaration of faith. By doggedly pursuing the search for sources of variation on all levels, such studies could gradually show us *how* the organism works as a unit and take us beyond the mere recogniton that this unitary principle exists. They could continually raise questions about various possible levels of causal determination in the explanation of particular responses.

A second methodological consideration to which I would like to draw attention is the principle of *experiments in nature*. The phrase "experiments created by nature" expresses a way of effectively manipulating a variable without having to elicit it artificially or to vary it systematically within a single individual. A point previously stated—that each individual can be placed quantitatively on several personality dimensions—reminds us that "nature" provides the researcher with specific "manipulations" of any variable in question. These dimensions include such rubrics as "rapport" (for example, passive-compliant, passive-demanding, and so on), "defensive structure" (for example, inhibition, intellectualization, compulsiveness, repression), and so forth. Recalling also our assumption about the continuity of normal and abnormal conditions in each of these factors, pathological conditions might be sampled when we wish to obtain extreme quantitative representations of one, two, or as many of these variables as we are able to define.

Through appropriate clinical measures, all levels of personality activity, including variables observable mainly in the therapeutic situation, can thus become accessible to investigation. Manipulation is achieved, first, through judicious selection of cases characterized by relatively fixed quantities of the personality variable being analyzed (independent variable): aggression, passivity, anxiety, and so on. Second, it can be achieved by keeping these quantitative values of the independent variable *constant* and allowing associated variables to vary in their natural context. If, for instance, anxiety were chosen as the independent variable, then, through clinical and psychological-test criteria of anxiety, individuals who represent different degrees of anxiety would be selected. The effect of this sort of "quantitative manipulation" on the dependent variable would be noted. In each case, the independent variable would be *held constant* either in terms of fixed antipolar groups—that is, a nonanxious and an anxious group—or, if continuous measurements are possible, in terms of degrees of anxiety.

In this procedure we have not abandoned the traditional principle of manipulation of the variable; only the *manner* of manipulation has been altered. This procedure is no less experimental; manipulation and variation are simply accomplished in a fashion more congenial to the clinician's assumptions about his data (assumptions of interaction and interdependence) and in a way that now permits him to investigate areas of the personality structure that could not be approached with the traditional experimental method. In fact, Brunswik, in an important monograph (1947), has pointed out the inadequacies of conventional experimental design even within a nonclinical framework. His proposal for a revised experimental model also emphasizes the features of holding constant independent variables while allowing others to vary, and of successive omission of factors in the process of establishing relationships. This process is for him critical in demonstrating what he calls the "representativeness of experimental designs."

Returning to the two principles that we have postulated, we can now see that the course of an essentially clinical experimental investigation of personality proceeds from an analysis of individual differences, including selection of relevant hypotheses and variables for experimentation, to projection of such hypotheses in "experiments in nature," to selection of significant variables for further quantitative measurement and establishment of functional relationships. We are, of course, rather far removed from the last stage of such research, owing to the primitive state of our understanding of personality dimensions and of techniques of quantitative measurement.

I have emphasized only methodological implications of the "clinical attitude." There are conceptual ones as well, but I cannot go into them in this chapter. One such implication may, however, illustrate more concretely the scope of the clinical postulates that I have outlined, in particular the dictum that individuality (the gestalten) may be evident at all levels of a person's functioning. It is possible that such familiar sensory properties as absolute and differential thresholds may have adaptive significance: For example, they can be of "protective" use to the individual, serving to invite or "keep out" stimulation either by raising or lowering the level of minimal or differential excitation. We may then ask whether this protective function manifests itself in typical forms when different modes of defense predominate in the personality. Is the typical contraction of the hysteric's world abetted by a particular patterning of threshold functioning? In persons in whom repression is a favored mode of establishing equilibrium can we expect to find that absolute and differential sense thresholds are typically higher? Just as armor may be considered an artificial device for "raising the pain threshold," so does it seem possible to impute similar significance to the stimulus-limiting efforts of certain modes of defense (Reich, 1949).

Mounting evidence points to the pertinence of such concepts

as ego integration and modes of adaptive control for understanding variations in sensory functioning and individual differences. Bartley (1946), in a survey of accumulated knowledge in the field of visual perception, points out that the weight of evidence has made it compelling to search for controlling processes of total personality functioning to fill a gap created by the inadequacy of attempts to account for many phenomena by peripheral mechanisms alone: ". . . it is neither structure nor local process that poses the ultimate problems but rather the performance of the individual." Such concepts of ego organization as "defense," the strategy of "individual differences" and "experiments in nature," should be helpful in exploring the limits of the widely recognized but still unverified suspicion that causal ties exist between "peripheral" properties of the sensory apparatus and more general principles of ego organization. Such studies represent still another attempt to extend clinical considerations to what has hitherto been a no man's land for the personality theorist.

Chapter 5

The Personal World Through Perception

A focus upon perception is for most psychologists secondary to an interest in persons; perception is a convenient wedge into that larger problem. Our target is a theory that can lead to laws of *perceivers*, rather than to laws of *perception*, a theory concerned less with linking generalized field conditions or states of motivation to perception in general than to the organization of people. Rather than asking what effects values or needs have upon perception, we want to know how people are *constructed* to cope with values as stimuli of behavior.

Perception is a key area for the study of individual organization. The work of Ames (1946–1947) and Cantril (1947), which comes from the boldly conceived functionalism of Helmholtz (1910); the data amassed by Hilgard (1951); the pioneer efforts of Murphy (1947), Bruner (Bruner & Goodman, 1947; Bruner & Postman, 1948), and their associates, and of Brunswik (1934) provide evidence that purposes, aims, and intentions suffuse the very act of perceiving. All this work challenges the idea of "internal requiredness" or autochthony in the stimulus field, of "field structures" so compelling as to have predestined and universal effects independent of personal intent. It has also helped to bury the older conception of an autonomous perceptual system capable of study apart from the total system of the person, an idea born out of myopia toward personality theory. Clinical observation has certainly assisted at this interment. The hysteric's scotoma toward the objectionable, the paranoid's sensitivity to minute nuances, the depressive's distortions of body image—the clinician can provide any number of instances of perception giving faithful service in handling censored wishes. Perception is *the* point of reality contact, the door to reality appraisal, and there is no doubt that especially in perception are the selective, adaptive controls of personality brought into play.

But to pile demonstration of purposiveness in perception upon demonstration is not enough, nor is it enough even to show the different qualities and distortions of percepts, of "hypotheses" and "subceptions," and to trace them to needs or values. Such activity brings us no nearer a theory of *personality*, for it still deals with the nature of *perception*—how *it* is capable of being influenced, how it *can* serve purposes. Our sights must go beyond perception itself to the different requirements, demands, and claims of personality structures.

REQUIREMENTS FOR A PERSONALITY THEORY OF PERCEPTION

The touchstone of any personality theory is how well it accounts for *differences* among people. In meeting this criterion, it is not enough to note differences, to classify contents and responses. Another step is necessary: The theory should give us principles—dimensions—that lend meaning to variations and suggest regulative principles of which each variation is only an instance. If external factors affect a person, we should direct ourselves to his *coping with* them through his singular filtering processes rather than to the effects themselves. We may call this concern with the structure of a person a *vertical* approach.

A generalization about personality is always *vertical*, in contrast to the *horizontal*, cross-person, and nonsystemic generalizations so common to social-psychological thinking. The horizontal approach levels people and considers only the uniform or "general" effects of a situation. Its typical focus is upon *what* is seen—the content of a percept—rather than upon *how* it is seen, the personal organization that frames it. It ignores the "vectors" of personality organization that direct response and reduce the authority of the stimulus field. The horizontal approach does not typify only the classical theories of autochthonous perception; it has also carried over to most current functional theories. Even an outlook as purposivistic as Ames' treats the "purpose" in an act of perceiving as if it were inevitable in the particular situation and the same in all persons. For Ames, "purposes" vary with the situation rather than with the person; he makes little provision for differences in purpose in the *same* situation. That is why his and most other functional theories of perception are only starting points for, but are not themselves, theories of personality.

Two major questions face us here: Precisely what must we assume about the *structure* of personality to justify our studying it through perception? How can we best take systematic account of individual differences in perception so that they become data for a personality theory?

Most personality theories treat the appraisal and mastery of reality. This function of *reality testing* mediates between inner demands and outer imperatives. The equilibrating mechanisms that a person develops constitute his *ego-control system*. It is this system about which perception can tell us most. All theories of adaptation assume in one way or another that functioning is directed toward resolving tension and toward reaching an equilibrium between the inner and the outer worlds; perception is regarded as helping to accomplish these states. But they are not solely perceptual matters, for all the components of response—perception, motor processes, thinking—are put to use in the effort to achieve equilibrium. If we take seriously the idea of the "organism as a whole," then we should find consistency in how all these functions work. This claim is something to be demonstrated, of course, but it would be difficult to think of coherence in a person if it were not true. This crucial tenet is required of any theory of personality that would encompass perceptual theory; it is the only basis for finding the study of perception relevant to the theory. Conversely, if analyses of perception are to have any relevance to personality theory, they must disclose how the control principles, the equilibrating mechanisms, appear *in* and *through* its functioning.

In speaking of equilibrium I want to avoid a common but unfortunate mistake that follows from relying too much on physical models: treating equilibrium as a fixed and inevitable state to which the person always returns and that takes similar forms in all people. In this view, given the *same* "field conditions" and the *same* "needs" in the *same* intensity, the final state reached in that field and the processes for reaching it will be the same for everyone (Hochberg & Gleitman, 1949). This view is the hallmark of the horizontal approach: The "person" is like a balance that comes to equilibrium in exactly the same way no matter what is being weighed.

The concept of "equilibrium" is useful if we recognize that the point of balance and the means for reaching it are different for different people. Perhaps it would be better to substitute for "equilibrium" the word "solution," or "balance" itself, meaning the more or less "steady state" that a person reaches as he resolves a task, a problem, or a stimulus in his own way. What determines the form of the steady state as much as anything is the favored and stable means of tension reduction that the person settles upon. One man's "equilibrium" in another man's discomfort. This precept is basic, and we must begin with it.

Our goal, then, is to seek in perceptual structure the matter-of-course avenues by which a person resolves imbalances or disequilibria and to infer from them his central controls.

The entire functionalist emphasis—as expressed in the work of Ames, Bruner, and Brunswik—testifies that the directedness and purposiveness of perception are in the very *act* of perceiving. If we look at the perceptual system, we find a number of properties that offer possibilities for control by the ego system; they serve ends and answer adaptive requirements. Such properties as thresholds, perceptual latency or recognition time, brightness, and size constancy are favorite topics for textbook chapters. All of them may be variants of a more basic property of "hypothesis forming," as Bruner suggests, or the developing of schemata, or of adaptation levels, in Helson's terms (1948). Considered from the point of view of the perceiver, however, they are "tools" or "potentials" to be used in any situation to which he adapts. These qualities of the perceptual system I have described elsewhere as *adaptive properties* (Klein, 1949).

But these "adaptive properties" are provided by the physiology and anatomy of the perceiving system. They are the *givens*, and all perceivers have them; no one with an intact perceptual system is without thresholds, the quality of latency, the capacity to "schematize" or form adaptation levels. The disclosure of such properties was an important event in the history of psychology, and equally important are the more recent demonstrations that they can serve purposes, needs, and values. But to stop there is merely to reaffirm a clinical commonplace—that it is indeed possible for "personality to influence perception." Yet most functional emphases have stopped there. We *know* that only certain people scotomize, only certain people develop psychogenic anesthesias, and only certain people accentuate valued stimuli (Klein, Schlesinger & Meister, 1951). The perceptual apparatus lends itself to adaptive control; its properties are used variously. To sum up, people develop stable modes of meeting the world (ego controls). These controls and the connections among them, both within persons and among persons of the same type, are the "dimensions" of the ego-control system. The next advance should show *in perceptual terms* how the modes and patterns of perceiving express the claims of ego controls.

Perceptual Attitude

For want of a better, we have tentatively adopted the term "perceptual attitude" to identify these key principles.[1]

---

[1] I use "attitude" in a different sense than its usage in American psychology, particularly social psychology, in which it usually implies a quite specific *content* and a direction toward or away from an object. In this

A perceptual attitude is a personal outlook on the world, embodying in perception one of the ego's adaptive requirements. A style of reality testing is expressed through it. It expresses a broader control principle that makes comparable demands upon other systems besides perception. Because it tries to specify more general principles of ego control in perception, this attitude supplies the needed conceptual tool—or intervening variable (MacCorquodale & Meehl, 1948)—for focusing personality theory on perception. It gives us a means to account for how and in what respects people differ, and in so doing it allows us to generalize about persons both in perceptual terms and in personality principles. It carries us a step beyond mere demonstrations of selectivity and purposiveness, and leads us to look for individual variations and for different kinds of equilibrating mechanisms in people.

We shall better understand the implications of perceptual attitude through descriptions of several specific attitudes that are being studied, but to help fix the concept in mind I shall mention one. It is *sharpening*, a tendency to be hypersensitive to minutiae, to respond excessively to fine nuances and small differences, to exaggerate change, and to keep adjacent or successive stimuli from fusing and losing identity. I shall give further examples of perceptual attitudes, but their meanings will be clearer if first I summarize certain of their general qualities that reach to the ego-control system itself.

As a Solution to an Adaptive Task. Attitudes that we call "leveling" and "sharpening" are ways of resolving disequilibrium when the task is to cope with "differences." There are probably other attitudes or "solutions" that could be applied to this same

---

common meaning it carries no implications of formal personality structure. But my use of it is precisely in the latter sense, as a genotypic principle of control, with no ties to specific content and no necessary relation to particular conflicts or stresses, and having counterparts in all forms of cognitive behavior. As the common meanings are so difficult to ignore, the reader will do well to couple "attitude" with the German *Anschauung*, which better implies the broader meaning.

task. I am not sure how best to represent formally all those that we could conceivably observe in certain types of situations. Our own definitions are influenced by *quantitative* differences among people, and this fact has led us to think of attitudes as ranging from "more to less" along a continuum, as from "leveling" to "sharpening." This approach may be untenable when we learn more about those people who are now the "in-betweens." The various attitudes may be *qualitatively* different, and it may be uneconomical to think of any two as "opposites." There is some evidence even now that the so-called "sharpening" attitude is not simply "opposite" to leveling.[2] Perhaps it is better to think of a *cluster* of unique solutions than of a single linear dimension. But the simpler scheme of a continuum anchored by seeming opposites is workable enough for now, and my illustrations will refer to "dimensions" of attitudes. We must keep in mind, however, that the question of continuity is far from settled.

As a Style of Organization. Perceptual attitude imparts the flavor to an act of perceiving, the organizing theme or leitmotif of perceptual sensitivity. The "sharpening" attitude, which I shall discuss more fully later on, demands, in effect: "Be alert to all shades and nuances. Let nothing slip by unnoticed." This response should show itself in many tasks and all modalities. A type of order is conveyed by it, what Angyal (1948) calls a "system principle." For instance, when we speak of the circularity of something (regardless of what) we mean a formal principle or motif of organization—the equidistance of points from some center. In the same way, when we speak of sharpening, we do not imply a particular perceptual content but a formal principle that shapes the percept; the theme is accentuation, the highlighting of differences.

As a Syndrome or Pattern of Adaptive Properties. The extent to which adaptive properties participate in a percept is not always known. If it were, we could base our definitions on them, for every variation of an adaptive property acquires its color from a perceptual attitude. Properties that we call "schematiz-

---

[2] [See Gardner *et al.*, 1959; Gardner, 1964a; Israel, 1966.]

ing" and "inherence," which I shall describe later, take special forms in sharpening and leveling. The particular patterning of adaptive properties that express an attitude we call a *syndrome*. Most of the time we do not know the adaptive properties in a situation, but, if we understand the kind of solution reached, then the perceptual attitude is definable nonetheless.

As an Expression of an "Executive Directive" of the Ego-Control System. Perception is only one facet of the controlling ego system, but through it we see the manner of working of the entire system. In this sense, a perceptual attitude has "purpose," but by this I mean only that it expresses a control requirement, a regulative principle. It acts very much as a "selective valve" regulating intake, what is or is not to be ignored. Its immediate "purpose" is only what it succeeds in accomplishing; for example, in leveling the purpose is the obliteration of differences, in sharpening a heightened sensitivity to them.

Parallel attitudes presumably appear in "learning" behavior, in motor activity, and in other functions of the ego. The ego system is independent of any one *part* system, yet its principles pervade them all. It is possible that certain kinds of people, for example hysterics, need overvalent or "technicolored" stimuli for effective learning. This kind of learning behavior may be parallel to leveling in perception; in other words, tendencies in two very different areas of behavior may be offshoots of a single ego-control principle. But we must leave such cross-functional definitions for the future. As our focus at present is on perception alone, our definitions had best remain anchored there. Eventually, a more inclusive model of the person's total functioning may allow us to convert perceptual attitudes and their counterparts in other systems into a single set of general principles of control.

One implication of perceptual attitude deserves a special note. We are encouraged to think of attitudes as having concurrent forms in patterns of physiological behavior, for example in electrochemical activity of the brain and in muscle-tonus phenomena. The concept of perceptual attitude, or *Anschauung*, frees us from the notion of levels of behavior, each organized rather independently of the others. It suggests that what we mean by levels of behavior is really only the multiple expressions of an ego control in operation, and it suggests also that physiological description can enrich our idea of it. The "reducing" of psychological to physiological laws in this way becomes a meaningless issue. There is not physiological behavior and psychological behavior; there is only *behavior*. The levels we speak of are only *conceptual* levels arising from the methods chosen for studying behavior; they are not reflected in the organism itself. The structure I have outlined gives physiological considerations, especially individual differences in such phenomena, a place in a theory of personality. It makes it possible to unify, with parsimony, behaviors not previously reconciled.

Empirical Derivation of a Perceptual Attitude

Obviously, our propositions about the ego-control system are too crude to allow a purely deductive approach to perceptual attitudes. For this reason, our hypotheses have often developed in an informal way—from curiosity about certain phenomena, quirks of data, hunches from clinical experiences, intuitions of subjects, and suggestions in the literature. Most of the time we have followed our noses and let the data lead us to organizing principles that might account for them. The most common starting points are, however, worth special mention.

A favorite point of departure has been individual differences in performance on a task emphasizing one or several adaptive properties. Through a close study of the extreme groups on such tasks, tentative formulations about attitudes are made to account for the differences. We then seek other perceptual tasks that will highlight these attitudes, and attempt by a process of internal validation to see whether the separation of our groups is maintained. This process leads to redefinition of the attitudes in somewhat broader terms. Following this process of confirmation and formulation in *perceptual* terms, we are ready to seek concomitant aspects of the attitude in clinical descriptions, in motor or physiological behavior, and in other functioning.

We can also start from a hypothesis about an ego-control

principle derived from clinical experience, translate it into perceptual terms, and then proceed in the manner just outlined. The starting point is a matter of convenience. My examples will furnish illustrations of both kinds of approach.

Before turning to illustrations let me summarize briefly. We began with the supposition that the organism continually wrestles with and seeks equilibrium between two sources of tension, its inner strivings and the demands of reality. In this task the ego puts perception to use, as it does other systems. Perception lends itself to use by virtue of its "adaptive properties." But these properties, common to all perceivers, are employed idiosyncratically; the personal styles in using them for reality appraisal I have called *perceptual attitudes*. That is as far as we have come. With this conceptual framework in mind I shall describe three sets of attitudes that have been derived and studied at the Perception Laboratory of The Menninger Foundation: leveling and sharpening, attitudes of resistance to or acceptance of instability, and physiognomic and literal attitudes.

SOME PERCEPTUAL ATTITUDES

The Dimension of "Leveling" Versus "Sharpening" of Differences

Holzman and I first studied the set of controls that we call "leveling" and "sharpening" in a situation that was as neutral, as anonymous, and as "contentless" as any the psychophysical tradition can conjure up. The starting point was an experiment in visual "schematizing" that had to do with the way people organize and integrate their impressions of the sizes of squares (Klein & Holzman, 1950; Holzman, 1954). When we began, there was no idea of "leveling" and "sharpening" in our minds. We were asking only, What sorts of solutions do people reach when they have to cope with stimuli that continually but gradually change in size? We felt that such a situation was "open" enough to draw a wide range of responses and left room for a variety of solutions to appear.

Our method was to project, one at a time, fourteen squares

ranging in size from two to fourteen inches. After looking at a square, the subject judged its size. At first only the smallest five were shown, until each had been judged three times. Then, without the subject's knowledge, the smallest square was taken out of the series, and square 6, which was larger than any in the first series, was added. In this way, by progressively subtracting the smallest square and adding a larger one, we gradually shifted the series from the smaller end of the range to the larger, until all fourteen squares had been exposed, making a total of 150 judgments.

The situation had none of the characteristics of those that involve so-called "projective techniques." It involved no erotic content, excited no mysterious conflicts, triggered no special traumata or stresses. Most of our subjects, almost all of them psychiatric patients, found the test rather easy to cope with; it was even absorbing to some. At the very worst it was monotonous. Our assumptions did not require stimuli that were pointedly symbolic or calculated to make contact with concealed layers of needs and wishes; we assumed that a person brings to bear in any kind of situation what for him are "preferred" ways of dealing with reality. This assumption is strategic for our method: Perceptual attitudes can be derived and studied in the laboratory, with no hard-to-reproduce conditions of conflict or significant content required. Only the *formal* aspects of situations concern us at this stage.

I cite one of the most relevant findings, concerning the extremes of our group, for these people became the key subjects: Some kept pace with the changing squares and judged size accurately. At the other extreme were those who responded to change very slowly; they kept underestimating more and more—they "lagged." The extent of this "adaptive lag" was such that at the close of the experiment some were judging a square of thirteen inches as being only four inches!

How to account for this lag? It was as if the "lagging" group preferred to ignore, deny, or suppress differences, to "level" them all to uniformity. Though the squares, when placed side by side, are obviously different, when seeing them successively these people managed to obscure the differences and to reach the stability of sameness. It was as if they had developed an early preconception that "all the squares were small" and this idea served as a "background" to pull all stimuli toward it, for all squares were judged to be small without much regard for actual distinctions.

In the group that shifted appropriately, an opposing formula seemed to be at work. These people seemed less enslaved by such a preconception of the series; they were better able to consider each stimulus in its own right, and appropriately. They therefore appreciated and noted change. Stability for them meant not suppressing change and difference but being alert to it.

As we looked further, we found that among those who lagged inaccuracy was particularly great when a square was no longer vivid, that is, when it was neither largest nor smallest in a series but somewhere between. Only when a square was conspicuously different and larger than the others did the lagging subjects keep track of it. When it lost its novelty and became integrated into the series, embedded in it and "lost in the crowd," they were unable to tell it from the others. Accuracy increased once more when it became the smallest and again a prominent square in the series. One subject dropped more than 90 per cent in accuracy when the square moved from being the largest in the series to the next largest! The nonlaggers were much more accurate at the beginning and lost less accuracy as a square moved through the series.

At this point the ideas of "leveling" and "sharpening" arose; we began to seek other situations for validation. Perhaps decreasing accuracy as the square lost its novelty reflected a difficulty with "embedded," as opposed to vivid, stimuli; perhaps people who lagged would also find it harder to extract a particular figure from a masking context. We used Thurstone's version (1944) of the Gottschaldt figures to test this hypothesis. The task was to locate a simple figure hidden in a more complex one. The laggers did indeed find this extraction task more difficult than did the nonlaggers.

We next used the familiar childhood puzzle of finding hidden faces in a larger picture. Again our levelers found it hard to penetrate the camouflage and to "extract" the hidden faces. The sharpeners easily spotted the hidden faces. In fact, in one case this acuity seemed to reach such unusual projective proportions that picayune details were elaborated into faces.

We carried our reasoning further. In the leveling group the preferred tendency should have been to reduce the salience of figure against ground, to level the differences between them. To test this hypothesis, we made use of an observation by Koffka and Harrower (1932) that a contour increases the saturation of a figure; in segregating a figure it tends to "heighten" the qualities within it. A black figure looks "blacker" when its contour is firm. We call this effect "inherence," a term suggested to us by Fritz Heider.

As we expected levelers to obscure rather than to highlight differences, we supposed too that "inherence" would receive less play in their perception. Contours would be less effective in setting off figure from background for them. Their tendency would be to dilute a figure to make it more congruent with the background, and the reverse tendency would characterize the sharpeners, for whom saturation of the figure would be increased by the fact of segregation alone.

To test this hypothesis, four small squares of different tones of gray were superimposed on nine different grounds, and subjects compared them with standards ranging from white to black. The firm contour should have made the stimuli seem darker than they actually were. In nearly every case the figures were, in fact, judged to be darker. But, more important, this tendency was weaker among the levelers, for whom segregation did not increase saturation as much as it did for the sharpeners. To sum up, the levelers seemed to diminish differences in the perceptual field.

Let us pause for a moment. We began with a single task, our schematizing test, and we tried to account for individual differences by formulating an opposed pair of attitudes. Then, branching out to other situations to which these attitudes seemed to apply, we developed a more comprehensive principle to which we could refer the results in all these situations. In this procedure we have looked for intrapersonal consistencies from one task to another; our focus has been the perceiver and how he organizes experience in his own way. The findings have, from the beginning, pointed to *individual* prediction.

We defined the control principles in perceptual terms; we did not immediately correlate individual differences with personality "traits" or diagnostic labels. Such premature correlations are more often frustrating than revealing. They suggest important ties but tell us little about these ties. Our procedure anchors perceptual attitudes to sets of coordinate phenomena and thus avoids the confusions that arise in correlating incoordinate phenomena.

Validation of these attitudes is now far enough along for us to examine their ties to clinical behaviors. In describing the properties assigned to an attitude, it should be remembered, we suggested that it should express a control principle of the ego that gives personal color to the function of reality appraisal. We should expect to discover this principle in clinical descriptions too, though it might be couched in terms more congenial to clinical practice.

Our first step was exploratory: We gathered a large number of descriptive statements about some thirteen traits defined by Murray (1938), for example, needs for dependence, independence, dominance, aggressiveness, and so forth. We asked our subjects' therapists to designate their most and least distinctive qualities, using the sorting method known as the Q technique. In this way we obtained a patterning of these traits for each subject. We then summarized the relative prominence of the different descriptive traits in each extreme group.

The description of the leveling group followed a pattern that we call "self-inwardness." It consisted of a retreat from objects, avoidance of situations requiring active manipulation, exaggerated needs for nurture and succor, self-abasement. The avoidance and minimizing of distinctions and nuances in the perceptual sphere thus seemed to have a parallel in an avoidance pattern in everyday behavior. Such qualities were much *less* frequent in the sharpening group. The opposite tendency toward "self-outward-ness" included traits that are manipulative and active; it characterizes people who generally found competition and exhibitionism congenial, who had high needs for attainment, who energetically and often aggressively pushed themselves forward, and who had a great need for autonomy. The leveling group was, however, more unequivocally linked with "self-inward" qualities than was the sharpening group with the "self-outward" items. In the sharpeners "self-inward" and "self-outward" items were about equally represented among salient qualities, but as a group they were well separated from the levelers.

That is as far as we have carried our empirical studies of this attitude dimension, enough to give it preliminary definition, but there is already evidence of its generality and a hint of its ties to some central parameter of ego functioning.[3]

Figure 4 shows some of the relations implied in the concept of perceptual attitude, using the leveling-sharpening dimension as an example. It is a sort of conceptual map that diagrams some speculations about the possible links of these attitudes beyond the perceptual sphere itself. First, it places leveling and sharpening within the broader context of the ego-control network operating in perception; it defines only one dimension among a number of control principles. In one sense these attitudes are intervening variables linking individual differences in one situation to those in others and to the larger design of a control system. As we think of this system as unified and ordered, we suppose attitudes to be interrelated in any single person; we could regard them as his "type." But I must pass up this problem in typology. The diagram, then, projects a view of the structure of only one set of attitudes—the leveling-sharpening dimension. It shows its internal validation and expresses the idea that perceptual attitudes are unique patternings of adaptive properties defined through consistencies of behavior in a number of situations. The adaptive

---

[3] [Substantial work has been done on the leveling-sharpening dimension since our first experiments; see Gardner *et al.* (1959) for a later orientation; Gardner and Lohrenz (1960), Israel (1966), and Lovinger (1969).]

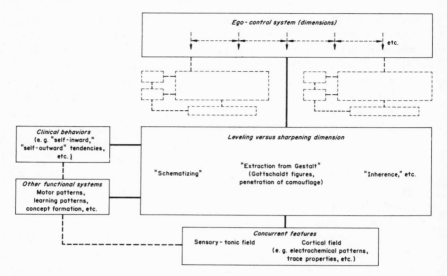

Figure 4 "Conceptual Map" of the Leveling versus Sharpening Dimension*

* The boxes, except for the one labeled "ego-control system,"
indicate areas of behavior where it is possible to look for patterns
akin to leveling and sharpening in percepton. These links are shown
by solid lines. Dotted lines indicate congruencies that may eventually be found among the so-called nonperceptual behaviors. They
are as yet completely unexplored, but their existence is also deduc-
ible from the conceptual scheme. Other perceptual attitudes are
also indicated by dotted lines; these give a perspective of the whole
ego-control system. A similar mapping out of relationships is possible for each of these other attitudes.

properties included in our tests are called for convenience
"schematizing," "extraction of a gestalt" (Gottschaldt test and
Penetration of Camouflage), and "inherence."

From the validation of the leveling-sharpening construct in
perceptual situations, the diagram leads us to look for wider
affiliations. Of course, we have only a hint of them now. On
one side a bond with clinical descriptions is shown. Earlier we

said that perceptual attitudes are only representatives in perception of pivotal ego controls; they may have parallels in other functions. Were we able to go beyond the phenomenological constraints of our definitions, we might be able to give these definitions highly generalized forms from which we could deduce their special cast in each response system, perception as well as others.[4] Even now our descriptions of perceptual attitudes offer starting points for interpreting the meaning of individual differences in other areas of functioning. This possibility is shown in Figure 4 by the connection to congruences of leveling and sharpening in motor and expressive behavior, in learning, in concept formation, and so on. A person's consistency in each of these spheres is a major research problem for the future.

Other possible manifestations of leveling-sharpening are suggested in the validation program pictured in Figure 4. We may suppose that the leveling attitude is also defined by a set of distinctive electrocortical events and accompanied by particular variations of postural tonus. If it were possible to record reliable individual differences in these phenomena, we might arrive at descriptions of the attitudes in such terms.[5] To cite one possibility: At various times it has seemed that analysis of schematizing behavior touches common ground with research in the time error and through it with neurophysiological conceptions and the study

---

[4] [In this connection see the study of relationships between leveling and sharpening and properties of the "orientation reflex" by Israel (1966).]

[5] [The work of Israel (1966) and J. Silverman (1964a, 1964b, 1964c, 1967) is directly relevant to the program of construct validation outlined here. Israel's most recent work (1968) takes an impressively long step toward psychophysiological specification of the leveling-sharpening principle. It relates leveling and sharpening tendencies to different states of orientation indicated by response patterns of deceleration or acceleration in heart rates. This study unites the psychological conception of leveling and sharpening with the functional meaning of the heart-rate response first developed by Lacey (1959; Lacey et al., 1963). It further suggests that an important and hitherto unexplored point of difference between levelers and sharpeners is in the processing of emotive stimulation.]

of "satiation" effects (Köhler & Wallach, 1944). It is not inconceivable that what we observe as a "leveling" attitude might also include the set of cortical events that Lauenstein (1932) reports as "trace assimilation." We may ask whether assimilative tendencies of the time error would be particularly manifest in our leveling group.

Attitudes may have still other concomitants. Perhaps the diverse perceptual attitudes of schematizing and other situations are accompanied by typical patternings of muscle tonus. Our construct leads us then to an interest in the sensory-tonic events to which Werner and Wapner (1949) and Purdy (1935) have assigned fundamental importance in perceptual experience and to wonder about the significance of individual differences in these behaviors.

Our model thus brings so-called "autochthonous" and "peripheral" factors within the orbit of personality theory. The organismic framework of Figure 4 tells us that it is too limiting to speak of "physiological behaviors" and "psychological behaviors." It is better to think of modes of regulation or control that provide the mold for a person's functioning, which we can describe in a variety of ways. If we were to achieve all the alliances pictured in the diagram, we would have a set of laws for an ego directive as it operates within the total structure of the person.

The Dimension of Tolerance Versus Resistance to the Unstable [6]

Curiosity about apparent movement led us to another set of attitudes. We call them tentatively "tolerance" and "intolerance" for the unstable or the equivocal. Apparent motion, or the phi-

---

[6] [In subsequent work on this dimension the designation "tolerance for the unstable" was replaced by "tolerance versus intolerance for unrealistic experiences." The latter term seemed to embody more accurately the phenomenological and behavioral qualities that emerged in correlational studies. A fuller treatment of the dimension appears in Gardner et al. (1959). See also studies by Klein, Gardner, and Schlesinger (1962), and Segal (1967).]

phenomenon as it is often called, has a long history, but questions about the ease or difficulty of the experience and the reasons for it in the personalities of people are new.

The phi-phenomenon is a common experience in daily life: in a motion picture, in the moving neon arrow outside a bar, in flitting lights around a theater marquee. In these instances the exposure of stationary stimuli at a critical interval gives the impression of movement. We know that the experience depends on several factors—the brightness of the lights, the rate of the flashes, the distance between the lights, and so on. Certain combinations of forms are more readily seen as moving than others. Two figures of no clear-cut form yield a broader range (between "alternation" and "simultaneity") of apparent movement than do two distinctly formed stimuli. Also, when the two figures are identical, perception of movement is easier, that is, the figures seem to move at a wider range of speeds than do two figures that are different. When the two figures not only are similar but also exhibit plausible movement, as in galloping horses, the range is greatest of all.

For our purpose what seemed most striking was that people differ in the *ease* with which they experience movement whatever the stimuli are. It is definitely more comfortable for some than for others. Such "facts" of individual differences are in themselves not startling; they have been reported many times. But what do they tell us about the control and selective functions of perception? What kinds of "solutions" result in such differences? That is, what problem faces a person in the apparent-movement test? What ways of "solving" it are open to him, and what are his favored answers? He must look at two alternating figures that become harder and harder to see as such as the alternation rate is stepped up. He must either compromise with what he knows and organize the two as one form that he sees as moving, or strain to keep seeing the field as he *knows* it to be, as consisting of two distinct, alternating stimuli. Now, we supposed that an important aspect of reality testing for some people, a requirement that they impose on reality, is that it remain stable and unchanging, even rigid, especially in its outward aspects. In order for such a person to be comfortable, things must appear as they are *known* to be; he desires stability above all. It is as if the outward forms, the shells or containers of experience, in distinction to their "depth" or emotional meaning, must be preserved at all costs; they are his anchors in experience.

This enslavement to form came out clearly on the Rorschachs of a group that had trouble seeing movement (Klein & Schlesinger, 1951). We grouped our subjects according to their handling of forms on the Rorschach. We found that those who were very concerned with sharp forms, who were reluctant to project more than the most obvious meanings onto the inkblots, who played it safe and did not elaborate percepts, gave us the narrowest ranges of movement. Those who fantasied and projected freely—even too freely in some cases—or permitted themselves to tamper with the given form of the blot gave us our broadest ranges of movement.

Thus, an attitude that was reflected on the Rorschach in reluctance to project or fantasy, in refusals to attribute to the blots qualities that were known not to be there, and in difficulty in adopting an "as if" attitude was also working in the apparent-movement test. Two forms appear that the subject knows are not really moving. As the speed of alternation increases and the field becomes harder to organize, rather than accepting the easy compromise of seeing one stimulus moving, he resists. The experience of apparent movement violates the integrity of what he knows. Such subjects have indeed reported the experience as uncomfortable; they "did not want it to move." We might say that movement means equivocation, "unsurety," to use an expression of Ames', that only a tenacious clinging to the forms as known could prevent. These subjects are *form-bound*. Among our other group the experience of movement was easily accepted, and we called them *form-labile*. Experiencing movement is, in fact, an easier way to organize the field once a certain rate of stimulus alternation has been reached.

The apparent-movement phenomenon, then, offers a chance to observe the degree of dependence upon "form" in reality appraisal. The two stable states are the experiences of alternation at very slow speeds and of simultaneity at very high speeds.

During alternation the two forms are seen separately, and the integrity of each is maintained. Between these two states there is an equivocal state of disequilibrium. Ease in experiencing movement indicates a readiness to tamper with forms in order to bring about stability. It is harder to make this compromise when the two forms are unlike and movement thus harder to experience.

The attitudes that lead to form-lability and form-boundness can be shown in other than the apparent-movement experiment. Extreme reliance on form perhaps reflects a still more general intolerance of instability of any kind. There are at least three other situations in which this hypothesis can be tested. In one we induce a distortion of the entire visual field with aniseikonic lenses that distort the retinal image. This distortion develops gradually, and people vary in the time they take to recognize it. Some never do report any change. They resist the unfamiliar and hold fast to what is habitually stable. A second test involves the well-known experience of autokinesis—the "illusory" movement of a pinpoint of light in a dark room. Again, stable frameworks are removed and disequilibrium induced. Will a person *force* the light to remain still when other supports are absent, or will he accept the movement experience? Still a third situation measures the flicker-fusion threshold. Pilot studies suggest that those who show constricted apparent-movement ranges also show lower flicker-fusion thresholds. The experience is less one of direct dependence upon form itself for reality testing than of a need to stabilize an unsteady field. Our form-bound people appear to be uncomfortable when they face such instability and hasten to resolve it. The overall attitude that we have abstracted from three related experiences—phi-phenomenon, flicker-fusion, and Rorschach[7]—we have tentatively called *intolerance for the unstable or equivocal.*

---

[7] A methodological point deserves note. In using the Rorschach, we tried to avoid a dubious but popular practice in clinical research. There are few convincing demonstrations of clear-cut links between cognitive patterns and Rorschach score categories, yet the Rorschach, like the Stanford-Binet years ago, often turns up as the validating instrument in research designs.

It would not be surprising if many members of our form-bound group who show general intolerance for any kind of equivocation were clinically describable as rigid, pedantic, compulsive persons.[8] We have concentrated on the form-bound group because the experience and the attitude involved seem more nearly unitary. Among those who are *not* characterized by form-boundness we find some who are truly form-labile—that is, who really disregard formal requirements, "project" freely, and flout reality in an extreme manner. But we also find those who would be better described as "flexible" and who can simply tolerate a greater degree of *Ungestalt*, to use Stern's term, without discomfort. Our form-labile group is, therefore, not as homogeneous as the form-bound group seems to be. The complexity of the form-labile group is apparent only in qualitative observation, not in the scores. Our dichotomy is therefore probably oversimple—the result of ranging quantitative scores along a single continuum and thus obliterating some qualitative distinctions. Incidentally, attitudes toward unrealistic experiences, like all the attitudes we have worked with, are not in themselves pathological, though they may be exacerbated in pathology. Both our extreme groups ran the gamut from normal to psychotic.

As with our leveling-sharpening dimension, we need not stop with the perceptual definition of an attitude and its clinical

---

Worse, by circular reasoning, such validations of *other* measures by Rorschach categories are occasionally cited as validation of the Rorschach itself! Our use of the test was dictated solely by our attitudinal hypothesis. We did not rely upon the Rorschach as a "criterion" to "explain" the behaviors that occurred, nor did we use it to determine the personalities of our subjects. We applied *to* the Rorschach a hypothesis about a control principle, and the test was only one of a number of perceptual situations in which the control principle might operate. Our hypothesis was independently derived, free of bias toward Rorschach interpretation, and capable of testing by other means as well. In this application there is perhaps a paradigm for validation of the Rorschach itself and for developing a clearer picture of the ego-control principles expressed through it.

[8] [See Gardner *et al.* (1959) and Segal (1967).]

correlates. It can perhaps lead us to congruent forms in other functional systems and to multiple forms of expression, as seen through the probes of different methods. Far from being the end of our search, the isolation of an attitude provides only the groundwork for further investigation. Earlier I offered one possibility: Is an excessively form-bound person unusually "compulsive"? [9] Another question is whether a particular patterning of sensory-tonic events accompanies the attitudes, a possibility suggested by Werner's theory (1945) that movement is a sensory-tonic experience. Still another question is whether a particular kind of brain injury, to the frontal lobe, for example, invariably results in form-boundness, bringing in its wake particular satiation effects and patternings of sensory-tonic events, as well as certain personality qualities. Werner and Thuma (1942) did indeed find that for the brain-injured the perception of apparent movement is especially difficult. Interest in the effects of brain injury thus has a logical place in the study of an ego-control principle.

The Physiognomic Versus the Literal Dimension

A third set of perceptual attitudes has its roots in well-known observations that percepts are often subtly suffused with emotional or expressive qualities (Kouwer, 1949; Werner & Thuma, 1942; Zietz & Werner, 1927). Inanimate objects or events seem to move, become motivated, and assume expressive and "human" auras. "An object is just as sinister as it is black; in fact, it is sinister first of all" (Katz, 1948). A flickering light is described as "dancing." A schizophrenic feels as he enters a room that "the door is devouring me" (Storch, 1924). No doubt everyone has his own favorite examples. Colors often have emotional qualities. It is said that "green is smooth and especially agreeable . . . red is very disagreeable, exciting, obtruding, aggressive, produces nausea." Goethe is quoted to the effect that "yellow-red has an intolerable power; it is active. It seems to penetrate, to pierce the

---

[9] [See Gardner *et al.* (1959), Klein, Gardner, and Schlesinger (1962), and Segal (1967).]

eyes" (Goldstein, 1942). All these experiences involve a preference for the dynamic and emotive rather than for the static and
literal.

The physiognomic experience itself has been fairly intensively studied (Arnheim, 1949), but its relation to the control
system of personality has not been stressed. How much reliance
do people place on the physiognomic or on the matter-of-fact? On
what does their preference for one or the other depend? How else
do people for whom one or the other is typical differ? Such
questions about the organizing *attitudes* that such experiences
reflect shift interest away from the mere cataloguing of physiognomic experiences. The older work went no further, trying only
to show how it is possible for objects to acquire physiognomic
connotations—the mechanics of such an investment.

There are broad hints that physiognomic experiences have
the wider importance suggested. Werner (1940) reports greater
or lesser preference for physiognomic experience in different
ethnic, developmental, and pathological groups. He believes it to
be more typical of "primitive" forms of thought organization. He
thinks that in development we shift from a high reliance upon
physiognomic thinking in childhood toward "geometrical and
technical" thinking in adulthood. He believes too that in regressive states the ego falls back upon a highly physiognomic organization. Bizarre physiognomic experiences are common among
schizophrenics (Storch, 1924). Hanfmann (1939) reports that one
schizophrenic grouped small, thin, and yellow blocks together,
saying, "Don't you think they look sick?" To be able to perceive
physiognomically is probably essential to rich and responsive
communication between people. But extreme reliance upon it
might be pathological. Its complete *loss* may be accompanied by
narrowing or dulling of emotional responsiveness of the sort that
is so frequently observed in the brain-injured.

Tests [10] of this dimension in the study of individual differences are being developed. Eventually we may be able to apply the

---

[10] [Dinah Rubinstein (1952) made a promising start on this development;
more recently Morris I. Stein developed a test of physiognomic sensitivity,

construct-validation process already used on other attitudes and to trace relations to other forms of behavior ("personality qualities").

The tests include an "active" and a more "passive" physiognomic experience. The subject is asked to draw a line that is angry, happy, loving, and so forth, following a procedure used by Lundholm (1921), Krauss (1930), and others. In the majority of such "free" or "active" productions that we have taken from people of different sexes, age groups, and statuses, there are great similarities. Anger is most usually expressed in a heavy angular or broken line, resembling a conventionalized lightning flash. There is intense pressure in the pencil stroke. A "peaceful" line is unbroken, uniform, and symmetrical. Lines expressing the quality of loving are nearly always round, often a circle, or two rounded lines that touch. Previous work has centered on such uniformities, but our interest is mainly in the equally important variations. We are trying to scale the differences found, to develop criteria of facility: which moods are hardest to convey for which people. We also take into account stereotypy of response, deviations from the usual, and so forth. Of what importance is similarity among a person's responses to all these words, complete failure to differentiate among anger, sadness, or loving in drawing lines? From a clinical point of view it is perhaps a danger signal. But, even when using this test with clinical application in mind, we must look beyond to its possible predictive significance for other situations.

In a second test, subjects try to identify from a mixed group of lines those that are most appropriate to each feeling. The designs used are "typical" for each mood found in the large group tested with the first task. The second, more "passive" task must be evaluated with similar stress upon kinds of "errors," disagree-

---

which was later used (Rosett, Robbins & Watson, 1967, 1968) in work on cognitive style. Tests developed by Scheerer and Lyons (1957) are also relevant, but to my knowledge have not yet been used for validation of this dimension.]

ments with convention, and difficulty with particular feelings.[11]

Let me go a little way beyond what we have actually explored to point out a few possible links to other behaviors. Perhaps a gift for physiognomic organization is implied in behavior usually described as "empathic." Perceptual components are ignored in speculations about "empathy," most of which have emphasized motor "identification." But the coloring of percepts by subtle affects may be a precondition of "empathic" experience. The physiognomic-literal dimension is also pertinent to the measurement of subtle changes in ego functioning that follow upon lobotomy. Frank (1950) has reported that lobotomized persons show unconcern, insensitivity, or ennui in interpersonal relationships, that the experience of subtle sentiments and empathy is reduced, and that a general flattening of emotional life occurs. If these findings are correct, the physiognomic capacity should also be weakened or otherwise affected. Lobotomized persons might find the *requirement* to perceive physiognomically quite difficult and might depart from conventions or show other deviations. There is some early evidence that they do, but our study has only begun. Although this particular investigation has an immediate practical goal, the findings may yield clues to physiological concomitants of the physiognomic attitude. Possibly one requirement of a physiognomic capability is an intact frontal lobe.

Actually, we have already studied a few persons with gross frontal lesions with this question in mind, and their drawings reveal striking impairments. In one case, the patient's literal and concrete responses to physiognomic tests were particularly dramatic; at no other point in the usual clinical battery of psychological tests (Rorschach, Wechsler-Bellevue, and so on) was such a striking impairment revealed. (There had even been some question whether there were *any* psychological effects from the frontal lobectomy that had been performed on him.) This patient's productions were completely lacking in variety and took such literal forms as the drawing of animals. When he was told that he did not have to draw an actual picture but could use any kind of ex-

---

[11] [See Rubinstein (1952); Scheerer and Lyons (1957).]

pressive line, he proceeded to *write* synonyms like "shy" for "timid" and "romance" for "loving." He revealed an almost complete incapacity for the physiognomic attitude; clearly, it plays no role in his life. If the physiognomic attitude in some form is one requirement of emotional communication and empathy, then we should not be surprised by the emotional poverty that this patient showed under clinical scrutiny. Further work may reveal that such an impairment typically occurs in frontal-lobe injury, though the literalness of this lobotomized patient is the most extreme we have encountered.

IMPLICATIONS AND PERSPECTIVES FOR THE FUTURE

These three examples of perceptual attitudes have, I hope, given an idea of the importance of this intervening variable. I have far from exhausted its implications; neither have I summarized all the attitudes that we have worked on. It is perhaps possible, however, to appreciate more fully how such attitudes bridge the gap between perceptual data and personality theory. They do so not by a jumping of levels in which perceptual variation is linked to clinical traits but by directing us to organizing principles in the perceptual sphere itself that give it consistency. They focus upon what horizontal approaches usually overlook, the internally consistent "perceptual character" of each person.

To recapitulate my thesis: Ego control takes form in perception through what I have called "perceptual attitudes," special ways each person has of coming to grips with reality. They are pervasive and are not applicable only in situations of stress or conflict. As formal mechanisms they can be studied in the laboratory; they are demonstrable in quite neutral circumstances and in the various cognitive functions.

I would like to call attention to some implications of the concept of attitudes for the psychoanalytic concept of defense. Psychoanalysis is perhaps the only theory of personality to give systematic recognition to formal, structural controls of functioning—for example, the defense mechanisms—and it is important to see how the formal controls that we have described for perception fit with the psychoanalytic scheme of things.

On first glance, perceptual attitudes do seem to share certain of the properties usually assigned to "defenses." Like defenses, they are coping mechanisms at the disposal of the ego, means of "resolving" tensions and of bringing about stability. Like defenses, they are of several kinds because the requirements for tension reduction differ among people and among situations. In fact, we might suggest that the defenses observed on the clinical level are counterparts of the controls that we are looking for in perception. In making this analogy, we have in mind a rather general conception of defense that refers not to "defense against something" but to means of tension reduction. For all we know, of course, perceptual attitudes may, like defense mechanisms, begin in psychosexual fixations or traumata. But we must by-pass such genetic considerations.[12]

There is one difficulty in relating these two concepts. Even though it is possible to think of perceptual attitudes as collateral with the defenses of psychoanalytic theory, we have avoided the term "defense," especially in the sense of the well-known defense mechanisms. The reason is the differences of method that the two concepts reflect; perceptual methods of investigation are radically unlike those that gave birth to the classical concept of defense mechanisms. "Methods define concepts," and psychoanalytic concepts are no exception. We therefore distinguish between the *concept of defense* as required by the psychoanalytic model of ego structure (Frank, 1950; Hartmann, 1939; Hartmann, Kris & Loewenstein, 1946) and the *defense mechanisms* derived from and defined by clinical observation. The point is that the concept of attitude fills requirements for perception

---

[12] [Chapter 6 is relevant to this issue. The most suitable framework for conceptualizing defenses and other forms of ego control is still a moot issue. A fuller treatment of the topic appears in Chapter 1 of Gardner *et al.* (1959); see also Rapaport (1957a), Gardner (1964a, 1964b, 1965), Gardner & Moriarty (1968), and J. Silverman (1964a, 1964b, 1964c, 1967).]

research in the same way that the concept of defense does for clinical observation. The differences in origin should warn us not to expect particular attitudes to translate into particular defense mechanisms. It is pointless to expect *direct* analogues of "repression" in perception. Repression, though seemingly unitary enough to clinical observation, may, in a different method of observation, reveal several constituent mechanisms. At this stage, concepts are best linked to operations, and we shall call the cognitive controls inferred from our observations by the more noncommittal term "perceptual *attitudes*." Their possible correspondence to classical mechanisms of defense provides an interesting point of departure for future research.[13]

The crucial aspect of our approach is its firm basis in perceptual data; attitudes are hypothesized not through *analogy* to clinical concepts but through a process of internal validation. We thus avoid the tail-chasing procedure, which Krech (1949) has justly criticized, of accepting clinical conceptions uncritically as standards by which to interpret the meaning of the perceptual datum, but which themselves remain untouched by it. As attitudes are tension-reduction devices in the service of reality mastery, they must draw the clinician's attention as "means of delay and control." This idea may not result in the "changes" in psychoanalytic theory that Krech (personal communication) would like to see, but it must certainly cause an extension and refinement of one aspect of it—the conception of ego controls—and it also has importance for a more general theory of personality as well.

I want to call critical attention to the currently favored method of linking individual differences in perceiving to "personality traits" or diagnostic categories. At the risk of sermonizing, I underline the essential emptiness of this approach for a theory of personality beyond a certain demonstrational value. A correlation is important for systematic theory if it does one of several things:

---

[13] [See Holzman and Gardner (1959), Schlesinger (1954), Gardner and Long (1962), Benfari (1966a, 1966b), and Wolitzky (1967b).]

points to a link *between perceptual behaviors* and thus contributes to the induction of an organizing principle, that is, a perceptual attitude; illuminates a concomitant aspect of a perceptual attitude, that is, establishes a link between the formal organization of perceiving and that of other *functional* systems; or indicates a relationship of integrative mechanisms within the person. It is hard to see how simply to find that observed variations in perceptual behaviors correlate with schizophrenia or with "introversion," even in the order of .95, contributes to these goals. At the most, the correlation *implies* a stable dimension with consequences beyond the perceptual sphere itself, but it does not itself reveal the critical organizing principle.

The snare in correlating perceptual behavior with "traits" is the belief that it can disclose a tie with events *outside* perception. But "traits," or diagnostic categories, are usually literary concepts, the tatters of outworn typologies or global behavioral descriptions, with practical use but no *functional* specificity. A "trait" may, in some instances, be merely another and more literary way of labeling perceptual behavior, so that what seems like a correlation of two sets of independent events may be only a correlation of two ways of reporting a *single* cognitive process. Are "introversion" and "passivity" kinds of cognitive organization, motor organization, perceptual behavior? Very often a correlation with traits is attempted without the crucial intermediate step of accounting for individual differences in the perceptual behavior through perceptual principles alone. Neither the perceptual datum nor the clinical datum is clarified by the correlations. An example is the type of study that correlates "preferences for colors" with anxiety. In itself the correlation offers no information about the *perceptual* principles that account for variations in color preferences or about the functional meaning of "anxiety." One might as well correlate moonbeams with cobwebs.

The problem in clinical research, then, seems to be that it has been too much concerned with correlating any correlatables in the search for differential diagnosis, and too little concerned with *process* and functional specificity and with models of total functioning that would make such correlations the bases of laws of the individual. That is why one often feels about clinical research as if it were a motley arrangement of curios, no matter how glittering the individual items. The correlations described in connection with the leveling and sharpening attitudes deserve some of this criticism. They *do* have a demonstrational value in pointing to consistency within the person of an organizing principle isolated in perception—indicating that leveling and sharpening have significance beyond perception—but they do not by themselves advance us toward the goal of defining the ties to other functional systems. A brief survey of the gaps in the picture will suggest the future course our work must take.

First, we can say as yet practically nothing about the relationships *among* attitudes within any one person that would make it possible to describe his ego-control system as a whole. A perceptual attitude is only one of several adjustment devices available to him. All of them must be seen in some kind of systemic arrangement that we can designate as his *type of ego structure.* In other papers Schlesinger and I (this volume, Chapter 4; Klein & Schlesinger, 1949) have sketched the outlines of a future typology and laid down certain empirical requirements to avoid the pitfalls that trapped type theories of the past. Practically nothing can be said now about types, and here is a major question for the future.

Second and even more serious is our present difficulty in distinguishing among attitudes. Even our most general definitions seem tied to certain test situations. Because the tests are different, the various attitudes are defined in terms best suited to them. Such definitions in incommensurate terms give the impression that the attitudes are themselves actually different, but we have as yet no way of checking whether they are.

The ideal solution would be to redefine perceptual attitudes in accordance with a hypothetical model of total ego functioning, one based, say, on a theory of automation (for example, McCulloch, 1948; Ashby, 1947). Such a redefinition would permit us to go "beyond phenomenology" toward perhaps a more parsimonious definition of control principles not only for perception but for all functions. There is no time here to choose among the possible models. Putting together leads from Bertalanffy (1950, 1952) and Rapaport (1951a, Part 7), I shall say only that the most promising one seems to be a "vertical" scheme of the perceiver, endowed with the properties of an "open system" in self-regulation.

Third, I have spoken of each attitude as a "preferred mode of control." But what "triggers" one or another attitude in any situation? For example, some of our more disturbed patients have responded to the apparent-movement situation in a highly phys-iognomic manner, contrary to usual reactions of others. To phrase the question differently, what determines the "choice" of an attitude in a situation requiring adaptive responsiveness? This question is probably as open as that of the choice of a defense mechanism or neurosis.

Fourth, there is another loophole, one shared with the entire functionalist position, in considering perception as the vehicle of adaptation and reality appraisal: accounting for synthetic, crea-tive, and other-than-adaptive activities of man. We sometimes speak as if reality appraisal and control were the essence of ego functioning, but this view is probably too narrow. To say that all a person's behavior serves the ends of reality control and mastery certainly does not convey the flavor of his life or even of his perceptual world. As a friend once remarked, the exquisite deli-cacy of a piece of lace is not captured by the statement, "It rips easily" (it has "weak defenses"!). The delicacy of the lace is also a positive quality, and even present perhaps *because* of the nega-tive one. The analogy holds for our conception of the ego. A model based solely on adaptation excludes the leisurely, the contemplative, all those activities that take reality and needs for granted: Experiences of "awe," of "mystery," and of "wonder-ment" are completely unrecognized. Despite this gap, we are describing a vital facet of man, his controlling agencies, certainly one of the preconditions of all ego activity. For this reason the matter merits the exclusive attention we are giving it for the time being.

Fifth and finally, I have spoken of perceptual attitudes as "stabilized" modes of control, thus applying a static term to what is really a dynamic process. Our picture of "a system that comes to rest in a familiar form" is the only one that our present scheme provides, yet it tells us nothing of how easily attitudes within the person can be changed, how flexible they are, how easily they can be manipulated. Within the "perceptual character" we know nothing yet of special mechanisms directed to particular contents or traumata, of perceptual "resources" that become available in the fright of battle or in the heightened emotion of any sharp break with everyday living. Would these situations bring out *other* "solutions"? But, even recognizing the importance of such "resources," can it be that consistencies within the person still call the turn to some degree? In the central consistencies of a person, we have at least one basis for claiming that perception *is* personality.

Chapter 6

Need and Regulation [1]

CONTROL PROCESSES: AN OVERSIGHT IN MEASURING NEED

Needs push, but, as with any force, there must be limits. Behavior is not altogether, in Murray's words, waiter and pimp to the tyranny of need. I would like to present several lines of theory and evidence showing the value of disengaging two sets of variables in the measurement of motivation: on the one hand *needs*, on the other *cognitive controls* (or, as I shall call them later, *delay mechanisms*). The muddle in many efforts to define the role of needs in behavior and to understand need as the generator and helmsman of behavior may come in large part from neglect of a critical set of variables: regulating structures that modulate, facilitate, inhibit, counteract, and otherwise qualify the discharge of need tension in behavior.

---

[1] The experiments upon which this paper relies so heavily were carried out in the Laboratory of Social Relations, Harvard University, during my stay there as visiting lecturer. Ann Salomon, John S. Rodrigues, Jr., Jean Mandler, and Gudmund J. W. Smith were prominently involved in the work. Dr. Salomon in particular was a main collaborator throughout.

The issue has been well expressed by Murray:

According to the nineteenth-century conception, the human mind is like an inanimate and impartial motion-picture film which accurately records the succession of physical events. It is a percept-registering or fact-registering organ, with the attributes of a scientific instrument. The introduction of the concept of tendency (animal drive) however, required that this notion of the mind be modified so as to embrace the function of *selection*. Out of the passing medley of physical patterns the brain picks out those which are pertinent to the reduction of hunger pangs and of sexual tensions. . . . That these are among its functions can hardly be denied, but if we attend to them exclusively, studying only those proceedings in which the governing organ yields to, or is pushed around by, this or that viscerogenic tension, we shall fail to observe that the mind has ways and interests of its own. (1951, p. 446)

For present purposes it is important to define need in a way that will help us to coordinate it with the concept of cognitive controls. As I shall use the term, it conveys a "want of something," a demand for work that pushes the organism to some sort of consummatory behavior. Following Lewin (1946), it is helpful to express these qualities in a hypothesis of a *force*, having the properties of *intensity* ("tension"), *direction* toward an object, and *modifiability* of tension as reflected in experiences of relief, pleasure, and satisfaction. This conception of need may not cover all instances in which the term is used—for example, creative needs—but it conveys the most usual connotations and seems especially appropriate to the applications that I shall deal with. The main point about need in this sense is that we detect its presence in one of three ways: through consummatory actions (like eating), through some measure of direction (such instrumental acts as running, attending, and so on), or through themes and contents in thought related to the need. When we speak of the "effects" of a need we mean in part an altered direction of thought that expresses the facets of the need. All of these considerations define only the quantitative aspect of needs; qualitative distinctions lie outside the immediate purposes of my discussion.

What are the motivational characteristics of a cognitive control as distinct from those of a need? First of all it exerts force. Like a need, it directs, but its central feature is not a discharge in consummatory actions that bring "gratification." Rather, it functions to resolve an immediate adaptive requirement. Its appearance in particular forms and directions of the cognitive process we may also call a *cognitive attitude*. When a cognitive control is activated to cope with an adaptive demand and especially when a barrier to need satisfaction is present, such processes of control may also serve to tame the need itself; they may engender *delay* of need gratification. Behavior, then, expresses both the pressures of needs and the forces that counteract, qualify, or facilitate their gratification in keeping with a coping strategy that is invoked to meet the requirements of reality.

As we shall see later, such regulative strategies are especially evident in circumstances of enforced delay or impediment to immediate gratification, that is, in barrier conditions. A barrier can be physical, social, or moral (Wright, 1937). As in the experiments to be described, it can be simply a freely accepted, temporary restraint created by an experimental instruction. The qualities and contingent properties of barriers are important considerations in determining the manner in which cognitive controls govern the paths and strategy of need satisfaction. Depending on the perceived nature of the barrier, its qualities (like whether it is inner or outer) and its strength (as from insuperable to easy), the steering effect that cognitive controls or cognitive attitudes exert upon need may take differing forms: They may reroute the approaches to need-satisfying objects; they may alter the consummatory process; they may modify the intensity of the need itself; or—a possibility sometimes overlooked—they may draft the energy of the need to some other adaptive intention prominent in the situation. Some of these properties of controls appear in the experimental situations that I shall describe later. In all of them, the cognitive process is the vehicle through which the coping principle is expressed.

Accepting these considerations, we must wonder how "pure

need" can ever be tapped or how any single piece of behavior can be measured for so-called "intensity" of need alone. Not only is the intensity of a need hard to gauge if we fail to take account of controlling mechanisms; we can hardly reach correct conclusions about the quality of a need, its effects as an inciter of behavior, or even its presence. Before going on to experimental examples and to more detailed considerations of the properties of cognitive controls, it is necessary to look more closely at some puzzling issues that the variable of a cognitive control may help to clarify.

STUDIES OF EFFECTS OF NEEDS UPON COGNITION

Psychologists have recently been asking, To what extent and in what form does a need organize the cognitive field? The question is important because it is a battleground for clashing theoretical positions. One point of view assumes that the cortical field "has definite predilections for certain forms of organization and imposes these upon the sensory impulses which reach it" (Lashley, 1949, p. 466). For instance, Wallach (1949), a prominent spokesman for the Gestalt position, maintains that motives can steer the course of cortical organization only in a phase of cognitive organization that *follows* the initial stage of "perceptual process formation," that is, only in the stage of communication of what he calls "process" with "trace." From this point of view perception (meaning process formation alone) is uninfluenceable by needs. A need has to influence *something; some* conversion of the stimulus configuration must first take place, as in figure-ground formation, recognition of reversible contours, and the like, before any influence by a need state can occur. In short, a need must bend to basic perceptual formations; its influence is definitely subordinate. A contrasting view is implied in many demonstrations purporting to show the inescapable steering influence of needs and values in perception (for example, Bartlett, 1932).

Neither point of view adequately accounts for all the facts. Woodworth (1937) has pointed out that the Gestalt position fails to take into account what he calls nonspecific "situation-sets" that precede process organization yet exert a selective influence upon response. Indeed, the Gestalt position as represented by Wallach seems to hinge mainly on the *logical* priority of process formation, as dictated by the Gestalt model of the cognitive process, and not upon direct evidence that perceptual formations are unresponsive to need states.

Perhaps more important are experimental studies that seem to question whether process organization is as narrowly confined to the impersonal pull of object patterns as is claimed by Gestalt theory. Several studies report reliable individual differences in some of the very phenomena (like closure and assimilation) that, according to Gestalt theory, characterize primary perceptual formations (Holzman, 1954; Postman & Bruner, 1952). This evidence should not of course obscure the soundness and importance of one central implication of the Gestaltist's argument: that there are *structural limitations* to the influence of need. We accept the idea of such structural limits; we ask only whether they must be considered solely a matter of stimulus configuration or whether there may not be another type of relevant structure. Holzman and I have tried to broaden the Gestalt point of view to include the possibility that regulative styles of personality organization are reflected in individual differences at the level of process formation itself (Holzman & Klein, 1954). The possibility arises that "perceptual attitudes," as we have called them (Chapter 6), constitute one source of restraint (and therefore influence) upon drive organization. They may be essential components of strategies for coping with reality and therefore important in the control of needs.

The motivation-centered approach is equally incomplete. First, it recognizes no *limits* to the influence of a need. Second, it is theoretically untenable. Studies using this approach have usually been cast in a simple stimulus-response mold; the experimenter adopts "intensity" of need as the independent variable and perceptual response as the dependent variable. He then treats the resulting perceptual effects as depending entirely on *stimulus properties of the need*. Although perceptual organization *can* be modified by needs (within limits), this approach has produced embarrassingly contradictory reports on the *direction* of such effects upon cognition. Some studies show alterations in one direction; others show opposite—or even no—effects (Ansbacher, 1937; Bruner & Postman, 1948; Carter & Schooler, 1949; this volume, Chapter 4; Lambert, Solomon & Watson, 1949; Mausner & Siegal, 1950; Murphy, 1947). More impressive than evidence for or against general effects is the puzzling complication of sizable individual differences that are almost invariably present. One clue to a possible source of these differences appeared unexpectedly in a study I did with Schlesinger and Meister (Klein, Schlesinger & Meister, 1951). We noticed consistencies in the direction of errors in size estimation; perhaps more important, we found that a subject's consistency in errors on "neutral" symbols persisted even in the presence of emotionally loaded symbols. This finding raised the possibility that response to need or drive is consistent with, indeed merely emphasizes, a "typical" directional tendency present within the organism. These and other findings seem to undermine claims of *generalized* effects attributable solely to needs.

The facts of individual differences and intraindividual consistency tell us that perhaps people are organized differently to deal with needs, that perhaps styles of control check the effects that needs will have in different reality contexts. Behavior—cognitive response—perhaps expresses the impact of *both* need and control.[2]

EFFORTS TO MEASURE "INTENSITY" OF NEEDS

Need is often treated as an independent variable, a *stimulus* whose quantitative aspect, like the brightness of a light source, can be varied and whose "effects" can be measured. But efforts to treat needs as physical stimuli run afoul of a dilemma. For the energy source of a need, unlike a light source, is the organism itself; intensity can only be inferred from behavior. The stimulus

---

[2] [See Jenkin (1957).]

character of the need must inhere in some quality of organismic response. We cannot eliminate this problem by defining needs in terms of the arousing circumstances—hours of food deprivation or the like—because there is no basis for assuming a firm relationship between initiating circumstances and intensity and quality of need. That is why Tolman found it necessary to distinguish between drive and need; he defined need as a response, a "readiness to get to and manipulate in consummatory fashion (or to get from) certain . . . types of object" (1951, p. 288). From this point of view a need can exist without any corresponding drive (as when a depressed person eats without being hungry) and a drive without any corresponding need (as in *anorexia nervosa*).

When we resign ourselves to the fact that we are dealing with some form of response, it is illusory to expect, as many experimenters do, that variations in some *single* behavioral index (like running or approach behavior) will provide a measure of pure "intensity" or of "pure need" for that matter.

In discussing the difficulties of applying behavioral indexes of intensity, Tolman seems to recognize the importance of regulative mechanisms:

. . . another difficulty, especially in the case of human beings, is that these latter tiresome animals seem to be able to cover up, repress, inhibit, or distort their drives so that when you put them in the presence of the standard goal-object they refuse to go to or consume it, in any obvious, overtly measurable way—in spite of the fact that *you* know that they do suffer from the given drive or need. Thus, for example, one can put a hungry, but overly well-mannered child in the presence of food, and he may refuse to eat. (1949, p. 363)

It is, by the way, common even in clinical evaluations to describe needs in terms of intensity without considering that the particular indicators used also reflect regulative mechanisms. For instance, test responses are often the basis for referring to "strong" oral needs, "strong" passive needs, and so on. This practice implies that the massing of *contents* or themes around particular needs expresses mainly the urgency of the need itself, an assumption subject to the same limitations described for laboratory criteria. It is difficult to escape the fact that all such indicators of "intensity" are responses, and that these may reflect the "force" not only of need but also of other organismic directives with similar channels of cognitive expression.

Let me illustrate the ambiguity of behavioral criteria from a series of experiments on thirst. For reasons that I shall make clear later, we selected subjects who showed opposite tendencies in the way that they handled intrusive and provocative symbols related to the need. Now, the conventional question would be, was thirst equally intense among the subjects? The question is unanswerable because it is impossible to decide beforehand on logical grounds that any one of *several* possible indicators of need gives a truer picture of intensity than does any other; on some of these indicators our groups were indistinguishable, yet on others they were decidedly different. For instance, our subjects all rated experienced intensity of thirst at various points during the long experimental session. They also rated the pleasantness of thirst-quenching and "neutral" objects. The relative attractiveness of the two types of symbols for the sated and thirsty groups was then compared. Thirst by these criteria seemed to be greatest in most subjects toward the end of the session, and the two thirsty groups were pretty much alike on both types of ratings. Another barometer of intensity is behavior *after* the experiment. Again, the two groups of thirsty subjects behaved in the same way, invariably lingering at the water cooler planted outside the laboratory room or at a nearby coke machine; in contrast, the comments and behavior of the sated groups were far more casual. However, although the ratings, fluid consumption, and other indicators assure us that, without doubt, all thirsty subjects "wanted water" and that the attraction of thirst-reducing objects was definitely enhanced by thirst, no one of these measures or all together seemed more unequivocal in connoting "intensity" than other plausible indicators unrelated to them. For example, agreement among thirsty subjects on the ratings contrasted with the wide range of expressive behavior that appeared *during* the experiment. The variations ranged from loud and continuous complaining and histrionic clutching of the throat to, in most cases, apparently casual and quiet acceptance (which at first provoked uneasy doubts that our technique for inducing thirst was really doing the job).

Moreover, there are still other behavioral signs of thirst that cannot be ignored. The experiments created a *barrier* to gratification, and subjects were expected to perform adaptive tasks despite thirst. It is reasonable to examine the *adaptive efforts* of our subjects under these conditions for additional measures of intensity. Judged with this yardstick, our thirsty subjects again behaved quite differently among themselves, as we shall see. Measurement of need obviously cannot be reduced to issues of intensity alone.

Need, then, is regulated—not necessarily out of existence but at least into definite channels of expression and influence in keeping with the reality context. How it will worm its way into behavior will depend on other conditions in the situation in which it is active, and measurement requires us to evaluate these conditions in order to determine the presence of need and its "intensity." This much is certain: It is misleading to expect or claim that a single piece of behavior—whether instrumental response or consummatory act—is the exclusive expression of the intensity of need alone.[3]

THE PSYCHOANALYTIC CONCEPT OF "DELAY"

Before turning to more concrete experimental demonstrations of cognitive controls in the regulation of need, I shall pause over the concept of delay in psychoanalytic theory, for it was this concept that generated the idea that thought processes are intimately concerned in the regulation of drive.

Freud first used the concept of delay to describe the regulative function of certain events intervening between arousal of drive tension and its release (if release occurred) in a consummatory response. These intervening events affecting "discharge"

---

[3] [See also Vinacke (1962), Wolitzky (1967a).]

grow out of both conflicts surrounding need gratification and the immediate context of reality claims.

Freud supposed that certain structural "givens" and maturational developments—such as "memory traces," a conducting medium for energy transmission, thresholds, secretion structures, and so on—create the capacity for delay and are its first vehicles. He included also the structures that are responsible for such functions as attention, judgment, notation, and the like (Freud, 1900, Chapter 7).

Freud assigned the major role in the evolving and differentiation of control processes to a process of transformation of energy distributions, analogous, as Rapaport puts it, to "a river, which where it is slowed down builds up sand bars to slow it further" (1951a, Part 7, p. 695). Freud called this development "binding" and its outcomes "anticathectic" organizations, which have their own energy supply and engage in functions that are relatively independent of the parent source. They now serve as delaying structures, activated when heightened need tension occurs. Each such derivative becomes itself the basis for a new controlling organization, and a hierarchy of controls eventually develops. The workings of these controls are to be found in the products of thought itself—in forms of cognitive behavior.

Freud conceptualized this organization in its totality as the secondary process, to be distinguished from "mobile" energies striving for discharge—the primary process. "Secondary" refers to the organism's second most important requirement for its well-being—that of controlling drive energies—which develops on the heels of efforts toward furthering its "primary" requirement —that of discharging drive energies. At the heart of psychoanalytic theory there is, then, this conception of two major organizations of thought, one in which drive satisfaction dominates thinking and another governed by the requirements of adaptive efficiency. The former is reflected in such qualities of thought as "prelogical" formations, condensations, displacements, symbolizations, and transformations without spatial, temporal, and causal constraints. Secondary-process, or rational, thought is constantly tuned in to the temporal and causal organization of the "real" world. The distinction between these two systems is summarized by Freud as follows:

> All that I insist upon is the idea that the activity of the *first* ψ-system is directed towards securing the *free discharge* of the quantities of excitation [pleasure principle], while the *second* system, by means of the cathexes emanating from it, succeeds in *inhibiting* this discharge [delay] and in transforming the cathexis into a quiescent one, no doubt with a simultaneous raising of its potential. (1900, p. 599)

The total system of arrangements within which such controlling organizations are established is called the "ego." In this sense —the psychoanalytic sense—the ego has no connotations of a homunculus. It is a hypothetical concept that refers to an arrangement of processes concerned with the regulating, modulating, and delaying of need satisfactions, with reality appraisal, and with reconciling reality claims to those of drives and inner values.

We may infer that "adult" behavior is partly a matter of differentiation of such structural arrangements that make possible delay of need satisfaction. Controls under barrier conditions may thus range from virtual absence, as in explosive discharge (typical of infants in the form of diffuse movements, restlessness, and other signs of urgency, including even hallucinations), to a multiplicity of controls finely attuned to deal with varying reality requirements. Perhaps a great limitation of motivational research with lower animals is that it deals with organisms capable of only a limited range and variety of delay possibilities. (Reports have suggested that the Berkeley rat does sometimes show these high qualities. They do not seem to be the rule for rats generally, however.) Studies of somatic needs in rats seem to deal with the infant prototype of motivation—heightened excitement and diffuse "beating on the walls" reactions—with perhaps a narrow range of individual differences within the species.

The psychoanalytic conceptions briefly reviewed here have a wider orbit of connecting assumptions that I must by-pass for present purposes. The theory as outlined by Hartmann (1948) and Rapaport (1951a, Part 7) is still hardly more than a preliminary sketch for a more detailed canvas.[4] The main point that I want to stress is that Freud's conception of primary and secondary processes provides a broad setting for conceptualizing a *variety of forms of controls*. A second important feature is its provision of a framework for conceptualizing regulative tendencies that affect the impact of needs on behavior through the workings of a person's perceptual, memory, and thinking activities.

Clearly, the issue of regulative processes and their influence upon needs is inescapable. But it does raise a problem in *measurement*. If both needs and delay mechanisms share the same cognitive channels of expression, how can we separate them for measurement? Are such coping mechanisms measurable at all? How can we separate their effects from those of needs? Can we demonstrate that they subject the same need to different fates?

Some Experimental Demonstrations

I should like to approach these issues of measurement through several experiments on the effects of thirst in different settings of cognitive control. The critical issue, of course, as far as our present purpose is concerned is not so much arousing need as eliciting and isolating modes of coping with the reality context in which need appears. Because it might help to clarify earlier studies, especially the persistent puzzle of individual differences, we confined ourselves to an experimental setting familiar from need-cognition studies of the past.

In such studies need is commonly treated as *agent provocateur*, as potentially disruptive, as inducing error. A typical study by Bruner and Postman (1948) required size estimations of disks to which were attached motivationally significant symbols quite irrelevant to the task of size judgment. In such a task the symbol provides no effective aids or clues to judgment; indeed, it is well for the subject to ignore it if he can. Injected in this fashion, need is an obstacle to efficient response, a disruptive "distraction." But it would be a mistake to think that need *inevitably* plays this role

---

[4] [See Rapaport (1957b), Gill (1967), Holt (1967a), Hilgard (1962).]

when aroused, an implication all too easily drawn from many studies. Obviously there are circumstances in which hunger, thirst, or fear mobilizes the organism to high peaks of efficiency in the service of need. Nevertheless, this type of experimental situation is useful for revealing certain forms of cognitive control in action as mechanisms of delay. It raises the question whether or not there are characteristic ways of handling irrelevance, and the further question of how differing ways of coping with intrusive and irrelevant stimuli alter the impact of need upon behavior.

Our strategy was to select people who responded in two contrasting ways to interfering, task-irrelevant stimuli; to activate a need (thirst); and then in both groups to measure its effect upon responses to various tasks involving two kinds of intruding symbols—some related to the need and others with no obvious relation. Symbols appeared in such a way as to be potentially disruptive. Ten such situations were used, including the Bruner-Postman size-estimation task that had played so large a role in earlier conclusions about need-perception relationships, tachistoscopic recognition of peripheral objects surrounding an attractive thirst-reducing object, free associations to a thirst-related word and a "control" word, incidental recognition and recall, distance discrimination, reproductions of designs from memory, and others.

A word should be said about the experimentally induced need. Thirst seemed ideally suited to our purposes. Its main advantages are that it is one of the least conventionalized of basic needs, being relatively little complicated by ritual and social fashion in its gratification, and that it is easily induced.

We provoked thirst by feeding subjects a dry but attractive meal, consisting of spaghetti with a hot, spicy sauce, heavily garlicked and salted; peanut butter on salted crackers; dried, very salty herring; and anchovies, topped off by a dessert of salted peanuts and dry chickpeas. (In pilot studies we first tried to induce thirst by means of the drug Banthine, but it proved unsatisfactory, as some subjects reported dry mouths but felt no thirst.)

The meal was served attractively and at noon. There was no

sound basis for requiring subjects to eat a certain minimum, and they were allowed all they wished. Everyone found the meal quite tasty and finished at least the standard first serving. Most subjects ate several helpings of the spaghetti.

Invariably the meal provoked a request for water, which was, of course, denied. This refusal was usually met with good-humored resignation, and even protests were colored more by histrionics than by anxiety. After all, Harvard University undergraduates are prepared for anything from psychologists; our subjects, at least, were resigned to machinations of all sorts, and they knew that the deprivation could be only temporary. Besides, they were being paid. Although insistent, their thirst was never desperate.

A further word about laboratory-induced needs is relevant. As I have emphasized, needs are in part cognitive events, and the perceptions and understandings of the experimental setting must contribute to the actual form of a need. In all laboratory experiments of this sort, there are unspoken assumptions about protection from real harm; annoyances are definitely understood to be temporary. In our studies thirst inevitably occurred, but the setting probably reduced its urgency. In general, the total situation had the following attributes: a persistent, somewhat annoying, but moderate deprivation; a temporarily erected "barrier" or delay to the alleviation of this irritant; and acceptance of the temporary delay. It is important to mention these perceived qualities of the situation as a caution against any tendency to generalize our results to *all situations* in which thirst is a factor. But, although the situation is not really parallel to most situations in which one is preoccupied with thirst, especially those involving duress, it is probably true that the larger part of the motivational fabric of daily life is made up of precisely such mild and temporary deprivations that must be lived with. Therefore, although not paradigmatic of the thirst need specifically, the experimental situation does seem to typify a kind of deprivation or temporary delay familiar enough to adults. Needs that brook no delay, for instance a child's hunger, or thirst experienced in the desert, are exceptions, not the rule, in our lives.

The critical task on which we obtained our extreme groups was a color-word interference test that originated in Jaensch's laboratory in Germany, was first used by Stroop (1935) in this country, and was later modified by Thurstone (1944).[5] Each subject had to say aloud as quickly and accurately as possible the *colors* red, green, yellow, and blue, in which incongruent color *names* had been printed. For instance, if the word "red" appeared in blue ink, he was to read "blue." The task thus pitted against each other two response tendencies: an inclination, encouraged by experience, to read the word, and an inclination to follow the immediately relevant instruction to concentrate on the color and ignore the word. There were ten lines of ten words to a page; the colors appeared in a fixed random arrangement. Two other reading tasks preceded the critical task, and provided bases for evaluating performance: a page of color names printed in black and another consisting of color slabs alone.

Of the 100 students tested, two main groups of twenty each were selected by means of criteria developed in pilot studies; they represented extremes in interference proneness. That is, although all forty were equally quick in reading colors alone, one group, the high-interference group, had a great deal of trouble ignoring the word context of the color-word test and took longer to read the colors than did the other, the low-interference group. Half of each main group was assigned to a thirsty group, half to a sated group, making four groups of ten people each. The final groups, then, were of ten "high interference" thirsty subjects, ten "high interference" sated subjects, ten "low interference" thirsty subjects, and ten "low interference" sated subjects. All groups were given the entire battery of procedures, including self-ratings of thirst.

Now, what happens to need in such test circumstances? How do people go about "making the best of it"? How do "handling" techniques vary in the different groups? I shall highlight the results for three test procedures—size estimation, tachistoscopic

---

[5] [See Jensen (1965), Jensen and Rohwer (1966).]

recognition, and free association—and I shall dwell on a fourth procedure involving incidental recognition.

There was a limitation in the design of our studies, which were mainly exploratory. The first experiment of the series on size estimation had primarily a demonstrational purpose—to show, for instance, how "proneness to distraction" by irrelevancies may contribute to the disruptive effects of a need. In this particular task and in some of the others we had no firm reasons at the outset to expect specific directional tendencies in one or another group. Some tasks *were* planned according to guiding notions, however. The results of a pilot study thus led us to expect certain directions of error in the size-estimation task, and from these expectations came some preliminary ideas (lightly held but present) that determined the particular forms in which we cast our tachistoscopic and free-association procedures. For the most part, however, the procedures were planned with no clear expectations of the kinds of consistencies that would appear within our groups. Nor did we have any preformed ideas of how to conceptualize whatever differences between groups we might find. Instead we chose to do this job inductively, by weaving the various instances of difference into the most (seemingly) economical and internally consistent arrangement. This ad hoc procedure was somewhat disciplined by our decision to rely only on substantial differences in linking task to task. Even so, this procedure is an uneasy one, with the ever-present risk that sampling error will create an interpretive fiction. There is some reassurance in the fact that the sampling of test procedures and the response indexes were sufficiently diverse to test most of the generalizations about the generic styles shown by the groups on *all* these tasks.

Reproductions of Size

The size-estimation task required two kinds of judgment, perceptual and memory. It had special interest as a starting point for us because it has caused much controversy, producing contradictory findings about directional effects of needs, as well as impressive individual differences (Bruner & Postman, 1948;

Carter & Schooler, 1949; this volume, Chapter 5; Lambert, Solomon & Watson, 1949; M. B. Smith, 1952). In the *perceptual* condition the subject adjusted a variable circle of light until it appeared equal in size to the standard disk placed at his left. The disks were slightly smaller than a half-dollar. Upon them appeared symbols that were either thirst-related (a coke, a highball, and so on) or neutral, and matched in size, brightness, and color. There were twelve disks, and a total of forty-eight judgments was required: The subject made four adjustments of the comparison field to each disk, two in an ascending direction toward equality and two in a descending direction.

Figure 5 shows the direction of error for the various groups and treatments in the *perceptual* condition. The first thing that strikes us is that the high- and low-interference groups separated cleanly in *direction* of error: The high-interference group markedly underestimated, and the low-interference group overestimated. These trends appeared in both the thirsty and sated conditions. Another feature, one that is not shown in Figure 5, is the appearance of these group tendencies on *both* neutral and thirst symbols. Analysis of variance showed that the distinction between the high- and low-interference groups was the single most cogent influence upon error. Need itself—thirst—was not independently significant but only in interaction with the group distinction. Need seemed only to exaggerate a mode of coping that was already present in the sated condition: In the high-interference group the thirsty subjects underestimated more than the sated subjects did, and in the low-interference group the thirsty overestimated more than the sated did.

One feature of Figure 5 is important because of widespread skepticism about need-cognition results. The totals for the *combined* thirsty and sated groups tell us that, if we had posed the issue of need-perception effects in the usual way, asking what the *general* effect of a need upon perception is, the conclusion would have been "no effect!" For when we look for an overall tendency in the combined results of all thirsty subjects compared with all sated subjects—disregarding the high- and low-interference distinction—we find a net effect of zero. This conclusion is some-

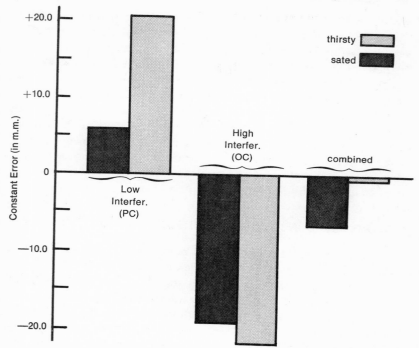

Figure 5 Mean Constant Error of Size—estimation in "Low Interference" (PC) and "High Interference" (OC) Groups when Thirsty and Sated

times reported, but it is just as misleading as the conclusion that a *particular* effect invariably follows need arousal.

Several ancillary findings deserve notice. High-interference subjects performed with greater individual consistency—less erratically—than did low-interference subjects; this difference was especially great between the two thirsty groups. Differences also appeared in the gap between adjustments made from the ascending and descending directions. This interval was much narrower in the high-interference subjects.

In the *memory* condition all subjects, thirsty as well as sated, tended to overestimate. Overestimation was, however, significantly greater in the low-interference subjects, regardless of the presence of need. This result is interesting in that it illustrates how a group difference persists within the limits and error tendencies that are peculiar to a particular adaptive task, in this instance, recall. A "remembering" task in itself seems to produce errors of overestimation, but within this functional restriction the differences that appeared between the high- and low-interference groups were highly consistent with those that occurred in the perceptual condition. Overestimation was *less* in the thirsty high-interference group than in the sated high-interference group. That is, this thirsty group overestimated in the memory condition, but the direction of the tendency was in line with its tendency to underestimate in the perceptual condition.

CONTROL BY CONSTRICTION AND FLEXIBLE CONTROL

All these results suggest the importance of cognitive control, but they do not define the *regulative principles* that underlay and produced the correlations between the color-word test and size estimation in these high- and low-interference groups. As both groups of subjects made errors, though in different directions, it is apparent that the terms "high interference" and "low interference" do not describe the generic styles or regulative principles that produced the phenotypic forms of high and low interference in the one situation and under- and overestimations of size in the other.

What clues may we draw on in describing these general response tendencies? I shall touch on only a few features of the data that seem to provide meaningful hints of the cognitive regulative principles that characterize high-interference subjects. Not all the attributes that I shall describe were completely clear to us from the size-estimation and color-word task data; most of them seem, in retrospect, to have been evident in the behavior produced in these two situations, but my descriptions are colored by data from other tasks that I shall describe in detail later. Full explication of the generic styles would require detailed scrutiny of the test situations. For the moment, however, I shall stress those propositions that seem to fit the size-estimation and the color-word results, as well as the results of a survey of "everyday behavior tendencies" culled from a questionnaire that all subjects filled out.

The findings for the high-interference subjects—errors in the direction of *underestimation,* especially evident in the thirsty group; a *narrow gap* between adjustments from ascending and descending directions in the comparison field, suggesting that these subjects traversed the whole range of possible settings more thoroughly before giving their final judgments; and *lower individual variability*—all suggest a tightened or suppressive form of control, perhaps reflecting efforts to keep judgments in line with whatever external sources of information, cues, and anchors were available in the stimulus field. Underestimation—particularly in a context of low individual variability—was perhaps the outcome of a concentrated effort to focus on certain features of the stimulus field and to exclude others, to limit awareness to the boundaries of segments of the field, particularly the most relevant segments, in this case the diameter of the circle.

Bearing in mind that these subjects were especially thrown off by the color-word task, it seems reasonable to assume that this tendency to "package" a stimulus coincides with efforts to reduce overlap among the boundaries of organized units of the cognitive field. This process would be especially evident in the size-estimation task, in which the instruction offers encouragement to do precisely that. But the color-word task presents a *physically inseparable* overlap of inconsistent organizations. In the face of this insurmountable obstacle to isolation, it is reasonable to expect those who are especially *intolerant of overlap* (as in ambiguity) to be particularly disturbed by the intruding field.[6]

This line of reasoning suggests that efforts to reduce overlap, to segregate and increase the definition of objects in the field, are guided by firm standards of what is "real out there," empha-

---

[6] Reading time for the high-interference group systematically increased in the course of reading the page of incongruent color-word combinations. Far from improving as the trial proceeded, they tended to get worse. [See Loomis and Moskowitz (1958).]

sizing objectively verifiable anchors and cues. It does not seem far-fetched to suspect that, in this orientation to reality, distrust and suppression of hunch and affect as bases of judgment would be the rule. Extending speculation a bit further to what seems a logical possibility, we may expect high-interference subjects to hold the reins tightly on communication and affect; even if they admit feelings into consciousness, they do not easily communicate them.

In such a setting of constricted control, what would be the effects of a need and of provocative, need-related symbols in the stimulus field? Underestimation was particularly evident in the thirsty, high-interference group. Perhaps heightened need intensifies efforts to preserve firm boundaries among objects in the cognitive field. Control over the pressure of need might thus take the form of even greater effort to achieve a compact organization of the stimulus field. It does not seem far-fetched also to expect that, when such suppressive efforts are directed at need or affect, sensitivity to need-relevant stimuli will actually be heightened, with the aim, not of allowing, but of preventing, their influence upon organization. Need, in short, should intensify efforts to maintain a clearly articulated stimulus field.

These hypotheses were subjected to more detailed scrutiny in the other experimental procedures. On the face of it these possible qualities of the high-interference subjects resemble clinical descriptions of compulsiveness, and we explored this connection in a rather crude test, a self-rating inventory that contained a number of everyday instances of compulsive behavior. The subjects' reports encouraged the belief that compulsive tendencies *are* especially strong in high-interference subjects. That is, the high-interference subjects disclosed themselves, for example, as concerned with precision and meticulousness, with tendencies to overvalue order and to be acutely uncomfortable with disorder, and to categorize reality intellectually rather than to organize it in terms of affective predilection. Other scales in the inventory were developed around the issues of communication and release of affect; these results too encouraged the same impressions and stimulated further hypotheses about the other cognitive tasks that I shall briefly describe.

The self-ratings of the low-interference subjects were more ambiguous and did not provide clear clues to the regulative strategy that produced such apparently diverse trends as absence of compulsiveness, low interference in the color-word situation, and consistent overestimation on the size-estimation task. One quality that appeared is, however, perhaps worth stressing: These subjects' responses on the inventory revealed them to be rather freely expressive emotionally, suggesting a certain volatility that may have contributed to the higher variability of their judgments on the size-estimation task. It may be that they allowed a broad and shifting array of cues, including momentary intensifications of feeling about the thematic contents of the disks, to play into the organization of their cognitive fields. The data from other test situations that we shall consider seem to suggest more strongly that flexible selection, governed pretty much by objectively *permissible* tolerances in a task, was a key quality in their performance.

Clearly, the original designations of high and low interference are too bound to the criterion task to embrace the regulative tendencies that unite various qualities of performance. To suggest the more generic qualities just hypothesized, we have labeled the regulative pattern of the high-interference group *constricted control* and the other *flexible control*. I shall use these terms in describing the performance of the two groups of subjects on other cognitive tasks.

Tachistoscopic Recognition of Peripheral Stimuli

The results on the tasks discussed so far suggest that need-related stimuli take on different significance in the two main groups. In one a concern with what is "really out there" and with the firmness of boundaries suggests efforts to divorce drive-related cues from the organization of response. But this suppression does not necessarily mean absence of influence by drive. Admittedly, we are speculating at this point, but it seems possible that a constant effort to distinguish the promptings of need from objective fact and external anchorages of judgment might increase rather than dull sensitivity to need. In short, constricted control might also imply sensitivity to what has to be suppressed and shunted aside. Perhaps stimuli that bear connotations intimately associated with an existing need state actually exert a momentary "fascination" effect.

Brief exposures of stimuli in a tachistoscope seemed to offer a way of highlighting such an unrecognized "pull" exerted by a need-related stimulus. Brief exposures do not allow detailed scanning on any single trial; if an attractive need-related stimulus were centered in the stimulus field, attention, especially in the constricted-control group, might fall first upon the center of the field and hamper recognition of stimuli placed on the periphery. That is, a portion of the exposure time would be taken up by the pull toward the center, hindering peripheral recognition. It would also follow that the constricted-control subjects would take longer to overcome this centering tendency over a *series* of exposures.

To make certain that our need-related stimulus was indeed dominant in each subject's awareness, we presented the tachistoscopic task in two phases. The purpose of the first phase was to precondition attention to the center of the card: The stimulus card was blank except for a gaily colored strawberry ice-cream soda drawn in the center. This card was shown at subthreshold exposures that were gradually lengthened until recognition occurred. Following this phase, the critical stimulus card was inserted. The soda again appeared in the center, but around it in a concentric arrangement extending to the periphery were placed various letters and numbers. On a gridded report sheet subjects indicated the positions of figures identified during each exposure. They were instructed to identify as many items as possible on a single exposure. The card was shown twenty-five times. Exposure time on each trial was one-tenth of a second, which was found to be safely above the recognition threshold for the soda alone in all subjects. I shall discuss only those features of the results that are the most relevant to the propositions described earlier.

We developed a method for determining the most probable *locus of fixation* on any one trial. The procedure assumes that the exposure time was too brief for significant eye movements to occur, and that the most probable fixation point was the geometric midpoint of the figures reported on the grid sheet for any one trial. Of course this point is very likely only a crude approxima-

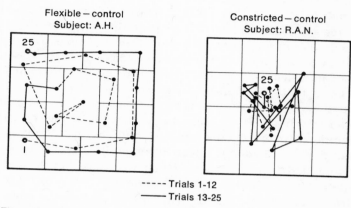

Flexible — control
Subject: A.H.

Constricted — control
Subject: R.A.N.

----- Trials 1-12
———— Trials 13-25

Figure 6 Fixation Patterns of Two Thirsty Subjects: A Flexible Control and a Constricted Control

tion of the actual fixation position that photographs of eye movements would disclose, but it served our purpose.

For the most part, only minor differences between the two sated groups appeared. Differences between the two thirsty groups were highly significant, however. The thirsty flexible-control group generally made many more fixations *outside* the central portion of the card. Figure 6 shows the fixation pattern of a member of each thirsty group to illustrate the tendencies typical of each group. The charts show the progression of fixation from the first exposure to the last. By following the line from exposure 1 (heavy dot) one can observe the scanning strategies of the two subjects for the twenty-five trials. The constricted-control subject clearly hovered around the center in all trials; the fixations of the flexible-control subject extended more and more into the periphery, so that during the second half of the exposures fixations were farther out than at the beginning. One point deserves mention: The procedure did not allow us to identify the specific pull of the soda itself, as compared to some other equally striking but non-thirst-related stimulus. The results do, however, indicate the particular effect of the need condition in the two groups.

Accuracy of recognition over the twenty-five trials also differentiated the thirsty groups. We compared the groups on correct item recognitions, using only the trials in which an item was correctly recognized for the first time. In this comparison relative efficiency on items immediately surrounding the soda was compared with efficiency on items farthest in the periphery. Again it was clear that peripheral recognition was substantially more efficient in the thirsty flexible-control group than in its sated counterpart. In the sated group the greatest percentage of correct recognitions occurred on central stimuli; in the thirsty group recognitions were equally effective for *both* central and peripheral stimuli. The most striking result was thus that flexible-control subjects were *especially efficient* under thirst conditions. By contrast, the thirsty constricted-control subjects, though also slightly more accurate on peripheral items than the corresponding sated group, were not nearly as much more effective on the peripheral items.

Is greater peripheral efficiency the result of greater total output under thirst conditions? A check of this possibility indicated no significant difference in output for thirsty and sated groups, whether flexible or constricted in control. It is evident, then, that more systematic scanning of the card was the basis of the efficient recognitions of the thirsty flexibly controlled. Also important in these considerations is the fact that *fabulations* (invented or grossly misplaced items) were actually fewer in the thirsty flexible-control subjects than in the corresponding sated; on the other hand, in the thirsty constricted-control subjects, fabulations were significantly *greater* than in the corresponding sated, indicating that the thirst condition was especially disruptive in these subjects.

To sum up, the overall efficiency of the *thirsty* flexible-control subjects exceeded by far the performance of their sated counterparts, as well as the performance of the constricted-control subjects. Their fixation tendencies were more patterned and systematic, they had more peripheral fixations, they produced fewer fabulations, and they correctly recognized many peripheral items early without loss of efficiency on inner items. By contrast, attraction to the centrally placed soda on the card was heightened in the constricted-control subjects; they produced fewer circular or systematic fixation patterns.

The Trend of Free Associations

These styles were further highlighted in the free associations of the two groups of subjects, in which need again left different imprints. As we have seen, sensitivity to need and efforts to control or contain its effect seemed to characterize the performance of thirsty constricted-control subjects. Would the "centering" effects disclosed by the tachistoscope also appear in the associative behavior of the constricted-control thirsty subjects?

The experimenter spoke two words to the subject, first the word "dry" and then the word "house." After each word the subject was asked to report for three minutes "everything that comes into your mind—words, sentences, images, thoughts." They were told that the stimulus word was not meant to limit them in any way but merely to "start them off." Each subject's protocol on "dry" was classified into content categories, thirst-related and not. First, each protocol was broken down into "idea units" (an idea unit was defined as the least number of words that could stand alone in a single thought or idea). As interest in these data centered on the frequency of themes related to thirst, seven categories were established, six representing thirst-related themes and one including all "distant" themes. The seven categories were *thirst sensations, thirst satisfiers, dry circumstances, wet circumstances, word play* (using the word "dry" idiomatically or in slang associations like "high and dry," "dry goods," and "Mrs. Dry"), *distant but relevant references* (like "Arizona," "Egypt," and "jungle"), and *nonthirst references*. Because of our main concern with thirst, many formal qualities of the nonthirst-related responses were ignored, and attention was confined to the question of whether associations were captured by the need state. For the same reason rather obvious symbolic references to other needs and motives were ignored.

The differences between the groups in the frequency of non-thirst ("distant") responses were striking. The constricted-control subjects—both thirsty and sated—clustered in a tight orbit around the stimulus word; that is, their images clung to obvious connotations of dryness and thirst. Even the sated constricted-control group exceeded the thirsty flexible-control group in clinging to more obvious symbols and connotations of the stimulus word! Clearly the sated flexible-control subjects strayed from obvious connotations of the stimulus word much more easily than did any others.

That this "centering" tendency was a stylistic characteristic and not a special product of the word "dry" was confirmed by a similar clustering tendency around the word "house." In classifying responses to the word "house," interest was again centered on how closely responses were linked to the stimulus word. Four categories were formed: *direct references* (to the structure of houses and rooms), *references to contents and surroundings* (furniture and household items), *references to home or household*, and *nonhouse-related responses*. Again, the flexible-control subjects exceeded the constricted-control subjects in the percentage of departures from the stimulus word. It should be mentioned that in total productivity—sheer number of idea units—none of the differences among the four groups on either "dry" or "house" were significant.

Two-way analyses of variance were carried out on each of the content categories for each stimulus word. Of the seven content categories for "dry," only the results for the word-play category were significant; of those for "house," only the category of references to home or household showed differences. By far the most important variables were groups (types of cognitive control) and treatment (thirsty and sated).

Clearly, then, the clustering of associations around the immediate stimulus was the single most distinguishing feature between the constricted- and flexible-control groups. It is also clear that this "stimulus centering" was a *generalized* characteristic of the constricted-control subjects, as on *both* stimulus words and even under sated conditions their clustering tendency was greater. From these results alone, it does not seem that thirst substantially increased preoccupation in constricted-control subjects with the stimulus word "dry," but it should be remembered that the percentage of stimulus-centered responses was already very high in the sated constricted-control group.

Evidence from another direction, however, disclosed an exaggeration under thirst of this funneling tendency in constricted-control subjects. This exaggeration was revealed in the number of instances in which thirst-related associations broke into the associative stream to *house.* These intrusions often appeared quite dramatically and unexpectedly. For instance, a subject would be going along talking about the particulars of a house when suddenly out would pop references to "a rainy day," "a swimming

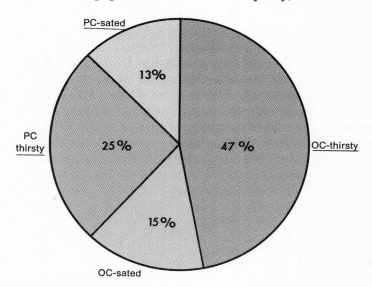

Figure 7 Percentage of all Thirst Responses to "House" given by each Group (Total number of thirst responses = 113)

pool," a "humid desert," a "cool refreshing drink," and the like. Such intrusions related to dryness and thirst were much more frequent in the thirsty subjects with constricted control. This finding is shown in Figure 7. (As productivity did not differ among the groups this type of summary is possible.) About half of all such intrusions appeared in the thirsty constricted-control group. This proportion is particularly impressive because, as we have seen, distant flights of association were so uncommon in these subjects. Again, then, we see that need has a distinctive effect but one entirely consistent with a person's typical means of cognitive regulation.

The following protocols illustrate the tendencies just described: the stimulus-centering tendency in a constricted-control subject and the intrusions of thirst-related responses in an otherwise stimulus-centered protocol on the word "house." An example is also given of the manner in which flexible-control subjects strayed from the stimulus.

Dry Subject A. Y.

constricted-control (thirsty)

Wet./ Thinking my mouth is water./ Thinking of a desert./ Lots of sand./ It's raining./ Thinking of that man lying down./ Thinking of that thing that looked like an overturned chair./ The wagon in the background/ and the tree./ Thinking of a lake./ A sponge wet with water . . ./ wiping the water off the sink at home./ Thinking of how it feels when it's raining [pause]./ Thinking of a sort of misty rain./ Thinking of "w-e-t" wet./ What the word looks like when it's spelled./ I remember I saw it when I was reading those colored words./

House Subject C. R.

constricted-control (thirsty)

Well, I think of my aunt's little red house at Ipswich/ and *summer cottages* in general/ and our own house in Morristown/ a nice house/ and gracious living/ nice rugs./ Christmas tree for some reason/ Christmas tree and all the presents under the tree./ *Summer outside . . ./* the driveway./ Chopping trees down in the woods./ A deer in the woods/ and a little valley behind our house./ A log cabin we once built out there./ And some signs we hid in the ground/ and went out and got again./ We hid all sorts of things—/ secret messages/ keys/ objects./ Fall in the woods./ Beautiful golden color of the leaves/ and the trees themselves with a curious kind of bark—/ elm, is it?/ A bird's nest in the tree./ And I think of birds in the sky./ *Lazy warm summer day.*/ And our neighbor's house—/ so different from ours./ It has a curious stairway/ and a stone floor on the bottom./ Hard cold stone that I always thought unsuitable for a house./ And the rug in the living room/ and their *swimming pool* in the back./ *Summer*—/ *warm day*/ and *bugs*/ and *offensive days.*/ Vegetable garden in which I *sweat*/ and tomato patch where I worked./ And a *lake* where I used to go as a kid./ It's very *murky warm insipid water*/ with *seaweed* at the bottom you get caught in if you dive./

Dry   Subject G. F.

flexible-control (thirsty)

Wet . . ./ wet roses in the springtime . . ./ rain/ water . . ./ California . . ./ "how dry I am."/ Kind of fizzles out there./ Thinking of how, when I had an image of a glass of water in front of me, it was very cloudy/ because in the dormitory the water comes through that way/ and you have to wait about five minutes before it clears up./ Wondering when I'll see my girl again./ Perhaps the end of this week./ I don't know./ Gotta see my draft board too./ T'hell with them though; they can wait./ Yeah, this week I think./ I don't know if I will or not./ I never decide till the last minute anyway/ so I don't know why I bother thinking about it so much./

Incidental Recognition of Thirst-Related and "Neutral" Words

The last set of data that I shall discuss has to do with incidental recognition of need-related stimulus words. These data interested us particularly because they again disclosed a tendency for thirst to facilitate adaptive performance in thirsty flexible-control subjects. In this task subjects read two new color-word pages; the colors (red, green, yellow, and blue) appeared this time in different word contexts. One page had fifteen thirst-related words (like "parched" and "wet") randomly dispersed in the different colors over the page; the second page had fifteen neutral words equated to the thirst words for frequency of usage and length. As in the original selection task, subjects read colors and tried to ignore the words. But following this test, without any prior warning, they were tested for recall and recognition of the words. The recognition-report sheet contained the correct thirst-related and neutral words mixed in among equal numbers of incorrect thirst and neutral words, permitting us to check not only correctness but also the tendency to confabulate.

Recognition of thirst words, although greater than for neutral words in both constricted- and flexible-control groups, was generally superior among the constricted-control subjects. That is, the constricted-control subjects were less effective in conforming to the primary adaptive requirement of ignoring the words while reading colors. As reading time was longer in the constricted-control subjects (as we should expect from the selection criteria), the effect of reading time upon recognition score had to be ruled out. Although a moderate correlation of .33 was found between reading time and recognition, it was not of a magnitude that could account for the considerable differences found between groups. Thirst itself did not differentiate the groups on the measure of correct recognition; relative superiority in recognizing thirst words was nearly the same in the two thirsty subgroups.

That thirst *did* have a distinctly different effect in the two thirsty groups appeared in the results on *fabulated* recognition (the tendency to choose words not on the original pages). The number of false recognitions of thirst words was unusually high in the thirsty constricted-control group. The sated constricted-control subjects averaged 13 percent, compared to 56 percent for their thirsty counterparts. The two flexible-control groups reached about the same level—a slight difference of 3 percent separated them. From the higher recognition scores of constricted-control subjects, sated and thirsty, it might appear that they were "taking more chances" than the flexible-control subjects were, which would create a greater likelihood of both correct and incorrect responses. But this inference, it should be noted, is inconsistent with these subjects' performance on the other tasks. It seems particularly unlikely for the sated constricted-control subjects, as the total number of recognition *errors* in this group was not unusual, thirty-four compared to twenty-seven for the sated flexible-control subjects. The fabulating tendency in the thirsty constricted-control group seems to have been a highly specific consequence of thirst.

Thirst in constricted-control subjects thus tended to induce errors on this task. But, although it lulled constricted-control subjects, it seemed to enliven flexible-control subjects, whose overall errors were fewer than those of the sated groups. It seems that thirst mobilized even more selectiveness than usual in flexible-control subjects; it apparently marshaled in them a more effective orientation to the task. These indications of a facilitative effect in the flexible-control group are especially interesting in demonstrating again that need is not necessarily disruptive of cognitive organization. It will be recalled that in the tachistoscopic task also thirst facilitated the performance of flexible-control subjects; their peripheral recognition under thirst was better than the performance of the sated flexible-control subjects. We are tempted to infer that in the flexible-control subjects need tension can be "recruited" to assist in the resolution of more immediate reality claims. Of course, it is obvious that this finding needs to be checked in further studies of *intraindividual* changes from sated to thirsty conditions, for our conclusions are limited to the *group* comparisons between sated and need conditions.

PROPERTIES OF COGNITIVE CONTROLS AND IMPLICATIONS FOR MEASUREMENT

I should like now to take stock of some general properties of cognitive controls and to draw some implications for measurement.

First, cognitive controls, or cognitive attitudes, are, like needs, *directive*; they exert a selective influence on the cognitive field. But they are not linked, as needs are, to a range of satisfying objects; they are created by the impact of adaptive problems for which they become instruments of resolution.[7]

Second, although they serve an equilibrating function, cognitive attitudes do not necessarily eliminate or reduce tension. They equilibrate in the sense of resolving an imbalance created by a problem, an instruction, or a reality requirement, but they are not tension-reducing in the sense of producing momentary quiescence; in fact, they may at times increase tension. The facilitating effects that appear with the flexible-control attitude show how equilibration can maintain tension rather than eliminate it through release or tension reduction.[8]

---

[7] The close relationship to Allport's instrumental attitudes is worth noting:

> . . . it must be admitted that *some* attitudes seem to be merely directive and not motivational. For example, when a subject comes to a psychological laboratory he is motivated by curiosity, emulation, or obedience (themselves deep-lying attitudes), but he may assume additional attitudes which are incidental to the occasion. The *Aufgabe* which he adopts, for instance, is not itself the motive in the situation. To press a key when a red light appears is an attitude but not a motive. This attitude merely directs or guides a course of conduct which has been otherwise motivated.
>
> It seems necessary, therefore, to distinguish two type of attitudes: one which is so organized and energized that it actually *drives*, and the other which merely *directs*. Both of these types are conditions of readiness-for-response, both are in a sense dynamic, for both enter into the determination of conduct. The first, however, is specifically *motivational*, the second (which includes besides the *Aufgabe* such "postures of consciousness" as are involved in skills and in the manner and modes of response) are merely *instrumental*. The true motive underlying an instrumental or directive attitude is often some other driving attitude, or sometimes it is of so primitive and unorganized a nature that it may be called instinctive. (1935, pp. 21–22)

I am indebted to David Rapaport for pointing out the close similarity between Allport's approach and the one outlined here.

[8] Hartmann (1939) has stressed that regulative processes represent different types of equilibrating tendencies and points out the insufficiencies of trying to reduce regulation to a unitary tendency toward equilibrium or homeostasis. Although all controls or delay mechanisms are assumed to be

Third, cognitive controls can involve a variety of cognitive functions, such as memory and perception.

Fourth, we infer them not from symbolic content of percept, memory, or fantasy, as we do the presence of need, but from *formal qualities* of behavior, that is, from the particular ways in which responses to the stimulus field are organized. Cognitive controls thus may involve and organize such basic processes as *schematizing* or conceptualizing behavior, *mapping* (see Tolman, 1948), *absolute and differential thresholds, anticipation, attention, concentration,* and so on. Elsewhere we have labeled the structural properties used in cognitive attitudes "adaptive properties" (Klein, 1949).

Fifth, because we detect cognitive controls through formal qualities of response, it does not matter whether experimental stimuli are neutral or "loaded," as long as an adaptive requirement has been so carefully built into the situation as to elicit the particular attitude. Even certain favorite standbys of Gestalt demonstrations of "required" laws of organization have been relevant to some studies, like those of time-error phenomena (Gardner, 1953; Holzman, 1954; Klein, Schlesinger & Meister, 1951) and the phi-phenomenon (Klein & Schlesinger, 1951).

The action of cognitive attitudes upon need can be summarized: Cognitive controls determine the manner of distribution or "rerouting" of need energy in conformity with immediate reality. They check *direct* need satisfaction, functioning as delay mechanisms. At various points in this chapter, I have indicated that concern for the interlocking of need and control may provide important research leads. Intriguing questions arise. Is the influence of a cognitive control and of a need independent of the type of need? What are the effects of needs when special defenses appear? How do "oral defenses" interact with the restrictions imposed by constricted control? These questions also extend into developmental issues.

"equilibrating" in their effects, the energy deployments and requirements differ. No single homeostatic principle is adequate to encompass these different forms.

The distinction between need and cognitive control implies that it is necessary to approach motivational measurement of any behavior through the two avenues of *formal* characteristics of response and *content*, a strategy that owes much to techniques of clinical test interpretation developed by Rapaport (Rapaport, Gill & Schafer, 1945–1946) and Schafer (1948).

This distinction is important even to proper evaluation of questionnaires and rating scales, a consideration often overlooked in the usual emphasis on content in the use of such instruments. When assessing compulsiveness, for example, through a questionnaire, surely we must recognize a difference between watching a person turn a doorknob six times as he leaves his house and his telling about it on the questionnaire. His *manner* of telling is potentially as revealing as the fact itself. A questionnaire is essentially a *communication*. How he answers, the form required of him for answering, and, if ratings are required, his rating behavior—all of these should qualify any judgment about the significance of content alone.

This caution holds true in any test situation in which needs are active, as in a TAT test. *How* needs are provoked to arousal, what communicates them, the reality problem posed by the *form of the test situation* itself—all must be brought into the evaluation of the vicissitudes that need has undergone.

I have treated cognitive attitude as an intervening variable, as a device for explaining consistency in a person's cognitive behaviors. For measurement purposes we should clarify its links to antecedent conditions. Our conception of "antecedents" or the "stimulus situation" differs from accepted usage in stimulus-response theories, in which antecedent conditions are usually physical attributes of the stimulus. This interpretation of stimulus is not helpful in describing the circumstances that bring stylistic tendencies into play. In our data, it would be hopeless to look to similarities in the physical qualities of the tachistoscopic situation and the association task to account for intraindividual consistencies.

It is more profitable to assume that the "antecedent conditions" of a cognitive control are the *adaptive requirements of a task* as the subject understands them. A hypothesis about a cognitive control is always a hypothesis about what the control *accomplishes*, and the strategy of experiment is to select situations designed to elicit a particular control. This strategy makes it possible to expect generality of response on a variety of tasks that differ widely in their physical attributes. If they pose similar adaptive problems, the chances are that they will arouse similar kinds of controls. For the study of personality and individual style, it is much more economical to seek generality on this basis than through physically identical situations. It fits the dimensions of our data and inspires questions about personality consistency that are foreign to S-R theory.[9]

Of course, the problems of learning and the nature of "stimulus-response" connections still exist for us, but in a necessarily different form than in S-R theory because our conception of what is learned differs. The "learned response" we are dealing with is not simply motor habit, correlated with certain physical qualities of stimuli, but cognitive dispositions for which broadly equivalent ranges of response properties are the expressive vehicles.

ARE COGNITIVE ATTITUDES "DEFENSES"?

Throughout this discussion I have avoided the term "defense." It is unnecessary to equate cognitive controls with defen-

---

[9] Maslow strongly expresses the same view:

. . . the organization of the personality is to be understood in terms of the problems facing it and what it is trying to do about them. Most organized behaviors then must be doing something about something. In the discussion of personality syndromes we should then characterize two specific behaviors as belonging to the same syndrome *if they have the same coping aims with respect to a certain problem*, that is to say, *if they were doing the same thing about the same something*. (1943, p. 527, italics added)

ses, and it is a decided advantage *not* to consider defense as the prototype of *all* control, a tendency that early psychoanalytic discussions unfortunately encouraged. There is no time to trace more recent developments in psychoanalysis that have forced modification in this view; they have, however, gone beyond earlier preoccupations with defense.

"Defense" is a useful construct to refer to modes of mastering anxiety provoked by conflicts among needs or need derivatives. In this usage, defense is knowable through its antecedents in conflict and through the sanctions and restrictions it imposes in regard to certain sources of drive satisfaction. Like all controls, defense is, of course, a form of thought organization, but its identifying mark is its function of resolving conflict and of closing channels of gratification.

The regulative controls in our experiments are not made of this cloth. They place no particular sanction or restriction upon need-satisfying *objects,* and they appear when quite "neutral" stimuli are involved. They subjugate need to immediate reality requirements, but the aim of the need itself is not affected. Nor is arousal of cognitive attitudes powered by conflict among needs. We might even call such attitudes "conflict-free" styles of regulation.

This separation is not hard and fast, but it is clear enough, I think, to make defense and cognitive attitude independently useful as intervening variables. It also creates new and intriguing departures for experimentation. What are the effects of needs when special defenses—in addition to cognitive attitudes—enter the picture? In our experiments on thirst, for instance, conflicts over oral gratification could have been a complicating factor, invoking special defenses as well are reality-attuned cognitive attitudes. Is it also possible that certain defenses are more or less likely to develop in the context of certain cognitive attitudes? Is the defense of isolation equally possible in the people we have designated as employing constricted and flexible control? The distinction between the concepts also provides a firm basis from which to approach current speculation on organization of the ego system, for we can ask whether or not "conflict-free styles"—cognitive attitudes—themselves originate in defenses and achieve autonomy from them.

Another salutary effect of distinguishing between defense and other modes of control is to force us to specify just *how* a piece of behavior is defensive every time we use the term in experimentation. That is, we must demonstrate its antecedent conditions of conflict among needs and the restrictions imposed upon need-satisfying objects. It also requires us to partial out influences of other modes of control. Most of the confusion in discussions of so-called "perceptual defense" comes from such operational failures.[10]

There is still another advantage in distinguishing defense from other modes of control: freeing the concept of control from the charge leveled against defense that its aim is always negative. Adaptive controls can lead to quite creative reorganizations. Freud's conception that thought is "experimental action" involving delay of impulse discharge certainly allows for this possibility (1900, Chapter 7). The psychoanalytic model of delay of need satisfaction and the distinction between the primary and secondary processes offer a broad framework in which to conceptualize, in terms of functions, a variety of controls beside

---

[10] It is doubtful that many phenomena called "defensive" in the experimental literature can be legitimately so interpreted. For instance, a heightened recognition threshold does not inevitably have a defensive intent; it can also reflect the type of habitual cognitive control that we have considered here. Usually studies that attempt to define "defense" in such operational terms never specify just what the defense is directed against, what conflicts contribute to the behavior, or what restrictions on need gratification are served by the behavior. It should also be pointed out that operational definitions of defense in terms of specific *behaviors*, rather than in terms of antecedent conditions of conflict, are only pale reflections of the original psychoanalytic concept. In general, the central fault in experimental applications of the concept has been failure to draw any systematic distinctions between defenses and other forms of adaptive control.

defense (see Bibring, 1943; Hartmann, 1948; Rapaport, 1951a, Part 7).

I have concentrated upon some immediate issues of measurement and have underscored a working distinction between need and control. Any detailed particulars of how need and regulation of need interlock must, of course, wait upon an embracing scheme that will adequately conceptualize organismic regulation.

Chapter 7

Cognitive Control and Motivation

Some years ago my co-workers and I proposed a concept of cognitive control that would center attention upon a person's typical strategies of perceiving, remembering, and thinking (Klein & Schlesinger, 1949; this volume, Chapters 5, 6; Holzman & Klein, 1954). We suggested that such inveterate regulative tendencies—*cognitive attitudes*, we eventually labeled them—might account for some of the differences among people that always appear in perceptual and cognitive studies. Later it became clear to us that a variety of cognitive attitudes contributes to consistency in a person's behavior, and we have taken note of such a structural arrangement of cognitive attitudes by calling it *cognitive style*. In proposing these concepts of cognitive attitude and style, there was at the back of our minds a feeling that, although motivation-in-perception studies were rectifying older sins of omission, they were also assuming that an intense enough drive can bend all cognitive structures to its aim. No one had committed himself openly to such an overstatement, but empirical work seemed to be moving steadily toward it. Some way had to be found to provide in theory for effective perceiving without renouncing the possible pervasiveness of motivational influence upon thought.

The behavior patterns in which we sought evidences of cognitive attitudes seemed clearly to reflect direction in thought, but as we learned more about them it also became clear that they lacked the characteristics ordinarily ascribed to drives. For instance, a rather common notion of drive is of goal-directed behavior involving, in Tolman's words, a "readiness to get to and to manipulate in consummatory fashion (or to get from) certain . . . types of object" (1951, p. 288). Yet patterns of cognitive attitudes seemed by no means committed to particular objects, nor were they linked in any clear-cut way with particular forms of satisfaction. Cognitive attitudes seemed purposive without having the character of a drive demanding satisfaction. They had much in common with what Gordon Allport (1935) has called "instrumental attitudes," for they involved not so much *what* a person was typically seeking (drive satisfaction) as *how:* his ways and means of seeking it. In fact, they could in some measure account for individual differences even in the innocuous, sexless, contentless, aggression-free tasks of the unglamorous psychophysical experiment.

It dawned on us that our most reliable estimates of such individual controls were actually made in settings that ensured optimal performance, relatively uncomplicated by anxiety and by connotations of conflict in the stimuli. That is, when subjects felt involved without being threatened, their patterns seemed to stand out. It seemed best, then, to consider the purposiveness in cognitive attitudes in terms suited to their most obvious accomplishments in behavior, rather than as an expression of drive. Such attitudes are ways of making contact with reality in which intentions are coordinated with the properties, relations, and limitations of events and objects.

Thus conceived, cognitive attitudes seem to resemble what psychoanalysts have called "character defenses." To regard them as "defenses" could, however, be misleading because they are not obviously tied to specific demands or conflicts, as the precise meaning of "defense" should imply. Although in particular experimental conditions they seem to help bring about drive reduction (as in the way a hungry person typically goes about getting his food) or to bring about behavior that can be viewed as defensive, these results do not really reflect the essence of the cognitive attitude; they are secondary outcomes. Furthermore, to view them in specific terms of drive reduction or defense, first, leaves unexplained their apparent reflection of highly generalized forms of control, as likely to appear in a person's perceptual behavior as in his manner of recollection; second, fails to take into account that the activation of one (rather than another) cognitive attitude depends more upon the adaptive *task* with which a person has to cope than upon the drive tension of the moment.

Working from the psychoanalytic assumption that thought originates in the enforced postponement of drive satisfaction (Freud, 1900, Chapter 7; 1911), I found it useful to consider cognitive attitudes as contributing to drive activity in a secondary way, not necessarily defensive, by modulating, facilitating, or inhibiting the effects of a temporarily active drive upon behavior (this volume, Chapter 6). They seem to ensure that drive-organized behavior will also be realistic behavior, for they represent strategies of reality contact that are probably the outcomes of a person's repeated efforts to deal adequately and economically with classes of situations typically encountered en route to drive satisfaction. If the problem of motivation were merely how to activate the organism, cognitive attitudes would be irrelevant to drives. But motivation involves directed behavior—some perceivable change that meets subjective standards of adequacy, of a workable fit with the nature of things. If a given result is to be achieved, behavior must have not only a motor but a steering wheel and a map—both of which cognitive attitudes supply.

The study of cognitive control in drive activity (this volume, Chapter 6) seemed to encourage this thesis. The main purpose of the investigation was to discover how thirst would affect the cognitive performance of subjects of differing cognitive attitudes. We found that thirst *generally* did produce deviations in cognitive behavior, but in different ways in the two groups. The effects of drive thus seemed more understandable when we knew the requirements of a task and the cognitive attitudes relevant to it.

There are evidently limits to how far drives can bend cognitive behavior, limits imposed in part by the situation, in part by the objects with which a person must deal, and in part by the cognitive attitudes called into play by the adaptive problems confronting him. The experiment seemed to tell us that drive, with its associated situation sets, goal sets, and incentives, calls most of the tunes, but not the tempo or the style in which they are played.

There seemed, then, good reason to postulate two bases of regulation in behavior: control structures having what we may call an *accommodative* function in behavior—that of coordinating intentions and the structural matrix of objects and events—and drive structures, which give behavior segments either an instrumental or a consummatory significance. This distinction proved to have its troubles, however. The main difficulty was how to describe the "force" of drive independently of its partners in interaction. Try as we would, it was impossible to define the pushing or impelling quality of thirst apart from the cognitive tools of perceiving and cognition that it presumably pushes. Further reflection on the nature of thirst in our experiment created doubts about the wisdom of conceiving drives simply as pushing agents that produce behavior. Thirst, like the so-called "higher" needs, is evidently very much a cognitive event linked in some way to somatic deficit, though not necessarily requiring such a deficit for arousal; but it does always involve intentions and conceptualizations as well as a range of consummatory objects. Clearly, a more adequate conception of drive should embrace both the delaying principles *and* the specific object aims, goal sets, and intentions implied by the concept of drive.

The study gave us a useful perspective on the issue of directedness in behavior. It emphasized for us that behavior reflects direction and control but that it is not exclusively at the mercy of the demand aspect either of drives or of environmental forces. What is clearly called for is a conception of regulation that provides for guarantees that thinking and behavior will accommodate internal demands while being simultaneously responsive to adaptive intentions and to the inherent structural arrangements of things and events. Instinctual danger, remarked Anna Freud

(1936), makes a man wise. By being responsive to drive aims and to reality alike, thought and behavior paradoxically achieve a certain freedom from both masters (Hartmann, 1939; Rapaport, 1957b).

CONTROL STRUCTURES IN DRIVE

I shall try to place these component motivations of thought in a somewhat more workable relation to one another within a general conception of drive. Admittedly, the proposals are speculative and tentative, but there is no escaping the necessity for keeping step, however haltingly, with the empirical developments of the last decade that have made more glaring the insufficiencies of older conceptions of drive. Of course it is hazardous to hope that any theory or concept can provide a sacrosanct shelter in these times of rapid empirical discovery. But such discovery calls for an acceleration of theory building, not for a retreat from it. As Hebb remarked, theorizing today is like skating on thin ice; one must keep moving or drown.

The conception of drive as an independent entity triggering internally propelled selective behavior came about at a time when concepts of purpose and intention had to be grafted onto an unwilling host of psychological theory. It brought into psychology, however, a fundamentally unspecifiable force, descriptions of which often retreat to the metaphors of an energy language. Other defects also seem obvious now. For one thing, it is impossible to define the drive presumed to interact with cognition without involving in the definition the very structure supposedly driven. Hebb (1949) and Jacob (1954) have argued—and our results certainly bear them out—that even a so-called "somatic drive" like thirst cannot be defined solely in terms of tissue lack. The dehydrated condition of the body would not itself create a call for water if it were not for some kind of relating (cognitive) activity associated with the somatic tension. It is also difficult to reconcile a conception of an independent pushing agent with the fact that behavior is differently organized in different people, even when it shows the integrative pull of the same goal set or incentive. Nor is it easy to reconcile it with the fact that behavior, though selective, responds quite efficiently to existing environmental arrangements.

It seems more parsimonious to follow the lead of Woodworth (1918), Woodworth and Schlosberg (1954), and Hebb (1949) and to include within the meaning of "drive" first, the "relating" processes (the meanings) around which selective behavior and memories are organized and in terms of which goal sets, anticipations, and expectations develop and, second, those processes that accommodate the relating processes to reality. In this way drive can be defined solely in terms of behavior and thought products. Emphasis is thus where it belongs; in Hebb's words, upon the directedness, patterning, and timing of behavior, these three being, after all, the essential problems that provoked motivation concepts in the first place.

In speaking of "drive activity" we imply the existence of an appetitive requirement for appropriate stimulations of a certain range and class. The first characteristic of drive is that it involves a goal set, a requirement for appropriate object qualities. Drives bring the organism into readiness for certain things, certain meanings. A drive, then, is essentially structured around relational and conceptual activity. Conceptual activity may be said to have a *recruiting* and *priming* effect upon behavior. The *priming* effect consists of strengthening, through activated concepts and memories, certain sensory stimuli and not others, and of predisposing thought and behavior toward or away from particular objects and events. The conceptual activity may be said to have a *recruiting* effect in providing a framework for ordering registered sensory events. In short, drive is a construct that is useful in expressing a demand for something, rather than an urge toward something. We could call this demand the *recruitment* and *priming* aspect of drive structure.

In the sense that drive activity may be said to recruit objective facts into the organism's fund of experience, we can also speak of stimuli as signals and mediators of objective facts. As any object is actually a complex arrangement, only certain impingements register as stimuli (signals), and only certain properties of an object are experienced as such. Drive activity is in part defined by this selection. Perception is indispensable to this selection, and percepts thus reflect the relevance of objects to drives.

A drive, however, is said to be adaptive only when its manifestations respect, so to speak, the inherent organization of distal events and objects, and this limitation brings us to the second characteristic of drive structure. In most contexts (at least in normal waking life), we bring the attractions and repulsions provoked by drive activity into some realistic relation to environmental probabilities and to the opportunities that situations present. Behavior *accommodates* itself to the logic of things conveyed through the senses. A crucial component of this accommodation process, to which Troland (1932) first called attention in his concept of "retroflex," is a sort of back action of the environment on the cortex; that is, changes of behavior provoked by contact with segments of reality are themselves perceived, and the consequences of the contact can be reported to the cortex in terms of benefit or injury, leading to reinforcement, facilitation, or inhibition of the behavior change.

Cognitive structures are indispensable to this general accommodative effort, involving an informational return from one's actions upon objects, for they are provided with means of imposing an order upon receptor events that accords with the relatively constant attributes of objects and events. Perceptual experience amply testifies to this fact. Regardless of recruitment by active drive aims, perception seems assured of a certain essential independence by certain structuring processes that are directly responsive to objects and relations; for example, tendencies to *Prägnanz* in experiencing forms, one-sidedness of contour, and the like. Indeed, all the tendencies to which Gestaltists have called attention in their principles of perceptual grouping and form illustrate this autonomy of perceptual processes.

Particularly impressive evidence of the intimate coordination of perceptual experience with the actual properties of objects themselves appears in Ivo Kohler's studies (1951, 1953). In experiments modeled on the classic studies by Stratton (1897), he observed the effects of wearing inverting prisms for months at a time. Eventually subjects showed great improvement in visual-motor coordinations. The most striking findings, however, were the clear-cut indications, after the long period of motor rehabituation, that the visual field righted itself *perceptually*. The learning that obviously occurred involved *perceptual* accommodation to *actual* properties of the external spatial framework.

That such coordination occurs in every purposive commerce with reality structures seems to be an inescapable fact. That is, the activity of drive consists not simply of arousal or even of readying the organism for particular goals. It includes specific ways of dealing with the environment; it involves accommodative structures. Because cognitive attitudes describe a person's typical accommodative patterns in dealing with reality, they are best viewed as integral aspects of his drive structures; they are initiated by any intention (not necessarily conscious) that calls for realistic appraisal and assessment.

Behavior, then, embodies priming, recruiting, and accommodative functions. Drive aim, drive consummation, and mode of cognitive control are simply different vantage points from which to view the *same* behavior.

If we consider behavior from a developmental point of view, this conception also implies that modifications of drive aims and of accommodative structures go hand in hand—essentially the view of Piaget (1936). For him, psychological reality is a product of action and feedback out of which schemata form and change. He shows how "abstract intelligence," in the form of ideas, derives from "sensorimotor intelligence," which is rooted in inborn reflexes, among which are the sucking reflexes. The ideas that develop around the sucking reflex illustrate this process. In the early stages of infancy an object does not exist in its own right; it exists only as something to suck, and objects are not distinguished functionally. In recruiting objects, however—in giving them meaning as sucking objects—the active sucking schema changes and refines itself, and the sucking movement changes with different objects. Much of our learning comes down to such accommodative differentiation.

THE BEHAVIOR SEGMENT IN ACCOMMODATIVE ACTIVITY

The accommodative side of drive activity—the "reality principle" in operation—deserves closer scrutiny, for it is there that cognitive attitudes and styles can be observed. I should like to offer at this point a definition of the natural boundaries of a segment of adaptive behavior. They may be said to consist of sensory, cognitive, and motor events linked in a pattern of activation that terminates with a particular change that is experienced as "adequate" to the initiating intention (Troland, 1932).

Even when drive recruitment is clearly present, it cannot account for all selection and choice in behavior; selection has another source in adaptive intentions. An intention that requires us to deal with things and relations as they are narrows responses to certain properties of objects and events and to the restraints they pose to action upon them. A thirsty person still considers differences between the *picture* of an ice-cream soda and the real thing; in an experiment he is generally capable of judging size without giving way to the desire to drink. Intention initiates the back-action process referred to earlier; it endows certain behavior changes with potential influence, and they in turn enhance or inhibit behaviors that favor or bar the intention, as the case may be. Specific intentions may themselves be modified or refined by such informative back action, even as all processes in this interplay serve a single recruitment aim. In any one adaptive segment, an intention and its associated goal set start the process. As behavior encounters objects, modified intentions generate new changes. But the revised intentions remain commensurate with the initiating goal set and adaptive intention. If my intention is to navigate a motorboat to the opposite shore, I must "intend" to press the starter, guide my progress to avoid other boats, and so on, although the main objective does not waver.

Selecting the appropriate behavior segment that exemplifies a cognitive attitude is not an easy matter and is always a more or less arbitrary abstraction from a more comprehensive adaptive effort. For purposes of analysis, we may consider such a unit to be any segment of behavior, gross or minute, of long or of short duration, that is bounded by an initiating intention on one side and a behavioral change *experienced* as fulfilling the intention on the other. On this basis a unit may take minutes or span years. In any event, the unit chosen will have the initiating and terminal characteristics described.

I want to emphasize one feature of this conception: Its stress on *experienced* fulfillment as the natural terminus of an adaptive behavior segment. The mere attainment of an objective without awareness of it as such is not enough to terminate an action having adaptive intent. A behavioral change may be entirely adequate to the intention that gave rise to it—that is, it may actually attain the intended objective—but the attainment may not be *experienced* as such, and the behavior will then continue. Examiners are familiar with the response pattern on the Block Design test of the Wechsler-Bellevue in which a subject unwittingly arranges the blocks in the correct solution, fails to perceive its correctness, and upsets it. There are also familiar instances in which confirmation is experienced prematurely, and action terminated—but in error. In still another variation, a subject's standards of adequacy may be too high; he simply will not accept *any* perceived change as "adequate." There is a real advantage, then, in distinguishing *awareness* of attainment of a goal from the fact of behavioral change alone. The distinction gives us a basis for expecting cognitive styles to be different when standards of "adequacy" or of an acceptable "fit" are different (note, for instance, Gardner's evidence, 1953, of generalized dispositions for broad or narrow equivalence ranges in discriminative behavior). An incidental implication is that the *experienced* attainment may be crucial in learning, that is, in the "reinforcement" of behavior, on the theory, as Woodworth (1947) has developed it, that adequate *results* of his activity are likely to be more impressive to the learner than his motor responses or perceptions en route. Now, if cognitive style contributes to such experiences of confirmation, it may also be expected to affect the course of learning.

An operational definition of such a frankly subjective experience of attainment presents, of course, easily recognizable difficulties. What is an acceptable criterion of such awareness of "adequate" change? The experience may consist of some indication by the subject that a choice, a movement, a perception, or a judgment he makes is "okay," "good enough," "big enough," and so on. Whether the experience of attainment should be a *perceived* change or some indication of the subject's *reflection* or *judgment* upon the adequacy of a behavior change is a difficult problem and must be decided within the framework of actual

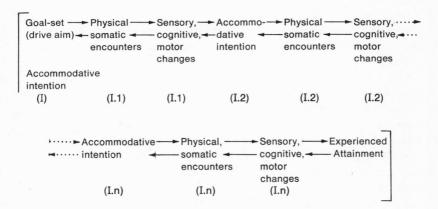

Figure 8 Adaptive Behavior Segment

investigation. But, difficult as it may be to decide upon such operational criteria, I do not think that we can ignore the problem. The main issue is not a preference for a subjective indicator when a behavioral one might do, but of recognizing that *whether or not a subject is aware of the significance of a change makes a difference in his subsequent behavior on a task.*

Figure 8 summarizes the supposed behavioral unit that emanates from the active, recruiting matrix of an accommodative intention (I), and that terminates in a behavioral change experienced as confirmatory. The adaptive behavioral unit is pictured as an extended series of events *outward;* arrows also point in the *reverse* direction to indicate the recruiting force of the initiating goal set and its associated accommodative intention. The symbols "I.1 . . . I.*n*" refer to modifications in adaptive intention resulting from successive environmental encounters and from the altered situation continually revealed by perception. Terminating the sequence is a behavioral change experienced (through perception, thought, or imagery) as attainment. Note that action and thought are not conceived in any rigidly fixed sequential relation.

In this conception of action upon and back action from objects, the main thing is *not* that stimuli produce motor activity but that they induce a *change* of activity terminating in an *experienced* result—a change in behavior that stimulates the receptors and that may be perceived or otherwise experienced. At the same time, the terminus of an adaptive behavior unit is not simply a response—motor or otherwise—as conventional S-R conceptions would have it but also the experienced attainment of aim.

In an adaptive behavior segment, perceptions and actions are united solely by the requirements of an intention; both contribute to the intention, and therefore both are interpretable on the same terms. Motor response does not necessarily *follow* perception. Neither is it necessarily the executor of perception, although it is an indispensable component of a more comprehensive adaptive effort. Motor activity can have different functions within the overall strategy employed en route to the terminating change. In the Object Assembly test of the Wechsler-Bellevue test, trial-and-error movements may provide opportunities for *perceptual* restructuring; the subject may move a block and *then* see the crucial relation. Ivo Kohler's studies (1951, 1953) offer vivid testimony to the possibility that motor rehabituation may actually be an important *antecedent* condition for restructuring the perceptual experience itself. The role of perception and motor activity in reflecting the adjustive requirements of intention is lost when we rigidly adhere to the older model of stimulus, followed by perception, followed by motor response.

We are by now so accustomed to defining our units of cognitive analysis in terms of varieties of qualitative experience—such as *perception, memory, imagery, judgment*—that we may over-look their embeddedness in the total sensorimotor exchange. We usually take perception or motor activity, rather than the inte-grated adaptive unit itself, as a dependent variable. It is not fruitful, however, to restrict descriptions of a cognitive attitude to the motor or to the perceptual components of the more inclusive behavior sequence. The level of analysis of a cognitive attitude must be the total accommodative sequence implementing a goal set, not simply that aspect of it that is "perceptual" or "mem-ory" or "motor."

To review the main considerations up to this point: The behavioral unit appropriate to the study of cognitive attitudes is the patterned sequence of behavioral events that eventuate in an experienced attainment. The child's creeping after a toy exemplifies such a complex yet integrated unit of responses; back actions from objects en route provoke new stimulations, inhibit some, facilitate others, and finally produce a terminal experi-enced attainment. The integrating factor in an adaptive behavior unit is the goal set—the objective or aim (for example, to judge size in an experiment or to find food when one is hungry). Within this orientation determined by goal sets, the cognitive attitude unfolds *in* the reaction. "Cognitive attitude" refers to the organiz-ing principle that is exemplified by this interplay of action and transaction and by the internal standard determining what is considered an *adequate* perceived result.

The idea of drive as a *meaning-inducing* field of activity implemented by *accommodative structures* makes it easier to use the concept of drive in accounting for behavior. First, it elimi-nates the idea of an unanalyzable push "interacting" with proc-esses that have no basic relation to it. Second, it makes it possible to regard control structures as themselves an aspect of drive activity and to expect that goal sets will be affected by the ac-commodative activity of these structures. Third, it accords well with the notion that cognition, which involves concepts and categories, is always motivated, and at the same time warns us that motivated cognition is not always—in fact, most of the time need not be—"distorting" and "autistic." Fourth, any behavior segment may be looked at from the point of view of the developmental level of drive aims and the level of accommodative strategy reflected in it. Accommodative strategies—cognitive attitudes and styles—are presumed to undergo developments that parallel changes in drive structure (that is, goal sets and associated conceptual structures); they include those accommodative modes associated with early drive organizations, as well as highly differentiated later modes. Finally, it allows for the possibility of *regression*, as well as development, in cognitive behavior. At any single developmental level, actions express the ratio of recruiting to accommodative activity reflected in them. When behavior reflects maximal recruitment and minimal accommodation, it is not likely to be adaptive. Examples of such a mode of response are the hallucination of drive objects, the symbolization of representations, condensations, and other forms of what Freud has called primary-process modes of thought. Regression involves recruitive activity of drive aims lower in a developmental hierarchy, which move thought and behavior in accordance with earlier, less differentiated stages of drive organization.

The paradox pointed out earlier of an effectively oriented organism that is yet pervasively motivated is resolved in this conception of drive. Our view of drive structure as combining accommodative and recruiting functions tells us that autonomy from drive aims and from stimulation can be only *relative*, for the recruiting activity of drives provides insurance against capricious steering of behavior by environmental stimulation. On the other hand, drive aims always involve instrumental and accommodative structures of thought. Complete imperviousness to environmental stimulation implies only recruitment in response to drives; accommodative activity prevents such coerciveness. The workings of a drive structure thus entail delay. Every cognitive process *potentially* has implications for drive organization; every drive involves cognitive controlling structures.

ACCURACY AND EFFECTIVENESS IN MOTIVATED PERCEIVING

I should now like to consider the issue of accuracy in perceiving, so that it will be possible to see how cognitive attitudes and styles may guide perception and cognition in various ways while each remains in its own way adaptive and motivated. Discussions of motivated perception have been confused by the assumption that if perception is accurate it cannot be determined by drive, that accurate perception is somehow less "subjective" and therefore less expressive of personality, which refers to the idiosyncratic determinants of experience. Presumably, then, only in "wrong" or "distorted" perceptions would we find the influence of drives and personality dispositions.

First, let us be clear that demonstrations of effective perceiving do *not* indicate absence of motivation. Perception is always part of a larger *adaptive* act that brings some but not all qualities of objects into our experience. We are not randomly and helplessly responsive to stimuli; drive structures are fundamental guarantors of selectivity.

Even the typical psychophysical experiment in which maximal accuracy is sought is not free of motivated selection. Rather, the experimental setting creates what we may call a "motivational reduction screen," which hopefully cajoles a subject into maintaining a particular intention as a basis for reporting what he sees. Sometimes the screen is not effective, and other motives peek through. Certainly the subject's report is conditioned by this fact. For instance, in one tachistoscopic experiment, Morris Eagle was testing subjects' recognition limens, using gradually increased exposures of a simple line drawing—a triangle. As exposures lengthened, one subject kept repeating that he saw "nothing." He gave this report so far beyond the usual limits that the experimenter became suspicious. He himself looked into the tachistoscope, and the triangle appeared clear as day. He again showed the triangle and asked the subject what he saw, and this time he received the response, "Nothing, only the same old triangle." Had he been seeing it for some time? "Yes," the subject replied. Why had he not said so? The subject replied, "Well, it didn't seem reasonable to me that you would have built such a complex, huge apparatus just to show a little old triangle."

The example illustrates the active process of sifting and choosing among alternatives that always narrows a subject's report of his perception. It is also possible to show that sets and interests are involved in the perception itself, even when it faithfully reflects constant features of a physical stimulus. Zangwill (1937) has shown that different preparatory sets produce different perceptions of the same contoured surfaces and that later inability to recognize these stimuli is traceable to differences in the earlier perceptual contexts. One of his stimuli had a double hump. When the subject was prepared to see animals, the contours typically were perceived as animal forms (for example, camel); when the subject was prepared to see "mountains," a corresponding translation occurred. This experiment tells us that motivation does not simply create perceptions out of whole cloth, nor does it simply distort; its influence consists in coordinating receptor information with the interest of the moment and with the concepts appropriate to this interest. Perception is directed and organized in terms of aims and goal sets, even when it yields experiences that correspond pretty closely to the structure of something that is really "out there."

The Zangwill study also tells us that perception is very much a *conceptual* process, even though closely coordinated with the structural logic of things and with environmental probabilities. Professor Boring (1953) tells of a biologist friend who showed him drawings of the same microscopic specimen before and after the discovery of chromosomes. None of the drawings showed chromosomes before; there were plenty to be seen afterward! Essentially the same point was made experimentally by Wallach (1955) in connection with gradients in the density of texture, which Gibson has shown are so crucial to the perception of slant (1950b). Wallach demonstrated that either set or recognition is needed to make texture an effective stimulus for perceived slant. As he puts it:

This is not to say that texture gradients have nothing to do with perceived slant. Rather it is that memory and set serve to make the texture gradient effective. . . . Such a memory is brought into play either through recognition of familiar objects that are usually seen at a slant or by a set. A set may be due to experimental instructions as in Gibson's research or to preceding exposures as in our own experiments. Once a texture gradient has become effective, its steepness can then influence the angle of the perceived slant.

An experiment reported by Pieron (1955) also neatly illustrates this close tie between perception and conception. Put a plumb line in front of your eye while you are wearing Ivo Kohler's prisms (which invert the visual field): the string will at first appear to climb miraculously and then will seem to descend, and the weight to lower. Apparently, given gravity as a frame of reference, we experience our vision as "wrong"; then perception corrects itself. In this instance, even though perception is clearly accommodative, it is also very much a conceptual activity.

A basic confusion in speaking of accurate perception in absolute terms is to mistake a finite number of characteristics of an object or event (perceivable by the experimenter) for the totality of what is *potentially* perceivable. The apparent oneness of an "object" is deceptive. An object comprises complex relations, some experienced, some not, depending on availability of the concepts basic to the perception. Because our concepts are more limited than is the actual number of properties of things, we see at best only part of the world in every so-called "accurate" perception. "For when you come to think of it," muses Thomas Mann's Felix Krull, "which is the real shape of the glowworm, the insignificant little creature crawling about on the palm of your hand, or the poetic spark that swims through the summer night?" "Accuracy" can refer only to the degree of correspondence between a percept and a *single* attribute of an object and only to a measurable degree at that; it has nothing to do with seeing the "whole" object.

The history of art and science gives fair warning that we ought not to be betrayed by the directness of our perceptual experience into thinking that our concepts, and therefore our percepts, of any "single" thing can ever be complete. Today's conventional, workable reality is tomorrow's barrier to exploring different aspects of the same things. That is why the artist's unceasing efforts to discover new forms in nature can be regarded as also basically destructive; he must destroy well-worn conventions in viewing reality in order to "create" (to "see") new forms. (It is no accident that artists test low in object constancy.) The artist tries to make perceptible those properties of things ordinarily relegated by habitual aims and goal sets to an irrelevant periphery. His perception is not necessarily more accurate than is conventional experience; his different viewing orientation gives perceptual prominence to properties that have at most a purely mediational role in ordinary effective perception.

This fact helps explain why contemporary works of art may often provoke experiences of unpleasure and discomfort. Relations brought to our consciousness by the artist may contradict familiar indisputables in our perceptual life—tacit assumptions regarding periphery and center that anchor conventional, provenly effective perception.[1] The price we pay for efficient perception is partial blindness. The artist, like the scientist, supplies the categories and concepts that will become tomorrow's conventional perceptual realities.

Therefore the concept of accurate perception can be especially mischievous if it leads us to assume that there is a finality to perceptual development, a plateau in what *can* be seen. Perception pursues meanings, not exhaustive accuracy or totality. The course of perceptual development is not toward achieving the limits of discriminability or exhausting the perceivable qualities of objects but toward developing successive working models of objects and events. The fact that most of our perceptions repre-

---

[1] Such feelings of aversion are certainly not wholly explained by the experience of contradiction, however. Possibly they also reflect a reaction to unconscious drive aims activated by the artist's focus, as Ehrenzweig (1953) has suggested. Meanings on several levels, each in a different drive matrix, may be apprehended.

sent coordinations with physical stimuli, as psychophysical studies repeatedly show us, must not keep us from recognizing that "literal" perceptions are still *selected* perceptions.

It is also necessary to keep in mind that effectiveness is a developmental matter. Perception is *differently effective* at different stages of development; it is not necessarily *less accurate* at earlier stages than later on. As drive aims change with development, perception reflects changes in adaptive purpose and different conceptual structures; standards of effectiveness change. The perceptions that "satisfy" the child, that coordinate his behavior with the relations within and among things, differ from those that the adult requires. For the *child's* developmental stage and in the tasks that he sets himself, *his* perceptions may be no less effective (and in that sense no less accurate) than are those of the adult simply because they are different. The child for whom the emotive expressiveness of a form is more insistent than its details of texture and shape is not less responsive to what is actually in the stimulus object. His perceptions may seem inaccurate to an adult world that judges him by a conventional standard. If "accuracy" is to have any sensible meaning in perceptual theory it can refer only to effective coordination between the properties of things and our concepts and perceptions of them; *stage* of development partly defines criteria of "adequacy" or "effectiveness."

This understanding gives us a basis for conceiving of *regressive perception*. Altered perceptions in unusual states of consciousness (under mescaline, for example) may often revive earlier developmental orientations which give a fresh slant on things in the present—coordinations with physical properties that adult pragmatic concern for effective, adaptive perceiving has come to exclude. Regressive perception may activate a once adaptive but discarded conceptual matrix of psychophysical coordination—a rule of organizing experience. Seeing things in a novel way from an earlier perspective is not necessarily seeing them in a wrong way, in any absolute sense. Regression involves the adaptive aims associated with earlier goal sets and concepts, but with them it invokes earlier adaptive means. Therefore not all instances of retreat from advanced developmental positions should be taken as a helpless capitulation to drive satisfaction at the cost of adaptation.

These considerations of effective perception illuminate the adaptive character of cognitive attitudes and styles. To say that they are adaptive means not that they provide, in different degrees, an accurate translation of reality but that they provide in each instance a *workable fit*. The concept of cognitive attitude alerts us to the individually varying standards of such a practical fit in the "feedback" strategies that guide perceptual, cognitive, and motor activity. It provides for the fact that persons differ in how "accurate" perception must be in order to be *effective* for the purpose at hand. In order to meet a subjective standard of "big enough" or "small enough," cognition musters complex processes that make possible perceptual contact with the sizes, slant, and colors of things, and it incorporates these processes into a larger selective strategy that includes appropriate conceptual and motor activity. The significance of feedback in such a strategy is that it coordinates the phases of perceptual-cognitive-motor activity with drive aims, on the one hand, and with environmental structures and probabilities, on the other. Different phases of an adaptive action would, then, be expected to reflect the larger organizing strategy. We should not be surprised to find that the rate at which figure-ground differentiation occurs or the extent to which small differences are ignored or heightened in awareness varies from person to person —yet that each tendency exemplifies an adaptive rule or strategy.

A psychophysical study conducted at the University of Stockholm by Johansson, Dureman, and Sälde (1955) illustrates the point. To most observers, the perceived motion of a single object moving in a visual field increases considerably when a second object moving with the same speed in the opposite direction is introduced. Subjects differ, however. The scores of some subjects in the experiment indicated that the static frame of reference was dominant in perceived movement, of others that the influence of the second moving object very much predominated. That these opposing trends reflect more comprehensive adaptive strategies is suggested by the fact that individual differences in this simple task were also related to social attitudes of withdrawal and isolation. The experiment demonstrates a stylistic influence upon a basically stable psychophysical function. It also highlights the possibility, too often ignored in personality studies, that cognitive style may be profitably explored in psychophysical investigations of the correspondences of physical stimulation to behavior, and not only in studies of highly equivocal stimulus conditions that encourage projective-type responses, which are usually presumed to be the only circumstances for observing personality attributes.

Effective perception does not mean uniform perception among people; similarly, individual differences in perception do not necessarily imply "distorting" mechanisms. *Scanning, leveling,* and *field independence* (Schlesinger, 1954; Holzman, 1954; Witkin *et al.*, 1954), though distinctive reality orientations, are still, for the subjects involved, "adequate" modes of making sense of reality, modes appropriate to adaptive intentions.

STRUCTURE OF COGNITIVE ATTITUDES AND STYLES

I turn now to a closer look at cognitive attitudes and their arrangements in cognitive styles. A detailed summary of empirical studies of specific cognitive attitudes and styles has been made by Gardner *et al.* (1959). Here I shall limit myself to a few general characteristics of these control structures, to some of the principles followed in detecting them in behavior, and to a few of the research possibilities generated by the concept of cognitive style.

A cognitive attitude describes a way of organizing a transmitted array of information. The organization may take place in the course of peripheral transmission, though the evidence is still scanty; the loci of cognitive attitudes are more probably to be sought beyond the sensory projection areas (Bruner, 1957b; Osgood, 1957). They have the status of intervening variables and define rules by which perception, memory, and other basic qualitative forms of experience are shaped. The empirical limits of the assumed generality of cognitive attitudes and styles are at present by no means clear, however (this volume, Chapter 5).[2]

A cognitive attitude is triggered by a *situation*, a requirement to adapt, not simply by a physical stimulus. In order, then, to detect the control components—the cognitive attitudes—in behavior, we must know a person's explicit intentions and the circumstances to which he must adapt, particularly the *options* offered by the situation in question. Intention implies, for one thing, that certain qualities of *awareness* and not others are involved in the adaptive effort; one can be set to discriminate *perceptually*, or to *remember*, or to *image*. Intention also restricts the range of behavioral possibilities that a person will consider relevant. For many intentions, simply noting the presence or absence of something will be adequate; other circumstances and different intentions may require deeper probes. Intentions establish the premises of coordinations with environmental events. A Rorschach card shown in the usual way ("What might this be?") poses a problem for which innumerable strategies are appropriate. One can range from responses closely anchored to *perceptions* to frank inferences and judgments of vague possibility. Were the same stimulus card presented with the instruction "Find all the animals on this card," it is by no means certain that the cognitive attitudes called forth would be the same as in the first instance. For measurement the intentional matrix of a task is all-important. Obviously, when response options and intentions are limited, the range of possible cognitive strategies is limited also. It would be foolish, except in pathological instances, to expect the cognitive attitude of leveling to appear in the action of switching on a light. Of course, many situations are of this class, a single intention coinciding with a single option.

Clearly, a person can take up different cognitive attitudes of varying appropriateness to different tasks and intentions. The particular cognitive attitude most typically exhibited by a person is not necessarily the one that is most appropriate to a particular situation or adaptive intention. Indeed, pathology in cognitive

---

[2] [For reviews of findings on generality in recent years, see Gardner (1962), Gardner, Jackson, and Messick (1960), Gardner and Moriarty (1968).]

control consists perhaps in just such failures of coordination between cognitive attitude and adaptational requirements. In an apparent-motion situation, one schizophrenic subject kept seeing the movement of two squares of light as "a penis darting back and forth." The physiognomic propensity illustrated in this response may relate to a distinctive cognitive attitude, as other studies have indeed suggested (this volume, Chapter 5); [3] but in this instance it was inappropriate to the task defined by the instructions. Different cognitive attitudes can, however, be equally effective and can lead to *varying*, equally "veridical" experiences.

Some Process Components of Cognitive Attitudes

Cognitive attitudes may be studied through processes that seem to be fundamentally involved in adaptive commerce with environmental structures. I shall limit myself to two such processes: *attention deployment* and *anticipation*.

Attention Deployment. In speaking of attention cathexes I am using Freud's conception of an amount of cathexis that a proximal stimulus must attract if it is to become conscious (Freud, 1900, Chapter 7; 1911). Availability and deployment of attention cathexis are presumably vital matters in the development and maintenance of cognitive structures (Rapaport, Gill & Schafer, 1945–1946; Rapaport, 1951a, 1957a).

Consider the consequences of high or low availability of the fixed amount of attention cathexis. One could argue that hysterics have to maintain so high a level of anticathexis (to maintain repression) that there is not sufficient attention cathexis available to form new concepts. Attention cathexis ensures the necessary "feedbacks" of perception and action until such time as the object has acquired a representation; attention cathexes can then be released to other adaptive efforts. In this way it is analogous to the wooden scaffolding and molds that hold poured cement. If you keep them on a sufficient time, they can be removed, and the cement will still hold. When there is insufficient attention

---

[3] [See also the more recent study by Rosett, Robbins, and Watson (1968).]

cathexis, the gradient of dissipation is great. Attention cathexis in this view would thus play a crucial role in the building of stable concepts.[4]

A cognitive attitude that we call *scanning* (Schlesinger, 1954) shows a distinctive quality of attention deployment. In scanning, attention is broadly and intensively deployed. The scanner is aware of a broad array of background qualities of a stimulus field. His investment is intensely incorporative, characterized by a sustained close look. The consequences of this deployment of attention cathexis in cognitive behavior are many, and they lead to successful predictions of degrees of object constancy (scanners easily take on a retinal attitude) and of facility in recognizing embedded figures (the Witkin embedded-figures task, 1950). It is interesting, by the way, that practically all the myopic subjects in one of our samples were strongly characterized by the scanning attitude. Paradoxically, these myopics were hyperaware of small stimulus differences (Gardner *et al.*, 1959).

Other studies disclose that the scanning attitude involves not only intense concentration on the central task but also an indiscriminate peripheral sensitivity that renders many aspects of the field available to conscious recall. A study of incidental recognition by Holzman (1957), using the Müller-Lyer illusion, found that scanners could quite accurately reproduce the areas bounded by the arrowheads in the stimulus despite the fact that they had not been "set" beforehand to acquire this information.[5]

Other cognitive attitudes that my co-workers and I have studied also involve distinctive patterns of attention deployment. Holzman (1954) found that the *leveling* attitude was characterized by a tendency toward loss of identity of successive stimuli. On the color-word interference task (see this volume, Chapter 6),

---

[4] [This proposition is central to Rapaport's attention-cathexis theory of learning (Rapaport, 1959b). For a further explication of the theory, as well as relevant experimental findings, see Schwartz and Rouse (1961), and Schwartz and Schiller (1970).]

[5] See also the more recent studies by Benfari (1966a, 1966b) and Holzman (1966).]

the levelers' performance slowed progressively over a period of time. On a time-error task they showed a steep gradient of dissipation of incoming stimuli; compared to *sharpeners*, their successive judgments of weights were therefore more affected by an interpolated stimulus.

Anticipation. Accommodative structures include patterns that guide the selection of concepts and steer action. These we call *anticipations* or *sets*. They define the range of alternatives for which a person is perceptually or cognitively "ready." Anticipations are crucial to the coordination of concepts with objects and therefore to the development of control strategies. Different patternings of anticipations seem to be reflected in the various cognitive attitudes.

Levelers and sharpeners differ in their ability to shift from one set to another. The capacity to alter anticipations in accordance with slight gradients of stimulation contributes to the sensitivity of sharpeners to gradual changes in size in a series of squares (Holzman, 1954). G. J. W. Smith and Klein (1953) presented subjects with a succession of Gottschaldt designs in which one of two test figures was embedded. When a design containing the *second* figure was shown, levelers perceptibly slowed up; they did not easily give equal weight to the two alternatives after the run of designs that contained only the first figure.

Another cognitive attitude that we have studied, *constricted control*, also reflects a distinctive anticipatory pattern, which showed up in conditions in which subjects had to cope with perceived incongruency (this volume, Chapter 6). In trying to resolve an ambiguity, some subjects tended to lean heavily upon certain easily apprehended physical features of the situation; when instructions allowed them to choose among conflicting cues to steer judgment, they tended to favor the more directly confirmable ones. In a test of sensitivity to an apparent-motion situation, their motion thresholds were determined in large measure by the experimenter's authoritatively given explanation of "reality" in the situation (that the objects were not really moving); their motion thresholds were relatively high (Gardner *et al.*, 1959). The anticipatory pattern of the more flexibly controlled subjects under conditions of perceived incongruity tended to be one of uncommitted readiness.

Adaptive Consequences of Cognitive Attitudes

I have described *cognitive style* as an arrangement of cognitive attitudes, constituting another structural level of personality. One reason is that we have found correlations between cognitive attitudes and certain behavior tendencies that are not easy to understand by the defining principles of the specific cognitive attitudes alone. Possibly such behavioral correlates reflect a superordinate level of organization of which the cognitive attitude is itself a component. One basis for conceiving of this possibility is to think of certain types of behavior as a *secondary adaptation* to a cognitive attitude after continual and repeated reliance upon the attitude. For instance, the leveling attitude produces an oversimplified world. The leveler adjusts to this internalized representation of the world, and the manner of doing so becomes itself an aspect of his cognitive *style*. Cognitive style may describe the accretions of adjustive qualities that arise as a result of continual applications of the basic cognitive attitudes. The characteristic blurring of temporally extended stimuli among levelers could lead to relatively impoverished conceptual structures. Applying a fundamentally limited set of categories that "work" for him, the leveler could conceivably feel no further need for "close listening." The associated qualities of ingenuousness and naïveté and the experiences of surprise that we find quite frequently in levelers are conceivably secondary consequences of the attitude. Style refers to a level of organization in which such secondary developments from a person's various cognitive attitudes coexist in a balanced arrangement.

When we turn to those people of whom the *scanning* attitude is typical, it is clear that with them a too close attentional investment—the hard, close look—could have secondary consequences of another kind. For one thing, as Bruner (1957a) has pointed out, the price of the long, close look is a slower identification and categorization of relevant details; a crucial loss can occur in the small interval available for adjusting. Possibly anticipation is also impaired because close inspection prevents speedy appraisal of alternatives. It is perhaps not surprising that doubt, uncertainty, and mistrust are prominent accompaniments of the scanning attitude.

These and other correlates of cognitive attitudes stood out when we investigated different "person clusters," each containing a heavy representation of scanners (Gardner *et al.*, 1959). In one of these clusters, scanning appeared with *sharpening, narrow equivalence range in categorizing,* and *constricted response to ambiguity.* A distinctive cognitive style characterized the scanning subjects in this attitudinal context. The dominant impression that this group gave was of intense control and inhibition, with very pronounced intellectualizing tendencies and pervasive experiences of ambivalence, mistrust, and expectations of being hurt. They regarded the world as a source of malevolence and danger and were generally pessimistic about the present and the future. They seemed preoccupied with issues of mastery, and they were intensely self-absorbed (for example, they made an unusually large number of references to body parts on the Rorschach). They felt guilty and dissatisfied with their achievements, and their contacts with objects and people were darkened by aggression. At the same time they were intensely absorbed in the rejecting and threatening world of people and things.

SOME INVESTIGATIVE APPLICATIONS

First of all, style of commerce with environmental structures and its stability may be an important safeguard against regressive behavior. An interesting step has been taken by Holt (1960) toward extending predictions from cognitive style to evidences of "regressive" thinking. The departure points of his work are the assumptions, derived from psychoanalytic theory, that the course of drive development is toward progressively more differentiated levels and that there is a potentiality that thought will revert to earlier modes of drive-organized thinking ("primary-process" modes of thought, in Freud's terms). Holt argues that the dispositions to primary-process forms of thought and the varieties of such reversions are perhaps dictated by the conditions and possibilities afforded by cognitive style. He has developed a set of indexes of amount, type, and manner of control of primary-process thinking in Rorschach responses. Preliminary findings indicate that subjects with contrasting cognitive styles are also distinguishable on the indexes. Comparing constricted- and flexible-control subjects, he found a distinct trend: Flexible subjects gave slightly higher percentages of drive-directed content and an average of twice as many formal manifestations of the primary process. Constricted subjects tended to respond with drive content and with signs of disturbance or else flatly, as if unconsciously or naïvely. In contrast, the sexual or aggressive contents in the flexible subjects' Rorschachs were typically couched in ways more acceptable as social communication (Holt, 1960). Possibly, then, cognitive style has an important role in either limiting or providing opportunities for thinking to revert to primary-process modes. This suggestion holds out the possibility that cognitive style may be helpful in understanding individual variations in the "regressed" behavior often brought about by mescaline and LSD-25.

Second, structures, once formed, seem to require appropriate supplies of stimulation—a required frequency of contact with particular realms of objects and properties of objects (Hebb, 1955a; Piaget, 1936; Rapaport, 1957b). Drastic alterations in the level of environmental stimulation—too low or too high— can cause adaptive structures to lose their effectiveness. This loss is strikingly suggested by the McGill University studies on the effects of isolation (Bexton, Heron & Scott, 1954; Hebb, 1955a, 1955b) and by Lifton's descriptions (1956) of "thought reform" procedures in Communist China. Depriving accommodative structures of their required optimal level of stimulation perhaps makes it possible for behavior to be dominated more easily by the recruitment aspect of drives, and to regress to developmentally earlier cognitive styles.

Presumably, drastic changes in stimulation would wreak havoc upon cognitive attitudes and styles, but in different ways. If the requirements for adequate or optimal stimulation vary in different cognitive styles, we would expect stimulus deprivation of the kind used in the McGill studies to produce predictably different effects. There is evidence that levelers organize stimulus sequences according to low common denominators of object structures (Holzman, 1954; Gardner *et al.*, 1959). We also find that leveling subjects tend to show little curiosity. The optimal stimulus requirement set by this adaptive strategy may be different from that for the scanning attitude, which is typified by absorption in detailed perceptual contact with objects and events. Scanning imposes greater demands for varied and frequent stimulation, and it seems quite possible that wholesale and prolonged removal of stimulation may quickly devastate developmentally advanced thought and produce a regressive pattern. Leo Goldberger's studies (1961) of individual differences in the effects of sensory deprivation help to illuminate the role of cognitive attitude and style when opportunities for adaptive "feedback" are thwarted by restrictions of stimulation.[6] Situations of either extreme reduction or oversupply of stimulation provide opportunities to study the protection afforded by cognitive attitude and styles against the domination of thought by the recruitment aspect of drives and to track the regressive consequences of radical deprivation or stimulus overloading.

Third, controls involve the monitoring, sifting, and reduction of stimuli conveyed through the senses. We used to take it for granted that such "gating," as Bruner (1957a) calls it, occurred at the higher centers alone. Reception itself was supposed to be indiscriminate, subject only to the structural limits of the receptor surfaces. Hebb (1957) tells us that a good deal of such sorting may occur prior to cortical "encoding" and "decoding." The ex-

---

[6] [More recent reports support this expectation. Holt and Goldberger (1959), Goldberger and Holt (1961b), and Goldberger (1966b) report findings relating leveling, constricted control, and Paul's (1959) memory style of importation to various maladaptive responses to isolation. They also report, as do A. J. Silverman *et al.* (1961), consistent relationships between field dependence and negative isolation effects.]

traordinary sensitivity of the sensory apparatus makes it reasonable to look for such a screening process before transmission to
the cortex; otherwise, cortical channels to the higher centers
would be hopelessly jammed. Freud (1920) envisioned a "protective shield against stimuli" that accomplished the first filtering of
stimuli, and this idea was the basis for his postulation of "pre-ego
defenses." An experiment by Hernandez-Peón, Scherrer, and Jouvet (1956) demonstrates the possibility of a filtering process at
the receptor surfaces. They were able to show in cats that spike
potentials in the cochlear nucleus, elicited by audible clicks,
disappear when a distracting object (like a mouse or a fish odor)
suddenly captures the cat's attention, as if the auditory stimuli
were selectively "blocked" at the cochlear nucleus itself rather
than at the higher centers.

Some of the tests in our studies of cognitive attitude suggest
that the selective action of some cognitive attitudes may reach
back even to the level of proximal stimulation and the receptor
surfaces themselves. The hypersensitivity to stimulus details in
the scanning attitude indirectly suggests this possibility.

Evidence of cognitive controls in sensory gating processes
comes from another quarter. Several studies (Klein et al., 1958;
G. J. W. Smith, Spence & Klein, 1959; Bach & Klein, 1957) have
employed the technique of producing a subliminal stimulus by
exposing two stimuli briefly and in rapid succession so that only
the second of the pair can definitely be seen. The consciously seen
form—the second of the pair—then takes on a different appearance in certain respects from when it is seen alone, an effect
evidently induced by the preceding masked stimulus. This influence has been found, however, to vary with more general
reaction tendencies of the subjects. Though the relations between
these response dispositions and what we have called cognitive
attitudes and style have not yet been worked out, it is possible
that adaptive controls of this kind may affect the intake itself, as
well as the organizational fate, of receptor excitations.

I have tried to review some issues of control structures that
participate in behavior, and their relation to drives. I have tried
to show their basis in the unceasing accommodative exchanges

that spring from motivations. Yet we are only at the beginning of an adequate conception of control structures, their relations to one another, and their composition. How structure itself is to be conceived is an overriding issue. The efforts of Floyd Allport (1955), Piaget (1936), and Hebb (1949) are perhaps the most powerful wedges yet driven into this problem. Then there is the question of the nature of the system in which structures develop, a matter at the very heart of theories of personality integration. We are moving toward an eventual model of a hierarchy of subsystems, each a governor of those below yet each, like perception, preserving a certain autonomy from those above. A crude analogy would be the relation of a bay to the larger ocean of which it is an integral subsystem, its *relative* independence vouchsafed by its land outlines, which give its current distinctive qualities, but nonetheless subject to insistent events of the more embracing ocean system. The fascinating theme of personality itself, at once its paradox and its achievement, seems to be its ties both to drive aims and to environmental structures and probabilities—and its relative autonomy from both.

PART THREE

CENTER AND PERIPHERY IN MOTIVATED THINKING

Chapter 8

Consciousness in Psychoanalytic Theory: Implications for Research in Perception

By now psychoanalytic theory has touched almost every frontier of psychological inquiry. Many refinements have been wrought in the tripartite model of ego, superego, and id, so that it is easier to make contact with other theories and with data about the most disparate psychological functions. In turn, as psychoanalytic theory accommodates itself to the newer developments and to different sources of new data, an even greater modification of its earlier terms and propositions must occur. Its exclusive reliance upon the data of the consulting room is lessening; it has become a more gracious host to information from many settings, including the laboratory. One result has been a more explicit concern with psychoanalysis as a *general* theory of behavior rather than exclusively as a therapeutic or so-called "clinical" one.

The most striking extensions of the theory have occurred on the issues of adaptation and reality testing. Rapaport (1959a) and Gill (1959) propose, for instance, that a complete psychoanalytic account of an item of behavior requires the addition of the "adaptive point of view." This emphasis has catalyzed a growing interest in the mechanics of thought and perception as "tools" of adaptation. As propositions begin to develop around the so-called "conflict-free" aspects of behavior (Hartmann, 1939; Rapaport, 1951a, Part 7), around structures that reflect primarily the imperatives of reality rather than those of drive, and around structures that achieve, in Hartmann's words, a certain degree of neutralization or independence from their drive origins, it becomes ever clearer that the proving ground for these propositions must be the study of thought processes. And so we see a growing interest among psychoanalytic theorists in findings of the academic laboratory about processes of cognition.

The crucial importance of perception for a general psychoanalytic psychology was recognized by Freud. In 1896 he wrote, "If I could give a complete account of the psychological characteristics of perception . . . I should have enunciated a new psychology" (Freud, 1887–1902, p. 175). Yet until recently this matter has rested pretty much the way Freud left it in the model that he sketched broadly in *The Interpretation of Dreams* (1900), *Beyond the Pleasure Principle* (1920), "A Note upon the 'Mystic Writing-Pad'" (1925), and in his recently published ruminations in the "Project for a Scientific Psychology" (1895). From these beginnings, from Hartmann's programmatic survey in his *Ego Psychology and the Problem of Adaptation* (1939), and from Rapaport's more recent synthesis of these beginnings (1951a, Part 7, 1959a), there is emerging a conception of ego organization that would deal with cognition without overlooking motivation. Even more important, the program of the newly emerging "ego psychology" *requires* a detailed exposition of perceptual and cognitive processes in order to fulfill its objectives.

In this chapter I shall treat only one of several conceptions of psychoanalytic ego theory that seem to be profitable for research in perception: the theory of *consciousness and awareness*. At the same time I shall dwell upon certain research trends, growing out of the psychological laboratory, that may have a unique potentiality for sharpening and refining the psychoanalytic theory of consciousness. Like all useful theory, psychoanalysis must stumble in the wake of factual discoveries, as well as pointing the way for new ones. In this way the synthesizing power of the theory is nourished by actual phenomena while providing a perspective from which to assess their organismic significance.

REGISTRATION OUTSIDE AWARENESS

I shall first describe some studies, both old and recent, that are illuminated by psychoanalytic propositions about consciousness. The phenomenon involved in these studies is the activation or registration of meanings (call these "trace systems" or "schemata") by external stimuli that are themselves too weak or marginal to capture notice; the stimuli are thus "subliminal," or "unrecognized," or "incidental," or "indifferent." Such registrations of marginal stimuli may occur simultaneously with registrations that are perceptually experienced, that is, registrations of which one is *fully aware*. Second, these studies are concerned with the distinctive impact of subliminal (meaning not experienced in awareness) registrations upon thought.

The basic phenomenon has been frequently reported. As far back as 1896, Binet described experiments on the critical questions: "First, what are the unconscious stimuli that may affect the normal consciousness of the subject; and second, under what form do these stimulations penetrate consciousness?" (1896, p. 209). Binet anesthetized a young girl's neck against tactile sensations; when he pressed an engraved steel disk against the area, she was unaware of his doing so. When she was asked to call up an image and draw it, however, her drawing showed with remarkable fidelity the outlines of the disk with its engraved design. The subject's drawings of the stimulus are reproduced in Binet's book.

Urbantschitsch (1907) asked subjects adept at producing eidetic images first to describe in detail their perceptions of pictures as they were viewing them. The stimuli were then removed, and the subjects were asked to call up images of them. Many details appeared in the *images* that had not previously appeared in direct perceptual reports upon the stimuli. Urbantschitsch describes a striking example of subliminal activation (registration) that he encountered in a myopic subject. From standard optical tests and the subject's conscious report, it was obvious that certain details of the stimulus (which was like a Snellen chart) could not be "seen." The same subject, however, produced an image with many details very close to those that he had not been able to recognize in direct observations of the chart. Current studies of similar phenomena can profit from Urbantschitsch's description of the transformations to which such subliminally registered material may be subject. In several instances, originally unrecognized details emerged in peculiarly multiplied and transformed ways, modifications that today might be considered indicative of primary-process modes of thought. The most striking conclusion that Urbantschitsch distilled from his studies is that "sometimes a previous sensory stimulation first comes into consciousness when we get an image of it and only then do we realize that we have heard or even seen something, which up to that point had remained completely unconscious."

Related phenomena have been the objects of more recent studies (Kubie, 1943; Lazarus & McCleary, 1951; J. G. Miller, 1939, 1951; Pustell, 1957; Razran, 1955). Diven (1937) and Lacey and Smith (1954) have been able to condition "discriminations" without awareness. Furthermore, they have been able to show that such subliminally conditioned discriminations have quite different extinction and generalization characteristics than have "conscious" ones. The main phenomenon seems fairly well defined: Of the multiple impingements upon receptor surfaces, many more achieve some kind of subjective representation than is evident in the thought products and behaviors of which the subject *is* fully or even partially aware.

The significance of transient, momentarily unessential, and unnoticed registrations in thought becomes striking when we consider the phenomenon of *day residues* in dreams. Freud cited examples in which the day residue had been a fleeting glimpse of something that had hardly entered awareness. He suggested that "indifferent perceptions," as he called them, have a distinctive role in the workings of the dream, perhaps significantly different from that of conscious perceptions in the "waking state." Freud remarked about his dream of the botanical monograph:

The first of these two impressions with which the dream was connected was an indifferent one, a subsidiary circumstance: I had seen a book in a shop-window whose title attracted my attention for a moment but whose subject-matter could scarcely be of interest to me. . . . In the manifest content of the dream only the *indifferent* impression was alluded to, which seems to confirm the notion that dreams have a preference for taking up unimportant details of waking life. (1900, p. 174)

We can understand Freud to mean that incidental registrations are more easily fused into a wider orbit of meanings than is a conscious percept; they can be condensed and displaced more readily than can a consciously *intended* perception, and it is perhaps these characteristics that give them a unique status in thought.

Take also the example of a dream that a patient reported to her analyst: She goes to a funeral. She does not know the person who is dead. At the funeral she sees her therapist. In the course of associations it turns out that the day before she had been browsing in the library and had happened upon a sociology textbook. She had glanced at the chapter headings, one of which was "Mourning and Bereavement." It had made no impression at the moment, at least none to distinguish it from other chapter titles over which she *did* pause. Her associations then led to ruminations about her dead husband. Had she mourned him enough? Was she glad to be rid of him? The sequence of events suggests that certain object qualities had registered even though they were quite irrelevant to the patient's conscious intention at the time of looking at the book; the impressions persisted in memory and were *active*, that is, drawn into the orbit of highly valent thoughts, wishes, and motives that were carried into the dream.

These examples show, first, that we are a great deal more receptive to the world around us than we are aware: The senses are restlessly active, and their range extends far beyond the immediate pragmatic purposes of looking and listening. Second, the examples show that such "incidental" activations persist and are engaged by the continuing stream of thought. And, third, they show that such registrations are subject to transformations in ways that perceptions in awareness are not, or not as easily.

Freud did not pursue further the leads suggested by his offhand remarks about "indifferent" perceptions. He seems not to have distinguished among different types of incidental or peripheral intake, a taxonomical problem that has still not been systematically explored. Nor does he seem to have considered the role in dreams of such varieties of "incidental registrations": those arising from the anatomical periphery as compared with the center of the field, registrations below awareness, the incidentally "noticed" but trivial impressions, and the centrally noticed but unverbalized impressions. We do not know, for instance, whether "subliminal registration" of tachistoscopic stimuli is but a special, perhaps extreme, case of peripheral intake.[1]

Until recently, little systematic attention has been given to the general importance of the day-residue phenomenon for theories of perception. An offshoot possibility of equal interest has also been overlooked: that incidental registration may affect thought in waking states as well as in dreams. Here is an example of a rich clinical concept left fallow because of a methodological impasse. To trace in detail the correspondence between dream and day residues, and between incidental registrations and waking thought, we must have the conditions of stimulation firmly in control. To this task, the therapeutic situation hardly lends itself.

This problem may perhaps account for the fact that Pötzl's experiments, to which we now turn, were among the very few that intrigued Freud and for whose possibilities he expressed enthusiasm. The neglect of these experiments by psychologists for so many years is one of those inexplicable caprices of the *Zeitgeist*. Pötzl (1917) was the first to demonstrate experimentally that the manifest content of dreams draws upon exposures of stimuli too brief to attract notice. In his basic experiment, he showed his subjects landscapes very briefly—for about 1/100 of a second—and had them describe and draw what they had seen.

---

[1] [In this regard see Eagle, Wolitzky, and Klein (1966).]

The subjects were asked to come back the next day, and to take particular note of any dreams that they had in the meantime. In the dreams they remembered and drew, Pötzl looked for indications of unreported components of the stimuli. He found them abundantly present. Pötzl drew the conclusion from his data that what had *not* been noted in the immediate report of the stimulus was more likely to appear in dreams than what *had* been noticed.

Support for Pötzl's main conclusion has come from recent studies by Charles Fisher (1956, 1957; Fisher & Paul, 1959), by Luborsky and Shevrin (1956), and, in certain respects, by Hilgard (1958) and by workers in our laboratory at New York University (Bach & Klein, 1957; Eagle, 1959; Klein *et al.*, 1958; G. W. J. Smith, Spence & Klein, 1959). Like Pötzl before him, Fisher required subjects to describe and draw what they saw after brief exposures (1/200 of a second). Then, if a subject brought in a dream the next morning, he was asked to associate freely to elements of it and also to draw scenes from it. From this material, from standard techniques of dream interpretation, and from detailed clinical information about the subjects, the motives and wishes of the dreams were reconstructed and the protocols and drawings analyzed for instances in which elements of the experimental situation (the stimulus picture, as well as other conditions of the experiment) had actually registered, that is, had achieved structural representation or phenomenal form, and had been worked into the presenting surface of the dreams.[2]

Numerous elements of the stimulus picture (portions both

---

[2] [These studies affirming Pötzl's claims have been severely criticized by Eriksen (1960) and Johnson and Eriksen (1961) on methodological grounds. Haber and Erdelyi (1967) confronted these criticisms in perhaps the most painstaking and carefully controlled study so far attempted on the issue of the effectiveness and recoverability of a subliminal stimulus. They reaffirm the main conclusions of the work reported by the earlier investigators. In the authors' words: "The present findings have confirmed the feasibility of recovering into conscious awareness perceptual material of which the perceiver is initially unaware. It has been shown, moreover, that much of this below-conscious material, whether preconscious or unconscious, continues

reported and omitted in the original response) as well as themes involving the experimenter himself appeared in the dream fabric, taking on the special meanings of the dream motif that had been aroused by the experimental situation. Not only did surface qualities of the stimulus pictures register, like texture and form, but also causal and symbolic relationships in the experimental setting. For instance, one of the subjects reported a voyeuristic, exhibitionistic dream that alluded to the cameralike aspect of the tachistoscope and the "Peeping Tom" quality of fathoming a teasingly brief exposure. Fisher has also demonstrated that registrations outside awareness may emerge transformed in *images* that come to a subject's mind in the waking state (Fisher, 1957; see also Fisher & Paul, 1959). Modifications and condensations similar to those appearing in dreams were detected.

At New York University we have carried inquiry about nonconscious registrations another step: How and in what ways do subliminal registrations affect *thought in a waking state* and within what limits? A chance observation in the laboratory gave birth to a technique that made this type of inquiry possible. Using a three-field tachistoscope—a device that alternately projects two stimulus figures upon a mirror placed diagonally across the field —we showed two different forms, an A figure and a B figure, in rapid succession at the same point on the screen. Provided that the rate of succession is sufficiently rapid, the *first* (A) stimulus of the pair is *not* seen, and the second one (B) is. Obliteration of the A figure occurs even after exposures that are ordinarily long enough to allow recognition when it is not succeeded by the second figure.

This phenomenon, which we have obtained with everyone tested, though its limits vary among subjects, opens the way to the study of induced subliminal effects. Possibly the A figure, even though it is not seen, exerts an effect upon conceptions of the B figure that the subject *is* aware of. If so, it becomes possible to vary systematically the *meaning* of the masked A figure and to

---

to exert a significant influence upon the perceiver's behavior—in this case, fantasy productions of the free-association type." (p. 626)]

look for distinctive effects of such meanings upon the consciously perceived second figure.

Can *meanings* be "known" at subliminal levels, independently of the perceived B figure? And do such subliminally given meanings influence thought in ways distinct, as Pötzl suggested, from those of conscious perceptions? Other studies in our laboratory suggest affirmative answers to both these questions, though the effects are by no means simple, universal, or easily detectable. One study (Klein *et al.*, 1958) revealed that subliminally presented sexual pictures and symbols affected conscious impressions of faces. The effects were complex and were mediated by certain characterological variables, like the subject's self-image and sexual identity. Nevertheless, the changes resulting from the various pairings of subliminal and supraliminal forms seem inexplicable unless we assume that the subliminal forms had been registered and meaningfully elaborated outside awareness. The experiment seems to show that what the subject was *aware of*—his *perception*—was influenced by what he was not aware of, a registered form outside awareness that did not attain perceptual identity. Something in the process started by the first stimulus, although not sufficient to excite recognition in awareness, evidently contributed to the final percept.

In a more recent study (G. J. W. Smith, Spence & Klein, 1959), we were able to demonstrate even more decisively that subliminally activated *meanings* can affect the course of perceptual awareness in the "waking state." This time we used *words* instead of pictured figures as subliminal stimuli, in order to rule out the possible effects of contour. The subliminal stimuli were the words "angry" and "happy." They appeared subliminally in conjunction with a male face, which was clearly seen. Again the face changed subtly in the two pairings. Impressions of the face when the word "happy" preceded it subliminally were more pleasant and positive, and in the "angry" series more unpleasant and negative.

Three other interesting findings turned up. First, the effects of the subliminal registrations did not always appear in the verbal descriptions of the face; sometimes they affected the *speed of response* to the face. If verbal comments showed no particular effects of the subliminal stimulus, effects appeared instead in the response time, with some subjects answering more quickly to the subliminal "angry" stimulus, others more quickly to the "happy" stimulus. In addition, the subliminal words seemed to have different effects on the perceived figure according to their distance from the point of recognized meaning (operationally, the percentage level below recognition threshold). The subliminal stimulus was shown at gradually increased exposures, and we found that differences were more striking when the stimuli were presented either well below the level of recognition or just before they reached recognition level. Finally, the effects depended upon certain general reaction tendencies of individual subjects. Some of these variables were readiness, or ability, to give oneself up to fantasy or to communicate fantasy; degree of distrust or resistance; passivity toward thinking; and tolerance for overt expressions of hostility.

Essentially the same effects appeared in studies conducted in our laboratory by Eagle (1959), who used an aggressive theme as a subliminal stimulus, and by Bach (Bach & Klein, 1957) and Fox (1960). Fox devised still another technique for exposing a subliminal stimulus, a stereoscopic-projection method that permitted *prolonged* exposures of subliminal stimuli (in contrast to brief tachistoscopic exposures); the subject was asked to describe the clearly perceptible face in the presence of the superimposed subliminal stimulus.

In these studies it seems clear, first, that subliminal registrations activated an array of meanings and that concomitant conscious impressions of a form involved these meanings; second, that the impact of the subliminally active ideational schema— outside awareness—*was discernible in different channels of expression, verbal and nonverbal.*[3]

I have selected only a few examples of experimental develop-

---

[3] [For several reviews of experimental studies related to these propositions and for more recent developments in theory, see Pine (1960, 1961), Eagle (1959), Fisher (1960), Spence (1967). See also this volume, Chapter 14.]

ments around the issue of subliminal registration that are hard to incorporate in conventional theories of perception yet seem to me comprehensible within the psychoanalytic conception of consciousness. Viewed in this light, they carry important implications for a theory of perception. Before turning to some of these implications I would like first to consider some propositions in the psychoanalytic theory of consciousness itself.

CONSCIOUSNESS IN PSYCHOANALYTIC THEORY

Rapaport (1956) has pointed out that Freud never consolidated the several formulations, made at widely separated times, of his theory of consciousness. For instance, he never systematically integrated the "economic" or energy conception of his "picket model," to use Colby's term (1955), in *The Interpretation of Dreams* (1900) with his formulations in *The Ego and the Id* (1923). As Rapaport puts it:

The next logical step would have been to state the obvious—that all that which had so far comprised the system Consciousness now becomes the function of the structure termed ego, and then to explore the position of this *substructure* in the structure of the ego. This step was not taken—as Freud clearly acknowledged in his posthumously published *Outline of Psychoanalysis*. Conscious, preconscious, unconscious were again considered mere qualities of no dynamic import. (1956)

Newer ideas of the energic structures of ego organization try to give consciousness precisely such import. Rapaport (1959b) in particular is responsible for reviving Freud's early idea of consciousness as a *cathexis- or attention-dispensing function of the ego system*. In Rapaport's conception this is coupled with the notion that ego structures influence the deployment of attention. Basic to the theory is the assumption that an energic quantum—attention cathexis—is responsible for awareness; its amount is determinate at any given time; it can be mobilized and deployed among different structures responsible for different qualities of experience and feeling—the different ways in which we can be aware of things. Hence, both amount of attention-cathexis and pattern of its deployment among component ego structures determine conscious experience, and different configurations of the deployment of attention cathexis describe different *states of consciousness*. In any state of consciousness, awareness is like a light playing on dark waters, subject to disciplinary forces. The light can be bright or dim, sharply focused or diffuse; the experiences it produces can vary qualitatively as images, perceptions, or memories.

Note that this point of view does not identify consciousness with a *particular* quality of experience. It is different, therefore, from the popular notion that identifies consciousness simply with awareness of external events. In fact, it was Freud's attempt to get away from this popular conception that led him very early to describe the dispensing of cathexis by means of his metaphor of a super "sense organ" that receives input and then doles out cathexis. By refusing to equate consciousness exclusively with awareness of the external world he could then suppose that internal events, as well as external ones, can become conscious, that cathexes can be withdrawn from the external to the internal, and that conflict between the two can determine where attention cathexes are to be invested—in short, that there can be a *strategy of deployment of cathexis*. Conceiving of a cathexis-dispensing, Consciousness structure enabled Freud to view clinical events in a distinctly new way and to deal with the phenomena of conflict.

Freud later felt compelled to give up his conception of consciousness in the connotations of a capital C. The reason was that his model of a Consciousness *system* had to do too many jobs. It had to refer simultaneously to the *quality* of a thought content—the nature or mode of experiencing it—that is, consciousness with a small c; at the same time it had to refer to the *structure*—Consciousness—that endows a thought content with this quality. When it became obvious from the clinical data of resistance that the structure Consciousness can give rise to contents that are *un*conscious (with a small u), the scheme had to go. He replaced it, as we know, with the conception of ego and id systems. With this, conscious, preconscious, and unconscious referred simply to qualities of experience, and all three can occur in the ego system. In shelving the idea of a cathexis-distributing structure, however, Freud lost the seminal power of the theory's assumption that only so much cathexis is available for the activity of thought and no more, that different patterns of its distribution define different states of consciousness and that differences in the qualities and contents of awareness are associated with these variations in cathectic deployment.

As Rapaport has pointed out, Freud did not take the step of noting that the very quality of "being aware of something" and the modes of this awareness (for example, whether the experience is perceptual or occurs as an image, whether it has the quality of recollection or of judgment, and so on) can vary as changes occur among the energy distributions that constitute the ego system. Such a view requires the notion of different cathectic organizations governing the distribution of attention cathexis, thereby endowing an idea with a qualitative guise, either of a perception, an image, or a memory.

Contemporary ego theory views ego structures as means of delaying drive gratification. This has made it possible in turn to conceive of a variety of energy distributions with a distinctive influence upon cognitive behavior, including experienced qualities: energy systems constituting the component thought functions themselves, for example, perception, memory, imaging, and the like, each making for distinctive qualities of experience; mobile (unbound) energies that together describe the varieties of drives; bound and neutralized energies that together describe different kinds of reality-adaptive motivations; anticathectic energy distributions that together constitute different kinds of defensive organizations; and, finally, those as yet inadequately described energy distributions that constitute different kinds of adaptive cognitive styles or strategies of thought organization, exemplified in the work of Holzman (1954), Gardner (1953), Schlesinger (1954), and Paul (1959). In this general conception of cathectic organizations, the mobile drive organizations are associated with primary-process modes of thought, whereas the relatively neutralized drive regulations characteristically give rise to secondary-process modes of thought and behavior.

I am aware of the very schematic flavor of this listing of energic structures within the energy model of psychoanalytic theory. My main purpose is simply to indicate the means available in psychoanalytic theory for describing different *states of consciousness*, definable as distinctive patterns of cathectic distribution, each reflecting and vouchsafed by the existing balance among drive, defense, and other controlling structures of the ego system.

In this framework, then, consciousness becomes a conceptual convenience referring to the existence of structural means of dispensing attention cathexis in varying amounts, giving rise to a pattern of awareness—the available parameters in which experience can occur, the distinctive ways in which it is possible to experience an idea. Awareness, in this view, is no unimportant epiphenomenon but has an adaptive import defined by the controlling structures that affect the deployment of cathexis. One cannot speak of *a* "consciousness" or even, strictly speaking, of *a* "preconscious," without keeping in mind its context of ego organization and the particular parameters of awareness that distinguish it.

One implication of this conception is that the organizations affecting perceptual experience in those states of consciousness loosely called the "waking state" are not indigenous to all perceptions in *all* states of consciousness. The limits of perceptual experience are defined by the structural characteristics of the state of consciousness in which it occurs. The "waking state" of consciousness of a cooperative subject in a laboratory psychophysical experiment is dominated by a distinctive pattern of controlling structures peculiarly suited to reality testing. It is a pragmatic organization, probably a high-level developmental derivative of repeated efforts to control discharge of drive, and of the evolving of detours from more direct and unrealistic modes of gratification. The range of experience of which the laboratory subject is capable in this particular "waking state" is highly differentiated. He is able to experience something as a fact, as an assumption, as something to be negated, doubted, hoped for, and so on. His awareness allows him to distinguish a memory from an image and from a perception. In the state of consciousness characterizing participation in the usual laboratory experiment, such modes of awareness reach a high point of efficiency and acuity. In fact, the capacity for awareness of the difference between a perception and a memory was, for Freud, one of the central components of the reality-testing function. A pragmatic object-orientation predominates. In other states of consciousness the parameters of awareness are different; the dream state, for example, is characterized by a more restricted range of possible and distinguishable experience.

It seems that, for registrations to acquire *perceptual* identity in the "waking state," they must be "recruited" to *reality-attuned schemata*. In the dream, the pragmatic rules of efficiency no longer apply, but we still *perceive*. What rules perception *there*, however, is in considerable degree a different adaptational principle, the pleasure principle. As in the "waking state" of laboratory performance, perception in the dream is still subject to conceptual schemata that shape the experience. But in Rapaport's words, the many connotations of things that remain "mercifully hidden from our waking cognition by defensive and controlling organizations . . . are 'recruited' (to use Hebb's term) to the dream theme by dream cognition" (1957a, p. 646). Perception in the dream is governed by different rules, by the principles we know as the primary process. Rapaport has shown how different states of consciousness may vary in this respect and has proposed a classification of the parameters of awareness by which to distinguish different states of consciousness.

In this view, perception is an experience that is not unvarying from one state of consciousness to another. For all the immediacy and experience of direct contact with things in themselves that it gives, perception, in contrast to imaginal modes of experience, is also a cognitive event, framed by a context of meanings or concepts. Both the *capacity* to "know" objects perceptually and the *meaning* given by perception will vary from one state to another. Both range of perceptual content and intensity of perceptual experience will vary according to the balance of activated drive, control, and defense. In the "waking states" perceptual quality seems to be granted, most of the time, only to sense-conveyed registrations for which reality-effective concepts are available. We tend to perceive only what is adaptively relevant to our pragmatic transactions with things and events.

Such reality-effective concepts would be any that have a proven utility in coordinating personal intentions with the logic of reality structures. An example is the object-constancy principle, in which similar things, varying in size, are seen as displaced from each other in depth. Because it is at the service of concepts, however, perception in "waking states" usually shows us less the completeness of things themselves than the frameworks, the reality-oriented schemata, into which things are cast.

IMPLICATIONS

Now let me return to some implications for the experiments described earlier.

First, the experiments show that *registration* must be distinguished from the different *experiential qualities* in which we may be aware of things and of events. The processes responsible for phenomenal registration seem to be independent of those that govern attention deployment—the means by which we become aware of things in a distinctive quality. Registration and perception seem to involve distinct processes. Furthermore, the attributes of objects that are potentially registerable without awareness are, as far as we can tell now, at least as varied as the object qualities that we are able to perceive in waking states, perhaps more so (Fisher, 1957; Fisher & Paul, 1959; this volume, Chapter 3), but obviously this matter is one for empirical research. An object or an event is actually an aggregate of multiple units: surface properties, movements, relations, and causal properties. If we think of an object as an array of such units and relationships, it is conceivable that certain of its properties will be perceived (one will be perceptually aware of them) whereas others may register but not be perceived. Judging from the scanty evidence at hand concerning the possibilities of registration without awareness, a wide variety of the surface qualities, relationships, and units constituting things are potentially registerable.

Experimental evidence suggests quite extraordinary efficiency in this registration. The structuring process that accomplishes it apparently picks up a great deal, concerns itself in awareness with little, and in action with still less. Registration is much less selective than would appear from the immediate concerns of observable action and reaction. (The results, incidentally, seem to support Freud's contention that barriers are more disciplinary and selective on the *outgoing* side of an organism's behavior. Getting *into* the system seems to be less difficult than emergence in awareness.) It is advantageous, then, to distinguish registration from perception.

A second point must be stressed. Perception is a distinct quality, the experience of being in contact with "things as they are." We must assume, then, that for a registration to be experienced as a *perception* it must be endowed with an additional and distinctive cathectic quality. In short, although attention cathexis seems to be a necessary condition for perceptions to occur, it seems not to be a sufficient condition, for there are other qualitatively distinct modes in which objects may present themselves in awareness. Freud spoke of *perceptual cathexis*, which can raise an idea to perceptual intensity. This concept sharpens the issue and also, of course, the mystery of how much is registered and by what mechanism, and of how such incidental registrations may acquire the quality of perception. What determines whether the experienced registration will be "recovered" in the form of an image or a percept or in some nonideational matrix altogether —an action, for example?

Third, the studies point up the crucial role of *state of consciousness* in determining the structures of perceptions and registrations. The studies I have described have been carried out for the most part in a special kind of waking state typical of laboratory settings. All the findings are conditioned by that fact. This waking state is a frame of mind in which the subject finds himself trying to be accurate and therefore highly selective, to achieve in his responses a balance between his perceptions and the claims of logic and experience, and to cast his experiences in a form that will make them readily comprehensible and easily shared by the experimenter. The latter is particularly important in the detection of subliminal effects, for the fleeting impression, the difficult-to-verbalize experience, easily fall by the wayside. That such a condition of consciousness imposes limits on subliminal influences is also suggested by Fisher's report that registrations are easier prey to transformations when they are *imaged* than when they are perceived. In waking states typical of the laboratory, the workings of primary-process mechanisms are more likely to be observable in images than in perceptions. However, when a subject is led by various means into a reverielike state in which he "loses" himself in the stimulus, increased responsiveness to subliminal registrations results.

In general, it seems likely that subliminal registrations are incorporated into a variety of schemata (meanings), perhaps layered in depth and complexity, and that they are subject to transformation either in primary- or secondary-process terms. In waking states, these active schemata may affect *various channels of behavior*. The critical factor that determines how registrations are worked over, what meanings are assigned to them (whether in terms of the primary or secondary process), and in what qualitative form they are recoverable in awareness (as *perceptions* or as *images*) is the *controlling structures characterizing the state of consciousness of the moment*. In certain states of consciousness registrations would emerge in awareness in the context of images dominated by the primary process, whereas perceptions would not be so dominated; in other states of consciousness (as under mescaline) *both* perception and imaging would show such primary-process transformations. I have cited evidence that registrations not accessible as perceptions in the waking state of an accuracy-oriented laboratory subject are recoverable as perceptions in a dream. In the laboratory context such registrations appear to be recoverable mainly through a different quality of awareness—as images.[4] In such a waking state perceptions reflect schemata that are adaptively consonant with reality and are less conducive to primary-process transformation. Imagery even in this waking state is evidently less subject to disciplining reality schemata than is perception. Freud (1911) took note of the functional significance of different modes of awareness. In his opinion, qualities—modes of awareness—direct cathexis; they act as regulators that "made it possible for the mental apparatus to tolerate an increased tension of stimulus while the process of discharge was postponed" (p. 221), which is why he considered the capacity to distinguish a perception from an idea a most important criterion of effective reality testing. The capacity is virtually lost, for instance, in dream cognition. His idea does not eliminate the possibility that perception in waking states may be released from such reality-adaptive schemata and that perceptions of a primary-process character will appear. Murphy's work (1956) on autism suggests this possibility. In general, however, there seems to be a greater likelihood that in waking states such transformations occur more readily among registrations outside awareness and in presentational modes *other* than perception.

The fact that registrations can take different forms in awareness—either as images or as perceptions—raises interesting questions about the relative advantages of different states of consciousness for the recovery of subliminal stimulations. Subliminal registrations seem less amenable to voluntary *recall* and do not emerge directly as percepts; recovery of subliminal input does seem to be more easily achieved, however, by asking

---

[4] We do not know whether other techniques of inducing recovery may be more effective in the usual waking state. An attitude of passive receptiveness may facilitate it. We know, for instance, that long-term confinement in bed may result in the unchecked emergence of "foreign" ideas in awareness. [See Fiss' more recent findings (1966) that relaxation and low arousal facilitate recovery of subliminal registrations. An earlier study by Fox (1960) also pointed to the same conclusion.]

subjects to image (see Chapter 9). Dream, hypnotic, hypnagogic, and mescaline states perhaps make it possible for a relatively undifferentiated slice of registered experience to be reexperienced with an intensity that can be accomplished in the usual waking state only by those who have the capacity for eidetic imagery. As reality contact and reality requirements are minimized, attention cathexis can be deployed to registrations, which can be brought to awareness in a *passive* manner, as are eidetic images. It is possible that all ways of minimizing reality-adaptive intentions— for example, reducing postural supports for discrimination, inducing distractions, producing a state of passive receptiveness in which thoughts "take over" (in contrast to an active, attentive condition conducive to "producing" thoughts)—may facilitate emergence of subliminally registered contents.[5]

In considering the kinds of transformations to which incidental registrations are subject and the vicissitudes of awareness from one state of consciousness to another, we touch upon matters that concern inventive and creative thinking. The observation that to create a new order you have to destroy a familiar one seems to me a good characterization of inventive and creative thought. Ordinary workaday awareness paradoxically serves an efficient and sensitizing yet blinding function. Otherwise our lives would have little stability. For the most part, conceptual contact with the objects, places, and events that we encounter takes place at the level of their most readily identifiable practical meaning. The conceptual schemata that dominate cognition in our work, our relations with others, our encounters with objects have a proven utility; we therefore have a stake in them, and we prefer to cling to them for efficiency and economy (Ghiselen, 1952). The thought forms dominating awareness provide us, at the least,

---

[5] [Lloyd Silverman's reports that responsiveness to subliminal inputs is strikingly evident in schizophrenics are especially relevant to this point. His findings suggest that the features of consciousness suggested here as conducive to subliminal effects may typify the schizophrenic's waking state (L. Silverman, 1966; L. Silverman & Silverman, 1967; L. Silverman & Spiro, 1967, 1968).]

with a relatively unchanging and *persisting* world of things—an unchanging background for the effective *control* of things. But the reality-adaptive schemata that ordinarily guide awareness can easily hinder sensitivity to unfamiliar forms and to transformed ideas, by the very fact that their main function is not to promote discovery but to buttress predictability—to provide insurance against the irregular and the unfamiliar.

The ways in which many painters work point up the highly schematic character of our usual reality-adaptive perception. It is well known that artists surmount the established laws of constancy in order to "see" new forms or latent forms in objects. A painter devotes painstaking care to hidden form combinations of objects. His is a continuous scrutiny of the multilayered hierarchy of the innumerable arrangements constituting what we call an "object." For the artist an object is not a single, unitary entity but an ordered array of form elements and relations. A chair, for example, is a particular organization of volume, color, texture, slant, physiognomic qualities, and so on. The artist scans the field for such object properties, forms that in the ordinary circumstances of our waking life have only the status of mediators (cues) and are rarely the *direct* aims of purposeful perception. In purposeful perceiving, several different cue properties (like texture and brightness) provide *redundant* indications of a single, aimed-for thing quality (like slant). For the artist, in contrast, the very forms that usually have only the status of mediation in reality-adaptive perception become *objects* of perception. It is his deliberate search for such "irrevelant" (in the sense of not usually commanding awareness) forms and his becoming aware of them that accounts for his lower-than-average tested object constancy. The artist's vision in a sense destroys the familiar schemata that order perception; he breaks through the constancies in order to focus on hidden qualities in our familiar world of constant objects. The artist's sensibilities provide an example of the potentialities that exist within us for an enlarged perceptual awareness of the properties of things and for "perceptual growth."

Certain forms of creative endeavor and innovations may,

therefore, require by-passing the well-worn schemata of the usual waking state. Schilder (1924) long ago suggested that, at the fringes of awareness, what we have referred to as the coding of registrations and transformations may more easily occur in terms of other schemata precisely because the inhibiting effect of the system ordinarily sustained by attention cathexis is less influential. This suggestion leads to the interesting possibility that the emergence of subliminal cues in an altered state of consciousness will facilitate problem solving. Behind it is the assumption that thought outside of awareness "applies the premises and asks the questions from which reason grinds out the conclusions" (Gerard, 1956).

When "freed" from awareness, registrations may, even in the usual waking state, undergo transformations analogous to those of dreams, and such transformations may *indirectly* influence perception. In dreams, forms are fluid and fuse easily; they do not have the precise and single meanings of adaptive perceptions. Superimposition is possible. In the waking state of a subject oriented toward effective action, perception may have, to use Ehrenzweig's term (1953), a "bump-erasing" function (described by the Gestalt laws of figural formation), whereas incidentally registered forms may not. Without the constraints of pragmatically oriented awareness, a form may have the "bump-*creating*" effect helpful to certain kinds of creative activity. By the same reasoning, the well-known laws of good continuation, closure, and so on would hold for the *perception* of figural forms but would not necessarily hold for *incidentally registered* forms. In general, Fisher's studies and our own seem to show that the peripheral, or incidental, nature of a form endows it with certain potentialities that it no longer has when it has been disciplined by the reality schemata characterizing awareness in the usual waking state. These possibilities must be scouted in future research.

The experiments on subliminally masked stimuli that I have described require us to assume that the subliminally activated structure that affects conscious thought is a complex one. This structure includes the registered contours and gradients in an ideational matrix, their qualities of use, symbolic equivalence, and motivational links—in short, their meanings. The effective stimulus upon conscious thought is not simply the perception of the physically given unit but its total psychological representation in and out of awareness following registration. It seems that the traditional description of responsiveness to stimulation, based on the narrow perspective of events in the laboratory waking state, requires revision. The sequence seems rather to be stimulation of the organism's sensory surfaces, registration, cognitive recruitment of the registered stimulation to various conceptual schemata, and *emergence* of the reaction—partly in a particular mode of awareness (perception or imaging), partly on other behavioral levels, and partly through motor facilitations of the various conceptual schemata.

Through this picture of the sequence of cognitive events, we move closer to resolving the paradox created by the motivation-in-perception studies of recent years: How is it that, if motives influence perception, we can perceive so effectively? The answer seems to be that motives are constantly governing cognitive organization but that the motives involved may vary on a hierarchy ranging from reality-coordinated intentions and their associated conceptual schemata to primary drives and their schemata. The drive level presumably also governs the extent to which secondary or primary processes are involved in these elaborations of registrations. Furthermore, a proper evaluation of the incursion of motives in the cognitive act *must take into account the organization of the particular state of consciousness in which it occurs* and the types of controls that characterize it. It must provide for the fact that reactions to registrations and to perceptions can take different behavioral forms and that the participation of the primary process in cognitive activity can potentially occur in all these forms, if in different states of consciousness.

Novel problems are brought into focus by bringing psychoanalytic conceptions to bear upon the data that I have reported. There is the question of what is potentially registerable outside awareness. There seem to be indications that a large variety of thing properties are potentially registerable. Are they all equally registerable outside awareness? Furthermore, which registrations *persist?* Do they all achieve structure as "traces"? If some do and some do not, what are the rules of elimination? Although a wide range of registerable thing qualities is suggested by the results I have mentioned, the conditions of registration and of the persistence of registrations are by no means well understood. In the apparent immediacy of our perceptual awareness, the problem is not an obvious one. The basic question is, When in the workings of the eye, for instance—at what state of the integrative activity of the receiving mechanism—does an impingement become a registration and the registration in turn become converted to a percept, memory, or image?

The studies that I have described disclose considerable individual differences, consideration of which I have omitted for lack of space. Evidence is accumulating that cognitive behavior in waking states is subject to quasi-stable structures of control that lend consistency to a person's cognitive behavior. These structures must also be taken into account in refining predictions of cognitive behavior in waking states. Possibly the individual differences observed in the effects of subliminal registrations are in good part traceable to this source. Previous studies, for instance, show that such habituated cognitive controls determine the likelihood that certain types of proximal organizations of stimuli will occur in a person's perception, thus influencing his discriminative sensibility. It is possible, as well, that they condition the variety, vicissitudes, and effects of subliminal registrations. Luborsky and Shevrin (1956) are carrying out pioneer studies around this issue.[6]

Perhaps I should stress a bit more one general implication of the research that I have described and of the psychoanalytic model of consciousness: the possibility that the laws of perception developed in the academic experimental laboratories are specific only to a particular state of consciousness and that their functional importance must be understood in terms of the struc-

---

[6] [More recently, Luborsky and Shevrin (1962), Shevrin and Fritzler (1968a, 1968b), Shevrin, Smith, and Fritzler (1969), Stross and Shevrin (1968).]

ture and dominant orientations of that particular state. The particular state of consciousness is the one characterizing behavior when conscious intentions are to master, to communicate, and to evaluate the properties of things—a state mobilized in an extreme form in the usual laboratory perceptual task. Psychophysical studies bring to bear on response a state of consciousness that guarantees an effective *appraisal of reality*, sharp distinctions between wish and reality, the certain and uncertain. *It is on results in this state that perceptual theorists have based their laws. Very possibly most of the laws so far formulated are valid for this state alone.*

For instance, the Gestalt principles of figure and form are helpful to the reality functions that must be served in the waking state. Wallach, a prominent Gestalt theorist, points out (on one of the rare occasions when a Gestalt psychologist has allowed himself a functional interpretation) that the grouping processes governing perception are protective, accounting for the stability of simple perceptual processes and their resistiveness to transformations by need tensions (Wallach, 1949). One might say with Brunswik that the laws of good continuation, of closure, and of figure and ground are efficiency principles peculiarly adaptive to our commerce with reality.[7] In psychoanalytic terms, these laws describe the secondary-process forms of perceptual experience. It is possible that the principle of least effort or of *Prägnanz* and the laws of figure formation are essentially the perceptual counterparts of more general regulative strategies of thought in particular waking states (though there is by now good reason to suspect that perception in all waking states is not altogether free of characteristics more commonly found in dreams).

In general, psychoanalytic theory, in contrast to Gestalt theory, assumes that cognition in the usual waking state includes *one class* of cognitive elaboration, determined for the most part

---

[7] "Thus it may well be that all the Gestalt factors may be open to reinterpretation as externally imposed upon, rather than innately intrinsic to, the processes in the brain; they all would then appear as functionally useful rather than as whimsically 'autochthonous' " (Brunswik, 1956, p. 122).

by schemata attuned to intentions to cope with things as they *are*. It is easy to see why, in not allowing for different states of consciousness that also produce perceptual experience, Gestalt theory has identified perceptual experience with *particular* forms of organization, concluding that the *quality* of perception is necessarily and sufficiently linked to the forms the experience takes in the waking state common to laboratory performance.

But other equilibrating principles can dominate cognition too, and psychoanalytic assumptions about states of consciousness—and psychoanalytic conceptions of the pleasure and reality principles, with their associated modes of organization—provide for this possibility.

Psychoanalysis has taught us much about the "inefficient" (from the point of view of reality contact) directions that thought may take, which we know as the primary process (for example, condensations and symbolizations). Because perception is a cognitive event, an elaboration by schemata, it follows, as I have suggested earlier, that under certain conditions of release from reality contact registrations may be recruited to conceptual realms quite different from those that ordinarily dominate waking attention; the forms in perceptual awareness may owe much of their structure to more "primitive" drive schemata. This may be the essential paradigm for distinguishing mescalinization, dreams, and other states of consciousness. For reasons peculiar to the action of mescaline—particularly the pervasive *passivity* and paralysis of conation that it commonly induces—the usual constancies are undone; mescaline is conducive to an unstable world. One still perceives; perception shares with more ordinary waking states the essential quality of "being in contact" with things, but it has a distinctly different, adaptively inefficient character. It is not surprising, for instance, that subliminal registrations seem to be peculiarly likely to emerge into awareness as *perceptions*, not merely as images, in this state. Certain qualities of perceptual experience are unchanged in the mescaline state, and the points of difference and similarity between it and the usual waking state require close study.

It is easy to see why perceptual theories have had no room

for the assumption that much more information enters the system than is used, or for the possibility that such information may be subject to elaboration by two distinctly different systems of thought. On the face of it, the quality of perception seems irrevocably tied to the forms in which it is given; it is easy to assume that what a person perceives in the tense, purposeful, and adaptive laboratory state is the *full measure* of what he is actually sensitive to. For example, Gestalt theory has had much to say about figure and ground but little tolerance for the assumption of independent registrations of background forms. Köhler seems to hold that the background has no form and as such no psychological existence, as figure is the only form that is in awareness (1947). Forms may provoke retinal excitation and affect figural perception through such processes as contrast and assimilation, but only in this sense are they cognized. No meaning independent of the meaning of the figure is separately registered.

Similarly, other theories fail to provide for such independent registrations. Information theories of cognition, for instance, seem relevant only to the "sortings" and "matchings" that go on in connection with discriminative, adaptive intentions typical of waking states. The very concept of "redundancy" suggests that sensory input, to the extent that it is perceived, is brought into relationship with a limited range of meanings relevant to a task. Such a conception ignores the possibility that information that is redundant only to the concerns of awareness in the adaptively oriented waking state may still have a separate and quite independent status in the phenomenal field and be subject to recruitment by concurrent schemata.

Finally, I want to say a few words about the bearing of our discussion on some conceptual usages in psychoanalytic theory. The psychoanalytic model as it emerges from the crucible of our data seems to involve four assumptions. First, consciousness is a useful structural convention that permits us to speak of patterns of awareness—states of consciousness—capable of a wide range of variation even under waking conditions. Second, as a construct designed to describe the pattern of deployment of cathexis, it also provides for differences in *modes of experience*, the different ways in which it is possible to be "aware" of things. Third, registration is not limited to exteroceptive events. Interoceptive stimuli are also registered. Both kinds of registration are, however, subject to deployment of cathexis. Finally, the unit-forming process of registration is distinct from processes responsible for the qualities of our awareness of things.

The distinctions that we have drawn disclose a confusion in the frequently used concept of *preconscious perception*. In the strict sense of "consciousness" as a structural concept, the term "*pre*conscious" is more misleading than helpful. Because the modes and range of awareness can differ with states of consciousness, the term "preconscious" used without reference to its context of a particular state of consciousness has little descriptive value; it is necessary to specify "preconscious" in respect to what state of consciousness. Usually, however, "preconscious perception" simply means "registrations not in awareness." But because perception is a quality of experience distinct from other presentational modes of awareness like imagery, we cannot equate registrations outside awareness with perception. We can become aware of registrations in different presentational modes, as images and not percepts, for example. Perhaps the term *ception* conveys more adequately the idea of a psychic representation not yet committed to a particular quality of experience.

Emphasizing this conceptual confusion is not mere verbal finickiness. Proper and precise use of the terms "awareness" and "consciousness" alerts us to the productive possibilities that Freud opened up by relinquishing certain popular connotations of the term "consciousness." In speaking of registrations without awareness instead of preconscious perception, we are thus alerted to the superordinate organization—the state of consciousness—in which such registrations occur, the elaborations to which they are subject in primary- or secondary-process terms, and the controlling organizations that shape their emergence in different forms of experience, as images or perceptions, for example.

A rather common oversight in psychoanalytic discussions is also highlighted by the model. If we assume that far more registrations than we become aware of attain structure and persist, obviously there are processes other than "repression" (in the sense of "pushing out") that deny them awareness or attention cathexis. But what is the relation of such "nonconscious" events to repression in the usual sense? Psychoanalytic theory has tended to emphasize *repressed* contents and has ignored the wider array of unexperienced contents that may be simply the outcomes of perception and of other presentational modes in different states of consciousness, rather than of repression.

Obviously much more work is needed to exploit the potential of the psychoanalytic understanding of consciousness for dealing with one of the central problems of psychology—the range of human sensibility to meaning. Academic psychology has tried off and on through the years to slough off the problems of consciousness and unconsciousness, but the ghosts have lived on. Through the momentum provided by the structural concepts of current psychoanalytic theory and through recent advances in observational techniques, there is a real possibility that the ghosts will at last become manageable realities in the experimental laboratory.

Chapter 9

On Subliminal Activation

I am sure that the flood of claims and counterclaims about the alleged power of the subliminal must have stirred in all of us mixed feelings of amusement, bemusement, and irritation. Anxieties have been fanned, and the public clamor for shelters against the subliminal bombs is beginning to exceed pleas for protection against the far more tangible, real thing. Madison Avenue eyes this possible new frontier with alternate trepidation and fascination. The Brave New World seems at hand, with Aldous Huxley our Moses. Artful journalists, under pressure to produce one psychedelic effect after another in their blasé readers, have swelled the tide to a point at which, in this astrophysical era, fantasies about inner space threaten to carry the day.

Reactions to the claims for subliminal power have drawn more upon morals than upon fact and theory. In this respect, something of a tour de force was achieved in one shrewd fantasy by a writer for *Punch*. He envisioned the typical movie program of the future—at a drive-in, no doubt—at which the main attraction is an hour-and-a-half-long feature film consisting of a string of luridly colored advertisements for fancy-finned automobiles, soap, cigarettes, and other bonbons that advertisers tell us make life worth living. Out front, the audience, clapping in joy at its first view of the chrome-plated monsters, settles back happily, rhythmically chomping on a limitless supply of popcorn and swilling pop (vended automatically, of course, at each car seat). But lo! Far back in the isolated projection room the lone idealist, tense with fear, does his dirty work: Working with a second projector smuggled in behind Big Brother's back, he unfolds between the frames, at exposures of .001 of a second, Shakespeare's *Othello!* The fantasy brings us full circle to that most banal of truths from which moral controversy about science usually begins and where it inevitably ends: that the uses of science's products only reflect, they do not determine, the love or the hate in man's heart.

I find this thought neither interesting nor even elevating by now. For psychologists, the issues in so-called "subliminal," or as I prefer to call it "incidental," stimulation are far more fascinating and contain a far greater potential for fresh discovery if we stay within the confines of theory (scientific, not moral), of fact, and of deductions from theory and fact. That is where I propose to stay.

It would be nice to be able to say that the claims for the hidden stimulus have already been lifted out of the fog of moral argument and assessed on appropriate grounds of theory and fact. But the professional discussions I have read on the matter have not been very helpful. Most of the comments have been justified blasts at the obvious holes in research design—the perhaps fantasied research designs—in which the get-rich-quick entrepreneurs of the subliminal have couched their claims. Insofar as the experts have ventured into theory and previous research, they have leaned heavily upon studies of discrimination without awareness and of so-called "perceptual defense." These studies unfortunately miss the main issues. For whatever the commercial validity of the recent claims—and I predict flatly that it will prove to be nil—the issues they raise are genuinely novel and important. Yet these issues, far from being illuminated by the hundreds of studies of discrimination without awareness and perceptual defense, have actually been obscured by them.

These basic issues are, first, that an incidental stimulus may activate meanings (or trace systems or schemata) quite *independent* of those that are pertinent to the main directions of a person's thought at a given moment; second, that such incidentally or even subliminally activated meanings will affect *different* levels of behavior and *different* modes of experience than those to which conscious selective effort is directed; third, that the incidentally or subliminally activated meanings may have *delayed* effects, persisting and affecting behavior in situations and in states of consciousness quite removed from those in which the excitations originally occurred; and, fourth, that such incidental stimuli may acquire special properties by the very fact of their peripheral status in the field of stimulation, making it possible for such subliminal activations to have *distinctive* effects on thought as compared to stimuli that claim full attention.

Now there *is* a pertinent literature, there *are* current studies, and theory *does* provide leads directly to these issues. But in the two most recently published reviews (Adams, 1957; McConnell, Cutler & McNeil, 1958), one of them directly stimulated by the commercially provoked hubbub, I have looked in vain for any sign of recognition of this literature. I am referring to a line of empirical and theoretical development with shadowy origins in early work by Binet (1896), Urbantschitsch (1907), and others, which was brought into focus by Freud's discovery of the day residue in dreams and given renewed experimental life by Otto Pötzl's pioneer experiments (1917), later studies by Allers and Teler (1924) and more recent work by Fisher (1954; Fisher & Paul, 1959), Shevrin and Luborsky (1958), and by my colleagues at the Research Center for Mental Health (Eagle, 1959; Klein *et al.*, 1958; Pine, 1960; Smith, Spence & Klein, 1959). And there are available to us the general propositions of psychoanalytic behavior theory, epitomized in Chapter 7 of Freud's *The Interpretation of Dreams* and modified, extended, and amplified in many pertinent directions by Hartmann (1939), Rapaport (1957a, 1957b, 1959a), and others.

I have said that research incentive has been wizened and important phenomena obscured by restricting questions about subliminal stimulation to the issue of whether or not discrimination is possible without awareness—a favorite query of the last few years. The questions in such studies usually involve two considerations: the degree to which an experience (a discrimination, a recognition, a conditioned response, a choice) is swayed by contiguous stimuli presented at levels at which no verbal recognition is possible, and the extent of the subject's unawareness of the allegedly subliminal stimulus. Study after study has hovered over this second point: To what extent was the subject actually aware of at least *some* feature of the stimulus?

As far as an *experience of discrimination* is concerned, when a subject actively engages in an attempt to identify accurately a portion of a stimulus field, the evidence indeed seems to weigh heavily *against* the discriminability of a stimulus when no part of it is conscious. Discrimination distinctly improves as stimulus intensity increases, that is, as the subject has more consciously available pegs on which to anchor hypotheses about what is "out there." It seems clear from the convincing studies by Bricker and Chapanis (1953), Voor (1956), Boardman (1957), and others that it is impossible to discriminate—in the sense of a voluntary *intention to identify*—a part of the field without some partial conscious information from the stimulus. These studies tell us that previous claims of discrimination without awareness may have been based upon a failure of experimenters to specify the *partial* information that subjects were aware of and that enabled them to make better-than-chance discriminations of stimuli.

These critics have done us a valuable service in showing that we need assume not two kinds of discrimination but only one. Their conclusions teeter on the edge of overgeneralization, however, because of an argument that runs something like this: Only a discriminated stimulus can affect thought, and discrimination always depends upon the subject's having at least some information within his conscious grasp. Without some positive awareness of a stimulus, there is no effect.

This argument suffers from a flaw of many psychological explanations: It overlooks the subject's intentions. How much a person must *consciously* apprehend of the many stimulus excitations that enmesh themselves in his behavior is a relative matter, depending very much on what he is trying to do and what the situation requires of him. Different requirements are set in this respect when a person is actively *trying* to penetrate a field of stimulation—when his *aim* is discrimination—from those when he is, say, conjuring up a daydream in order to escape the dreariness of a lecture on subliminal stimulation. Awareness is most of the time selective, and it had better be. That socks, shoes, and trousers get put on in the morning, that these acts be *performed*, is the main thing, not that we be *aware* of the movements or of the order of movements involved. A discrimination *task* in the laboratory lays down a *special* requirement: that the subject report effectively and accurately on what is "out there." Sometimes this requirement is explicit in instructions; almost invariably the subject himself assumes it as soon as he is asked to tell what something *is*. Such an intention to discriminate is not a simple matter of perception alone. It is a complex orientation in which attention is finely tuned to the promptings of expectations and sets, aided and abetted by postural and muscular adjustments—all aimed at effectiveness and accuracy. Communicated response is governed by standards of adequacy (and these standards need not be conscious). In this context it is easy to understand the importance of a *perceivable* cue or signal; molding a *reliable* hypothesis and meeting subjective standards of adequate response require it to a certain minimal degree, a degree that probably varies among people and with different "cognitive styles." It reduces the range of the improbable; it helps to establish a hierarchy within the range of the possible.

The only point proved by the critics, then, is that an *intention to discriminate*, in Brentano's sense of a particular kind of orientation to a stimulus, cannot be successfully implemented until some critical, minimal segment of the field is consciously apprehensible. But we must be careful where we carry this conclusion. From the fact that an incidental or subliminal stimulus is inadequate for *discrimination* we cannot conclude that it provokes *no* activating effects at all and that it is effaced as quickly as it is registered, if it is registered at all. Nor can we infer from the demands of discrimination that *all* behavior contexts and confrontations with stimuli make similar demands for consciously accessible information.

Does the fact that *identifying* a stimulus requires at least some partial conscious information rule out the possibility that *some* information has been transmitted or, in fashionable terminology, encoded and ordered into schemata without awareness of it? Such a conclusion would be impetuous. It requires no experimental demonstration to say confidently that we are not aware of all the stimuli that we use in behavior. Such lack of awareness of mediating cues is common in perception. We recognize a face without noting the specific features; we throw and catch balls when their trajectories are far too complex for a physicist to predict. Most people know nothing of such cues as binaural time differences, yet they use them constantly and with excellent effect in perceiving the loci of sounds. Constancy phenomena testify to the same thing. The issue, in short, is not whether or not the subliminal can affect behavior, but whether or not the subliminal impact is observable in some variation of conscious experience other than an act of discrimination; whether or not it has an *independent* status in the sense that its cognitive effects run parallel to, without intruding upon, a *concurrent* act of discrimination; whether or not its effects are discernible in other situations and contexts of intention; and whether or not it is itself recoverable to consciousness when the usual premises of reality testing are in abeyance. It would help, therefore, if we were careful to separate *activation* from the *varieties of experience* in which the effects of activation are embedded.

This point is made in recent experiments carried out by Fiss, Goldberg, and Klein (1963; see also Fiss, 1966) and by Lapkin (1960) and Lippmann (1961) at the Research Center for Mental Health at New York University.[1] The Goldberg-Fiss experiment is particularly relevant because it grew out of an effort to test for discrimination without awareness. It shows that, even when a discrimination of a stimulus is not possible, the stimulus may still

---

[1] [See also Haber and Erdelyi's more recent work (1967).]

have an activating effect and may influence the course of another kind of experience, for instance, imagery. In the first part of the experiment, the subject knew that his task was to discriminate and knew the figures that he was to try to discriminate. Three figures—a triangle, a circle, and a square—were briefly exposed in a fixed random order; the exposures were gradually lengthened until parts of the figures were clearly discernible. Each time a figure was flashed, the subject was required to describe *what* he saw—a small part, a blur, or even a mere flicker. In addition, he had to *guess* which figure had been shown (knowing that it had to be one of the three). He had to report on every trial, even when all he could actually see was the merest flicker or shadow. It was found that, at those levels of exposure at which only a flicker or an unformed blur was reportable, the accuracy of guesses (discriminations) was no better than chance When exposures reached levels at which *partial* recognition of a figure was possible, success in identifying the whole figure increased but reached only marginal levels of significance. Only when stimulus exposures were long enough to make some part of the figure clearly perceptible were the subjects' guesses about the identity of the whole figure clearly better than chance.

We have here further substantiation of Bricker and Chapanis' main point (1953) that a successful discrimination experience is not possible unless the subject has some conscious grasp of a portion of the stimulus that he is trying to discriminate. This finding should not be surprising. Discrimination under laboratory conditions is guided by an attitude that we know as "reality testing." The subject prefers to work with information that can be consciously assessed and incorporated into a reasonable projection of the actual structure of objects and events. An effort to discriminate becomes a disciplined encounter with a field of stimulation for which *perceived* data have preeminent status. Its outcome is a distinct kind of discrimination *experience* with laws of its own.

But the experimenters carried the matter further (Fiss, Goldberg & Klein, 1963). May not these low-level stimuli, they asked, exert an influence upon some form of experience *other than* discrimination? The fact that the stimuli are insufficient for an effective discrimination experience does not touch the issue of whether they may register anyway and have a modifying effect on behavior and other types of experience. They tested this possibility in the second part of the experiment. In the square they put a double profile; within the circle they drew a clock (see Figure 9).

Figure 9

They then exposed each of these figures to the same subjects at an exposure time well below the level that, in the discrimination experiment, had provoked at most only reports of flicker in response to the square and circle. They exposed the clock figure twice at this brief exposure. Immediately afterward they asked the subjects to report any spontaneously occurring *images* and to draw them as best they could, following a procedure used by Allers and Teler (1924) and more recently by Fisher and Paul (1959). Then, the double-profile picture was exposed at the same exposure time, again with a request for images and drawings. It now remained to discover whether there was a significant intrusion of the double profile in the one set of images and of the clock in the other. Of course, the subjects did not know that their images were to be studied in this fashion. They believed that they were engaged in a different experiment—one on imagery—having nothing to do with the earlier discrimination task.

    The effects were assessed in two ways: First, judges evaluated the drawn images against the characteristics of the stimuli and then paired each drawing with its probable stimulus; second, they assessed this similarity quantitatively according to a check list of double-profile and clock properties developed in the previous, independent study by Fisher and Paul. The results were decisive. Five of the six judges showed a preponderance of correct placements of the images for the stimuli. On the check list, images produced after the double-profile exposure showed a significant preponderance of double-profile elements compared to images elicited by the clock stimulus. Incidentally, a subsequent check of the *discriminability* of the two stimuli (subjects were asked to guess, after an exposure of the same length as the experimental exposure, whether the clock or the double profile had been shown) produced no significantly successful discrimination responses.

The experiment indicates that a direct effort to discriminate a sector of a stimulus is indeed impossible unless some level of information is consciously accessible. It is equally decisive in showing that low-level stimuli may nevertheless register; that they may contribute to the organization of sequential thought; and that such activity is discernible *not* in an actual discrimination task but in some other variety of experience—in imagery relatively free of "reality testing."

In short, recent studies may have muted earlier claims for a distinctive discriminative agency outside awareness; they have not ruled out the possibility that behavior is affected on various levels, in various modes of experience, and in various states of consciousness by the activations induced by subliminal stimuli.

To appreciate these new dimensions of the problem of incidental stimulation, it is helpful to take a closer look at some neglected older studies. On the whole they provide more telling examples of subliminally induced cognitive activity than do most of the hundreds of recent studies that carry the additional burden of an unwieldy concept of perceptual defense. The Goldberg-Fiss study just described is only one of a line taking its cues from Binet, Urbantschitsch, and Freud. These earlier studies are important because they directly confront the issue of the delayed impact of incidental registration and because they raise the possibility that incidental stimuli acquire unique properties and affect thought in distinctive ways by virtue of the fact that they *are* incidental, they *are* in the background of the stimulus field, they do *not* command attention, and they evade the critical assessments of consciousness.

I should like briefly to draw attention to Freud's observations on the day residue in dreams, the significance of which has not been fully appreciated in contemporary experimental psychology. The phenomenon of the day residue involves the carry-over into dreams of incidental registrations of recent events. Freud gives many examples of fleeting daytime experiences that had captured hardly any notice at all yet became conspicuous in a dream the same night. He remarks about his own dream of a botanical monograph: "The first of these two impressions with which the dream was connected was an indifferent one, a subsidiary circumstance: I had seen a book in a shop-window whose title attracted my attention for a moment but whose subject-matter could scarcely be of interest to me" (1900, p. 174). The general importance of the day-residue phenomenon is that it concerns the effect on thought of transient, momentarily unessential, even unnoticed stimuli that nevertheless are drawn into an independently active field of thought, the consequences of which appear not when the activation takes place but only later in a dream. Freud made much of the remarkable fact that dream content draws upon the trivial impression or passing glimpse. He suggested further that such "indifferent" perceptions, as he called them, have a distinctive role in the workings of the dream, perhaps significantly different from those of focal impressions and perceptions, that is, registrations that we *are* aware of and to which we directly respond in the ordinary course of the waking day. "Dreams," he said, "have a preference for taking up unimportant details of waking life" (1900).

Pötzl's experiments (1917) were the first attempt to deal experimentally with the day-residue phenomenon (see this volume, Chapter 8). More recent, better designed, and more carefully detailed studies by Fisher and Paul (1959), Shevrin and Luborsky (1958), and others have refined and extended Pötzl's method and have strikingly supported his main conclusions. Recent

274 / Center and Periphery in Motivated Thinking

studies have been broadened to include different possible loci of effects in modes of experience other than perceptual—for example, imagery—and other states of consciousness besides dreams.[2] They have also expanded to include an interest in *transient stimuli* of all kinds, so that there is now a tendency to regard the so-called "subliminal" stimulus as only a special, perhaps extreme, instance of *incidental* stimulation (Pine, 1960).[3] All these studies also involve improvements in method over the well-known "recognition threshold" technique that has figured so prominently in studies of discrimination without awareness and of perceptual defense. Perhaps the most important feature of these studies, however, is that they frame questions about incidental stimuli from vantage points in the general psychoanalytic theory of behavior—not from isolated concepts culled from it (the rest banked off by heavy coatings of vitriol) but with attention to links among concepts within the theory. How the logic of inquiry is conditioned and enriched by this commitment is too long a story to recount in this chapter (see this volume, Chapters 3 and 8). Let me simply remark that the problem of incidental stimuli is illuminated in fresh and productive ways by such interlocking propositions from psychoanalytic theory as the relative participation in thought of controls, defenses, and drive; regression; activity and passivity; reality testing; and varieties of conscious experience.

The recent studies have centered upon three main questions. First, how and in what different ways do incidental stimuli affect conscious experience and other behavior—and within what limits? Second, what are the circumstances—the structural conditions of consciousness—in which such activations of meaning emerge into conscious thought and behavior? Third, do the inci-

---

[2] [See, for example, Fiss' study (1966) on recovery of subliminal stimulation under conditions of relaxation.]

[3] [Especially relevant is a study by Eagle, Wolitzky, and Klein (1966) on the effects of unperceived forms embedded in more dominant figures. An incidental background figure significantly affected imagery.]

dental activations have effects on thought distinct from those of stimuli that dominate attention?

It is impossible to dwell upon the detailed findings now available on these issues. The results are complex and subtle; the effects depend upon a great many variables such as associative connotations of the stimuli, conscious intentions, state of consciousness, and passivity of the subject. I can draw attention only to two main points of convergence in the findings. To begin with, it is now quite clear that an incidental stimulus may be enlisted in a train of thought that is quite independent of the task at hand. Its effects may not be immediately observable if the peripherally active train of thought has no point of contact with the thought operations of the focal task. The effects may therefore be *delayed*, and show themselves on levels of behavior and in states of consciousness with little similarity to the original context of stimulation and report. For those who like to be reassured about the condition of their psychological pie by checking it against the standards of neurological chefs, may I point out in passing that recent discoveries about reticular structures lend encouragement to the conclusion that activations may occur independently of concurrent perceptual experience.

In another point of convergence, the findings emphasize the importance of separating the *activating* effects of a stimulus from the modes of *experience* in which the stimulus may come to awareness. Perception is only one of various possible modalities of experience, and it is only one of several ways in which one may become aware of a subliminally activated meaning.

It seems to me more valuable to refer to the generic event in all these studies as *incidental* stimuli rather than as *subliminal* stimuli. The latter term would better be limited to certain operational means of rendering stimuli incidental in various contexts. The importance of a stimulus is not so much in its subliminal status as in the meanings and properties it acquires when circumstances relegate it to the periphery of conscious thought and attention (Eagle, Wolitzky & Klein, 1966). Awareness of a stimulus increases the possibility of its being subjected to the disciplined categorizing and assessment that are characteristic of adaptive thinking. It is for this reason that it seems to me less important to ask how far below awareness stimulation can occur and still produce an effect upon behavior than to ask in what ways and for what reasons *increased awareness* of a stimulus leads to *changes* in thought and behavior.

A critical consideration in assessing the effects of incidental stimuli is the conditions of *control* that characterize any particular state of consciousness. Psychoanalytically derived propositions about reality testing and attention and the balance of drive and control are again helpful (this volume, Chapter 8; Rapaport, 1957a). In certain states of consciousness the incidentally activated material may emerge to awareness in the context of images while perceptions show little evidence of it. Dreams, hypnosis, and hypnagogic and mescaline states perhaps enable a relatively undifferentiated slice of incidentally registered experience to be reexperienced with an intensity that in the usual waking state can be accomplished only in a passive frame of mind like that conducive to eidetic imagery. As reality contact and reality requirements are minimized, the prospects that incidentally registered material will emerge into awareness in passive imagery may increase.

In view of these considerations, it should not surprise us that the behavioral effects of subliminal or incidental stimulation are ordinarily *small*, and that they can be highlighted only in states of consciousness in which critical judgment and reality testing are much reduced. Anyone working on the problem of incidental stimulation would do well to give up any notions that the effects will be huge and explicit on just *any* level of response and in any task. The very forces that render a stimulus incidental to begin with also render its effects on behavior incidental, at least under the conditions of reality appraisal and pragmatic considerations that ordinarily characterize waking life. But certain corollary implications are equally important: Conditions of induced passivity, reduced reality testing, and reduced activity in thought—concepts that to my mind are crucial to a general theory of cognitive behavior—also enhance the effects of the incidental stimulus on thought and behavior.

In conclusion, a word about the so-called "practical" side of all this research: It is surely foolish to hope that a subliminal stimulus will preserve through its vicissitudes in peripheral thought the *single* meaning that the advertiser desires, that it will produce a *specific* effect consonant with this particular meaning on the *one* level in which the advertiser is likely to be interested —in the region of the pocketbook. There is no reason to expect a single impact on a single level any more than there is reason to expect it for a *supra*liminal stimulus. A comforting paradox confronts us: Reality testing, which so constricts awareness in the sense that it spares our attention from a great number of object properties with no bearing on the pragmatics of everyday life, has also a protective function. This same reality sense and reality testing prevent just any stimulus from exerting an uncheckable influence on behavior. Enslaved we always are—by ideas, by what people do to and for us, by the supraliminal and subliminal activations that they provoke. But a curiously indomitable element of critical conscious choice and delay intervenes in the selection of our masters, setting the limits and conditions of our enslavement to them. It is an element that is muted only by extreme changes in our commitment to reality.

PART FOUR

SUPPORTS OF
REALITY-ORIENTED THINKING

Chapter 10

Inhibition, Disinhibition, and Primary Process in Thinking

Disorders of thinking have in the past compelled the interest of psychiatrists and clinical psychologists by necessity and that of the experimental psychologist, in the splendid isolation of his academic laboratory, only by accident. Not so today. Bridge building between clinic and laboratory is more and more the rule, spurred by such experimental efforts as the McGill University studies of sensory isolation, by the Innsbruck studies of sensory disarrangements, and by pharmacological developments, to mention only a few.

Theory has not kept pace with experimental advances. Psychological theories have had a great deal to say about the orderly selectivity of everyday perception and cognition, given (or assuming) an optimally functioning organism, but not much to say about behavior outside the limits of adaptive effectiveness. That disordered behavior may reflect other orders of lawfulness is, if not as novel a general assumption as before, still an undeveloped one. Theory to guide the quest for such rules of disorder is relatively meager.

THE PRIMARY AND SECONDARY PROCESSES

Freud's distinction between primary and secondary processes (1895, 1900, 1911) offers a relatively untapped conceptual resource. Ernest Jones wrote, "Freud's revolutionary contribution to psychology was not so much his demonstrating the existence of an unconscious, and perhaps not even his exploration of its content, as his proposition that there are two fundamentally different kinds of mental processes, which he termed primary and secondary respectively, together with his description of them" (1953, p. 397).

On a descriptive level, primary-process thought is distinguished from secondary-process thought by different formal and content characteristics of the thought products. Primary-process thinking is unreflective and lacking in temporal orderliness; contradictory ideas are tolerated side by side; ideas freely shift about, and reversals of figure and ground occur easily. The greater the primary-process component in thinking, the more content seems to be ordered around libidinal and aggressive aims rather than around interests, values, and realistic intentions. Thinking that proceeds by rules of the secondary process, on the other hand, is reflective, shows time perspective, and employs concepts that are coordinate with actualities.

In principle, the distinction between primary and secondary processes can be carried over to specific thought functions (Schafer, 1958). For example, domination by the primary process means that memory is organized around drive aims; memory in the secondary process is ordered by conceptions of actual occurrence and pragmatic considerations. In *perception*, the primary process is characterized by drive-determined selection and earlier developmental organizations, the secondary process by a highly efficient coordination between experience and environmental arrangements. When *motility* is concerned, the primary process is shown in the unchecked release of impulse into action, whereas in the secondary process motility is modulated, subtly tuned to concerns of effectiveness and control.

Freud seemed to imply that the formal and content characteristics of primary-process thought are the products of certain thought-producing processes that he termed *mechanisms,* the most notable being *condensation* (which results in the fusion of two or more ideas or images), *displacement* (a shift of emphasis from one mental content to another), and *symbolization* (the replacement of one idea or image by another similar in various formal features but disguising a dynamically significant idea). The most detailed operation of these presumed mechanisms and the most vivid examples of the products they create are to be found in the dream, which for Freud was a kind of "pure culture" of the primary process. Primary-process thought and the mechanisms that underlie it are, however, by no means confined to dreams. Characteristics of primary-process thinking are also to be found in schizophrenia, reverie states, and other states of consciousness.

These more or less descriptive bases of the concepts are linked to more general theoretical assumptions. Primary and secondary processes are sometimes considered to reflect the existing balance between the pressure of basic drives for reduction and consummation, on the one hand, and considerations of effective reality coordination, on the other (pleasure principle versus reality principle). Thus it is said that in primary-process thought libidinal and aggressive energies are in a "mobile" state, their discharge being relatively unchecked in thought and behavior compared to their neutralized, bound forms in secondary-process thinking. Finally, primary and secondary process are sometimes taken as a gauge of the degree of autonomy of ego structures from environmental and drive forces. A great loss of ego autonomy from drives is reflected in primary-process dominated thought; on the other hand, rigidly emphasized secondary-process thinking exemplifies either an undue fealty of the ego to environmental fact or to be constantly geared for defense (Rapaport, 1950b, 1957; Holt, 1956).

It cannot be said that the conceptions of primary and secondary processes offer clear directives for experimental manipulation. It is not easy to specify the conditions that will produce thought with the descriptive imprints of the primary process. The difficulty lies partly in the fact that it is by no means justified to say that thought *products* answering the description of condensation and displacement always reflect the same thought-producing *mechanisms*—or even that it is best to refer them to mechanisms at all. Nevertheless, that particular mechanisms distinguish primary- and secondary-thought products is often gratuitously implied in such statements as, for instance, that the primary process can be "used" by the secondary process, that it is "overlaid" by the secondary process, that it is "held in check" by the secondary process.

THE FUNCTIONAL CONDITION OF STRUCTURES

It is possible to look at primary-process thought products in a rather different way, without reference to distinctive mechanisms. This point of view assumes that *one* set of structures and mechanisms, and one set only, is involved in thought, whether primary or secondary. Condensations and other formal properties of primary-process thought thus reflect the functional condition of structures that participate in molding a train of thought. Primary-process thinking would be the outcome of conditions that render certain structures inactive and release others to shape behavior. These critical conditions are *inhibition* and *disinhibition*.

This approach brings the conception of the primary process into juxtaposition with the structural point of view of contemporary psychoanalytic theory (Hartmann, 1939; Hartmann, Kris & Loewenstein, 1946; Rapaport & Gill, 1959; Gill, 1959). Psychic organization is assumed to be an arrangement of structures recognizable by their function (for example, perceiving, remembering, anticipating, intending). A function represents a relationship among many activated structures (analogous to the structural complexities of the accommodation-convergence functions of perception). Certain structures associated with functions capable of adapting the organism to the environment are given from the beginning: the abilities to perceive, to learn, to remember, to move, and so on. The development of these functions and their associated structures, however, is assumed to be intimately linked with that of drives—the forces that activate behavior and give it momentum. From the first, structures that guarantee some degree of coordination of drive aims with reality and action are present. Conflicts and environmental encounters, however, bring about modifications and new structures and, in fact, induce changes in the motivations themselves and in their instrumental means. There thus evolve ever more finely differentiated derivatives of drives, adaptive controls, and defenses. It is through the development of structures in relationships of function that the optimally adaptive organism acquires a certain relative autonomy from both environmental forces and instinctual tensions (Hartmann, 1939; Rapaport, 1957b). This cursory review of the structural point of view in contemporary psychoanalytic theory suggests an approach to primary- and secondary-process modes of thought in terms of the balance of inhibition (inactivation) and disinhibition (activation) among functions (and their structural bases) giving rise to variations of thought products.

Inhibition and Disinhibition

A good starting point for appreciating the distinction between inhibition and disinhibition is Freud's assertion that effective secondary-process thinking is essentially inhibitive. "All that I insist upon is the idea that the activity of the *first* ψ-system is directed towards securing the *free discharge* of the quantities of excitation, while the *second* system, by means of the cathexes emanating from it, succeeds in *inhibiting* this discharge . . ." (1900, p. 599).

The inhibitive aspect of thought is best known, of course, through the workings of defenses; the identifying mark of a thought process that serves defense is that it deflects or impedes the discharge of drives. Inhibition is not, however, to be identified only with defense; it is the hallmark of all effective and adaptive thinking.

Let me dwell a bit more on this point. When a structure is

intact and active, its accomplishments consist not merely in what it permits to happen but also in what it prevents from happening. Take, for instance, the behavior of someone who we say deals with things realistically. Such behavior involves channeling responses toward certain events and restraining other responses that are inappropriate to the objective. When we are hungry we do not cook our shoes, as Charlie Chaplin did in the brilliant fantasy depicted in *The Gold Rush*. Effective thinking—indeed effective action—always involves inhibition. *"Inhibition,"* wrote William James, *"is . . . not an occasional accident; it is an essential and unremitting element of our cerebral life"* (1890, Vol. 2, p. 583). In a now classic experiment, Hernandez-Péon, Scherrer, and Jouvet (1956) beautifully demonstrated the inhibitive essence of alert, attentive behavior on the neurophysiological level. They recorded the responses of a resting cat to rhythmic clicks of a stimulus by taking leads from the cochlear nucleus. A mouse was then brought into the cat's view. Cortical transmission of the still-clicking auditory stimulus was dramatically reduced! (There is some doubt whether it was altogether eliminated.)

Notice that the conception of inhibition here is different from the popular one, which implies rigidity and constriction. In this day and age inhibition is something of a bogey, suggesting the very antithesis of freedom. Yet it is easy to see that flexible, even spontaneous, behavior has to involve a patterning of inhibition to the extent that behavior remains faithful to realistic considerations. As Freud reminds us, delay of drive discharge, on which thought is based, and reflective thought in general are no less active for the fact that inhibition is their very essence. The crux of effective delay and of effective intentional thinking in particular is what is *withheld* from behavior. This fact provides a clue to disordered thinking. Functional breakdown is in significant measure characterized by the loss of inhibition or what we may call disinhibition.

It is this aspect of structure that plays an important part in the appearance of primary-process characteristics in thought products. When we speak of the disinhibited condition of structures, we mean the abdication of their function: The structures involved in the function are inoperative and incapable of realizing their formative potential in behavior. Disinhibition has two implications: grossness of function (temporary or prolonged), in which the selectivity that ordinarily characterizes the function is not evident in behavior, and release of other tendencies that have been kept in abeyance. Response capacities that are ordinarily checked by the functioning of the structures are now released to impose their organization upon behavior. From an experimental point of view there are two general means by which such disinhibition can occur: first, through assault on the structures themselves, either by prolonged disuse, as in Riesen's experiments on sensory deprivation (1958, 1960), or by direct cortical lesions, and, second, by disrupting the optimal stimulus conditions necessary for efficient functioning of the structure. Such externally caused disinhibitions are illustrated by sensory-deprivation effects and by the disorganized behaviors resulting from "delayed feedback" (W. M. Smith, McCrary & Smith, 1960). For instance, perceptual feedback is necessary for effective action. In delayed visual or auditory feedback, disinhibition is produced by disrupting the ordered flow of stimulation, even though the function itself and its structural basis remain intact (see this volume, Chapter 13). It is as if a dike were to become inadequate to the pressures of the sea against it, with a resulting inundation. The dike is functionally disinhibited; if its structure remains intact, however, it is again functionally adequate when the flood subsides. Of course, to pursue this analogy further, the flood may damage the dike, so that it may never return to its optimal level of functional effectiveness. Something of this nature was suggested by Freud when he speculated that persistent and unremitting repression might in time destroy the repressed idea itself (1926).

Disinhibition, in this view, does not necessarily involve dedifferentiation of structures—that is, either a collapse of the structures themselves or the regressive reactivation of primitive forms of the structures. To be sure, dedifferentiation of structures—primitivization—is one means by which a function may be disinhibited, but this condition of disinhibition is extreme, involving an impairment of the actual structures. There are, however, more benign circumstances of disinhibition, in which the function is in abeyance but the structures on which it depends are themselves intact, as in the temporarily nonfunctioning dike.

Primary-process forms of behavior, in their formal aspects, may be viewed as outcomes of the disinhibition of function. Recalling that the efficient operation of structures consists in their inhibitive power—what they temporarily or permanently keep out or make impossible or restrain from release—it is natural now to ask what forms behavior will take when these inhibitive features are lost; that is, what are the behavioral consequences of an inoperative function? Under these conditions, behavior will bear the imprint of what is released from inhibition.

Disinhibition and States of Consciousness

Let me illustrate this point of view with the dream—the "pure culture" of primary-process phenomena. It seems to me that, in the attention that has been devoted to the kind of thinking that is typical of dreams, an important point is sometimes missed, one that seems too obvious to mention yet must be kept firmly in mind. It is that the thought products of a dream take place in a distinctive context—a state of consciousness that involves extensive disinhibition of function. The situation was summarized by Freud:

The state of sleep does not wish to know anything of the external world; it takes no interest in reality, or only so far as abandoning the state of sleep—waking up—is concerned. . . . With the system Cs. thus uncathected, the possibility of reality-testing is abandoned; and the excitations which, independently of the state of sleep, have entered on the path of regression will find that path clear as far as the system Cs. where they will count as undisputed reality. (1917, p. 234)

The dream state, in other words, can be characterized in part by functions that are inactive—that are *not* represented in the molding of its thought contents. Some of these "negative" features of the functioning ego of the dream state are, first, abeyance of reality testing (as in loss of the capacity to match impressions with reality) and of the necessity for distinguishing perceptions from memories; second, a marked reduction of intentional and sequentially ordered thinking; third, minimal use of proprioceptive and exteroceptive feedback; and, finally, absence of volitional motor response accommodated to ideational experience. In terms of these absent functions we can appreciate more fully what *does* happen in the dream. We can even say that it is because of disinhibition that what does happen—the distinctive modes of organization of the dream—*can* happen.

An important consequence of the disinhibition of function in the dream state is that the organizing tendencies of drives and motives ordinarily held in check may make themselves felt. There is in the dream an approximation to what Freud (1895) termed "a complete expenditure of defense." The assumption that drives exert organizing force is, of course, a critical consideration here. Drives at whatever level of differentiation bring the organism into readiness for certain objects and certain meanings. They always, therefore, involve conceptual activity, which is, to be sure, more primitive and more inclusive the further down we go in the drive hierarchy. The important point is that this conceptual activity disposes thought toward or away from particular objects and their sensory indicators. With the extensive disinhibition of function that occurs in sleep, those motivational cores that are ordinarily effectively checked by optimally functioning defenses are in a better position to impose themselves upon ideation on their own terms. Of course, controlling structures are not wholly inoperative; the "complete expenditure of defense" that Freud considered the basis of primary-process products in their pure occurrence is a theoretical fiction. Nor is dream thinking steered exclusively by primitive levels of drive organization. The essential idea that I want to stress is that organizing cores are *released* into behavior as a consequence of the disinhibition of function.

Must we assume, then, that distinctive mechanisms are triggered in dreams? In view of the extensive disinhibition of function that characterizes the dream state, it seems unnecessary to assume that certain mechanisms not otherwise evident in behavior become ascendant. We need only assume that organizational possibilities are limited by the extensive disinhibition that characterizes consciousness in the dream state itself; the resulting condensations and displacements reflect the organizational level that is *possible*. Thinking goes on in the dream: We are aware of thought contents; we have experiences. But we need not suppose that they come under the aegis of mechanisms specially let loose for the occasion.

My point is a simple one: Behavior in dreams may be understood in terms of the removal of functional possibilities. Ideation is thereby cast into forms that express more directly than in the waking state the discharge aims of drives, although even in the dream these aims conform to limits defined by still functioning controls. The *forms* of thought in dreams are not themselves created by drives or let loose or excited by the drives, but reflect the balance of structural inhibition and disinhibition that characterizes the state of the ego in sleep. The *contents* of the dream may be explicable in terms of motivational forces; the *shape* of the dream's content is not. With respect to the role of drive in the ego state of the dream, it is the formal status of thought functions —the residual inhibitions and disinhibitions of function resulting from the conditions of sleep—that make possible drive determination of thought in the dream, not the other way around.

In this point of view, it is assumed that ego states are distinguishable by different patterns of inhibition and disinhibition and by the intrusion (release) of motivational forces and controls of different developmental levels. This assumption is consistent with Rapaport's conception of a continuum of states of consciousness (1957a), each characterized in part by a distinctive pattern of what we have called the "disinhibition of function" and the release of organizational possibility (see also Gill & Brenman, 1959).

Our approach makes us wary of assuming that formally similar thought products are the products of the same structures and mechanisms. It is most important to resolve this issue—whether the same genesis can be assumed for the condensations and ambiguities of a dream state, the involuntary condensations of a subject's responses on the Rorschach, and the condensations and deliberate ambiguities produced on call by a superbly gifted writer. (For instance, G. K. Chesterton wrote: "What the dickens shall I write about? I am not the Dickens who can write about anything.") *Functional incapacity* may be the basis of the dream; *cognitive style*, perhaps, of responsiveness to the Rorschach blot; and *skill or art* of the third.[1] The three may be correlated, of course. A stylistic tendency in responses on the Rorschach may indicate an aptitude or skill for condensation; it may even be useful in understanding how the person characteristically shapes the content of his dreams. It would be valuable to look closely at the correspondences and variations in a person's thought products in these widely diverse circumstances of primary-process manifestations.

Experimental Possibilities

On the basis that orderly adaptive functioning is inhibitive and that the disinhibition of function has unique behavioral consequences, it is possible to set up experimental conditions for the production of different facets of maladaptive thought. The paradigm of such an approach is systematically to make functions inoperative or ineffectual. A small example of the kind of strategy that may be employed is provided by Freud himself in his analysis of humor. Impressed by the inhibition characteristic of directed thought, Freud was naturally interested in the turns taken by behavior when such inhibition is surmounted—or, as I have expressed it here, in the behavioral consequences of disinhibition. On this basis, he accounted for the effectiveness of jokes:

Jokes . . . try to keep their expression as short as possible, so as to offer fewer points of attack to the attention. Secondly, they observe the condition of being easy to understand . . . [for] as soon as they call for intellectual work which would demand a choice between differ-

---

[1] It is in relation to the second possibility—the tapping of cognitive style—that R. R. Holt's work on the Rorschach seems to me especially promising; he is attempting to distinguish Rorschach responses according to primary-process characteristics (Holt & Havel, 1960).

ent paths of thought, they would endanger their effect not only by the unavoidable expenditure of thought but also by the awakening of attention. But besides this they employ the device of distracting attention by putting forward something in the joke's form of expression which catches it, so that in the meantime the liberation of the inhibitory cathexis and its discharge may be completed without interruption. This aim is already fulfilled by the omissions in the joke's wording; they offer an incitement to filling up the gaps and in that way succeed in withdrawing the joking process from attention. . . . While we are beginning to wonder what was wrong with the reply, we are already laughing; our attention has been caught unawares and the discharge of the liberated inhibitory cathexis has been completed. (1905c, p. 152)

Freud also suggested that disinhibition of executive intending (see Chapter 3) and of the reality-testing function might account for the effectiveness of his briefly used technique of encouraging associations and remembering by applying pressure on the forehead.

I am rather of opinion that the advantage of the procedure lies in the fact that by means of it I dissociate the patient's attention from his conscious searching and reflecting—from everything, in short, on which he can employ his will—in the same sort of way in which this is effected by staring into a crystal ball, and so on. . . . It is merely a question of getting some obstacle out of the way. This obstacle seems once again to be the subject's will, and different people can learn with different degrees of ease to free themselves from their intentional thinking and to adopt an attitude of completely objective observation towards the psychical processes taking place in them. (Breuer & Freud, 1893–1895, p. 271)

I shall close with two examples that illustrate, to my mind, the importance of disinhibition of function. The first involves the effects of attenuated stimulation—either subliminal or incidental —on thinking. Pötzl (1917) demonstrated that the manifest content of dreams draws upon exposures of stimuli too brief to attract notice. He found that contents of a briefly exposed stimulus unreported during the experiment were abundantly present in reports of dreams experienced the night following the experiment. Much other work (this volume, Chapters 8, 9; Klein & Holt, 1960; G. J. W. Smith, Spence & Klein, 1959; Pine, 1960; Spence, 1961a, 1961b; Fisher, 1956, 1957; Fisher & Paul, 1959; Paul & Fisher, 1959; Dixon, 1956; Shevrin & Luborsky, 1958) has explored conditions that enhance the recovery of such inputs not only in dreams but also in images, storytelling, and other forms of response.

One study by Fisher and Paul (1959) is particularly relevant to the issues of the disinhibition of function. They showed subjects a very brief exposure of the familiar double-profile figure, too brief to permit recognition. Then they asked their subjects to describe and draw any images that came to mind. The subjects were encouraged to respond freely and in relaxed fashion, without concern for the reasonableness and consistency of their images. The basic finding was that elements and properties of the undetected double-profile stimulus appeared in the subsequent imagery with a frequency far beyond chance levels. But there was more to the finding than that. Subjects produced images under two conditions—lying in a supine position in a darkened room and sitting in an upright position in a brightly illuminated room. Images produced under the first condition showed more impressive evidence of the briefly exposed stimulus than did those produced under the second. Fisher and Paul reasoned that the supine condition and dim illumination encourage the suspension of critical judgment and choice, a condition conducive to recovery of the stimulus. As realistic requirements of conscious report and experience are minimized, and as conditions encourage the suspension of automatic controls that usually guide and ensure a precise accommodation to reality, the prospects that incidentally registered material will emerge into awareness increase. The same reasoning, it should be noted, is behind the use of the couch in psychoanalytic therapy, and is also behind Freud's advice (1912) to analysts that the ideal listening attitude is one that temporarily suspends intentional, hypothesis forming thought.

Of course, such conditions are not by themselves conducive to the emergence of peripherally activated ideas, nor is it certain that they are the most effective in this respect. Darkness, like the analytic couch, may inspire opposite reactions; it may exacerbate defensiveness, control, and reality testing rather than disinhibiting these functions. Other studies (Fox, 1960; Eagle, 1962) have also found that a general stylistic disposition to suspend reality testing and to give one's self up easily to fantasy without anxiety is helpful to recovery of the stimulus. All these considerations are congruent with our impression that it is somewhat easier to influence the dreams of a sleeping subject with incidental stimulation than it is to influence passive imagery in a wide-awake subject in the laboratory. Again, the extensive disinhibition of function that typifies the dreaming subject's state of consciousness is the basis of this conclusion.[2]

My second illustration of the inhibition-disinhibition paradigm comes from one of the studies of sensory isolation that have been carried out at the Research Center for Mental Health by Goldberger and Holt (1958). The particular study involved fourteen subjects, who spent eight hours lying isolated in a sound-proof room under conditions of uniform stimulation, involving diffused light let in through halved ping-pong balls covering the

---

[2] [Recent attempts to modify dream content by exteroceptive stimulation present a more complex picture than this statement implies. It is evident from this work that the disinhibition of function alone in dreaming sleep may be insufficient to bring about alterations of dream content. There is evidence that dreaming sleep is indeed quite unresponsive to moderately intense but *meaningless* stimulations, for example, lights and sounds (see Rechtschaffen & Foulkes, 1965; Rechtschaffen, Hauri & Zeitlin, 1966; also Dement & Wolpert, 1958). The dreamer does, however, respond to stimuli of highly personal and emotional significance. Recently Bokert (1967) found that the dreams of thirsty subjects gave unequivocal indications of an auditory message presented during sleep ("Cool delicious drink of water"). It seems that a crucial condition for the appearance of an incidental stimulus in a conscious train of thought is congruence in the meaning of that stimulus with a concurrently active drive (see also Spence, 1967). Whether or not dreams are more responsive in this respect than "passive imagery" in a wide-awake subject is an issue still to be tested.]

eyes and a steady input of monotonous white noise through earphones. The finding that I single out for mention involves imagery and concerns the issue of when images are mistaken by subjects for actual perceptions. The visual imagery of some subjects became quite bizarre in isolation. But the subjects did not necessarily mistake these images, however bizarre, for *perceptions* of reality. On the contrary, such confusions were rare. The key to understanding the changes in isolation—the apparent paradox between bizarreness of imagery and relative absence of hallucinatory perception—is to recognize, as Goldberger and Holt did, that reality testing remained relatively unimpaired over the eight hours of isolation, even while disinhibitive changes were occurring in sensory functions involved in experiences of imagery. With the subject's capacity for *judging* the plausibility and implausibility of such experiences unimpaired, the vivid imagery became for him not more real but less so. Such images could, of course, be disturbing, but subjects did not mistake them for actual perceptions. Only when the reality-testing function fails will the more vivid image also be hallucinatory. Here, then, we have an instance of a function whose inhibitive manifestations remain intact even under stressful conditions, affecting, in turn, the experienced changes produced by the disinhibition of functions in other (sensory) regions of behavior.

CONCLUSION

The two sets of findings described epitomize the main emphasis of this chapter, namely, that state of consciousness and the balance between inhibition and disinhibition of functions characterizing it are crucial in determining the form and content of cognitive behavior. Laboratory studies of thought organization have traditionally been carried out under conditions of a special kind of waking state. Their findings are conditioned by this fact. The waking state of consciousness of a cooperative subject in the usual laboratory context is dominated by a distinctive pattern of controlling structures that are peculiarly suited to reality testing.

It is a pragmatic organization, a high-level developmental derivative of repeated efforts to discipline the discharge of drives away from unrealistic modes of gratification. It is a state of mind in which the subject automatically tries to be accurate and highly selective, to achieve in his response a balance between his perceptions and the claims of logic and experience, and to cast his experiences in a form that will make them readily comprehensible and easily shared by the experimenter. It is by intruding upon this orientation, through experimentally induced disinhibition of function, that we gain access to other-than-pragmatic bases of behavior and thought organization. I also see in the study of the disinhibition of function not only a way of understanding the arrangements of disordered, psychosislike thinking, but also a starting point for the study of the nonpragmatic significance of artistic form and its genesis.

Chapter 11

The Several Grades of Memory

For psychoanalysts the problem of memory has crystallized mainly around a concern with forgetting—and with forgetting narrowly construed as a phenomenon of repression. By "forgetting" I mean memory loss—a failure of retrieval or the inaccessibility of experience residues to awareness. The positive sides of memory processes—perceptual registration, coding, and consolidation, and qualities that distinguish the remembering experience from other modes—have generally not attracted interest, except for Freud's earlier speculative models of how traces are established and retained, which he put forward in "Project for a Scientific Psychology" (1895), in *The Interpretation of Dreams* (1900), and much later in "A Note upon the 'Mystic Writing-Pad'" (1925). With few exceptions (Lewy & Rapaport, 1944; Rapaport, 1942, 1951b; Kris, 1956; Schwartz & Rouse, 1961; Luborsky, 1967), these suggestions of Freud's remain unexplored.

The tendency of psychoanalytic writers to view memory in terms of forgetting and loss and almost entirely in terms of repression is not contradicted by the reminder that the conscious revival of the forgotten is, after all, a critical objective of psychoanalytic therapy. This concern was, of course, important to

Freud, as, for instance, when he experimented with devices for eliciting forgotten memories (see his early papers on hysteria, for example Breuer & Freud, 1893–1895). But Freud's focus on remembering proceeded not so much from questions about how traces are established (the learning and perceptual processes involved) and the processes of storage as from the question of how to make stored events available to conscious reflection. Freud seems not to have made much of the possibility that different ways of establishing traces and different modes of storage might themselves have a bearing on techniques of inducing remembering and of reconstruction. He did offer scattered hints on these matters, particularly in the early papers; he alluded, for instance, to the importance of state of consciousness and its affective concomitants in trace formation, especially in accounting for the formation of a repression and for its peculiarly persistent and tenacious effects on behavior. But there have been few systematic attempts to make capital of this hint in a theory of memory. It has never seemed as important to ask how traces of experience are *established* and what is the nature of such traces as to ask why an allegedly stored event has been forgotten, what has happened to the forgotten (repressed) memory, and how the long-forgotten can be resuscitated. The events of memory that are susceptible to the "pull of repression" tend to be regarded as vaguely passive processes, loosely referred to as the "memory function."

It is easy to see how the narrow view of memory as forgetting and of forgetting itself as almost entirely an outcome of repression came to prevail in psychoanalytic conceptions. The equation of forgetting and repression was etched into clinical practice by the early, since tarnished, assumption that the key factor in neurotic disturbance is a memory of an actual event—an experience residue isolated through repression that by virtue of that repression acquires preemptive power over behavior. In this assumption, the forgotten event is the troublemaker, and to divest it of its force it is necessary to alter its status as "forgotten." By the rules of clinical inference that govern the psychoanalytic session, what is repressed and why it is repressed take precedence, and this dictum is no less true today than heretofore.

Furthermore, the equation of forgetting and repression is probably endemic to the therapeutic situation generally. Forgetting as it appears in the psychoanalytic situation is, in fact, mostly of interest only in its nonadaptive aspects, for when a connection cannot be verbalized or when an experience remains unacknowledged as a memory it is not easy to deal with it therapeutically. Forgetting is a nuisance in therapy. Schlesinger (1964) has aptly pointed out, however, that normal forgetting is not necessarily negative and inadaptive. It is even an important factor in the continuing efficiency of memory schemata, as it is often "the normal result of the organizing process of memory which works through the continuous development of memory schemata." Although in this sense forgetting is not necessarily the enemy of memory, in the psychoanalytic situation it is too often the enemy of therapeutic progress. It is therefore not surprising that at this late date Schlesinger's reminder that not all instances of forgetting should be viewed as repressions can be pertinent for a psychoanalytic audience.

The persistent hold of repression upon memory theory is especially interesting when we note that the theory of repression is itself no longer confined to memory phenomena alone. Today the scope of repression is acknowledged to extend beyond simple isolation of early traumatic experiences. For that matter, it is not identified only with the "memory function." We speak of repressed impulses, repressed fantasy, repressed perceptions; also, and probably in contrast to Freud, of repressed affects (like guilt feelings) and repressed awareness of causes and connections. These are not simply matters of forgetting and of memory. But, although the regions in which repression can operate are now acknowledged to extend beyond the "memory function" alone, the earlier link of memory with forgetting through repression is still prominent.

It is therefore important to ask in what ways a more detailed concern with the adaptive side of memory functioning—remembering in its positive aspects—can alter and deepen our approach to memory phenomena generally and to clinically observable ones in particular. As an example of the possible fruitfulness of reversing the emphasis on "forgetting" to one upon "remembering," take recall of dreams. Freud entitled a section of *The Interpretation of Dreams* "Why Dreams Are Forgotten After Waking." This is generally the most popular question about dream recall, and it is reasonable to make this emphasis in therapeutic practice; certainly a forgotten dream is not as useful as a remembered one. But perhaps a fresh perspective can be gained on the *function* of dreams if we argue that forgetting is far from being the dynamically central event; *remembering* a dream is the exceptional event. Assuming, then, that forgetting dreams is the natural event, the interesting question becomes, How is it possible that we remember dreams at all, and what is the function of recall? Possibly dreaming and the *recall* of dreams have different functions; possibly recall depends on factors other than function. It may be more useful to *have* a dream than to *recall* it, as far as fulfilling the dream's function of drive discharge is concerned. It would then be meaningful to inquire about the special aims and causes of *dream recall*.

Contemporary ego psychology forces upon us a broader and at the same time more differentiated regard for the activity of remembering—a process quite independent of, yet subject to, repressive influences. Hartmann has written: "memory, associations, and so on, are functions which cannot possibly be derived from the ego's relationships to instinctual drives or love-objects, but are rather *prerequisites* of our conception of these and of their development" (1939, p. 15). If we take Hartmann's statement seriously, then the older idea of memory as simply the storage of immutable traces is no longer an acceptable model. Even if we put aside Lashley's rueful remark that he spent thirty years looking for the memory trace, only to discover that it is everywhere and nowhere (1958), the model allows neither for a developmental conception of changes in memory functioning nor for the possibility that memory may function adaptively in a variety of ways. Viewing remembering in its nondrive aspects, we are alerted to the possibility that a *variety* of functions are hidden beneath the enigmatic reference to "the memory function" with its implicit assumption that there is little else to memory than storage and little else to forgetting activity than erasure.

By considering memory as it contributes to behavior adequate to environment and drive—its adaptive aspects—contemporary experimental psychology provides a more differentiated picture of memory functions than that of the familiar psychoanalytic assumption of a unitary memory function. From a structural point of view, these functions may be seen as a succession of threshold levels, the surmounting of which is the condition for the occurrence of each function.

1. An essential condition of retention is a modality-mediated (auditory, visual, and so on) activation produced by an encounter or an event. *Registration* is an aftereffect or excitatory effect of such an encounter, extending to an associative structure or schema, that outlasts the duration of the stimulus. Not all inputs register in this sense—produce an excitatory effect—and not all that do register achieve the status of a trace or structured residue. Registration is thus a distinctive aspect of the process of remembering. Freud touched on this distinction in "Project for a Scientific Psychology":

Any psychological theory deserving consideration must provide an explanation of memory. Now any such explanation comes up against the difficulty that . . . after an excitation neurones are permanently different from what they were before, while, on the other hand, it cannot be denied that, in general, fresh excitations meet with the same conditions of reception as did the earlier ones. Thus the neurones would appear to be both influenced and also unaltered—"unprepossessed". We cannot off-hand imagine an apparatus capable of such complicated functioning. (1895, pp. 359–360)

The phenomenon of registration has received particular attention in experimental studies of the differences between stimulation capable of eliciting awareness or "report" on the one hand and unreportable excitatory effects of stimulation on the other (Pine, 1960; Fisher, 1960; Klein & Holt, 1960).

2. A second aspect of remembering involves not only registration of an encounter but *storage* or retention. Experimental stud-

ies have, however, disclosed that storage itself has two aspects that are fairly independent of each other—*short-term* and *long-term* (Broadbent, 1958). Conditions adequate for short-term retention of impressions do not ensure retention for longer periods. The experimental work that has developed around this distinction makes a complex story (Sperling, 1963; Mackworth, 1963; Postman, 1964; Waugh & Norman, 1965).

3. A third aspect of remembering is variously termed *coding, categorization,* or *location within schemata.* Organization of retained impressions within existing schemata of meaning is crucial to the continued use of stored experience. According to Lashley, "Fixation in memory is generally possible only when the remembered material forms part of . . . a dominant system. . . . We remember the content of a book, not in the author's words but in meanings which fit into previous knowledge of the subject" (1958, p. 536).

4. Finally, a critical aspect of remembering is processes of *retrieval* and *reconstruction.* A retrieved memory is the activation in the present of a former state of affairs. It is not necessarily *remembered. Remembering* includes, in addition, reexperiencing the awareness that occurred on the original occasion but is felt to be past. Only if an image is accompanied by some awareness that "this is something like what I felt then" or that "this is the way something looked then" can it be called "remembering." (Many experimental studies of memory are not necessarily studies of remembering in this sense, for remembering as a mode of *experience* is rarely a focus of inquiry.)

There are two aspects of the retrieval problem that should be distinguished: the *experiential* mode in which a memory is retrieved and the *state of consciousness* that forms the context of retrieval. We are indebted to Rapaport for his insistence upon the distinction between states of consciousness and modes of awareness and for the importance he placed on these neglected facets of thought organization in a proper accounting of cognitive organization (1951b, 1952). The distinction is often obscured in discussions of memory that are mainly absorbed in the substantive issue of memory contents.

Retrieval may take forms other than that of actually experiencing a retrieved content as a memory. It is not necessary for a memory or stored event to be experienced as a memory in order for it to influence behavior. Retrievals may be experienced as reconstructions but not as actual memories—for example aroused *beliefs* about past events—whereas actual *recall* involves the experience of an event in the mode of remembering. We also *act out* stored encounters as well as experience them as memories. The forms in which retained experience intrudes upon behavior and the processes involved in converting what is stored to memory *experience* specifically are thus distinctive facets of memory functioning; memory experience is only one aspect of retrieval or of the behavioral impact of stored experiences.

These distinctions among the modes in which stored events are experienced are important because they have much to do with the ways in which retrieved events are acted upon. Modes of conscious experience are attributed qualities of "realness" in different degrees, and the latter affect how we behave adaptively in relation to the retrieved event. Action in relation to an event will differ according to whether the event is perceived, imagined, or remembered. The perception of a chair is more likely to elicit an actual movement toward the chair and sitting on it than is an image or a memory experience of the chair.

Failures of reality testing and judgment often have to do with inappropriateness of *mode of experience* rather than with forgetting or actual failures of retrieval. One may respond to an activated stored representation of an event as something imagined, that is, without an accompanying sense that one is remembering and without, therefore, the sense of belief in its "realness" associated with a remembering experience. It may also happen, as clinical experience shows, that a vividly imagined event can be misexperienced as a *remembered* experience—and responded to accordingly (see, for example, Arlow, 1959).[1]

---

[1] The question touched on here is the extent to which the vividness of a memory experience can be taken as a valid indicator of actual past occurrence, a question dating back to Freud's early belief that the repressed

An important consideration in the problem of retrieval is the organismic state—*state of consciousness* (Rapaport, 1951b, 1952, 1957a; this volume, Chapter 8) or *ego state* (Niederland, 1964; Rubinfine, 1967)—that accompanies both acquisition of a memory in the first place and its later retrieval. Besides the mode in which the stored event is specifically experienced, there seems good reason to believe that different states of consciousness (alert wakefulness, reverie, and so on) provide different opportunities for activation of stored events, in differing forms, transformations, and experiential guises. In Rubinfine's summary:

As one moves on the continuum from the cathectic organization of full waking consciousness and its schemas which are conceptually organized and typified by secondary processes and close relationship to the reality principle, toward more dreamlike states, there is a regressive revival (cathexis) of more archaic schemas of ego functioning. These more archaic schemas are drive-organized and typified by the operation of primary processes, as well as reduction in self-awareness, and with their revival the distinction of self from non-self becomes hazier. (1967, pp. 200–201)

---

ideational contents of hysterical disorders were those of actual happenings. Later he discovered that such contents are more often fantasied constructions that, coming to light with affective intensity, are felt *as if* they were being reexperienced. It cannot therefore be assumed that the freshness of a re-presented idea reflects qualities associated only with remembering. Such an idea may owe its "wonderful freshness," as Freud put it, not to processes of memory but actually to those of repression. That is, vividness and affective intensity may be qualities sustained and even implemented by the repressive process. (For example, a sense of "familiarity" is likely to be attached to derivatives of the most deeply repressed ideas.) It is often more to the point to speak of a repressed *idea* than of a repressed memory; not only a memory, but also a fantasy (or rather the schema that serves as a basis for a fantasy) can be repressed. (See the more detailed treatment of this issue in the discussion of repression in Chapter 14.) It may be noted that related issues have been raised by Penfield's reports (Penfield & Rasmussen, 1950) of the experiences of subjects under temporal-lobe stimulation.

The importance of such states for the acquisition of memories is largely an unexplored issue, although it was early suggested (Breuer & Freud, 1893–1895; Ferenczi & Rank, 1925) that the peculiar intensity of repressed memories, of traumatic and affect-ridden memories, owes its qualities to the state of consciousness that initially accompanied acquisition. Conversely, reconstruction and retrieval may be contingent upon revival of the same state, a condition prescribed by Freud as an associative setting most conducive to the recollection of a dream (1900, pp. 101–102). Rubinfine (1967) and Niederland (1964) offer clinical examples of remembering that occurred in the context of such changes of "ego state."

Viewing memory, then, as comprising adaptive processes that convert experience to residues with momentary, short-term, and long-term usefulness in behavior, residues that are retrievable in various guises (of which memory *experience* is only one) and in different "ego states" or "states of consciousness," complicates the accustomed reference to the "memory function." It is, however, a vital beginning to implementing both the concept of autonomous ego functioning and such concepts as "recall" and "working through" in psychoanalytic therapy.

SOME IMPLICATIONS

When remembering is conceptualized in classes of function (trace making or registration, storage or retention, and retrieval), it becomes clear that *forgetting* itself need not be regarded as a unitary process; its behavioral meaning is different in each phase of the remembering process. In retrieval, forgetting may mean loss of the *remembering experience* of a retrieved event, without the implication that the memory is eliminated from storage or that retrieval through other modalities of experience, for example, imagery, gestures, or somatic displacements, is impossible. By the same token, forgetting may occur as an erasure that prevents long-term storage without loss of short-term utility. This kind of forgetting is, however, entirely different from forgetting in the sense of transformation within or assimilation to existing schemata. Finally, when we view memory in its positive structural aspects, certain questions about forgetting become quite meaningless and even absurd that seemed sensible within the simple conception of a unitary memory function. One such question is, Can something once remembered be forgotten? The question is meaningless if no specification is made of the particular memory function in respect to which forgetting is presumed to occur.

When memory is viewed as comprising several functions, the effects of repression can be seen to take various forms according to the function involved. It is reasonable to expect repression to operate in respect to some, but not all, aspects of memory functions. It is possible to conceive of repression at a *perceptual* level —that is, at the very process of registration or trace making. For instance, repression of perceptual registration could conceivably involve the actual desensitization of a receptor through inhibitory circuits whose influence extends from the cortex to receptor surfaces. Contemporary neurophysiological developments offer encouragement for such an assumption and thereby open the exciting prospect of a meaningful extension of the psychoanalytic concept of repression (Granit, 1955; Eccles, 1964; Diamond, Balvin & Diamond, 1963). Such experiments have suggested that stimulus inputs, presumably coded in the neocortex, can induce a cortically triggered inhibition of the receptor, temporarily restricting input from this modality. This process would prevent the type of reverberating playback that is necessary for registrations to acquire persistence in short-term or long-term storage.

Repression of already registered stimuli can also occur. We can visualize this process as an erasure that prevents the consolidation of a registration beyond short-term storage in the memory system. Or repression may manifest itself through transformations within the consolidation process of long-term storage itself. Freud once suggested that normal forgetting takes place through condensation and that "Repression makes use of the mechanism of condensation and produces a confusion with other similar cases" (1901, p. 134).

Rapaport (1951a) has proposed that memories can be stored

in *drive* and *conceptual* organizations (residues of adaptive encounters with the environment). A further aspect of repression in this phase of the memory process is therefore its effects on either or both of these classes of stored events.

Finally, repression may affect the *retrieval* function in distinctive ways. It may produce *total* inaccessibility of a memory to behavior, or only *partial* occlusion in the sense of disallowing identification of a memory as a *memory experience* ("my memory of . . . ," "my experience of . . ."). The latter is the most familiar effect of repression. Retrieval may still be evident, however, in such forms as *images* and *actions*, whose significance in relation to the repressed idea is not apparent to consciousness.

These considerations shift emphasis from the study of memory as a single function uniformly affected by repression to a more detailed search for *where* in the remembering process repression is being exerted. It makes a difference whether repression is effective at one or another point of memory; the behavioral effects of repression vary according to the phase of the memory process captured by it.

I have tried to emphasize memory in its *adaptive* aspects, as a many-sided process of registration, coding, storage, schema assimilation, and retrieval. One implication of this emphasis is that memory functioning may reflect different *cognitive styles* of adaptive strategy—what I have called "styles of secondary-process functioning" (this volume, Chapters 6, 7). It seems reasonable to assume that memory functions are enlisted in implementing such styles. This assumption attaches importance to individual differences in remembering behavior; we seek to understand them in terms of the generalized modes of control that characterize a person's ego system—his typical ways of processing inner and outer stimuli and his means of arriving at adaptive solutions to his encounters with stimulation. Following Hartmann (1939), we find it essential to speak nowadays of conflict-free, autonomous thought functions. But conflict-free adaptations need not all be identical. At least in the laboratory under conditions in which behavior is not easily related to conflict or defense, people respond to stimulation in characteristically selective ways. Differences among people on these perceptual and memory tasks are produced by equally adaptive and equally effective modes of resolving the tasks. It is as if secondary-process functions were themselves organized in terms of rules of economy—adaptive economy—that are independent of conflict, perhaps even of defense, and specifically of repression.

One such mode of adaptive control with which we have had experience in the laboratory is *importing*—a concept developed by Paul (1959) to describe a characteristic style in which once-learned verbal material is remembered. Importing as a strategy of remembering came to light when Paul found that some subjects regularly introduce explicatory or gap-filling material when the task is to recall stored material. Among subjects who rarely show such imported gap-filling elements, some show instead a tendency to widen gaps by stripping away; they *skeletonize* in remembering. Studies show that the importing tendency is a substantially general one in those who show it, appearing in a variety of verbal materials and in different memory tasks.

Whether an apparently cohesive style like the importing tendency originated a defensive solution of a childhood conflict and crystallized into an autonomous characterological tendency is, of course, a major issue. The reverse possibility must also be entertained, however. The choice of defense may itself be predicated on a predisposition for certain modes of arriving at adaptive solutions (Gardner *et al.*, 1959). Recent findings that importers seem to show characteristics more closely associated with hysterical dispositions than with obsessive-compulsive ones thus take on interest. Counterphobic and repressive tendencies seem to appear more frequently in diagnostic assessments of the importers (Paul, manuscript).

Styles of importing and skeletonizing also illustrate how forgetting and remembering can have either adaptive or nonadaptive significance. Forgetting need not be instigated by repression. In the skeletonizing tendency, it contributes to efficiency of selection. Importing and skeletonizing differ mainly in the means by which elements of memory are sharpened—in the one case by embellishments and an introduction of redundancies, in the other by an active forgetting process that strips away the less relevant. From the perspective of memory behavior as a reflection of cognitive style, forgetting can be regarded as an ego process that may assist storage and serve as one means of consolidating organization of recalled material.

Most of my remarks have been aimed at the necessity of viewing clinical phenomena of memory loss, remembering experience, and modes of retrieval within a broad conception of memory as comprising a variety of adaptive functions. A further objective in the development of psychoanalytic conceptions of memory deserves at least brief mention—that of bridging clinical observations and nonclinical experimental studies of memory processes. A difficulty in accommodating psychoanalytic theory to proliferating experimental data on memory is that what contemporary psychoanalysis likes to call the "structural point of view" is actually an explanation in functional rather than in causal-process terms. Explanation in terms of function is, of course, central to the psychoanalytic enterprise, even perhaps its unique contribution. Yet it is important to realize that, when we speak of "forgetting" or of "repression," we imply more than function; we also imply structures that behave in characteristic ways and, beyond that, a model of the actual processes of memory. To speak of the adaptive properties of memory is to speak of functions carried out by structures, but description of function is a long way from postulating the operational rules of the relevant structures. The "structural point of view" of contemporary psychoanalytic theory does not in itself constitute a model of structure in this sense.

An eventual systematic theory would have to encompass the functional attributes of memory to which psychoanalytic theory alerts us, within a general conception of the structures of memory processes. The data of forgetting and repression in the psychoanalytic situation will come to have a place alongside those from experimental laboratories when attempts are made to translate the functional explanations of psychoanalysis into a general theory of the memory *process* by which these functions are actually carried out.

Chapter 12

Blindness and Isolation

"It Isn't Fair" is a moving and sensitive report by Eveline B. Omwake and Albert J. Solnit (1961) on the treatment of a congenitally blind child. The case is unusual in a number of ways that merit close study, not the least of which are the innovative features of the therapeutic strategy that enabled the authors to surmount extraordinary obstacles to communication. But it is the ramifications of basic issues of affect and cognitive development that interest me here, for they are among the not-to-be-passed-up dividends of a profound case history, or of the rare experiment in which previously elusive variables are artfully manipulated and theoretical issues brought into sharper focus. Adding interest and importance to the case is the coincidence that the child's twin sister has normal sight. More pertinent here, however, is the relevance of the sensory handicap to the child's symptoms (which included extreme inhibition of touch and erotization of sensory experience), the relation between sensory deficit and stimulus deprivation that is vividly highlighted by the circumstances of the child's environment, and the implications of both handicaps for ego development generally and for affect and cognitive development in particular.

In order to be more precise I shall make a certain distinction. Omwake and Solnit at times describe the case as showing the effect of *blindness* on ego functioning. This claim, I think, obscures the fact that the case illustrates not one but *two* varieties of deprivation: a specific sensory restriction or deficit and an isolation from the environment—a drastic reduction of opportunities for assessing environmental facts and signals that has serious consequences for adjustment. The second deprivation seems to be an assault on the synthetic function of the ego itself, whereas sensory deficit alone is not. Examples of sensory deficit are blindness and deafness. Examples of stimulus isolation are cases of psychosis in solitary confinement and among language-isolated refugees (Solomon *et al.*, 1961; Lifton, 1961). The two kinds of handicap are not to be confused. Of course, perceptual deprivation is to some extent always a concomitant of isolation, one reason being that the human voice is such a significant part of total external stimulation. But the distinction is still there: Interpersonal isolation *without* sensory interference can produce symptoms; sensory deficit alone, without affective and interpersonal isolation, need not.

What is at stake in the second, more critical "deprivation" is the integrity of organizing rules or "transforms" that, on the one hand, make it possible to accommodate and conserve the redundant structure of the environment and, on the other, take part in the intrapsychic structuring of drives and drive controls.

The question is, To what extent are the evidences of retardation and deficit in the present case attributable to a type of psychological seclusion and to what extent to sheer alteration of sensory input?

As for the latter, we can, I think, safely say that blindness itself does not necessarily produce cognitive or affective stunting. There is very little evidence to support the idea that blindness imposes an upper limit on the potential development of the synthetic functions of the ego, or on the construction and differentiation of intrapsychic structures that enable the organism to act and think effectively and creatively. Very likely this development is somewhat harder to achieve for the congenitally blind than for others. By and large, however, the cognitive achievements of blind people lead us to conclude that vision is a *medium* or *carrier* of informational input, but not an indispensable one.

There is, indeed, good ground for believing, contrary to the popular idea, that blindness, even congenital blindness, is by no means as severe a handicap as is deafness, for instance. Tyler, summarizing the main evidence on intellectual deficits accompanying these handicaps, concludes, "Deafness, when it is congenital and complete, constitutes more of an intellectual handicap than blindness" (1956, p. 428). Of course, exact comparisons between the IQs of blind and deaf children, on the one hand, and of children in general, on the other, are difficult to make because of unavoidable modifications in test materials and procedures. On educational tests on all subject matters, however, there seems little doubt that deaf children fare less well. Even then, however, deafness seems to be a handicap because of a factor other than the modality restriction alone. As Tyler puts it: "A person who is completely deaf is most handicapped because of his failure to acquire language at the time most children are learning it. That there can be outstanding individual exceptions to these trends— Helen Keller for example—goes without saying" (1956, p. 428). (See also Dahl, 1965.)

From such work on the relationship of physical defects to intelligence we can surmise that nature has safeguarded the hegemony of the central nervous system over intellectual functioning through structural arrangements that reduce its dependence on particular modalities. The sense modalities are carriers of input for high-order integrative achievements, but they are mainly carriers rather than the indispensable organizers of this input. The synthetic function and its products in cognitive development are in this sense *relatively* autonomous of sensory modality. It is true, of course, that blindness is an extreme sensory handicap in that it cuts away a useful, perhaps even the most advantageous, avenue of information. But we should not confuse this lack with a complete cutting off of contact with events and objects of the environment and with opportunities for obtaining reliable feedback of action and perception without which the organism's integrity is threatened. The general conclusions are that only a physical condition that acts on the central nervous system itself will have a debilitating effect upon intellectual development, and that only a developmental handicap that severely curtails a person's opportunities for contact with his environment and for mastering language will have an irreversible, deleterious effect on intellectual performance.

It is in terms of the second kind of deprivation—restrictions of environmental contact—that the effects of blindness and of any other physical defect are to be assessed. These effects are not inherent in blindness itself but are reflections of an environmental insufficiency that in one way or another prevents the person from using compensatory input channels to sustain the synthetic function.

This more fundamental deprivation severely limits the organism's opportunities for building up and sustaining intrapsychic structures that subserve cognition, affect, action, and motivation. In general, an impoverished environment, with little variety and few opportunities for manipulation and discrimination, produces an adult with poor abilities to discriminate, stunted strategies for coping with requirements for detour and delay, and a poorly developed taste for exploratory behavior. Environmental opportunity, provided through stimulation of appropriate frequency and quality, is critical not simply for sustaining the functional efficiency of structures; it is also the "nutriment" of their development and differentiation. Appreciation of the stimulus context, its appropriateness or insufficiency, is central to the differentiation of drive structures and their ever more refined attunement to environmental possibilities, a consideration that has made for important modifications in psychoanalytic drive theory by Hartmann (1952), Erikson (1946–1956), and Rapaport (1960). All signs point to the conclusion that, unless certain forms of stimulation with learning take place at certain as yet unknown critical periods of a child's life, intractable consequences in adulthood are likely. It is this impoverishment, rather than the effects of sensory restriction per se, that is highlighted by the present case.

Omwake and Solnit's contention that a blind child might

develop a different "perceptual identity" from that of a sighted child thus needs qualification. I believe that conceptual clarity would be better served by linking the issue of "perceptual identity" to cognitive style, meaning a high-order organizational tendency represented *through* perception but not synonymous with a sensory *modality*. I do not minimize the handicap of visual deficit, but I do not see anything to preclude the emergence in a blind child of a cognitive style that would correspond in essential ways with that of a seeing child. On this point, it is to be hoped that further studies of the child's development will include a comparison of the perceptual styles of the sighted twin and the blind one. Such a comparison could go a long way toward clarifying the autonomous status of synthetic ego capacities in relation to sensory limitation. I shall come back to this point.

If we separate the matter of *modality* from that of *isolation*, it is possible to say that the visual apparatus is by no means indispensable to ego functioning. That highly developed models of spatial organization and environmental constancies can be achieved by the blind requires no demonstration, which alone speaks for this conclusion. By the same token, the existence of total blindness does not go far to account for evidence of ego defects and arrested ego development. I do not believe that blindness was a primary determinant of symptoms in the case under discussion; rather, blindness became involved in the psychopathology because of a more fundamental threat to the synthetic function. The nature of the isolation or deprivation that may have been involved in this assault is by no means clear, but that is where our discussion should center.

As a start, it seems to me important to recognize, first, that blindness is a challenge not only to the child who has to cope with the deficit but also to people in the child's *environment*. The consequences of blindness reflect the manner in which the challenge has been met. Blindness occurs in a world of sighted people, creating an obligation for the latter to provide the necessary information—and language—through available channels to sustain the *intact* synthetic functioning of the ego. The emergence of adequate conceptual systems is vitally mediated by language.

Given the tools of designation and language structure tailored to modality capacity, a whole world of conceptual possibility and control is opened. Helen Keller *cum* Anne Sullivan is vivid testimony to this fact.

These considerations argue for the special importance to the blind child of adequate ego surrogates in the person of the mother and those generally in closest physical contact with him. Effective ego surrogates at critical periods are vital for all children; for the blind and deaf their absence can be especially catastrophic to the development and maintenance of workable schemata of reality and of cognitive representations of drive tensions, the consequences of drive discharge, and drive control. I agree that there is probably a propensity to unusual sensitivity in the blind child, as Omwake and Solnit emphasize; an additional modality offers more *protection* as well as more *information*. I agree, too, with the authors' impression that the libidinization of hearing is probably a greater danger in a blind child than in a sighted child. But I emphasize that the essential factor is not the blindness but rather the maladjustive consequences of a vacuum created by inadequate ego surrogates. In the present instance, paramount in the creation of this vacuum were the mother's depression and the withdrawal of the nursemaid who, though responsible for both twins' care, clearly favored the sighted child with *active* ministrations. These difficulties would have been a heavy burden for even a sighted child to bear. Given efficient ego surrogates, a blind child can develop into a much more sturdy adult than can a sighted child reared in a context of affect deprivation. The most unfortunate fact of the present case is the coincidence of the two kinds of deprivation.

Now we come to the heart of the matter. What was the critical isolation or deprivation? What is the nature of the nutriment—the appropriate stimuli—of which the child was deprived? In what specific and critical respects were the mother's depression and the rejecting behavior of the nurse involved? Is the key consideration activity and passivity? If so, activity and passivity in what respects? Perhaps the critical failure of these persons lay in an uncommunicated lovingness. But why *should* this failure be crucial? In what specific ways is loving behavior vital for cognitive and drive development? And what is "loving *behavior*" precisely? Answers to these questions demand a level of detailed observation that it would be unfair to demand of the case report, and we must retreat to speculation.

To begin with, it seems useful to assume that an important nutriment for structure building consists of stimulus opportunities that permit the child to obtain informational returns from contacts with his environment—*a continuing feedback-evaluation process through which the child develops ideas of an anticipatable and predictable reality.* Through such a process and the structures to which it gives rise, there develop highly differentiated distinctions between self and other and self and environment. There are plenty of indications that such a feedback-evaluation process is critical in learning recurrent regularities of the environment (Anokhin, 1961). Surely the mother, as the environmental representative who ordinarily affords the most secure opportunities for trial contacts, is an important ancillary of the child's ego in this process. By precept, example, admonition, and assertion—as advance scout and guide—she has a major hand in enlarging a cognitive repertory that would otherwise be severely limited by insufficient motility.

The importance of the informative feedback process generally can be experimentally demonstrated. Disrupt, for example, the auditory feedback of speech by delaying for a fraction of a second the return of speech to the speaker's ear or have people wear lenses that invert the visual field. These circumstances set off an anxious battle for adequate feedback. This fact suggests that one of the prime sources of anxiety, in addition to drive eruptions and drive conflict, is states that threaten the adequacy of the synthetic function in the feedback-evaluation process—states in which conception and perception do not fit the environment in a manner that makes action possible or effective.

All these assertions can, I think, safely be made about the importance of feedback for the intrapsychic structuring of the environment. The feedback-evaluation process is even more critical, however, in a second respect that is, in my opinion, more profoundly involved in the deprivations suffered by the child: the development of fine shadings of affect and of drive control.

One of the important implications to be drawn from the psychoanalytic theory of affects (Rapaport, 1953) is that the *informational* components of affect experience—the "signal" aspect—are critically important to *drive differentiation* and *drive control*. It is through affective reverberations that drive tension is known, and it is through affects produced by drive-generated contact with the environment that the *consequences* of such contacts are in part recorded in structures of action and thought.

Say, for instance, that the child's action momentarily provokes irritation in the mother. This reaction reverberates in the child in an affective response that is directed toward both the action itself and the affective consequences that it had in the parent. A process of this nature seems to me crucial in the building of affective structures and affect differentiation. It is through the modeling of such affective structures that parental control is internalized. It is easy to see, furthermore, that affect signals so developed can become an important, even indispensable, means of monitoring drive tensions. And in thus influencing the control and directions of drive discharge, affect structures would participate in altering the character of the drive itself and be an important medium of drive differentiation.[1]

---

[1] [Recently Bettelheim has proposed a theory of autism centered on a process similar in essential details to the hypothesis offered here. Responsiveness to the feedback of autogenic movements and states, he believes, is critical to normal growth. Autism is a pathological outcome of an extreme miscarriage of this process.

What humanizes the infant is not being fed, changed, or picked up when he feels the need for it, though they add greatly to his comfort and feeling of well-being. Nor does irregular care necessarily dehumanize, though it will tend to make him dissatisfied with life or may cause poor development or sickness. It is rather the experience that *his* crying for food brings about *his* satiation by others according to *his* timing that makes it a socializing and humanizing experience. It is that *his* smile, or facial grimacing, evokes a parallel or otherwise appropriate response in the mother. (1967, p. 25)]

The utility of affect feedback thus seems to me in essential ways coordinate with that of exteroceptive and proprioceptive feedback. Internal means of monitoring the fit of affect signals to the control of drive are essential to drive development, in the same sense that there must be adequate monitoring of the fit of percepts and cognitive structures to action and thought. Together, these means seem to me the principal stabilizers of adjustment.

Here, then, perhaps lay the insufficiency of the mother and also of the nurse: in their deleterious effect on the differentiation of the child's affective experience, a differentiation ordinarily made possible through the fine shadings of mutual responsiveness that are involved in the physical contacts of active, unambivalently loving behavior. From the muted or gross responsiveness of the mother surrogates there emerged no clear informational returns on the consequences of drive-generated actions; no language of affect developed between them and the child that could serve the child in checking and guiding drive tension. I suggest that erotization of the child's tactile experience and hearing are to be traced to this failure of responsiveness. Note, for instance, the inert permissiveness of the mother to the tactile scanning of her breasts by the child. In short, the depression and guilt of the mother were serious in retarding the child's development of a language of affect helpful to drive differentiation and drive control.

At this point, speculation parts company with data and even theory, for little is known of the subtle language of affect communication through body contact suggested by this picture of a reverberatory interplay of drive tension and informative affect feedback. I believe, however, that the therapeutic successes so far achieved with this child lie in having provided on the one hand, through the transference, a means of monitoring affect and drive tension, and on the other hand, in the person of another ego surrogate (the teacher) greatly enriched opportunities for perceptual and cognitive control. It is interesting that in the course of time the child herself very carefully distinguished between these surrogates and seemed increasingly to recognize her need for both, neither being substitutable for the other.

Because of these considerations, it also occurred to me that understanding in the present case would profit less from studies of sensory isolation that have involved radical but temporary alteration of exteroceptive input than from Harlow's studies of monkeys reared with artificial (cloth and wire-mesh) "mothers" (Harlow & Comstock, 1961; Harlow & Harlow, 1961). Though I can only speculate, it seems to me that Harlow's studies exemplify the importance of the active, affective contact that I am trying to emphasize. Monkeys develop a fierce dependence upon their lifeless "mothers" of a sort not unlike the desperate clinging of our blind child, and even come to prefer them to their real mothers. The gratification and security gained from such a "dependable," always available, unpunitive "mother" guarantee anything but an untroubled adulthood, however. On the contrary, these monkeys eventually showed patterns that cannot fail to impress one as remarkably parallel to that of Omwake and Solnit's blind child in her first therapeutic contact.

The present case offers an opportunity for a study that I think would have considerable importance for the psychology of blindness. It is related to my earlier emphasis on the essential autonomy of the synthetic function, and it involves the question of the extent to which behavior reflects what my co-workers and I have referred to as cognitive style (this volume, Chapter 7; Gardner *et al.*, 1959)—the relatively autonomous organizational directions of a function that are not directly determined by instinctual pressures.

Blindness, I have said, is to be understood less in terms of the loss of visual functioning than in terms of the manner of organizing the information provided by the residual modalities. These organizing rules of personality and cognitive styles do not reside in the workings of the retina, nor of the cochlear nucleus, nor in the corresponding cortical centers of these modalities. Rather, the effects of blindness are more likely determined by structural properties of ego control that transcend channels of

sensory input and impose their organizational rules on the information provided by the intact modalities. Would it be possible,
therefore, to speak of field independence or field dependence
(Witkin *et al.*, 1954) or of leveling and sharpening, scanning and
focusing (Gardner *et al.*, 1959) in the blind?[2] I do not underestimate the fact that this particular child's struggle with blindness
cannot be divorced from the special conditions of her family
setting. Blindness may, however, take the behavioral course it
does because of organizational propensities that exist from the
first in any particular child. This question is related to how
personality tendencies themselves determine the manner of coping with blindness. Ordinarily the issue would be difficult to
approach directly. In the usual instances of blindness one cannot
know whether the personality tendencies observed are themselves secondary derivatives of the restrictions created by the
sensory deficit.

In this respect, the present case offers an extraordinary opportunity because the patient has a twin, reared in the same
household. Not much is said of the patient's sighted twin. It
would be most valuable to know in what respects, *despite* the
blindness, there are overlaps of temperament and cognitive style
in the two children. Offhand, we should expect vast differences.
But would not similarities, should we find them, be of equal
interest, especially in evaluating the consequences of the sensory
deficit? In terms of such overlaps, it would be enlightening to
evaluate the significance of blindness in the child's life space.

One other facet of the blind child's symptoms—the libidinization of sounds—deserves further comment. I have remarked that
the intellectual deficits of the blind are not as dramatic as the
seeing person's perspective on his world would imply. Yet there is
a major disadvantage that emerges vividly in the Omwake and
Solnit report and that the authors emphasize with sensitivity—a
disadvantage in adjustment arising not from the *loss* of information through the visual channel but from the *maximizing* of
informational possibilities in an overemphasized intact channel.

---

[2] [See Witkin (1965, p. 329, *n.* 15).]

Vision helps to reduce the encroachments of drive tension upon other modalities that are less well suited than vision for representing environmental structures. In this sense, a normally functioning visual apparatus shrinks auditory stimulation by reducing its status to that of a supportive medium for visually transmitted information and is an important asset for dealing with auditory stimulation defensively.

Finally, I should at least briefly spotlight another factor that gives blindness a special significance for this particular child. It is the peculiar dilemma of being a blind *twin*. We know from Arlow (1960), Burlingham (1952), and others that twins rebel against each other out of the necessity to affirm and assert *distinctions*. The situation in the present case is different; the blind twin must discover in what ways she is the *same* as her sister. From the urgency of her gropings to achieve a conceptualization of blindness, I suspect this consideration to be very critical. She has the same birthday, yet she has experienced unequal treatment, especially from the nursemaid. Surely twinship *and* blindness create in this child the problem of coming to terms with the bases and significance of her *in*equality.

Chapter 13

On Hearing One's Own Voice: An Aspect of Cognitive Control in Spoken Thought

A once-common grievance against psychoanalysis was that it seeks to base a psychology of normal behavior exclusively upon the events of abnormality. Developments in contemporary ego psychology, with its emphases upon ego autonomy, conflict-free functions, adaptedness, and the like, have made this criticism a bit anachronistic. Indeed, the focus on normal development in contemporary ego psychology is having an interesting by-product in the other direction—implications for a conception of abnormality. Hartmann's view (1939) that the development of primary autonomous functions proceeds from structural guarantees, present at birth, of coordination with an "average expectable environment," offers guidelines for understanding impairments of reality testing when this environment is disrupted. These implications do not supplant psychoanalytic theory's earlier and still central emphasis upon conflict, but they do supplement it in significant and useful ways.

An important feature of the "average expectable environment" is that response to organized change and to recurrent regularities in the environment goes on against a persisting, unchanging background of stimulation. There is a difference, as

Helson (1959) has put it, "between saying that a certain perception is more or less independent of immediately present stimuli and saying that a given perception is independent of the stimulus milieu in which the individual having the perception lives and develops. The first statement may be true; the second is not" (p. 573).

Undoubtedly one reason why such supportive stimulus conditions have been overlooked is that they are not themselves perceived. Persistent conditions of the environment tend to become stimulus zones of phenomenal neutrality in the manner, for example, that a homogeneously tinted windshield loses its color for the driver. It would be wrong to speak of these backgrounds of stimulation as "expectancy" levels or to say that the organism is "prepared" for them. They are not *psychological* stimuli as such, for they are not perceived as such, but they are critical for what *is* perceived and for perceptual stability. Perception specifies the environment, but it can do so only because constant background stimuli in the average expectable environment make possible, in Gibson's words (1959), stable, psychologically "neutral" zones in relation to which variations in the stimulus array can be distinguished. For instance, the gràvitational field provides a pervasive background of unperceived stimulation that is nonetheless a critical context of spatial orientation. Such a supportive, unchanging stimulus array contributes not only to the stability of object perception but also to constancy of the self as a perceivable object in space and time. Continued availability and constancy of unchanging background stimuli are presumed to be critical conditions of normal perceptual development. In Ivo Kohler's view (1956) the gestalt tendencies of perception, often believed to be native in origin, arise from and depend upon such constant stimulus levels in the environment.

The adaptive importance of nonspecific constants in the sensory environment is now coming more clearly into focus through experiments in which drastic changes are produced in the "average expectable environment." All of these experiments involve profound disruptions of background stimulation. Such wholesale and persisting shifts of stimulation have behavioral and phenom-

enological consequences. The unusual, the unfamiliar environment becomes the "average expectable" one. New sensory backgrounds are created, in the context of which the functions
governing reality contact must operate, as in stimulus isolation
and disarrangement studies (Goldberger, 1962; Goldberger &
Holt, 1961a; Held & Hein, 1958; Held & Schlank, 1959; Kohler,
1951, 1956), in studies of zero-gravity effects (Brown, 1961; Gerathewohl, 1962; Hanrahan & Bushnell, 1960), of immobilization
(Zubek & Wilgosh, 1963), and of disrupted feedback (Cherry,
1957; K. U. Smith, 1962; K. U. Smith & Smith, 1962). In all of these
situations, a persistent change or lack of homogeneity in external
background stimulation challenges the organism to develop new
neutral zones of psychological correspondence. For example,
Kohler's work (1951) on the effects of optical inverting lenses
shows that a persistent abnormality of optical stimulation leads
in the end to a reduction of this phenomenal abnormality; what
before was strange and abnormal in experience becomes "normal." Moreover, a reversion to what was previously optimal results in a temporary experience of abnormality.

By thus isolating an organism from its usual sources of
stimulation, we can attempt to gauge its relative autonomy—the
degree of independence of its functional repertory from particular levels and varieties of inputs. By studying behavior defects in
such circumstances we can try to observe how disturbance of a
part affects the rest of the living system—how much of normal
performance continues in the abnormal stimulus context. From a
psychoanalytic point of view, a particularly important feature of
these studies is that they involve disruptions of supportive stimulus conditions upon which secondary-process thinking ordinarily
depends. For instance, the altered conditions may make it more
difficult to maintain the inhibitions that are so fundamental to
reality-oriented behavior and secondary-process thinking. Because of its traditional concern with deviant behavior, psychoanalysis is favorably supplied with descriptive concepts for assessing
the quality and directions of behavior in the face of such disruptions. Assumptions about the behavioral consequences of a loss of

functional autonomy are aided on a descriptive level by such concepts as drive activation, defense, and control and by the complementary conceptions of primary- and secondary-process modes of thinking.

Among the taken-for-granted constant conditions of the average expectable environment it is likely that few surpass in importance the informative stimulations from self-produced movements —now popularly known as "feedback" (see Stein, 1965). An uninterrupted supply of unperceived, movement-produced stimulation appears to be essential in effective accommodation to changing environmental conditions. One is usually unaware of the guidance provided by feedback except when it is no longer available. Consider, for instance, the immediate response to wearing lenses that turn the visual field upside down, as in Kohler's studies mentioned above (1951). It sets off an anxious battle to obtain adequate feedback, suggesting that profound anxiety is experienced not only in the eruptions of drive and in drive conflict but also in conditions that prevent integrations dependent on the usual informational returns from one's own movements. In these conditions, conception and perception do not fit the environment in a manner that makes action possible or effective.

Norbert Wiener (1948) writes, "for effective action on the outer world, it is not only essential that we possess good effectors, but that the performance of these effectors be properly monitored back to the central nervous system, and that the readings of these monitors be properly combined with the other information coming in from the sense organs to produce a properly proportioned output to the effectors" (p. 114). Rapaport's comment (1950a) is pertinent: "On the way toward the discovery and conquest of the need-gratifying object, detours are made, and these detours are governed both by the need (and its derivatives) and the realities encountered. While the goal is sustained in the course of the detour, the momentary direction, the preferred path, is determined by 'feedback' of information. . . . The thought disorder of the schizophrenic . . . is amenable to description in terms of such disturbed feedback processes" (p. 332). One is reminded too of the dereistic directions of thought that occur when the attention function, so critical for effective feedback, falters during drowsiness.

In the present chapter I am concerned with one of the major avenues of informational feedback—the *auditory return of one's own speech*, the importance of being able to *hear* what one is saying while saying it. Specifically, I am concerned with the content and form of *spoken* thought when such monitoring is not possible. I shall propose that the afference of one's own speech is a critical factor in maintaining reality-oriented *communicated* thought—that is, thought conveyed through speech. If vocalization is to be effective, its success should, like that of all self-produced stimulation, depend partly upon the informative feedback to the speaker himself. The auditory return of speech may well be a critical source of this informative feedback, and perhaps even a vital condition for maintaining *sequential* order in spoken thought. I shall draw upon some observations from an experimental situation of vocal isolation that produces a substantial reduction in the auditory feedback from one's own voice. My emphasis will be on the regressive momentum generated by this situation and the evidences of primary-process thinking.

I start with a phenomenon that is, I believe, fairly common. A particular patient often falls into one of those all-too-familiar silences that, like speech itself, convey information. I am able by now to distinguish her hostile silences from the "my mind is blank" type. But there is another kind of silence that is neither. Our dialogue usually goes as follows: "Why are you silent?"

"I'm having unpleasant thoughts."

"And you are reluctant to tell them to me."

"No, it's that I don't want to hear them myself."

The patient is alluding to the echo of her spoken thoughts and its importance. We seem to be encountering a paradox. If she is *aware* of her "unpleasant thoughts," she is already "listening" to them and in that sense saying them. What can she mean by the statement that she does not want to *hear herself* say them? The crux of the matter is that by vocalizing a thought she makes it an external stimulus—gives it a perceptual, and therefore a tangible, quality; she makes it more real for herself as well as for me. The reality and impact of thought seem to be promoted by its vocalization. This example suggests, then, that whether speech is covert or overt is a critical factor in thinking. One is tempted to ask, Would she be able to state her thoughts to me more easily if she did not hear herself say them? But I am getting ahead of myself, for this question is actually the subject of a program of investigation that I shall describe in the course of this chapter.

There are, however, a few bridges to cross before we can appreciate the full significance of auditory feedback in spoken thought. They have to do with the *functions of voice in primary-and secondary-process thinking*, the *collaboration of voice and word in spoken thought*, the *distinction between silent and communicated secondary-process thought*, and the *importance of self as audience* for speech.

THE FUNCTIONS OF VOCALIZATION

Vocalization is above all a motor process whose importance, in psychoanalytic terms, is determined by the aims of drive and affect discharge, by the representational and expressive requirements of reality-oriented thought, and by defenses and other forms of control. Spoken thought involves qualities of voice, quite apart from the qualities of words themselves, that are responsive not only to audience reaction but to one's own thoughts and subjective states. This fact calls for a distinction between the vocal and the verbal aspects of speech. The untrained voice, as Gordon Allport (1961) points out, is a highly expressive instrument that can produce wide variations in pitch, timbre, and mannerism, including such fugitive and hard-to-analyze features as "intonation, rhythm, brokenness or continuity, accent, richness, roughness, musical handling" (p. 483). Furthermore, as a *motor* instrument, voice not only conveys thought; it is also capable of directly expressing emotional states and drives without the intervention of words. The distinction between vocalization and verbalization can be clearly appreciated if we note that, although most words are objectively oriented toward things and events, voice qualities are uniquely capable of representing bodily or subjective states, and in a fashion sometimes impossible to accomplish with words (Ostwald, 1960). A "trembling" voice and an "ecstatic moan" communicate what words often cannot express.

Glover (1925) gives an interesting account of how an oral personality disposition may shape speech:

. . . as with all other stages of development, we see reflected in *speech characteristics* and in the play with words the influence of the oral stage. . . . output [may vary] from extreme verbosity to extreme taciturnity: words are poured out in a constant flow or, on the other hand, there is a tendency to dwell on special phrases which are treated like choice morsels and rolled round the tongue. Ambivalent selection and use of words is also a striking characteristic and there is an obvious preference for the use of terms descriptive of mouth activities, particularly of biting activities, the effect being commonly described as 'incisive speech.' (pp. 33–34)

To be sure, words, *spoken* words, are the principal medium or carriers of thought. Whether one is engaged in silent thought, in speech, or in written communication, words are omnipresent. Psychoanalysts of course need not be reminded of the important function of words in speech and verbalization generally (see Loewenstein, 1956; Stone, 1961). It is words that give existence or reality to thought. In a tachistoscopic experiment, impressions are the more fleeting if they elude verbalization; as soon as one finds the apt word, the impression itself crystallizes, and the experience changes. So strong is the reality-giving power of words that, whenever we have coined a word to denote a phenomenon, we are disposed to infer actuality, some hard fact. Conversely, difficulty in naming can lead to an opposite impression and cause us to ignore phenomena. In William James' words, "It is hard to focus our attention on the nameless" (1890, Vol. 1, p. 195).

But it does not minimize the importance of words to emphasize also the relatively independent role of vocal qualities as carriers of thoughts. Words themselves acquire their sound component through their close functional proximity to the vocal apparatus; we *say* words in learning words. In directly involving a *motor* apparatus for the emission of sounds, speech goes beyond words by enlarging the means of coding thoughts and of conveying the affect and motive organizers of behavior. This factor sometimes lends a touch of artificiality to voiced expression, as when a patient says that he is not able to "express" his thoughts precisely. The manner of putting a thought into words on the psychoanalytic couch may often be off the mark of the thought itself. And saying a thought aloud often makes a difference, the sound of one's voice affecting the tone of subsequent associations.

Voice and Word in Discharge and Control

Freud had much to say about the role of voice and language in relation to the delay and discharge functions of structures. A most instructive source of Freud's views on this subject is his "Project for a Scientific Psychology" (1895), in which his conceptions of the secondary process and reality testing and of the relations of both to speech are spelled out with a specificity that he never matched in his later writings on these topics. His views are particularly interesting because, without using the word, Freud attributed great importance to feedback and the informative significance of the motor aspect of language, particularly in the disciplining and regulating of thinking.

In the "Project," Freud ascribes the functions of mental structures to two fundamental sources of behavior. The primary function of practical behavior is to *discharge* nonoptimal levels of tension arising from within the organism—those of endogenous origin, which he was later to call "instinctual drives." Among the methods of discharge those that bring about cessation of the stimulus are preferred and retained. The first developmental attempts at discharge follow, Freud says, "paths of internal change," either through hallucination or diffuse motor activation, as, for example, in the vocal activations of screaming. For the discharge aim—the primary function of psychic functioning—the musculature is all-important, and all pathways leading to motor innervation are ipso facto potential channels of discharge. Here then is one important function of voice. Quite independently of the verbal links it acquires, the vocal apparatus, because it is a motor structure, is from the very beginning a discharge channel. This capacity is originally independent of the word-making function with which it comes to be intimately associated in due course, and we must expect that its sound-emitting properties will retain this capacity of direct responsiveness to drive states and their associated affects.

Survival—"the exigencies of life"—says Freud in the "Project," dictates, however, that discharge not be indiscriminate, that it be oriented toward "indicators of reality" such that it produce an *effective* change in nonoptimal levels of tension. It is under the aegis of this requirement that the "secondary function" of regulating the "flow of quantity" and the apparatuses pertaining to it develop. The identifying characteristics of secondary-process thinking in the context of drive are inhibition, selective response to reality, reality-guided action, and a capacity for testing the appropriateness of a perception or a response against standards defined by intention. Effective performance of these functions delays discharge. The autonomy of secondary-process thinking, to use the terminology of contemporary ego psychology in stating this early idea of Freud's, is made possible by the person's ability to hold onto the effects of stimulation for some time before acting upon them. At the same time the motor apparatus must be capable of being *readied* for discharge; it must be capable of *partial* innervations such that small quantities of energy will serve as signals of the presence of the "appropriate reality," which will be quickly responded to with correspondingly appropriate and complete motor release. A crucial requirement of reality-oriented thinking and behavior in Freud's view, then, is that the apparatuses of discharge must be capable of responsiveness to *signals of contact* with reality. Affective response and the musculature, including, of course, the vocal apparatus, must develop links with a signaling system through which the full discharge potentialities of these structures are brought under control.

Here is where *words* in relation to utterance become crucial. Eventually, through what Freud called the "reports"—in contemporary usage "feedback"—of action (among which one must certainly include *auditory* reports as well as kinesthetic and proprioceptive ones), words through their association with vocal movements acquire the *secondary* function of signaling the appropriateness of a "passage of quantity" (1895, pp. 380, 388, especially 421–424, 444). In Freud's view, the importance of vocal associations of words lies in the fact that vocal links convert words into motor *surrogates* of action. That is, when sounds emitted by the vocal apparatus become associated with the word representations of objects, sound making becomes speech; speech acquires a *signal* function as "an indicator of action-reality." It is when vocalization becomes linked with words that speech becomes critically important in implementing reality testing— perhaps simply another way of saying that words in the form of speech make thoughts *real*. As one reflection of this view, Freud asserts that speech associations make it possible to establish traces of the outcomes of thoughts; linkages of thought with the *motor* components of words enable one to remember thoughts.

Vocalization can be used, then, partly to implement the release of affects and bodily tensions and partly to serve the secondary process in communication. From the direct motor expression of affect and drive states, vocalization advances into speech when sounds are coded into lingual forms that represent objective encounters with recurrent events and features of the environment. It is to be expected that the nonverbal aspects of vocalization retain their value as outlets of primary discharge through which drives and affect states are directly conveyed by vocal properties.

Silent and Spoken Thought

It will add to our appreciation of the functions of vocalization and particularly of auditory feedback in spoken thought to consider briefly the differences between silent and spoken thought.

It makes a difference in secondary-process thinking whether

or not it is carried out in the context of speech. When thought is silent but guided by the secondary process, its syntactical structure need not be the same as that involved in conversation or in writing (Lashley, 1951). In silent thinking tolerances of awareness are generally broad; that is, the number and range of thoughts one is explicitly conscious of can be extensive; effective or "correct" *outcome* is the all-important thing. Efficiency in silent thinking requires rejecting irrelevant lines of association that may spring into awareness en route to a desired terminal point, but the gamut of consciously apprehended, if fleeting, ideas and associations can be wide-ranging. One can take back a thought or a word more quickly in silent thinking than in spoken thinking. (And, of course, one can do so more easily in spoken thinking than in written thinking.) In silent thinking reversibility and range of awareness are thus much less restricted than in spoken thought; it is only the end result that puts the mark of the secondary process on the events leading up to it.

In *communicated,* spoken thought another order of events is involved—that of speech—and another requirement—the need to be understood by and to react to the audience. Because most of the time the speaker is seen as well as heard, additional functions must be performed by the speech apparatus—reaction to the audience and respect for rules of comprehensibility. The succession of words in sound must conform to a system appropriate to both the thought and the audience. The number of options for reversing the direction of thought is still considerable, but the rules and conventions for making oneself understood are also brought into play.

Spoken thought is therefore more affected than is silent thinking by the necessity for greater control over *peripheral lines of thinking*—over irrelevant, preconscious trains of thought that have verbal representation—and for preventing their access to utterance. Preconscious thought may be said to consist of a series of parallel and intersecting centers of activated ideas, only one of which has preferential access to the final motor path of vocalization. One of the important tasks of spoken thought is to maintain the dominance of a central focus of thought—to give verbal coherence to a train of thought without impediment from conflicting lines of thought. The voice helps. In communicated thought, control is accomplished not only through pauses but through forms of vocalization itself, as well as through the forms and content of language. Talleyrand is said to have remarked that the function of language is to conceal as well as to communicate, and this statement can be as true of voice qualities as of words. Inhibition and concealment in communicated secondary-process thought are served both by the properties of voice and by the forms and contents of words. Of course, there are also the more primitive or peremptory concealments determined by defense, and they too are assisted by vocal qualities. For instance, Fenichel (1945) describes instances of hysterical muteness in which vocalization is completely eliminated under the necessity of dealing with conflict-laden ideas. Usually, however, more benign forms of defensive *editing* occur, producing changes both in vocalization and in the forms of spoken language. It may be that the control or inhibition of potentially intrusive ideas is as important an accomplishment of speech as is its directly communicative function; it may indeed be a precondition of the latter.

One more function served by vocalization deserves mention —the maintenance of a sense of self. Man is both an acoustical generator and receiver; he hears himself in the act of producing sounds. The auditory component of vocalization makes it possible to distinguish covert from overt speech and one's own speech from that of others, distinctions that are surely important in providing a continuing reinforcement of the distinctions between oneself and others in the environment. Elimination of the sound of one's own voice can thus be experienced as profoundly isolating (Kubie, 1954, p. 454). On the other hand, vocalization can be a useful antidote to social isolation; men are prone to talk aloud to themselves when they have been alone for long stretches of time.

The Self as Audience for One's Own Speech

That speech is an *auditory* as well as a motor and language affair is often overlooked in speech analysis. The auditory return from one's own speech is one of the constant components of our sensory environment. Just as most of the time we take gravity for granted, so do we take for granted the fact that we hear ourselves when we speak aloud. To appreciate this auditory component and specifically the importance of auditory feedback it is well to remember that a speaker has two audiences—himself and others. As George Miller (1951) remarks: "Speech has the interesting characteristic that it affects the talker acoustically in much the same way it affects the listener. Since every talker is his own listener, it is as natural for a person to respond to himself as to respond to others" (p. 172). The sound of one's own voice is not a fact focally perceived from moment to moment but rather one of which one is subsidiarily aware—a constant background feature of the optimal stimulus environment of spoken thought.

This fact has enormous significance for the development and control of behavior and for the effective control of vocalization. A child must hear others before he can begin to listen to himself. He quickly learns, too, that there is a range of optimal speech intensities tolerable to others. The child must learn "not to speak loudly," to speak "properly," to give commands to himself (Luria, 1961). Control of speech volume continues to be critical; upon it depends the capacity to distinguish between making one's thoughts public and keeping them private. But the child must learn, too, to distinguish his own talk from that of others. In distinguishing between himself and others as audience, the child learns to separate *his* thoughts from those of others, an important basis for developing and maintaining a sense of intact and independent self.

Effective control in these respects depends upon the child's being able to monitor or edit his own verbal behavior; he must thus learn to appreciate that he is also part of the audience for his own speech. Zangwill (1960) points out that the infant's perception of his own speech sounds plays a most important part in the development of orderly speech. A neat demonstration of the developmental importance of hearing one's own spoken words is provided by experiments with children that have been carried out in the Soviet Union by Luria (1961) and his colleagues. They show that the child's ability to hear himself utter "stop" and "go" instructions plays an important role in the development of controlled behavior. When a child is told to press a rubber balloon as a colored light flashes, the instruction is ineffective until the child has been additionally instructed to call out the signal "stop" or "go" himself. Children between three and four succeed in controlling their reactions quite efficiently by accompanying them with loud vocal responses appropriate to the actions; to give a command to oneself *silently* is not as effective. In time the child does become capable of actively modifying the environment that influences him by using silent speech signals, but this development is fostered by a preceding phase of administering the signals *aloud*.

Awareness of oneself as audience for one's own speech is especially important in converting other people's commands to commands by oneself. It assists in converting prohibitions of adults into "the voice of conscience." Isakower (1939) has amplified the description of the superego function that Freud assigned to the "auditory sphere." It is when such "heard" words become words we also *say* aloud and *hear* that they become more meaningful to us. In Isakower's view, the auditory mechanism keeps us oriented in the world of conduct, as the adjacent vestibular apparatus does in the world of space. Not that audition is the sole architect of the superego, but the capacity to distinguish one's own from others' hearing of one's speech helps reinforce the distinction between oneself and the environment upon which the development of a firmly structured superego depends.

Loss of the capacity to distinguish self from others as audience is reflected in pathological disturbances in which the dividing line of covertness and overtness of speech is variable or weakened. In an extreme instance of such a disturbance, the inner promptings of a harsh superego are externalized as projected voices in auditory hallucinations. Freud's obsessional patient, the Rat Man, remarked: ". . . at that time I used to have a morbid idea *that my parents knew my thoughts; I explained this to myself by supposing that I had spoken them out loud, without having heard myself do it*. I look on this as the beginning of my illness" (1909, p. 162). Freud comments: "We shall not go far astray if we suppose that . . . this attempt at an explanation . . . 'I speak my thoughts out loud, without hearing them' sounds like a projection into the external world of our own hypothesis that he had thoughts without knowing anything about them; it sounds like an endopsychic perception of what has been repressed" (p. 164).

Such a failure in distinguishing thought and speech took the form of a delusion of reference in one subject in a study on the effects of mescaline. He reported that his thoughts had been so "loud" that surely everyone else in the room could hear them. He began to look quietly and sharply into the eyes and faces of those around him for clues that they were hearing what he was thinking and for evidence of silent condemnation. When later he was questioned about how his thoughts had "sounded," he likened them to the sound from a secretary's dictaphone: The head is filled with sound, and one can easily believe that, because what one hears is so loud, surely others in the room must hear it too.

An interesting pathological converse of losing the self-other distinction is illustrated in one patient's speech during psychoanalytic sessions. Speech in this patient was dedicated almost exclusively to control rather than to communication or expression, with a corresponding intensification of the controlling and concealing properties of speech. It was as if, in a depersonalized way, she let words and sentences go only after screening before, and censoring during, vocal release. The vocal and formal linguistic structure of her speech during therapeutic hours was like an elaborate veil designed simultaneously to reveal and to conceal, creating for the therapist continually intriguing problems of decoding its message. Ornateness, ambiguity, double meanings were typical. Take these examples: "There is something about wanting to be seduced on my part which in turn is linked to its opposite" (that is, to act as seducer). "One of us is no longer missing links" (referring, among other things, to an idea expressed long before that she felt "apelike"); "I touched his penis but not his unclothed penis"; "I anticipated a chocolate hunger" (referring to what she could eat as well as to the "black" mood that it would create); "I would assume that the threat of sanctions sits behind all this" (referring also to the analyst seated behind). The ornateness was not without charm: "To have a name is to be defined in oneself, and I was never at one with my name"; "This fantasy came out of a sea of amorphous thoughts"; a weblike summary thought: "We're both kind of grim here. I am, and you are too. There's not the least bit of lightening so that some perspective could be gained by the distance which humor allows. There is a too literal adherence to the surface meaning of language so that I am always trapped by what I say, which is something I don't always mean."

A ruthlessly exacting editing process is at work here, more appropriate perhaps to writing than to speaking. She leans heavily upon it for protection, and it produces qualities that would seem stilted even in writing; in the give-and-take of speech, they are bizarre. Far from losing a sense of herself as audience for her speech, this patient relies upon vocalization as a defensive reinforcement of it.

AUDITORY FEEDBACK IN MONITORING COMMUNICATED THOUGHT

Now we can turn to the central issue: the specific importance of auditory *feedback* for the maintenance of the secondary process in spoken thought. How significant is hearing oneself speak in the effective control and inhibition of preconscious trains of thought, and in maintaining the self-other distinction? One can be deaf to others and think effectively, but whether one can think effectively in speaking *aloud* without being able to hear one's own voice is an open question.

Reliance upon auditory feedback is not only important developmentally: It appears to be a crucial factor in the control of speech. One can demonstrate in a simple way the importance of hearing speech to the regulation of its pitch and flow. Marked disorders of speech result when the speaker's hearing of his own voice is delayed by a fraction of a second, so that he hears himself say one syllable while producing the next (Cherry, 1957; K. U. Smith, 1962). Some subjects are completely blocked; some can speak only very slowly. Distractibility may be involved here, but as Hebb (1958) points out: "This can hardly be simple interference, or distraction, because there are no such effects when the speaker hears other material, or in fact his own speech if the sounds are delayed by more than a second or so" (p. 62). That experimentally deafened subjects tend to shout also suggests that under normal conditions the sound of one's own voice plays an important part in controlling the quality of speech production.

All this evidence demonstrates the importance of the auditory return from one's own voice in maintaining serial order in speech. But what has auditory feedback to do with the regulation of *thinking?* If thought directs speech, then on what premise can we assume that vocalization, and the auditory self-monitoring of it, affect thought itself?

The capacity to adjust behavior to the perceived consequences of action is crucial to effective reality contact. When *spoken* thought is the form of behavior, then the pertinent feedback of this "action" comes from the auditory return to the speaker; it is an important adjunct of the speaker's knowing whether he has correctly conveyed the intended thought in speech. What one will say next depends upon some kind of implicit "okay" reaction to one's uttered words. Perceived discrepancies make it possible to change vocalization, the basic idea of an action-correcting feedback that itself remains in the background of awareness.

A reasonable proposition is that the auditory feedback from one's speech is important because of its contribution to what Skinner has aptly named the *editing* process in spoken thought.

A response which has been emitted in overt form may be recalled or revoked by an additional response. The conspicuous external record of *written* verbal behavior may affect the "speaker" before it reaches any "listener" and may be crossed out, erased, struck over, or torn up. The writer has reacted to, and rejected, his own behavior. . . .

Comparable "editing" of *vocal* behavior is more ephemeral and hence harder to describe. Withholding audible speech may seem to be nothing more than not emitting it. Some restraining behavior may, however, be detectable, such as biting the tongue or lips or holding the hand over the mouth. . . .

Subvocal behavior can, of course, be revoked before it has been emitted audibly. . . . Inadequate withholding, when there are strong reasons for emitting a response, may lead to whispered or mumbled or hesitant behavior of low energy and speed. (1957, pp. 369–370)

The editing of speech can be recognized in the formal structure of spoken speech, as in qualifying statements, pretended and involuntary slips, and formal qualities of vocalization like nervous laughter, colorless intonations, excessive talking, no talking at all, or stuttering.

Loewenstein (1956) has described the importance of the auditory perception of one's own speech and of what we call "editing" in the psychoanalytic situation. In general, how the patient sounds to himself will determine whether he talks or not, as well as what he thinks the analyst will hear. Through hearing himself vocalize, the patient controls his own reactions to his thoughts and attempts to control the reactions of the analyst. It seems safe to assume that hearing one's own speech provides at least an important support to the efficient monitoring of speech through editing and in this way assists in safeguarding the discipline of spoken, secondary-process thought.

Editing of speech may therefore depend in part upon the auditory return of vocalization, and may be rendered inefficient by inadequate feedback. When we take away this feedback, we may expect changes in the flow of speech and in the quality of thinking. Deaf persons are likely to talk slowly in part because it is more difficult for them to make the distinction between covert and overt speech. In people deprived of sleep, conversation may appear to observers as listless, shallow, and lacking in normal variations in loudness and inflection (Isakower, 1939; Oswald, 1962). It has been noted that as sleep deprivation increases, subjects seem less concerned with how well an interviewer understands what they are saying; they make fewer corrections of errors in their speech, apparently losing awareness of the changes in their own speech and in that of others. Auditory hallucination is also encouraged by such conditions. The consequences to speech of impairment in the feedback and editing functions are strikingly illustrated by the characteristics of speech *during* sleep. The speaker in sleep is not audience to his speech, and this fact affects the normal monitoring process of editing. Unable to listen, he cannot edit. As a result, the organization of speech in sleep does not follow the usual syntactical rules.

A wholesale reduction of auditory feedback from one's voice is somewhat analogous in its effects to those of the couch in the psychoanalytic situation. The upright position is important in sustaining the integrity of certain thought functions and operations. Undoubtedly a great deal of disciplined thinking can occur while one is on one's back—indeed, some people seem to prefer it. But there is no doubt that, by and large, the upright posture and associated tonic patterns of the organism are part of an orienting structure that is helpful to concentrated disciplined thought. When one is on one's back, the potentiality for alterations in the course of associations is thus increased, though, as we know, the reactions vary (see Kubie's important comment, 1954, p. 421). Similarly, we may expect changes in thought when the accustomed auditory return from one's own voice is taken away. As with use of the couch in the psychoanalytic situation, it is to be expected that vocal isolation will inspire different reactions. For some, *not* hearing one's own speech might facilitate the intrusion of peripheral lines of thought into the speech sequence, perhaps encouraging automatic talking analogous to automatic writing. Removal of auditory feedback may thus promote detachment and unconcern with reality constraints and an introspective involvement in the flow of one's thinking. In others, the loss of auditory feedback might produce doubt, indecision, anxiety, and blocking, or it may intensify in a compensatory way and control certain modes of reality testing, rather than reducing the effectiveness of reality testing altogether.

It is necessary to qualify this emphasis on the importance of auditory feedback in the editing and controlling processes of speech. I am far from suggesting that the sensory feedback of one's own voice is the sole instrument for monitoring spoken thought. Thinking is not to be identified with vocalization (Hebb, 1958; Lashley, 1951, 1954, 1958). Organization of thought precedes expression; vocalization is a possible but not inevitable accompaniment of thinking. To the extent that vocalization is centrally mediated, point-for-point monitoring may not be required. As Hebb remarks:

No one for example has succeeded in explaining a speaker's sentence construction, during the course of ordinary speech, as a series of CR's linked together by feedback alone, and there are strong indications that his thought processes run well ahead of his actual articulations. . . . Also, in some cases of aphasia . . . thought is not impaired in the way or to the degree that one would expect if it consisted only of muscular reaction plus feedback. (1958, p. 60)

It must be admitted that not much is known about the extent to which automatization of vocalization ensures continuity in speaking and thinking without auditory reception, nor is it known what qualities of vocalization are less automatic, therefore specifically requiring such aural monitoring. It must also be stressed that *listening* to one's speech is to be distinguished from *hearing* one's speech (see Polanyi, 1958). Focal attention is presumed *not* to be essential for vocal monitoring any more than focal awareness of one's locomotor movements is essential for the feedbacks upon which walking depends. It is plainly possible that the monitoring process of speech served by auditory feedback does not consist so much in specific word-for-word policing or of factual listening as in the detection of asynchronisms between a train of thought and its vocalization, in the manner, for example, that one corrects a spoonerism; one utters a spoonerism, *hears* it, and follows it with a corrective "Excuse me, I really meant . . ."

    It seems safe to say, too, that aural monitoring is less important to the discharge than to the communicative function of speech. To the extent that vocalized thought is drive-determined or affect-organized it is presumably less reliant on such feedback, for such independence is partly what is assumed to be a quality of peremptory primary-process thought in Rapaport's description (1950b).

VOCAL ISOLATION: THE CONSEQUENCES OF REDUCED AUDITORY FEEDBACK

We come now to a consideration of the effects of experimentally induced vocal isolation. I have said that, if hearing one's own voice in the course of speech is important for monitoring communicated thought, then changes in the character of spoken thought may occur when this process is interfered with. We can perhaps encourage the suppression of the self as audience by preventing or reducing the normal auditory feedback from verbal behavior. The possibility is intriguing from the point of view of discovering the conditions under which secondary-process thinking gives way in speech to more primary-process, or "regressive," thinking.

Our approach to this problem follows the paradigm that I described, attempting to induce primary-processlike behaviors by systematically undermining functional supports of reality testing, that is, by impairing sensory conditions upon which such functions ordinarily rely in secondary-process thinking. Drive-organized ideations ordinarily checked by optimally functioning defenses are then perhaps better able to impose themselves upon consciousness. In a context of generally weakened defenses, thinking may well bear the imprint of drive-organized ideation released from inhibition, or produce an exaggerated emphasis upon whatever forms of control are relatively intact (this volume, Chapter 10). With these considerations in mind, David Wolitzky and I (Klein & Wolitzky, 1970) investigated the generalized effects upon thought of a sharp reduction in the auditory feedback of one's own voice—a condition of relative vocal isolation.

There are several ways of interfering with auditory feedback: completely or nearly completely *reducing* it; *intensifying* it, as in plugging the external auditory meatus and thereby emphasizing the bone-conducted auditory return; *delaying* it; *accelerating* it;

producing *conflicting* feedback, in which the bone-conducted auditory return clashes with a synchronous side-tone (air-conducted) auditory feedback. Disturbances are likely to vary in these different circumstances, but we used mainly the first method —wholesale reduction of the auditory return *during the act of speaking.* If it is true that communicated, spoken secondary-process thinking is rendered difficult by the elimination of feedback from one's own voice, it becomes a matter of considerable interest to know how in these circumstances the *course of association* is affected.

The technique we used for reducing feedback is one that was employed by Mahl (1961) and consists of masking the speaker's voice by a band of white noise fed into earphones. The decision to mask the voice in this way was forced upon us by the difficulty of eliminating vocal feedback through bone conduction. There are two ways of hearing vocalization: through air-conducted (side-tone) stimulation of the basilar membrane and through bone-conducted vibrations of sounds generated by the vocal cords. Deafness to side-tone still permits bone-conducted hearing of one's own voice. Bone-conducted hearing is accomplished directly through the bony tissue of the skull. Sound waves cause the bones of the skull labyrinth to vibrate, producing vibrations on the basilar membrane, as in air conduction. If the ears are plugged, that is, if air conduction is excluded, a vibrating tuning fork with its shank held against the skull above the mastoid process of the temporal lobe can be clearly heard. The auditory receptor is much less sensitive to sound vibrations through bone conduction than to those through air conduction. Bone conduction seems, therefore, in Békésy and Rosenblith's view (1951), to have a purely supplemental function, important mainly in hearing one's *own* voice.

But nature's safeguards make for experimental complications. Admittedly there is no easy way to eliminate bone-conducted sound. Masking the voice by noise, for all the problems it raises in confounding the effects of noise and feedback reduction, is the most practical procedure that we have so far been able to devise. The white noise used has an intensity level of 100 decibels, which subjects have found tolerable after an adaptation period. In such circumstances subjects cannot hear themselves even when shouting—and some indeed soon begin to shout. The subject is alone in a small chamber, in a semireclining position on a couch with his feet up, facing a screen on which various stimuli are exposed from the adjoining experimenter's room. The experimenter appears in the subject's room after each test; the earphones are removed during instructions for the next test. Each subject is tested in the normal and masking conditions during a single session. In the experiment selected for discussion here, the order of conditions, as well as the sets of stimuli for each condition, were varied among subjects in a design that called for each subject to be his own control. The tasks given to the subjects included *imagery,* following each exposure of two surrealist paintings by De Chirico (each picture was exposed for ten seconds, followed by a three-minute response period); *responses* to one achromatic and one colored Rorschach card (exposed continuously through a three-minute period); and *free association* to four words (each presented visually for five seconds, with a two-minute response limit for each).[1]

Our eighteen subjects were mostly actors with whom we had a long acquaintance. They had been subjects in studies of the

---

[1] One of the few studies of experimental deafness is that by Hebb, Heath, and Stuart (1954). They studied the reactions of several subjects who went about their usual activities for a three-day period with their ears occluded. Although the effects resemble those of our study in some aspects, there is a vital difference between the experiments. Hebb's procedure occluded air-conducted sound but left bone conduction intact. Stimulation by the subjects' own voices was thus very likely exaggerated. The critical feature of our procedure was precisely in the masking of bone-conducted hearing. Obviously here is an important comparison of conditions to be made in future studies.

[Since this chapter was written, a study by Holzman, Rousey, and Snyder (1966) on the effects of auditory occlusion on free associations has appeared. Their results are strikingly in accord with the trend toward primary-process manifestations in our own findings.]

effects of LSD-25 (Linton & Langs, 1962) and of sensory isolation (Goldberger, 1962; Goldberger & Holt, 1961a). We knew a good deal about them, and we intended to relate their productions under conditions of vocal isolation to the knowledge that we had accumulated about them in previous studies.

I have described some of the main conditions of the study because it was evident to us that, although masking the subjects' voices seemed to be a critical factor in producing the effects we observed, there were other, equally critical variables that had to be taken into account before we could be comfortably certain of the specific contribution of the auditory-feedback variable. The loss of auditory feedback may very well owe its critical status to the effects of noise and the subject's personality. The noise accompaniment is important, a matter I shall return to, not least for its possible effects upon the arousal level of the organism. The combination of noise *and* loss of feedback may be conducive to a *feeling of isolation*, abetted by the relatively darkened room, which is known from other studies to be conducive to a more relaxed, passive, reverielike state of consciousness (Eagle, 1962; Kubie & Margolin, 1942; Kubie, 1945). Furthermore, we do not know the effects that changes of voice intensity itself in the attempt to surmount the noise may have on the quality of thoughts expressed.

For a detailed account of the effects produced under these conditions, the reader is referred to Klein and Wolitzky (1970). I shall confine myself here to some of the prominent currents that appeared in the results, mainly on the imagery task, and to certain dimensions of response along which striking differences occurred among subjects. I must also limit my account to the verbal aspects of thought. Obviously they form only part of the picture; voice qualities as well as words mediate thoughts, and the changes in intensity and quality of voice are surely among the most dramatic in the spectrum of effects. For instance, in some subjects the voice flattened, became guttural, and occasionally slurred. A fair number of subjects began to shout when they could not hear themselves, even against their judgment that they need not do so in order to be heard. In postexperimental interviews, subjects—shouters and nonshouters alike—invariably remarked that they had not realized how much they rely upon hearing themselves in ordinary speech. Many of the subjects also remarked that they were not sure that they had said the "correct word" or finished sentences; they thought that they were making errors of speech despite the fact that they knew what they were trying to say. As one subject put it, "I knew what I wanted to say, but did I say it?"

A majority of the subjects were more productive in vocal isolation than under normal conditions. It is interesting that this productivity seemed as characteristic of the extremely inhibited subjects as of the borderline, tenuously controlled subjects in the sample. It was not itself, however, indicative of loosened control or for that matter of imaginative content; productiveness and richness of imagination did not necessarily go hand in hand. Exaggerated efforts at control also appeared. One of our subjects, ordinarily extremely guarded and sparing in expressiveness, gave many more responses under vocal masking but with a strikingly exaggerated negation tendency in which time and again an assertion was countered by negating qualifiers. A few samples: "I don't think my mother likes X, but I see her anyway." "Her friend called me and asked me to his house for dinner; luckily I refused." The word "fangs," which usually brought forth a host of popular-level aggressive associations, was initially perceived by this subject as "franks"; even when the word was finally perceived correctly, it elicited only far-fetched reminiscences of Paris and "of horseback riding in Central Park."

Most subjects reported that their imagery was livelier and more vivid under vocal masking. One is reminded of similar tendencies under conditions of sensory isolation (Goldberger, 1962). Perhaps relevant is the fact that some of the subjects reported that they retreated into their own thoughts, a reaction they associated in later interviews with both the noise and the isolation from their own voices.

Images were scored for a variety of contents and for formal characteristics of language and speech. Drawing upon content categories worked out for the Rorschach by Holt and Havel

(1960), we scored the images for drive references, that is, for ideational contents suggestive of various forms of sexual pleasure —oral, anal, exhibitionistic-voyeuristic—as well as of aggressive tendencies. The classification provided for more blatant, directly drive-related expressions and for more socially acceptable, toned-down expressions. In addition, there were categories for references to remote events in time or space; for intense spatial experiences of vista or three-dimensionality; for expressions of strangeness and unreality; for reminiscences of childhood experiences or memories; and for bodily sensations—all in our opinion indicative of a reverielike loss of distance in the images. We called this group of responses *loosened ego boundaries*. Other category groups indicated *sensory intensity*—for example vividness and colorfulness of the imagery experience—and *explicit affect*. Then there were several categories of responses that seemed to carry moral overtones—expressions of guilt, punitive and retributive actions, illegality, Biblical and religious references—which we called *morality references*.

Editing tendencies in speech were also an important basis of scoring. One group of categories adapted from Mahl (1961), *speech editing*, included adjacent repetitions of words and phrases; incomplete sentences; aborted words or sentences changed in midstream; hesitant word completions (for example, "she was mour . . . mourning"). Word whiskers—*"uh"s and "ah"s*—constituted a separate category because Mahl found them to be uncorrelated with other "speech disturbance" categories. A third group of editing categories, called *language editing*, included qualifying expressions ("I think," "perhaps") and various forms of negation ("but," "do not," and positive assertions followed by expressions of negation).

We found a substantial increase in the number of drive-related contents among imagery responses under vocal masking. Although raw, blatant, or intense drive expressions appeared principally in our more tenuously controlled subjects, there was a strong tendency even among the relatively inhibited subjects toward drive expressions of a more socially acceptable, toned-down, or derivative nature under vocal masking conditions.

There were also more responses categorized as *loosened ego boundaries;* more frequent expressions of affect; and an increase in vividness of imagery. Along with these trends was a particularly intriguing tendency for drive expressions to appear in a moral context of "judgment," "retribution," "appeal," and "guilt." This trend is interesting in relation to the intimate link between superego and the "auditory sphere" argued by Isakower and others: [2] Such responses may range from harsh, punitive preoccupations in our tenuously controlled subjects, to more toned-down, abstract preoccupations with "responsibility" and "values" that characterize the protocol of an inhibited subject. There were, of course, considerable individual differences, but the group trends in these various aspects are reliable.

The effect of vocal masking was clearly not unidirectional in the responses that composed the editing categories. Because the three groups of editing indicators behaved in pretty much the same way in the comparisons we have made, I shall for convenience consider them in a single category of *speech-language editing.* A number of interesting trends appeared. Some subjects showed intensified editing under vocal masking; others actually showed a marked decrease—their speech proceeded with even fewer interruptions than normally. But there appeared to be a systematic basis for these varying effects of vocal masking upon editing: Whether or not editing increased under vocal masking was strongly associated with how much drive references increased from the normal control condition. Subjects for whom vocal masking produced more drive content in the responses in-

---

[2] Thus, Isakower: ". . . just as the nucleus of the ego is the body-ego, so the human auditory sphere, as modified in the direction of a capacity for language, is to be regarded as the nucleus of the super-ego." (1939, pp. 345–346) And Fenichel: ". . . the sensations that form the basis of the superego begin with the auditory stimuli of words. Parental words of admonition, encouragement, or threat are incorporated by way of the ear. Thus the commands of the superego as a rule are verbalized . . . accordingly, a person's relation to language is often predominantly governed by superego rules." (1945, p. 107)

tensified editing. Those with the smallest increase of drive contents in the images showed the fewest constraints upon the flow of speech. It appears that the reins on speech were held less tightly by subjects in whom drive expression was not very insistent under conditions of vocal masking. None of the other categories affected by vocal masking showed such stable covariation with drive content.

Analyses of the Rorschach responses disclosed a trend similar to that in the imagery responses. Of the eighteen subjects, fifteen showed an increase in the number of drive-related content scores under vocal masking.

It was our impression that the general effects of vocal masking described here appeared in a pattern of response consistent with our knowledge of characterological qualities of impulse control and defense in our subjects. There were few surprises in this respect.

Contrasting reactions to vocal masking, and the conformity of these reactions to character trends, can be illustrated in the results of two of our subjects. One was described in a diagnostic work-up as a "narcissistic character disorder with conspicuous schizoid features, reaching borderline proportions, and noteworthy hysterical tendencies." He was further described as having "important underlying phobic features with strained and brittle counterphobic defenses. His thinking can become loose, flighty, arbitrary, and peculiar." This subject had also proved to be one of the subjects most reactive to LSD-25, showing a great deal of regression, visual distortion, inappropriate affect, and bodily preoccupation. In the vocal-masking condition, he quickly lost distance from the stimuli, projecting himself into the circumstances he pictured in his images ("I am in the picture"). The protocol contained synesthetic responses, perseverations, explosive, sexually and aggressively colored affects, confabulations, perceptual fluidity, phobic responses, scenes of punishment and retribution, macabre and bizarre imagery with an oral-incorporative, leechlike quality. His voice became loud with urgent intensity. Afterward his face was flushed, and his whole manner suggested that he had experienced a considerable alteration of consciousness. The Rorschach cards also loosed a torrent of bizarre and violent imagery. Here are some typical responses: "like a rocket taking off"; "a woman's vagina with blood"; "it looks like raw flesh, like someone had an accident and the flesh is bare under the skin"; "two mouths, like parts of faces as if about to kiss, the two mouths look alike, could be men kissing or women kissing because the two mouths look so much alike"; "I see a time thing with sand running out as if time is running out." On another card two men were seen pulling at a woman, "trying to split her down the middle—splitting the seam," to which he added, "like the *world* was pulling the woman apart in two directions." Although his responses under normal conditions were qualitatively consistent with these responses, they were nowhere near as fluid and as wide open as under vocal masking.

A contrasting but equally distinctive effect of vocal masking appeared in one of our more inhibited subjects, described in the diagnostic work-up as a "moderately well-integrated, inhibited obsessive-compulsive character structure whose main defenses are of a constricting and inhibiting kind." Under vocal masking he too became more productive. But, along with the broadened scope of fantasy, highly colored by drive-related ideation, and many responses of childhood reminiscences, there also appeared exaggerated efforts to keep all these tendencies in check, for example by undoing and negation of the kind described earlier; by an editing tendency that took the form of changing the direction of a word or of a sequence of words in the middle of a sentence; by efforts to put drive-related material into a context of propriety; or by erecting elaborate qualifiers around the drive-expressive responses. The changes in vocal quality were equally dramatic and consistent in this subject. His voice moved down into the lowest basso registers; speech became slow, his words drawn out and prolonged, like "my-y-y," with many sighs, pauses, and word whiskers (ubiquitous "uh"s and "ah"s around the words). It is interesting that both subjects said later that they had been unaware of the changes in their voices. Both also reported that they were disturbed less by the masking noise than by not being able to hear their voices, and it seems that in contrasting ways they were making an effort to compensate for it, in one instance by shouting, in the other by emphasizing the low sound frequencies that would, to a certain extent, escape the masking by the white-noise band.

We are far from understanding the shifts along many dimensions that seemed to occur as a result of our experimental variations. More subjects, more experience with the technique, and a variety of experimental controls are called for. Although vocal isolation clearly had profound effects, it is too early to conclude that the marked reduction in auditory feedback from one's voice was the *sole* determining factor in the changes that occurred in the forms and qualities of voice and verbalization. Alternative explanations and qualifying considerations implicit in the experimental design still must be ruled out. There is, first of all, the issue of vocal isolation by means of a masking *noise*. The subjects were not really deafened; they heard noise, and it was very much part of the experimental situation. That is why I have been careful to speak of being "isolated from one's voice" rather than of "deafness." It is known that people differ in how easily they can suspend a reality-testing orientation in circumstances that strain reality testing and in the ease with which they can give themselves up to fantasy without anxiety (Eagle, 1962). Effects may well depend, then, on the state of consciousness induced, and on the manner in which the disrupted feedback affects one's sense of ego integrity and of reality in general.

On the other hand, if there is reason to think that the noise is importantly involved in the effects, it is also our impression that it derives its importance precisely from its association with vocal isolation. In the combination of the masked voice and the background of undifferentiated noise we may have created a peculiarly *isolating* condition that is conducive to a wavering of control and weakened reality testing. The combination of reduced informative feedback from the voice and the monotonic sensory background of noise could have increased the likelihood that peripheral thoughts and drive contents would achieve verbal form and may have provoked intensified defense through changes in vocal quality and forms of language.

More definite and varied conclusions, therefore, await further controls. There is also, of course, the question of how many of the effects will be replicated under conditions in which noise *alone* is present without impairing feedback. There is also the important issue of whether or not side-tone deafness accompanied by intact bone-conducted hearing (without noise accompaniment) will produce similar effects.

It is time to summarize. It makes a difference whether or not secondary-process thinking occurs in the context of overt speech. The difference is in the syntax of voiced communication which is carried not only by words but by the expressive and concealing capacities of the voice. But speech is an auditory as well as a motor-linguistic matter, in which the speaker is also his own audience; nature has provided strong guarantees that the speaker will hear his own voice. Possibly these guarantees reflect the importance of a background of uninterrupted auditory feedback from one's own voice for monitoring spoken thought, for helping to ensure synchronization between the logic of thought and its communication through speech, and for inhibiting peripheral lines of thought that otherwise would intrude upon conscious, purposeful thinking. If auditory reafferents of utterance are important for the monitoring process that keeps communicated spoken thought on track, then removal of this source of stimulation should impair the effectiveness of monitoring. One avenue to regressive tendencies of communicated thought would thus be the disruption of the supportive and informative feedback from one's own voice. Our experiments, accordingly, have been concerned with what happens to thinking when the monitoring function is impaired yet the person still has to communicate—talk aloud—his thoughts.

The conclusion is simply this: A radical reduction of the normal auditory input from one's own voice against a background of undifferentiated white noise has disrupting effects upon behavior, producing an increase of drive-related contents in thought and a concomitant intensification of editing tendencies in speech. The conditions are generally conducive to ego-regressive tendencies, including a movement toward primary-process thinking as well as exaggerated defensive and controlling emphases in thought process.

I cannot conclude without a remark upon the possibility that vocal masking may have some future use as a technical adjunct to psychotherapy. In the same sense that lying on the couch is not itself the basis of therapeutic change but provides an important condition for or encouragement to the appearance of undercurrents of thought, so associations under conditions of vocal masking might, with some patients and in carefully selected circumstances, be similarly useful. In promoting a widened orbit of associations it might be therapeutically advantageous for a patient to free-associate without being allowed to hear what he is saying. With some patients it might be a condition for promoting willingness to say aloud thoughts not otherwise easily expressed; for others it, like the couch, might occasion intensified defensive maneuvers. Of course, just as the decision to put a patient on the couch is not to be taken lightly, so would similar caution have to be exercised in using vocal isolation. And we are far from the degree of understanding that would justify such applications to therapy at this time.

PART FIVE

TOWARD A SYNTHESIS: A COGNITIVE MODEL OF MOTIVATION

Chapter 14

Peremptory Ideation: Structure and Force in Motivated Ideas

My topic in this chapter is the power of a train of thought, the capacity of an idea to take hold of behavior and to influence perception, imagery, symbolic construction, gesture, and action. It is one of the paradoxes of such a train of thought that it may gain in urgency from the very fact of being denied recognition and intentional acknowledgment—that its organizing theme evades reflection and recognition. I shall deal with the issue of intensity of ideation generally but shall emphasize the less obvious problem of the motivational intensity of a repressed train of thought. Such an active train of thought may assert its authority even while intention is pursuing a quite different course, as if mocking our illusions of intentional control. The unfolding thought, meant to point in one direction, also indirectly expresses the unintended message.

It is natural to call upon Freud for examples of active peripheral ideation.

I was called in to a consultation last year to examine an intelligent and unembarrassed-looking girl. She was most surprisingly dressed. For though as a rule a woman's clothes are carefully considered down to the last detail, she was wearing one of her stockings hanging down and two of the buttons on her blouse were undone. She complained of having pains in her leg and, without being asked, exposed her calf. But what she principally complained of was, to use her own words, that she had a feeling in her body as though there was something 'stuck into it' which was 'moving backwards and forwards' and was 'shaking' her through and through: sometimes it made her whole body feel 'stiff'. My medical colleague, who was present at the examination, looked at me; he found no difficulty in understanding the meaning of her complaint. . . . The girl herself had no notion of the bearing of her remarks; for if she had, she would never have given voice to them. In this case it had been possible to hoodwink the censorship into allowing a phantasy which would normally have been kept in the preconscious to emerge into consciousness under the innocent disguise of making a complaint. (1900, p. 618)

A powerful undercover idea may preempt behavior in various ways. It may, for instance, envelop a perception in a special aura of the kind experienced by Freud as he stood upon the Acropolis for the first time—as something vaguely familiar yet strange at the same time (1936). Elsewhere he spoke of the feeling of uncanniness as the reverberation of an idea or impulse repressed long before and now stirred by a perceptual encounter (1919a). In such experiences, he believed, the joining to perception of ideas, long "familiar" through having been deeply repressed, creates a paradoxical admixture of feeling in a single impression. The novel and strange seem inexplicably familiar, the consciously familiar inexplicably different.

Indirect reverberations of repressed ideation are, of course, standard clinical fare. Occasionally, but rarely even in clinical practice, one can actually make contact with generative ideas previously excluded from direct recall and experience. Then we see the phenomenon that Breuer and Freud (1893) described as the "wonderful freshness" of repressed ideas. Some years ago at the Menninger Clinic I witnessed several hypnotic sessions that have remained indelibly in my mind. The patient was a forty-three-year-old Negro soldier imprisoned for having murdered a prostitute while he was in military service; he was amnesic for the circumstances of the murder. He was also known to have made several necrophiliac attacks on dead bodies. The hypnotic sessions evoked a nightmarish web of long-forgotten terrors—of childhood seduction, of a terrifying occasion when he had been subjected to the exorcising of "evil spirits" by a voodoo doctor in the Louisiana bayou country, of grief and self-blame over the death of the only girl he had been deeply attached to—all leading in a logic too complex to report here to the murder, which he also finally recalled in the hypnotic sessions (Ehrenreich, 1960). The vividness and passion of the recollections were reflected in the altered state of consciousness in which he described them, in the high state of excitement of his writhing body and in his perspiring, terror-stricken face—these shook all who witnessed the scene. No ordinary memories were involved here; they reflected a rare eruption of *peremptory ideas*—ideas that in one dictionary definition of "peremptory" "preclude all doubt, question, or delay"; "admit no refusal"; they are true "imperatives." [1]

---

[1] There is a question, of course, of the extent to which the vividly recalled events were actually memories. In my view, it is more to the point to speak of a repressed idea than of a repressed memory. The equation of the repressed with memory dates from Freud's early belief that repressed ideational contents are actual experiences. Later he discovered that such contents are more often fantasied constructions that come to light with such affective intensity that they are felt *as if* they are being reexperienced. These ideas may owe their "wonderful freshness" not to memory but to the repressive power itself; vividness and affective intensity may be qualities sustained and even implemented by the repressive process. (For example, one might say that a sense of familiarity is likely to be attached to derivatives of deeply repressed ideas.) Not only a memory but also a fantasy (or, rather, the schema that serves as a program for a fantasy) can be repressed. Therefore, the freshness of a consciously experienced idea is not a quality unique to an experience of remembering. It may be noted that related questions have been raised about reports given by Penfield's subjects under temporal-lobe stimulation. This issue will be taken up later in the chapter; the theory of repression must be freed of the implication that it applies only

My own interest in the nature of peremptory ideation grew out of work on the effects of peripheral trains of thought on intentional and volitional thought (G. J. W. Smith, Spence & Klein, 1959; Klein & Holt, 1960; Pine, 1964; Spence & Gordon, 1967; Eagle, Wolitzky & Klein, 1966). The guiding premise of these studies is that, in addition to conscious concerns and focal intentions, there are concurrent trains of thought in a state of activation that also make claims on response channels. We may think of the experimental subject's behavior as prototypical of reality-oriented, intentional thinking. His action channels are responsive primarily to the experimental set and instruction, with responses programmed in terms of intention, and direction sustained and disciplined by information-giving feedbacks. It then becomes interesting to see the circumstances in which peripheral, nonintentional trains of thought exert an influence, the conditions for their becoming urgent, and the forms of their incursions upon intentional thinking. Through studies of incidental and subliminal stimulation, through conditions like sensory isolation (Goldberger & Holt, 1961a; Goldberger, 1962, 1966a) that weaken the domination of response channels by intentional trains of thought, and through conditions that interfere with supportive feedbacks (this volume, Chapter 13), we have ample indications that otherwise inhibited thought can enlist response channels. The more reason then to look into the conditions and bases of "force" in ideation— the motivational components of a train of thought—and, we hope, to arrive at a model that will be suitable for clinical phenomena as well.

My intention is to consider the cognitive aspect of peremptoriness; to indicate some of the ways in which ideas may acquire forceful momentum, the manner in which imagery and action may be programmed and undergo symbolic transformation; and to view as cognitive events those aspects of motivation that we call "discharge" and "intensity." In these connections, I shall try to describe some characteristics of a repressed train of thought,

---

to traces of environmental occurrence (see also the discussion of these issues by Paul, 1967).

treating repression as an active principle of behavioral organization that can have constructive, and not only pathological, features. I hope to show how repression may be a source of peremptory *motivation*.

MOTIVATION IN COGNITION

I propose to discuss motivation in terms of properties of a behavioral unit of ideation, affect, and action, and not in terms of "drive." To discuss drive as if it were a distinctive entity that "interacts" with thought creates all sorts of mischief. It is only as structured affective-cognitive-motor events that drives are knowable as motivations and definable at all. Inasmuch as motivation involves knowledge, it is cognitive. It lends significance and meaning to what we see and do (assimilation, in Piaget's terms), or it causes us to revise what we think we know (accommodation). Conversely, insofar as cognition has direction, it is motivated. A motive has consequences, and consequences involve ideational residues of actions, of affects, and of thoughts—all cognitive matters. Therefore, what is motivating about behavior and what is knowledgeful about motivation are one and the same. Motives in cognition are not motives "interacting" with cognition; to the extent that a thought records a directed relation of knower to object, to event, to self, and to other, it *is* a unit of motivation.

Although we must be sure not to forget the insights into motivation that psychoanalytic theory has given us, it seems timely to talk more about the ideational units in which drives are represented and less about purely energic or quantitative considerations that are by now customary in discussions of drives. The pitfalls of discussions pivoting upon considerations of drive energy have been discussed in adequate detail elsewhere (Herold, 1941–1942; Holt, 1965b, 1967a; Kubie, 1947; B. B. Rubinstein, 1967), and I shall give them only passing attention here. According to Freud, drives are specific energies, libidinal or destructive, with specific aims that decide the person's behavior. The purposiveness of a person's thought or behavior is thus ascribed to distinctive energies that drive him. Throughout his various conceptions of drives Freud retained this assumption of "intentionality" in drive energies.

From the point of view of consistency, it is difficult to conceive of energy as directionally specific. When it is set free in nervous substance in the form of chemical and electrical changes, it is specific only in the sense that it is evoked by specific stimulation and adopts specific pathways or regions. But it does not itself have a specific aim, goal, that is, a direction in which it is discharged. Therefore the theory of specific drive energies seems always to beg the question of direction. Motivation is a matter of accounting for changes in direction of behavior, and the problem seems more manageable if we start with the assumption, not that energy changes its quality, but that the same physical (neural) energy has changed its direction in traversing the structures that organize behavior. This consideration applies not only to sexuality but also to any so-called "drive." It makes sense to say, for example, that hunger is a result, not of hypothetical energic conditions within the organism that external reality can only modify, but rather of external and internal conditions of sensory stimulation with afferent and corticofugal consequences of transmission, inhibition, release of action structures, stimulation of experience and of qualities of experience—all matters of directed neural energy.[2]

It must be emphasized that none of these considerations means that an energy concept is of no use in psychological theories. Nor do they imply that *every* energy conception in

---

[2] Someone may yet actually show distinctive driving mechanisms for sexuality and aggression. Indeed, Jouvet (1961) and his colleagues may have discovered an activating drive process associated with the stage of paradoxical sleep, with which dreaming is intimately associated (see also Fisher, Gross & Zuch, 1965). The problem of how such "drive" activation is converted into cognitive counterparts (that is, "represented"), of how it becomes a motivational train of thought, of how, for instance, it participates in the organization of a "wish" (a cognitive structure) would still, however, remain.

psychological models is necessarily "vitalistic" in the sense that Holt (1967b) argues Freud's conception tended to be. I stress only that considerations of energy alone cannot provide a basis for describing motivational *direction*. If the conception of energy is used at all, there must be full recognition that it is a scalar and hence directionless; it must be structured and oriented.

I believe that it is more fruitful to approach questions of motivational intensity and direction by returning to the germinal insight with which Freud launched psychoanalysis: that a forceful *idea*—a cognitive structure—incompatible with other ideas is the main source of difficulty underlying hysterical neurosis. The central doctrine of the theory was that a *repressed idea* gives rise to the symptoms (Breuer & Freud, 1893–1895).

It may come as a surprise to be reminded that in Freud's earliest theories (1893, 1894, 1895) drive was not mentioned; he described instead a *non*specific energic quantity that (he implied) had to be directed. The facts of psychic trauma and conflict among ideas were all-important considerations in understanding the directions taken by the nonspecific energy. The result of conflict was a repressed but still active memory—the memory of a real event that was incompatible with the main body of a patient's socially and consciously acceptable ideas.

The conception that the motivational aspect of pathogenesis is essentially a *cognitive* organization tended to be obscured in subsequent theorizing about drives. The proposition that incompatible ideas owe their unique power to sexual involvement contributed, of course, to Freud's shifting his emphasis to a distinctive kind of energy that has its own aims, quality, and objectives. Even so, it must not be forgotten that to this day the central clinical (psychotherapeutic) *data* about drives are still thought products, mainly interpretable as unconscious ideas about sexuality and aggression that exert an imperious hold on behavior.

Following this precedent, then, we must find a way to conceptualize as attributes of cognition the properties of aim and peremptoriness that Rapaport (1960) named as two essential criteria of drive; we must state what these terms mean in the activity of thought.

To summarize: Motivation implies direction and intensity of activity. They are its core attributes. Motivation is not a matter of external stimulation or internal stimulation alone. To motivate behavior, rather than simply to arouse the organism, external stimuli must first become meaningful; the same is true of internal stimuli, or "drive." If drive is indeed unoriented, internally generated stimulation, it too becomes motivational only when it is cognitively represented, as in a wish, or within what Rapaport called the "drive organization" of memories (1951a, p. 630). Without such a mediating process, external and internal stimulation have activating but not directional effects.[3]

THE IDEOMOTOR SYSTEM: A MODEL OF A MOTIVATED TRAIN OF THOUGHT

I have said that the locus of motivation is to be sought within the structure of a train of thought. By a train of thought, I mean a temporally extended series of events linked to stimulation by exteroceptors and visceroceptors, to motor activity by affective and effector processes, and to one another by facilitative and inhibitive signals in a patterned sequence. I assume, too, that these structural elements of a train of thought are connected flexibly and not in a fixed anatomical network; the same elements in different permutations may participate in many trains of thought.

Figure 10 shows the essential formal characteristics of a relatively uncomplicated cognitive unit of motivation or a train of thought—an ideomotor system. The component structures, com-

---

[3] This approach is consistent with Schur's insistence (1960, 1966) that the term "drive" be used only for levels of development at which the "internal constant stimulation" is converted to *wishes* requiring gratification of such needs as mating and eating. In Schur's view, drive has meaning only at a developmental stage at which it is possible to speak of "wish," that is, the cognitive format of an active drive.

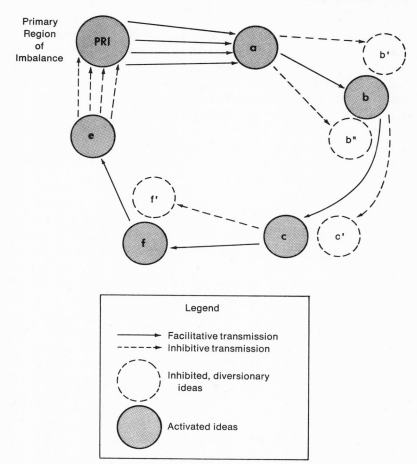

Figure 10 Showing Closure and Switch-Off Aspect of Sequential Events in an Ideomotor System

prising ideational and effector events, and the relations among them are shown simply as circles and directional lines.[4]

---

[4] Recent attempts to account for motivational events solely in terms of external stimulus properties without cognitive mediation are as incomplete and unsatisfying as accounts solely in terms of specific drive energies. Take

There are two main considerations: first, the nature of the components of the train of thought (its ideational, affective, and motor connections) and, second, the temporal organization of these components. I shall discuss the first only in passing, without intending to minimize its importance or intricacy. A train of thought involves receptive, affective, and motor components in relation to which environmental changes are produced and experienced, and in terms of which these changes are recorded. These components are, in effect, informational codes. They include records of past experiences and behaviors, including affective dispositions and tendencies of approach and avoidance associated with them. Actions are an aspect of the organized sequence of thoughts and vice versa. I also assume that conceptual codes include verbal components and, further, that words are an aspect of the *motor* component of an ideomotor system; words are surrogates of action. With Lashley, I assume that the process of thought is identical with that of action "save for the lack of facilitation of the final motor path" (1958, p. 540). Figure 10 does

---

the attempt to view curiosity as a matter of stimulus "novelty" and "complexity." Phenomena of novelty and complexity are difficult to encompass by reference solely to the physical stimulus. Ostow (1963) distinguishes between the experience of novelty arising from a fascination with the strange and a need to engage it on the one hand, and, on the other, the experience of novelty arising from an intolerance of the strange and a need to degrade it to the familiar. A sense of novelty may also develop simply as a short-lived orienting reaction toward the interruption of the familiar. "Arousal" or drive is undoubtedly involved in all these instances, but neither level of arousal nor the objective properties of the novel stimulus alone can yield predictions of the *behaviors* that will be evoked by the experience. What one does about the novel stimulus will depend in part upon the different motivational qualities that imbue the stimuli with novelty. As an instance of the second kind of novelty, Israel (1966) has reported that some people—levelers—may not only respond less frequently to a novel stimulus but even when they do respond may tend quickly to strip it of its novelty. In short, an experience of novelty is an affectively tinged orientation, carrying with it a potential disposition to actions of approach or avoidance.

not distinguish a train of thought consisting of pure ideation from one that is sensorily guided, nor does it represent error-correcting feedback or attention and consciousness, which distinguish an intentional from an unintentional train of thought.

This summary barely hints at the complexity of the structural elements shown merely as circles, but it must suffice. We shall move on to the main problem, the temporal or sequential organization of a train of thought and certain properties that define it as a unit. The motivational characteristics of aim and insistence reside precisely in these characteristics. I shall highlight only those properties of a train of thought that have to do with its direction and intensity. These motivational aspects derive from two features shown in Figure 10: *the self-closing pattern* of excitations within the structure and the segment called a *primary region of imbalance*.

Instead of treating a train of thought in the traditional manner, let us follow Hebb's lead (1949) and that of Floyd Allport (1954); let us think of the series of events constituting a train of thought as *completing a cycle*. This cycle (or, in Allport's terms, this train of happenings) is terminated in the region from which it starts. I mean that the pattern of events itself eventuates in stimulation that *terminates the excitations that instituted the whole cycle*.

The quenching of thirst offers an example of a self-closing cycle of activity constituting a motivation. The behavior cycle starts with dryness in the mucous membrane of the mouth and throat. There then ensue events (receptor, afferent, central, efferent) of searching for water, filling a glass, and drinking, which lead to water coming in contact with and stimulating the mucous membrane, thus lessening dryness. This stimulation continues until the excitations of thirst become less and less dense or, as it were, are switched off. In a motivated train of thought, behavior thus affects the events that instigated the sequence. It is assumed that as the ideomotor system comes to closure, the source of excitation at the primary region is *inhibited*.

The region of excitation where this patterned, self-closing sequence is initiated I shall call the *primary region of imbalance*.

As the events of the cycle are oriented toward the initiating excitations, it is the events of the primary region of imbalance that constitute the aspect of "intention" or the leading meaning of the behavioral events that make up the cycle. *Direction* of behavior is given by the self-closing nature of the events; the *intensity* of the unit is given by the density—the number, persistence, and unrelieved repetition—of events at the region of imbalance, as in the continuing requirements for appropriate stimulus conditions (external and internal) that would deactivate them. In short, the motivational aspect of a train of thought is brought about by a local increase or imbalance of stimulations in the ideomotor structure. The *density* of events in the structure is said to be particularly high at such a region.

The directional arrows of Figure 10 show the dynamic links among the event-structures of a motivated train of thought. This linkage can be brought about by three kinds of activation of the system's elements: *priming, facilitation,* and *inhibition.* In a train of thought the elements can be raised to a higher-than-usual level of excitation yet remain at a level lower than would be necessary to become stimulating or facilitative. This condition is called *priming,* a concept originated by Lashley (1951, 1954, 1958), and very similar to what Breuer called "tonic excitation" (Breuer & Freud, 1893–1895, p. 193). Presumably phenomena of set, readiness, and sensitization are behavioral indications of it. We might even speak of a primed event as a biasing either of reception, of transmission, or of effector release. Such priming can result from the *pre-excitation* of structural elements (as by exteroceptive input), from *simultaneous excitation* of elements adjacent to facilitated elements of the ideomotor system, or from the *aftereffects* of facilitation. Both receptor and motor elements are assumed to be subject to priming.

When an element is activated to a level at which it is not simply primed but is capable of stimulating adjacent elements, its transmitted effect can facilitate *or* inhibit. This assumption is a crucial feature of integrative processes in thought and is neurophysiologically plausible (see Eccles, 1964, who speaks of "direct antagonism of depolarization produced by excitatory impulses";

Deutsch, 1960; and Diamond, Balvin & Diamond, 1963). The integrative effect that occurs in the linking of one element to another by stimulation is thus assumed to result not only from facilitating stimulations but from inhibiting ones as well.

The primary region of imbalance can critically involve *affective states* to which terminal stimulation is directed. In such instances an affective change—an anticipatory affect—initiates the cycle; it is the focus toward which subsequent behavior is directed. Suppose a man meets a girl who strikes his fancy; she is pleasing to the eye, intelligent, congenial—all pleasurable qualities. Dwelling on her qualities not only intensifies their effects; it initiates others as well. *Not* seeing her begins to be *un*pleasurable. These affective anticipations are motivational. Together they inspire the wish to see her again. Instrumentalities of thought and action are mobilized to bring about the conditions that will satisfy the positive and negative affect arousals. An important characteristic of the requirement for balance in this instance is that it does not from the first involve simply the discharge of specific sexual tension. Eventually the imbalance may come to include this requirement as well (it may well become paramount). But at this early stage no issue of genital satisfaction need be involved, yet the attraction can be intense. The specific appetitive affects of the wish may vary, but in any case a change of affective state is prominent in creating the imbalance in the primary region (for a similar view, see Tomkins, 1962).

In the present model, the terminal stimulations are viewed as balancing, rather than as tension-reducing. This view is meant to provide for an important property of many motivations that is generally overlooked in tension-reducing models—what may be called an "aesthetic" component of a drive. When we are hungry for ice cream, we may want not simply ice cream, but a certain flavor and either in a cone, a sundae, or a soda. Wanting a meal often includes wanting to eat it in the proper restaurant, a certain quality of cooking, and the like. In our example of sexual attraction, the qualitative nature of the cognitive requirements of balance is not to be ignored. Not just *any* girl will do for this man. Furthermore, the density of the primary region of imbalance may include not simply a need for sexual release but other needs as well. For instance, the attraction may be such that the girl's absence triggers an inexplicable loneliness, a feeling of isolation, that only her presence can assuage. This feeling is not specifically sexual in the genital sense, but it does define the "meaning" of the girl's absence for the man. (That sexual attraction can be tied in with separation fantasies is a well-documented psychoanalytic fact.) If sexual release *is* a requirement, the release may itself be only instrumental, a means, for example, of providing a feeling of potency.

The point is that sexual gratification may involve attitudinal processes that were important in arousing attraction in the first place and that set certain conditions for terminal satisfaction. The behaviors that ensue from sensual arousal are, therefore, not simply means of reducing a quantity of accumulated tension in the seminal vesicles but means of achieving qualitative changes specifically appropriate to a complex initiating affective state. To speak of requirements for balance seems more appropriate to these qualitative considerations than to speak of tension reduction. The model does, however, encompass peremptory conditions in which imbalance in the primary event region has stimulated unpleasurable affect to such a degree that it is actually experienced as tension and in which terminal activity is directed principally toward modifying this intolerable experience.

Let me summarize the psychological state of affairs created by the primary region of imbalance and the self-closing nature of the ideomotor system. Motivation of a train of thought starts as a facilitating excitation in a particular event region of an ideomotor system. This excitation creates a requirement for completion. Without such a requirement, we have no "train of thought." Excitation proceeding from the primary region of imbalance steers behavior into efforts to bring about particular conditions in the environment (and in thought) that can reduce excitation in the initiating region—that is, to bring about feedback that will inhibit the initiating imbalance of the cycle. Such feedback includes reports of instrumental actions, perceptual events, memory events—whatever serves terminal *inhibition*, not necessarily the excitation of receptors. The primary region of imbalance acts as an organizer, a leading element that lends meaning to activity and thought; it sensitizes the person to stimuli and leads to information-producing actions. The primary region activates the train of thought to encode encounters (*assimilation*) for their relevance in terminating the stimulations that initiated imbalance. When no linking structures already exist to fulfill the requirement for terminal stimulations, the primary region impels improvisations of thought and action to produce such effects. (This point is discussed later on.) At such junctures, scanning, searching, and exploratory actions add new facilitations to the encoding repertoire. These additions refer to the *accommodative*, or learning, aspect of motivated thought. The achievement of terminal inhibition in the self-closing pattern is the relational aspect of a train of thought.

Discharge and Terminal Stimulation

Action upon desired objects in a motivational sequence is often called "discharge," particularly in psychoanalytic accounts. "Discharge" usually means a simple, and in principle measurable, expenditure of energy associated with a lowering of experienced tension; it is a wholly quantitative conception. In this sense, it is associated with Freud's concept of a hypothetical libido, or mobile sexual energy that can be turned from one object to another, depleted, impeded, and the like. Motivational satisfaction is often treated exclusively in such quantitative terms of energy equilibration and changes in an allegedly correlated state of psychic tension.

It is useful to recall that Freud was of two minds about the sufficiency of such a purely quantitative account of the vicissitudes of libido in satisfaction and discharge. Sometimes he took pains to point out that the attainment of pleasure is predominantly a *qualitative*, and only secondarily a quantitative, matter —one that involves coming into relation with objects that serve in effect as terminating stimuli.

We can therefore formulate a sexual aim in another way: it consists in replacing the projected sensation of stimulation in the erotogenic zone by an external stimulus which removes that sensation by producing a feeling of satisfaction. This external stimulus will usually consist in some kind of manipulation that is analogous to the sucking. . . .

This strikes us as . . . strange only because, in order to *remove one stimulus*, it seems necessary to adduce a second one *at the same spot*. (1905a, pp. 184–185, italics added)

"Sexual aim" here means seeking gratification afforded by a pattern of motoric stimulations associated with a sensual zone. Freud is expressing a view more akin to a balance conception of need satisfaction than to an energy-reduction conception.

In quantitative interpretations of discharge, pleasure and unpleasure are equated with falls and rises in "tension"; motivated behavior is then treated solely as changes in the quantity of tension and discharge as the reduction of tension. But again Freud underscored the inadequacy of conceiving drive aim in terms of simple variations in tension. For Freud, pleasure (satisfaction) and unpleasure (nonsatisfaction)—*affective qualities*—were much more important and closer to the central events of a motivational sequence than were rises and falls in tension. Furthermore, he was explicit on the point that they are correlated but not identical events: A rise in tension does not necessarily produce an increase in unpleasure, nor does a reduction of tension necessarily accompany experiences of satisfaction.

It seems that in the series of feelings of tension we have a direct sense of the increase and decrease of amounts of stimulus, and it cannot be doubted that there are pleasurable tensions and unpleasurable relaxations of tension. The state of sexual excitation is the most striking example of a pleasurable increase of stimulus of this sort, but it is certainly not the only one. (1924, p. 160)

And variations in qualities, rather than degree of tension, prevail in determining motivational direction:

Pleasure and unpleasure, therefore, cannot be referred to an increase or decrease of a quantity (which we describe as 'tension due to stimulus'), although they obviously have a great deal to do with that factor. *It appears that they depend, not on this quantitative factor, but on some characteristic of it which we can only describe as a qualita-*

tive one. If we were able to say what this qualitative characteristic is, we should be much further advanced in psychology. Perhaps it is the rhythm, the temporal sequence of changes, rises and falls in the quantity of stimulus. We do not know. (1924, p. 160, italics added)

In the present model, discharge is considered to be a *qualitative mater of matching appropriate stimulations*—of imbalance "quieted," in Freud's term, by stimulation occurring in the same region. Figure 10 tells us that the essential events of discharge consist equally of stop and of let-go actions. In this revised view, discharge simply means termination: It signifies that the concentration of excitations creating a primary region of imbalance has been dissipated through negating or inhibitory feedback. The all-important accomplishment of discharge is in bringing the organism into relation with such inhibiting stimuli. Excitation will persist while appropriate inhibiting objects are missing. Viewing discharge *functionally* in this manner, and disregarding its physical connotations of an energy release enable us to focus on its psychological significance.

From the point of view of energic quantity, discharge may at times involve an *increase* of energy expenditure and at times a *decrease*, depending on the action patterns involved. Furthermore, not every instance of motor behavior has a discharge or terminating effect. Whether or not it does depends on its relevance to the inhibiting feedback requirements of the primary region of imbalance. *Qualitative* relevance of stimulations, rather than reduction of a quantity of energy, is the crucial matter. This general notion of discharge is consistent with the principle that motivation has so often to do with object relationships—relational dispositions toward things, events, and people. Discharge refers to the action patterns that produce the stimulus objects to fulfill aims connected with such dispositions.[5]

---

[5] Genital sexuality may seem more congenial to a quantitative conception of discharge, for in Freud's theory the advance of sexual aim to genitality subordinates the pleasures of erotogenic stimulation to "the greater satisfaction" of orgasm. The special conditions of genital pleasure tend to en-

It is worth noting that this conception of discharge links up with Freud's theory that a wish involves a disposition to achieve a condition of "perceptual identity" with a memory of previous satisfaction:

An essential component of this experience of satisfaction is a particular perception . . . the mnemic image of which remains associated thenceforward with the memory trace of the excitation produced by the need. . . . An impulse of this kind . . . is a wish; the reappearance of the perception is the fulfilment of the wish; and the shortest path to the fulfilment of the wish is a path leading direct from the excitation produced by the need to a complete cathexis of the perception. (1900, pp. 565–566)

Gratifying a wish is thus preeminently a qualitative, rather than a quantitative, matter; this view is consistent with Freud's conception of terminating stimulation quoted earlier.

It is possible to see how a perceptual experience can be a means of discharge if we interpret discharge as inhibitory stimulation. Achieving an appropriate perceptual experience may promote actions or adjustments whose feedback will have an inhibiting effect on motivational excitation.

An interesting illustration is provided by Kaufman's observa-

---

courage analogies between discharge and orgasm, and Freud did define the "new" aim of genitality as a discharge of "accumulated chemical products." This definition was certainly not, however, his paradigm for a unified theory of sexuality covering all stages. The most consistent model is one that reflects his qualitative emphasis. At all stages, sensual pleasure is aimed for, although the qualitative conditions of arousal and terminal satisfaction vary. In the change of aim with genital sexuality, orgastic pleasure is preeminent, but the situation is not paradigmatically different; it is only the radical change in the *stimulus conditions* for gratification that make it appear so. The *highest degree of pleasure* is now attached to the final act of the sexual process. The conditions of orgasm become only another mode of *requisite stimulation* to achieve the pleasure aim. Freud's whole discussion of the conditions for pleasure emphasizes qualitative, not simply quantitative, considerations.

tions of "distress calls" in chicks (1960). He had observed that chicks isolated from the brood showed a gradual and substantial increase of these calls. In order to pinpoint the social factor in this phenomenon, he raised chicks in groups of two and after a time removed one of each pair, observing the chicks left behind in the home box. By the fourth day of isolation, distress calling was high. He then placed a large mirror in the box. The frequency of distress calls became significantly lower than that of similarly isolated chicks tested without the mirror. Kaufman comments:

. . . just the visual stimulus of another chick in the mirror was sufficient to suppress the rate of "distress" calls markedly. . . . "Distress" calls seemed to end as soon as the chick saw the mirror image. It would usually approach the mirror and peck gently at the mirror image. It would walk up and down the mirror with its own image. Finally, it would do something which in the test situation was otherwise quite rare, namely, it turned its attention to the food that was available in the box and began to eat. Periodically, the chick would interrupt its eating, look to the mirror, and then resume eating. "Distress" calls were few in number whereas "pleasure" calls were the rule. It was as though the visual image of the chick was not only able to suppress "distress" calls, but also made it possible for the chick to behave normally, which for a chick means to feed most of the time. (1960, p. 677)

The chicks' behavior is a good example of the "discharge" or switch-off effect of a visual perception.

The present model makes understandable how a *dream* can serve a discharge function, bringing about at least partial or temporary reduction in a state of need through events perceptually experienced by the dreamer. In a dream the particularizing effects of a peremptory ideomotor system are accomplished through symbolization. At a time when reality testing is impaired or suspended, object relationships or other gratifying states of affairs are brought about imaginally, making the needful thoughts less urgent.

An investigation by Edwin Bokert (1967) illustrates the point. Subjects were thirsty when they went to sleep, and he awakened them during the night in order to note the ways in which the thirst had intruded upon dream thoughts (the main objective of the study). Bokert found, first, ample evidence that thirst had indeed had an impact, and here we see the peremptory effect of a repetitively excited but inhibited response channel of an ideomotor system, in this case, thirst-reducing activity. Furthermore, though subjects did not spend any more time dreaming when they went to sleep thirsty than when they went to sleep satisfied, they had more rapid eye movements during their dreams in the former condition. Especially important is evidence of a switch-off effect of the dream content itself. The next morning subjects gave quantitative estimates of their thirst, and the experimenter noted how much water they consumed. These measures were then related to whether the dreams had had thirst-satisfying, nongratifying, or personally frustrating themes. The action in dreams of gratification involved mainly satisfaction or consummation themes. For example, one subject reported: "I seemed to be in a hospital again . . . the children were putting on a play . . . there was a small cafeteria . . . they were eating, and so were the nurses there . . . I was carrying around a glass of milk on the pediatric ward. I think I was drinking it. I also had a piece of cake."

In contrast, here is an example of a dream report classified as predominantly frustrating, in which a dream figure is thwarted: "A bunch of people were having an Orthodox Jewish party . . . some caterers brought in some stuff . . . two guys came with tea carts . . . one said, 'Everybody who is not an Orthodox Jew has to go.' Then I remember going out of this party."

Those subjects who had dreams with conspicuous themes of gratification actually drank less than did those whose dream imagery was preponderantly frustrating, and they also reported being less thirsty. We have here an example of discharge or terminal switch-off through symbolic activity [6] that has effects analo-

---

[6] This finding suggests another possibility: Perhaps dreams can have not only a need-reducing but also a reparative function, as in alleviation of injuries to self-esteem that occur during the day.

gous to those of perceptual feedback in bringing about a change in the motivating thirst pattern. (We would not expect such symbolic thinking to have long-lasting effects, though this matter is still to be explored.)

Intensity

Strength or intensity of a motivated train of thought—which at its extreme has the quality that we have called "peremptory" —is a matter of persistent, unrelieved facilitative events in the primary event region. Intensity refers to conditions making the terminal feedback to the primary region of imbalance *inadequate* to the instigating facilitative inputs there, conditions promoting *density* of facilitations at the primary region, and conditions *aborting* or interfering with potentially terminal feedbacks so that the facilitations of the primary region continually repeat; lastly, a by-product of these conditions is generation of *negative affect* or unpleasurable stimulation. Ideomotor activity provoked by such circumstances has a coercive hold on behavior.

Insufficient Feedback. Sometimes, although terminal feedback occurs, it cannot meet all the requirements for termination, as in a hallucinatory gratification, for example. Although such a perceptual experience does meet one of the terminal requirements of a state of need, it does not meet the others. Such a situation is probably reflected in Bokert's finding, described earlier, in which dreams of gratification appeared to produce a decrease in thirst. Such dreams may at best lead to only a short-lived surcease of the need, for the somatic facilitations of the need state are insufficiently affected; effective reduction of the need requires the balancing of more conditions than is possible with perception alone and without actual intake of fluid.

Density. Density is the *variety* of converging, but qualitatively distinct, events that create a primary region of imbalance. From the point of view of discharge requirements, it is the variety of matching feedback stimulations necessary to bring components of a train of thought into balance.

A somatic need may thus be more or less dense in the sense that the ideomotor facilitations involved in its arousal and the events culminating in its satisfaction can vary. For example, a need for food may arise simply from somatic insufficiency, whereas a denser need may arise from a humiliation for which the person seeks reparation through oral activity. The desire for food arising from straightforward somatic requirements leads to a relatively uncomplicated sequence of conceptual-motor actions and feedback. In such circumstances, even a small amount of food can be partially satisfying; half a loaf is better than none. As long as the feedback encounters no obstacle, the intensity of the wish is somewhat reduced. Things are different, however, when the search for food has a more complex motivation. When an injury to self-esteem stimulates oral wishes, food must soothe not only somatic insufficiency but also the painful affects of the psychic hurt. This complication in the primary region of imbalance—an increase in its density—complicates the conditions that will satisfactorily terminate the need for food. The food may have to be particularly filling, delicious, expensive, and so on. Similarly, the unrequited yearning of a lover calls for more than orgastic culmination if the attractions he is consciously responding to are embedded in fantasies of rejection, loss, and ego injury, for example. When one element of the sexual need is gratified, its other components may be left still seeking adequate feedback.

Inhibition of Terminal Feedbacks. Intensity of motivation develops when feedback is aborted, inhibited, or counteracted, especially when the conditions that will bring gratification are hemmed about by conflict and defense. Such circumstances give rise to paradoxical impulses of both an excitatory and an inhibitory kind. Anticipated pleasure may prime certain ideomotor channels of search, approach, and enjoyment. In case of conflict, however, inhibitory transmissions counter each such specific excitation of approach and perhaps even, in some measure, the anticipatory priming of an approach channel itself, thus making the avenues of approach less stimulable. Release may be inhibited without affecting priming. This source of intensity is, I believe, a crucial feature of the motivating situation in a *repressed train of thought*: A reduction may or may not be brought about in the stimulation of anticipatory gratification (the wish), but its direct switch-off through approaches to terminal objects is prevented. Circumstances of aborted feedback and the excitation of negative affect are central aspects of the motivational power of repressed trains of thought.

Unpleasant Affect. To the conditions making for intensity of a primary region of imbalance must be added a fourth source of peremptoriness in motivated thought: the excitation of unpleasant affect. The stimulation of negative affect may come about in a variety of ways. For instance, anticipated pleasure may itself stimulate a reciprocal negative anticipation of unpleasurable consequences, as in a guilt-ridden person to whom every success brings self-castigation. Earlier we met with another condition of affectively generated intensity, as when thinking of a lover intensifies the poignant unpleasure of absence. Another possibility is that continuous thwarting of anticipatory pleasure, as by insufficient feedback, unrelieved density, or continual counteraction, results in such an affective by-product as the stimulation of an "unpleasure center."

In general, when a primary region of imbalance stimulates negative affect, cessation of such unpleasure becomes particularly urgent. There ensue insistent efforts to achieve a situation in which the feedbacks from perception and behavior will terminate the negative affect. For example, when the thwarting of a wish becomes a source of unpleasure, the person may search for lesser satisfactions within the same domain, or change the stimulus context so that arousal of such wishes becomes less likely, or even redouble his efforts in the painful direction. The problem of how negative affect is handled becomes even more complex if the positive stimulations of anticipated pleasure are not easily stilled despite the unpleasant affect stimulated in their wake, a circumstance that quite typically arises with active, repressed trains of thought.

MOTIVATIONAL ATTRIBUTES OF REPRESSED TRAINS OF THOUGHT

A train of thought caught up in conflict and repression may be especially intense and motivating. Treating repression as a source of motivation seems paradoxical, for repression has come to suggest forgetting, a shunting aside of threatening contents. But to view repression simply in such negative terms is to overlook equally important properties of its motivational power. The forgetting that occurs in repression is quite different from the ordinary kind; ideas forgotten through repression have quite a different status from ideas subject to ordinary forgetting. Of the small daily outlays of money I make for carfare, lunch, and so on, I have for the most part no conscious recollection at night. I could, perhaps, recall how much I spend and for what I spend it, but ordinarily these minor acts do not have sufficient importance to keep their mental record long intact. But it is obvious that the process by which a *repressed memory* remains unconscious is quite different from the quiet and passive fading of impressions of insignificant events. When, for instance, a repressed wish produces a powerful compulsion or a blatant parapraxis, we cannot believe that it has lost its basic organization. Normal processes of wear and tear to which indifferent memories are subject have little effect upon the repressed memory, which, in Freud's view, stays bright and fresh though inaccessible.

Its very status as *repressed* is what gives such a train of thought special impetus and unique properties. As with any other motivated train of thought, repressed ideation in an activated condition compels sensorimotor adjustments. Despite this similarity, however, it has distinctive qualities that reflect the aims of repression.[7]

It will be useful to examine some features of repression before confronting the present model with them.

The *blocking of action* relevant to a wish is crucial once a repression has been established. In a typical situation involving an already structured repression, the approach tendencies of a wish are incompatible with aversive tendencies that are also

---

[7] For convenience, I frame this description of repression in functional terms of aims and objectives. I do not reject the possibility that the relationship can be stated cybernetically, in terms of a structural model with appropriate antecedent and consequent conditions.

activated. Approach tendencies relate to potentially suitable objects and positive affects; they are repeatedly triggered, and they constitute a persistently active disposition toward completion. At the same time, they are inhibited, so that completion is blocked. Presumably, anxiety is itself stimulated by the anticipatory primings of the wish; in Freud's words, anxiety is "a signal announcing a situation of danger" (1933, p. 85). Freud seems to have believed that such anticipatory unpleasure, one form of which is anxiety perhaps aroused along with the anticipatory pleasure, causes the inhibition. The dangers thus announced are more than enough to counteract the impulsions of the wish. (Freud called these cardinal dangers the "motives" of repression.) We are not conscious of the elements of a repressed idea, Freud taught, not simply because something is missing but because of an active counterforce, often called "resistance."

It is only to be expected that among the processes affected by repression are those that ordinarily assist approach, choice, and action—particularly awareness and attention. Freud assumed that focal awareness brings us closer to action: Therefore one means of warding off temptation is through the control of awareness and attention. The inhibition stirred by anticipatory anxiety affects conscious experience and produces such behavioral signs of cognitive failure as misconceiving, forgetting, and misjudging.

When a repressed wish is activated, incoming information related to the wish's fulfillment triggers an inhibition of awareness. In its extreme form, this inhibition makes unacceptable any perception, action, or memory, including its verbal links, that would potentially open a way toward gratifying but pain-associated fulfillment. Perceptual or other clues that can signal an opportunity for unwelcome consummation are dealt with by diverting awareness from connections to the wish and its associated pleasure. Not uncommonly in such circumstances, a person knows that he wants or fears something, but he does not know what. This feature of producing gaps in conscious experience is a crucial aspect of the repressive process.

Freud's emphasis on the inhibition of awareness in repression testifies to his respect for conscious processes in guiding action. Indeed, a principal psychoanalytic weapon for combating repression is to attempt to redirect attention and awareness to precisely those points of resistance that have been created by repression (Freud, 1916–1917).

Another way to describe the relevance of consciousness is to say that repression prevents us from *understanding the significance* that an event might have for implementing a tabooed wish. Failure to comprehend conceptual, perceptual, or instrumental links of a wish serves the defensive function of the repression. No clue must be comprehended if awareness of it would bring one closer to the tabooed consummation and its associated pleasure. One may even say that this failure of comprehension is the central accomplishment of a successful repression. A person may act in terms of a wish if he avoids painful affect by not recognizing it as such. Some forms of acting out, indeed, do have this property. The failure of comprehension can come about through one or another ego function, not necessarily through failures of memory alone. The required loss of comprehension may thus be achieved by a perceptual failure, by breaks in awareness of causal sequences, by miscarriages of judgment (producing attitudes of naïveté), and so on—according to what is best suited to the circumstances. Various strategies of interference with comprehension form the defining features of many defenses and symptoms arising from repression. A phobia is thus a behavioral pattern in which repression ensures through fear the failure to comprehend a wish and the quashing of actions necessary to satisfy it.

In this account and in the discussion to follow, it will be evident that I am regressing to a period of psychoanalytic theory in which repression was thought to be the basis of all forms of defense. I believe that there is economy in the older conception: a blocked wish associated with anticipated pleasure and unpleasurable affects (such as anticipatory anxiety) leads to substitute activities, corresponding in part to what later were construed as defenses and in part to surrogate forms of discharge of the wish itself. (The role of displacement in the process is discussed later.) Defenses, in this view, are a means or strategy of implementing a repression. For instance, an intellectualizing defense (Freud, 1916–1917, p. 288) at work in the psychoanalytic situation is a good example. In the unaccustomed position of lying on the couch and committed to free association, the patient feels the stirrings of unwelcome thoughts; automatically, a block is instituted, consisting of a flood of far-fetched, irrelevant ideation that operates as a kind of sanctuary. Other varieties of defense also become readily understandable as different ways in which repression is accomplished.

Earlier in the chapter I described an activated wish as involving an anticipated pleasurable affect. We must, therefore, ask about the status of this affect when a wish, though repressed, is in a state of activation. The dominant affective condition of a repressed wish is, of course, the unpleasure associated with fulfillment of the wish, one form of which is the anxiety that is anticipatorily excited. For Freud, this unpleasure was a cardinal fact of repression: Repression, he said, is a process of avoiding the carrying through of a wish whose "fulfilment . . . would no longer generate an affect of pleasure but of unpleasure" (1900, p. 604).

Freud goes on to say that *"it is precisely this transformation of affect* [into unpleasure] *which constitutes the essence of what we term 'repression'"* (1900, p. 604). This statement raises the question whether anticipatory pleasure is completely eradicated when a repressed wish is active. We need not assume so. Although it is, of course, possible that in some forms of repressive activity, anticipatory pleasure is completely done away with and the affect aroused is unpleasure alone, in others pleasure might continue to exist, but without awareness. Freud (1915b) did argue that an "unconscious *affect*" is a contradiction in terms—an argument he had rejected when applied to ideas. It seems to me necessary, however, to assume that affect, at least in its informational and signal functions, can exist without awareness. There are good clinical reasons for assuming it and no good reasons why we should not. Thus, either the positive or the negative affect, both, or neither could be more or less fully in awareness. Clinically, we can observe cases of each of these four types, ranging from the affect-ridden, stormy hysteric who feels both pleasant excitement and dread and understands neither, to the flat, inhibited hysteric who feels nothing. Furthermore, many activities best interpreted as *displacements* of repressed wishes seem to have pleasurable components, as if displacement itself accomplished a circumvention of the taboo on the specific object but not of the taboo on the pleasure associated with it—as long as its significance is not comprehended.

It thus seems reasonable to interpret Freud's statement in the less extreme sense: The essential aspect of repression is not that the pleasure once associated with wish fulfillment is no longer evoked but that this anticipatory pleasure is more than matched by anticipatory signals of the intolerably painful affect that will follow if the wish is fulfilled. At any rate, the status of the pleasure component of the wish may differ, creating variations in repressive activity according to whether or not pleasure is achieved. The motivational consequences of repression vary with the fates of the affects involved.

The facets of repression already described bring certain misconceptions of repression into proper focus. One is the common view that repression has strictly to do with memory and that its effects are mainly those of forgetting. This equation is probably made because of Freud's early assumptions, first, that repressed memories underlay neuroses and, second, that the undoing of repression in this sense alone is the main task of analysis. His later systematic accounts of repression (1915a, 1915b) do not confine the concept to the functional domain of memory, however. And, indeed, contemporary psychoanalytic objectives in therapy interpret the task of "undoing repression" in a way more in accordance with the broader conception just outlined—as a process capable of involving a variety of ego functions. To "undo a repression" can mean, for example, to bring about the perception and therefore comprehension of a causal link to which the person has previously been impervious.

Furthermore, even when the workings of repression do involve memory, it is misleading to refer to their effects as simply forgetting. The key point is that repression does not so much erase a memory as it prevents conscious access to memory and its verbal surrogates, resulting in failures of recall and recognition. But inability to recall is not necessarily the same as forgetting. Forgetting, at least normal forgetting, involves either temporary or permanent unavailability, the latter because the memory has been partly dissipated through absorption and assimilation within the continuing record of experience. Generally when a memory is repressed, permanent forgetting in this sense is prevented: "ideas which have become pathological have persisted with such freshness and affective strength because they have been denied the normal wearing-away processes by means of abreaction and reproduction in states of uninhibited association" (Breuer & Freud, 1893, p. 11). In the case of the necrophiliac to whom I referred earlier, the disclosure of material for which the patient had previously been amnesic showed not only that he retained early experiences but also that tendencies to action associated with them were rigidly linked to occurrences in his present situation. As Schlesinger (1964) summarizes: "Repression is as much a form of memory as it is a form of forgetting. It implies a form of memory storage which violates all the usual logical principles of memory organization." Not being recalled or recallable, the memories are not corrected and assimilated and, furthermore, are retained in a motivating (and inhibitory) capacity. Ideas experienced as peremptory, the signs of which are vividness, persistence, and affectivity, often show no obvious signs of originating in such repressed ideation.

Another misconception of repression is that it is simply a process of avoiding painful feelings. It is hard to see how an organism that blocked out awareness of everything unpleasant could survive, for the perception of pain and the remembering of painful incidents are necessary conditions of life. The only pain involved in repression is that connected with a tabooed wish; the pleasure associated with that wish is proscribed or associated with an intolerable anxiety. (One might speculate that experimental psychologists' focus on the assumed connection of forgetting with negative affect—completely neglecting the forbidden wish—is itself an instance of repression!) Of course, it is much more difficult to deal with a tabooed wish than with a painful affect in a laboratory.

So far, I have dwelt mainly upon the inhibitory activity of a repressed ideational system that blocks action, closes off comprehension of the wish, and mutes conscious echoes of approaches to the wished-for object. But Freud tells us that the impulse, though blocked, can remain active; the anticipatory components of the wish then require resolution. We must therefore give more attention to this second, more positive side of the activity—the consequences of repression for action. It is an aspect of repression that is sometimes neglected even in psychoanalytic discussions, perhaps because of a preference among theorists for examining its inhibitory aspect as a defense distinctive from others. Yet Freud said:

. . . we are inclined . . . to forget too readily that repression does not hinder the instinctual representative from continuing to exist in the unconscious, from organizing itself further, putting out derivatives and establishing connections. Repression in fact interferes only with the relation of the instinctual representative to *one* psychical system, namely, to that of the conscious. . . .

. . . it is not even correct to suppose that repression withholds from the conscious *all* the derivatives of what was primally repressed. (1915a, p. 149)

It is characteristic of the peremptoriness created by contradictory excitations of repressed ideation (incipient approach and perhaps even anticipatory pleasure, and contradictory avoidance and anticipatory anxiety) that it is, in Piaget's terms, primarily *assimilative* rather than accommodative in its behavioral effects. For him, the conscious implementation of a wish is an important accompaniment, even a requirement, of accommodative behavior. But in a repressed train of thought the accommodative processes of decision and choice are in abeyance. A repressed train of thought is usually impervious to changes wrought by interaction with the environment; it colors encounters with objects and events with its own meanings—the "pull of the repressed," as Freud called it—rather than being itself much modified by such encounters. Another way to put it is to say that the activity of a repressed train of thought is peculiarly resistant to extinction: ". . . the instinctual representative develops with less interference and more profusely if it is withdrawn by repression from conscious influence. It proliferates in the dark, as it were, and takes on extreme forms of expression . . ." (Freud, 1915a, p. 149).

An important point to remember, accounting for the varieties of assimilative activity induced by repression, is that the principal taboo is not necessarily on the pleasure experience itself but on the *content* or object of pleasure. It is possible, therefore, for the pleasure experience to be achieved through displacement while the person fails to comprehend what his good feeling really is related to. Conversely, some frigid, hysterical patients can indulge in promiscuous sexual behavior associated with incestuous fantasies if the sex is not experienced as enjoyable. Fulfillment of the act is dissociated from the pleasure and is therefore permissible.

Its nonaccommodative quality distinguishes the peremptoriness of repressed ideation from the pressure that can occur in a voluntary train of thought. In voluntary, or intentional, thinking, urgency of directed effort may be experienced in direct proportion to the obstacles encountered. When we make our way with determination toward an object, anticipation of outcome is another part of the "forceful" property of the idea itself. In a repressed train of thought, resolution of the anomalous pleasure-unpleasure impasse is the all-important objective, and it may override realistic considerations. As we shall see, it may induce symbolic transformations, if by this means the resolving feedbacks are achieved. Furthermore, experienced tension is not the measure of the peremptoriness of a repressed idea. In fact, action instigated by a repressed idea is often characterized by the apparent absence of intention and "pressure."

Let us now bring some of the descriptive facts about the activity of a repression a bit more closely into relation with the model that we have drawn of a motivated train of thought.

Arousal of the wish includes primings of representations of

gratifying objects, along with anticipatory pleasure. The primings create an assimilative field of sensitization to particular classes of stimulation; objects and events are encoded for their relevance to the wish. Activations are interrupted before they have reached the point of action, yet without affecting the reiterative, anticipatory priming. The inhibitory aspect of repressive activity determines that memories, perceptions, judgments are dealt with in a manner that will produce, at critical junctures of approach, failures of comprehension in regard to the wish-satisfying object and its associated gratification. Interruption—the inhibitory side of repressive activity—produces behaviors of the following kinds: gaps in awareness or failures of attention, as in failures of memory and perceptual scotomata; failures to comprehend connections, as in not seeing causal links, misremembering, or misperceiving; diversionary behavior that helps to evade or reduce painful affect; blocking of action, as in mutually canceling acts in which an approach is negated by an avoidance, or as in the kind of defense in which action is blocked by purely intellectualizing thought.

The intensity of a repressed train of thought arises from a unique condition of imbalance when inhibitory excitations block action and access to the circumstances of fulfillment, paradoxically ensuring continual increments of anticipatory affect. Although they are not consciously comprehensible, the component ideas nonetheless maintain their motivating and excitatory capacity.

A distinguishing feature of a repressed train of thought, as contrasted with other motivational states, is that it brings into the picture *two sets* of inhibitory processes: those that *block* the actions of fulfillment and those that *terminate or switch off* the excitatory conditions of the activated train of thought as a whole. Aroused anxiety does not turn off the wish but makes ordinary outlets unavailable; the wish's anticipatory approach tendencies continue to be active.

The switch-off of a *repressed train of thought* therefore has a unique requirement: It must occur without endangering the repression. Conditions that will cancel out the initiating excitations without allowing *direct* approaches to, perceptual contact with, action upon, or gratification from a wished-for object are sought. The inhibitory activity itself involves affective feedbacks that also influence the conditions of suitable switch-off or termination. With such paradoxical requirements, it is easy to see that an activated repressed train of thought compels unusual sensorimotor adjustments. Terminal events must be similar enough to the wished-for activity to make possible the switch-off, yet dissimilar enough to allow perceptual experience without the release of anxiety. This is a prescription for displacement. Displacements are typical by-products of repressive activity. As we shall see, there are several possibilities for surrogate termination—behavioral attempts that switch off the activation of the repressed idea yet evade the anxiety consequent upon direct fulfillment wholly or in part. Without threatening to undo the primary repression, successful defense in such instances alleviates the imbalances caused by it. Such alleviation reflects the synthesizing aspect of repressive activity.

Positive and negative affects contribute to the peremptoriness of a repressed train of thought. The interruption of an ideomotor system's activity is associated with unpleasure in various forms, anxiety being one and guilt another. The transformations of affect that occur in active repressed ideation are important to the latter's motivational effects. For example, some compulsions can be viewed as resultants of a pair of contradictory *affects*—the anticipatory pleasure of the repressed wish and the unpleasure originating in an ethical or aesthetic standard requiring that the wish be inhibited.

Some variations of repressive activity in respect to affect may be mentioned. First, in some instances *anticipatory pleasure is unaffected by the blocking of actions.* The inhibitions of repression need not affect pleasurable anticipatory stimulations, nor anticipatory primings generally, but only certain specific objects of pleasure. Displacement exemplifies such a condition when the pleasure-giving objects are beyond the "recognition span" of the

inhibitive process guarding against direct fulfillment. The behaviors terminating the cycle consist mainly of conditions that
consummate the pleasurable affect.

Second, there are times when *only negative affect is aroused
by activating the tabooed wish.* In such cases, the switch-off
behaviors that develop are not displacements of a gratifying kind
but are directed toward canceling the *negative* affect. Certain
forms of defense like *undoing* seem to be of this nature.

Third, activation of the wish sometimes produces *arousal of
both positive and negative affects.* The behavioral manifestation
of such a condition is illustrated in abulia, a condition in which
affects associated with love and hate are in continuous
opposition.[8]

Fourth, unrelieved activation of unpleasure may produce an
amplification of the negative affect to the point of painful tension.
The more cycles of activation a person goes through without
attaining satisfactory switch-off because of persistent repressive
activity, the more the impulses may excite unpleasant affect. The
persistent blocking and building up of negative affect can give
rise not only to anxiety but to a conscious experience of a tension
to be reduced (experiences of tension are not an inevitable development of repressive activity). Such an affective by-product

---

[8] The first effect of this strange constellation is a sort of weakness of will,
especially an inability to make decisions in matters pertaining to love, for the
unconsciously aroused hostility produces an inhibition in carrying out all
those actions for which love would be the compelling motive. Important and
decisive actions are thus put off, and those of minor importance are carried
out uncertainly, irresolutely, and without any sense of satisfaction and finality. In order to evade major love decisions, the patient typically concentrates
on matters preparatory to deciding. But even then irresolution and inde-
cisiveness display themselves, and he is unable to achieve anything final.
Sometimes the displacement activities give expression to a hostile impulse,
sometimes to a tender one, but the rule is that the activity that becomes
compulsive is of a sort to give the hostile and tender impulses a more or less
simultaneous release, and thus represents a sort of compromise between
them.

adds intensity to the repressed train of thought, creating an urgent requirement for terminal feedback—for stimuli that would switch off the negative affect. Such conditions of intensified negative affect, rising to consciousness in the form of an experience of tension, can result in impulsive acting out whose "aim" is not to gratify the pleasurable affect of the wish but to mitigate the negative affect itself—reducing the tension experience. Such acting-out behaviors may result in temporary termination of the aroused wish, followed by intense remorse.

This outline completes the picture of the motivational effect of an activated repressed train of thought. It has two important aspects: blocking of a conscious train of thought, and the production of switch-off behaviors through development of facilitative excitations. The former is motivational only in the broadest sense of the term, for it is the negating or inhibiting side of repression that interferes with the completion of an ideomotor cycle—the failures of comprehension in respect to ideas and actions that are congruent with the active, repressed idea. The second—partial terminations via displacement—is more strictly motivational, bringing about change of behavioral direction.

Figures 11 and 12 illustrate Freud's conception of the "pull of the repressed"—interference with closure of an ideomotor system brought about by repressed ideation. (How the repression takes place in the first place is not relevant here, for we are interested only in how an established repression can be motivating.) We recall from Figure 10 that a self-completing ideomotor system comprises ideational, perceptual, effector, and affective events. Imbalance can develop at different regions of the cycle; for example, the required feedback may be primarily perceptual, or ideational, or motor. Interruption of the ideomotor chain can also occur at any one of these links.

Figure 11 shows schematically two ways in which a repressed ideomotor system can affect an unrepressed one: either through interference with its first conscious events, the anticipatory and planning events (a), or through the perceptual phase (b). Reverting to our earlier example, let us assume that the unrepressed system has to do with a person's attraction to a certain girl. Or-

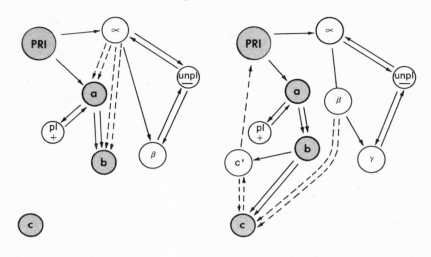

	Legend
————>	Facilitative
- - - - - ->	Inhibitive
PRI	Primary region of imbalance
a	conceptual component (e.g., anticipation)
b	perceptual component
c, c'	motor components
pl	pleasure center (positive affect)
unpl	unpleasure center (negative affect)

$\propto$ } Equivalent
β } unconscious
γ } components

Figures 11–12
Types of Repressive Interference with Ideomotor Systems

dinarily arousal at the primary region of imbalance involves more
or less conscious thoughts about her; it might include the thought
of asking her for a date (represented by *a*), accompanied by anticipatory pleasure (*pl*, a positive affect center); the next step
would be to prime a perceptual system (*b*) for the next sight of
her, so that the approach behaviors (*c*) could be initiated, leading
to the desired terminal feedback—that is, gratification of the wish
to make a date. But assume that the attractions of the girl in

question include a resemblance to the man's mother and therefore that the conscious wish system is also linked to a repressed oedipal one (a and β) with associated strong negative affect. When the repressed system is activated from the primary region, therefore, it may abort the *conscious wish* by an inhibitory transmission from a to a; in this case, the process will be blocked immediately, and even the facilitation of b will not take place. Alternatively, the wishful anticipations may occur; but even though they prime b, an inhibitory transmission from a and β, the unconscious image of the mother (perhaps abetted by the anticipatory involvement of *unpl*, the negative affect center), will so inhibit the perceptual schema of the girl as to make it unresponsive to external perceptual input. Although the subject thinks that he is eager to see the girl, he fails to notice her when the opportunity arises. Both of these interferences at the cognitive level may be regarded as instances of the spread of repression as in hysteria, producing what Anna Freud (1936) called a temporary "narrowing of the ego."

Figure 12 represents further alternative ways in which the repressed oedipal system may interfere with the subject's conscious efforts. He may be able to see his girl but then finds himself suddenly unable to approach her or to say to her what he really wants to say: The repressed system inhibits the specific action (c) that would switch off the primary region of imbalance (that is, gratify this immediate wish, which is, to be sure, only a derivative of a larger system not represented here). Notice that the interference with (c) may be of at least two types: direct inhibition, such as might occur in a hysterical aphonia, or the somewhat related displacement (c') in which the subject may, for example, compulsively "talk shop" with the girl and actually make it impossible for himself to say a word about more personal matters. This relation of mutual exclusion between (c) and (c') is represented in Figure 12 by a double arrow. In any event, the result is to exclude from awareness the original wish, so that the innocent set of ideas about making a date has in effect been "pulled . . . by the *Ucs*." (Freud, 1900, p. 547 *n*.) into an already repressed complex, whereas the " 'substitute by displacement' . . .

plays the part of an anticathexis" by preventing "an emergence in the *Cs.* of the repressed idea" (Freud, 1915b, p. 182).

The example bears some relationship to Freud's (1895) description of a hysterical compulsion, in which an activated repressed idea (*A*) induces through displacement an intense experience of another idea (*B*), the significance of which is lost to the patient herself. The idea (*B*) has become symbolic of the repressed one. Thereafter, in response to a stimulus from the outside or to an association that is more proper to the excitation of *A*, *B* comes into consciousness instead. *B* has become a compulsively powerful idea. When it is experienced, *A* is repressed. Freud (1905b) called a conscious idea of this kind "supervalent"; it preserves the repression at the same time that it becomes insistent. For every such excessive reaction in consciousness, there is, Freud said, a corresponding amnesia. In the example schematized in Figure 12, the man might in the future experience an incongruously strong impulse to indulge only in safe shoptalk with the girl—an inappropriately strong impulse that would maintain the repression of the oedipal system while incidentally allowing a small amount of gratification (represented in the diagram by a dotted line).

Note that the compulsiveness of the substituted activity is an example of how repression can motivate acting out. Notice also that the assumption here of feedback loops involving affective systems (*pl* and *unpl* in Figures 11 and 12) is strongly reminiscent of Freud's concept of the "key neurones" in his "Project for a Scientific Psychology" (1895). The resemblance is not coincidental.

One further point about displacement deserves emphasis. It is customary to view it solely as a transfer of *energy*. Such an emphasis diverts attention from the psychologically more interesting aspects of the process. If we consider displacement in purely functional terms, we see that the primary region of a repressed idea creates a demand for feedback that will switch off two types of transmissions: a disposition toward action in relation to objects, and counteractive, unconsciously represented dangers linked with the sought-after objects. To be a successful

defense, displacement must somehow serve this unusual requirement introduced by a repressed train of thought—of both inhibiting certain facilitative excitations (of anxiety) and of releasing its
terminating inhibitions only through indirection.

Modes of Displacement

The idea that repressed trains of thought reveal themselves
in forms of discharge, or, in the terms of the model, terminating
stimulations, makes it possible to view repression as a structuring process and not simply as a disordering process in behavior.
Successful switch-off of a repressed wish presents a special problem, as we have just seen. The stimulus conditions adequate to
switching off the conflicting excitations will be very different
from those that switch off an unconflicted wish. Substitutes must
be found that will satisfy both the facilitating and the contradict-
ing elements without jeopardizing the repression. Not just *any*
idea will do to bring about balance in the primary region; there
is always a range of equivalents that limits the serviceability of a
stimulus for displacement. There are, therefore, a variety of possible modes of displacement.

Some of these displacement modes may be summarized. I
shall not attempt to deal with them in the terms of the model,
except in a most general way, and instead shall limit discussion to
underscoring the qualitative rather than the quantitative nature
of the behavioral changes induced by displacement. What I am
about to discuss is descriptive, qualitative complexities that the
theory will have to encompass.

It need not be assumed that all of an ideomotor system's
response channels are uniformly affected in repression. Freud
(1915b) pointed out that the process of repression can disconnect
affect from *idea;* it can disconnect *verbal* connections from ideational and affective ones; it can inhibit *awareness* of the significance of an action while permitting the action itself. Although
inaccessibility to awareness and inhibition of activated action
tendencies are the main outcomes of repression, they need not be
simultaneously present. It seems reasonable to expect, too, that
the behavioral forms of a repressed idea will vary according to

circumstances of perceptual encounter. The completely dissociated idea would be an extreme case of repression—in which an entire ideational complex is denied all possibilities of switching off wish gratification and anxiety. Such a condition may be characteristic only of traumatic memories (Sears, 1936).

Consciousness of an experience may thus be intact but the associated wish is forgotten or inhibited. Or the action tendency may be *symbolically transformed* and its consciously experienced relation to a wish severed. This process often occurs in slips of the tongue; a train of thought not consciously intended is activated by the verbal stimuli generated in the course of an intentional sequence with quite another objective. The spoken words have a double value—as instrumental to the conscious intention and as a switch-off opportunity for the peripheral, repressed train of thought that is in a state of activation.

A common effect of repression and one reason for failure of recall is the severance of *verbal links* to an experience or memory. Because a primary objective of repression is to prevent action in terms of a wish, it is to be expected that verbalization of the experience will fall under the same prohibition, on the assumption that words are action surrogates. This prohibition is by no means the only or even an inevitable effect, however, for *verbal release* can also serve repression. The indirect switch-off tendency of a repressed train of thought may take the form of verbal behavior. For instance, one interesting mode of displacement can be that of metaphor. The economy of metaphorical constructions is that they can serve a double function—of conveying the meaning of an intentional train of thought and, simultaneously, that of a repressed train of thought. The interpretation of metaphor can thus be an effective way of tracking down the leading elements of a repressed idea.

Affective experiences can also provide appropriate conditions for discharging a repressed action tendency through displacement. Phenomena of fascination and curiosity—absorption in particular experiences, especially novel ones—may signify the activity of a repressed idea. It is an interesting and experimentally testable possibility that the motivational momentum of a repressed idea may lend a quality of novelty to perceptual encounters. (I owe this suggestion to Leo Goldberger.) If a stimulus resonates with a repressed idea, experiences that paradoxically reflect this equivalence while disavowing it may develop. Such a percept may provoke a feeling of "differentness," or of "significance," or of "novelty."

I shall cite an example of how an aura of intense yet inexplicable feeling can emanate from a repressed train of thought. On Palm Sunday a patient was overcome by sadness and unrest while doing a chore for her husband. She burst into tears and then thought, "What if I lose him; we are so very close." She was overcome by profound tenderness and grief and an equally profound sense of terror of anticipated loss. The mood persisted into her therapy hours for several days. She could see no sense in it. The immediate circumstances of her tears (the task she was doing) did not seem to be the essential key to her feelings. Her thoughts moved to the day-to-day irritations of her job, which led her to think of her mother and of continuing complaints about her mother, then of her father, who had died when she was ten—as it happened, on Palm Sunday. The connections among the holiday, her husband, and yearning and guilt over her father's death all emerged impressively linked to what she consciously felt was a senseless mood.

These considerations suggest that the motivating activity of a repressed train of thought need not be rigidly stereotyped. It may lead to improvisations of thought and action. It is useful to consider further how a repressed train of thought can act as an improvisational, even creative, force in behavior. Again, it is hard to encompass these possibilities in terms of the model at present. Nevertheless, the point that there is a creative aspect to the motivation induced by repression is still novel enough to merit simply descriptive elaboration.

Unconscious Fantasy

One basis of improvisational construction generated by repression is known to clinicians as unconscious fantasy (Arlow, 1961, 1963; Beres, 1962; Sandler & Nagera, 1963; Isaacs, 1948). Its features include a complex cognitive structure originating in circumstances of psychic injury that involve the thwarting of wishes or the arousal of unacceptable ones (childhood seduction, for example). Its cognitive aspects include more than wish fulfillment alone; the unconscious structure also involves prototypical representations of dangers attending the gratification of the wish, to which the ego responds with anxiety, the danger being the major factor inhibiting consummation of the wish (see especially Arlow, 1963). For example, an aggressive wish may carry the danger of destroying a loved object, or of retaliation, or of punishment (like mutilation or loss of love), as well as repudiations of conscience. The wish, as well as all these representations of danger, is given form in an unconscious thematic construction.

Clinicians generally believe that an unconscious fantasy is invoked under conditions of *current* threat, to self-esteem, for instance: when a person finds himself in a realistic situation corresponding to an earlier traumatic experience; when his realistic situation, though not traumatic, contains elements conforming to those of the unconscious fantasy, thus stimulating it; or when he is subjected to stress that causes a change in his state of consciousness and thus makes it possible for otherwise effectively segregated aspects of the fantasy to impose themselves upon behavior.

Once aroused, such a fantasy is motivational; it includes directives of approach and avoidance, of goal relevance and irrelevance, of behavioral selectivity generally. It acts as a guide to scanning and encoding in a fashion that Tolman (1948) described as the activity of a "cognitive map." There ensues a search for behavioral and perceptual equivalents that will repair the instigating conditions of experienced threat. In this sense, *unconscious fantasies motivate behavioral symbolization.* Specific symbols are features of environment made relevant to the particularizing activity of components of the fantasy, including wish and defense. In this sense, the unconscious fantasy is a peremptory ideomotor system that potentiates the environment for actions not originally associated with it. Such peremptory symbolizing has not been intensively investigated. A peremptory symbolizing action is one that gives stimuli positional values of relevance and significance within the ideomotor system. It is, therefore, essentially assimilative, rather than accommodative, in its effects.

A curious paradox of unconscious fantasy, in the clinical meaning of the term, is that its components are assumed to be highly organized yet its leading elements—gratifications sought and feared, dangers past and potential—are all dynamically unconscious. The term "fantasy," however, seems appropriate in that it affirms a state of affairs that exists only internally, although the person behaves as if it existed in objective reality.

This conception makes good clinical sense if we view this unconscious activity as the cognitive form of a dilemma, grounded in contradictory impulses and affects, and pressing toward solution through rearrangements of thought and action. The activated unconscious fantasy sets a complex problem for discharge because of the contradictory excitations it comprises. The switch-off must take behavioral forms that are realistically permissible yet must reduce the affective reverberations and dispositions of the activated fantasy structure. The aim of discharge is in a sense to achieve mastery over these contradictions, but a mastery that does not threaten or undo the repression; indeed, it is as if strategies of mastery were actually sustained by the repression. The resolving actions may be daydreams, or they may take the form of contriving circumstances in which the terms of the dilemma are actually lived out, or they may be worked out through the symbolizing activities of art.[9]

These features distinguish unconscious fantasy from the

---

[9] Such activities may become the basis of cognitive style. Zetzel (1964) describes two patients, observed over the course of long-term psychoanalytic treatment, who were characterized by well-habituated styles of seeking visual excitement, of excessive preoccupation with looking and prying, and of counterphobic search for horrifying situations with an almost conscious intention to frighten themselves. Analytic understanding showed these styles to be efforts to reevoke actual traumatic childhood experiences in connection with exposure to parental intercourse.

more visible phenomenon of daydreaming, a conscious sequence that leads to the imaginal gratification of a wish (see, for example, Singer, 1966). The difference can be summed up in the distinction between *dilemma* and *resolution*. The daydream often has a story quality: it begins and ends. In contrast, an unconscious fantasy is an active, internally structured *problem* that requires a "story" in life events that will, if not finish it, at least alleviate it. The unconscious fantasy is motivational in the sense of generating symbolic thought and action. A daydream may itself be one of its forms of behavioral manifestation.

It is this property of unconscious fantasy, of seeking resolution to a complex problem of discharge, that I have in mind when I say that its motivational workings have an improvisational aspect. Such an unconscious cognitive structure serves both as programmer and coder of experience: In terms of it events are understood and meanings assigned and symbolized. The salient structural fact about an unconscious fantasy seems to be that it constitutes a kind of internal reality in response to which a person acts under conditions that have provoked a painful injury to self-esteem; this "reality" creates perceptual, imaginal, and symbolic equivalents to the prototypical elements of the fantasy structure, inducing assumptions about outer reality. Improvisational activity arises from the necessity to achieve resolution of the activated conflicted elements under available stimulus conditions and within the person's present functional capacities.

Let me give an example. A colleague describes an incident in which a woman patient reported that, while in a department store shortly after leaving her therapy hour, she saw a woman who she was convinced was the therapist's wife, although she had never seen his wife. The idea took urgent hold of her in the store; she could not take her eyes off the other woman and strained to hear what she was saying, even had the idea of following her home. Analysis, of the incident disclosed that it had taken shape at the end of the therapy hour. Usually the therapist left his door open, but this time he had closed it behind her, and the patient had thought: "He has to call his wife. They are having trouble; what will they say to each other?" Jealous thoughts of being excluded came fleetingly to mind. She then "forgot" the whole matter. But the thoughts were by no means quiescent. Perception of the "wife" and the intense conviction that accompanied it fitted the train of thought triggered by being shut out at the conclusion of the hour. It satisfied curiosity about the wife while playing into the network of jealous thoughts and the wish to displace her. The delusional perception also had reparative value in alleviating the hurt of rejection, in that the patient cast herself in the powerful role of unseen observer.

Extended clinical contact makes it possible to track this type of repression-induced activity that is virtually inaccessible to short-term laboratory study—namely, fantasy-linked actions that prove to be attempts by a person to produce in his current life situation actual replicas of unconscious prototypical themes (Lipin, 1963). This may take such forms, for example, as reenactments of dreams of rejection (see Olden, 1941) or of repeatedly exposing oneself to dangers in efforts at mastering an early trauma or fear (see Bibring, 1943; Zetzel, 1964). In these instances, life circumstances and actions are so improvised as to recreate perceptually the contradictions of an unconscious fantasy, in respect to both wish and danger. *Replica-inducing activity* brings about analogues of the occasions that produced the original stressful situation—for example, a violent injury to self-esteem—that has somehow persisted as a potential motivator. Stimulus patterns that reiterate symbolically the essential situational format of the injury and its fantasied context are sought; they may even include a reproduction of the state of consciousness in which the stress originally occurred. Distressing past experiences are thus relived rather than remembered, and are worked out in relation to fantasied or actual efforts at gratification and mastery. Although occurring repetitively without a person's cognizance, such attempts to achieve circumstances that match perceptually and conceptually the unconscious prototypical situation may exact a considerable cost in effort and synthesizing capabilities.

It is easy to see how the coding and programming activations produced by unconscious fantasy could present a continuing problem in maintaining a veridical and accommodative contact with the environment. The problem derives from the possibility that in the emergency created by a profound injury to self-esteem, a peremptory fantasy can provoke defensive and symbolic transformations of environmental events. Whether this process involves efforts to replicate unconscious prototypical situations or takes other forms, the cognitive activity is essentially *assimilative*, not accommodative, in its motivational consequences. In such symbolic activity, the environment is *made relevant to* the particular tendencies of wish, danger, and defense that make up the fantasy. The symbolic activity potentiates the environment for actions not previously associated with it. It produces behaviors designed to be accurate not in the sense of science—of veridical portrayal of the world by intellectual activity—but in the sense of representing an inner world of emotional events (and their representational structure) that is every bit as real as the other.

Thus aroused, an unconscious fantasy can affect the learning process or produce a different kind of learning from the sort that is intended to bring about accommodative changes in cognitive schemata, as in the schoolroom. The coding properties of an active unconscious fantasy may create what Bruner has called "preemptive metaphors" (1966) that give the stimulation a too-personal significance that in turn interferes with the conceptual groupings that must be learned in the schoolroom. Unconscious fantasy may render such learning ineffective. The preemptive metaphor arising from unconscious fantasy can promote organization in the direction of overinclusiveness and overgeneralization; experiences tend to be programmed in terms of affective concepts of "things that can gratify me" and "things that can hurt me" (Rapaport, Gill & Schafer, 1945–1946). They become the basis for scanning and coding the environment for potential dangers and gratifications. In accommodative learning it is precisely such personal components that must be muted. If early learning is hemmed around by conflict with respect to, for example, parental approval and love, with the consequence that it becomes highly charged with unconsummated wishes, school experiences can become symbolically linked to the unconscious fantasy. Such school experiences acquire special potency because they help to sustain, and are in turn reinforced by, the fantasy. They may therefore prove to be especially stubborn and may intrude upon the child's thinking in the school setting (Bruner, 1966).

Intersections of unconscious fantasy with accommodative learning can undoubtedly affect development negatively. But they may also lead to strong interests and commitments, to an intensified involvement in segments of reality. I want to draw attention to the less pathological, creative cognitive by-products of the improvisational, assimilative learning that may occur under the aegis of repressed trains of thought. Because repressed ideas induce symbols, they may occasion fresh though unintended insights into the reality upon which they impose themselves—innovative restructurings or symbols that, though serving as resolutions induced by the arousal of unconscious fantasy, also provide constructive by-products: fresh reorganizations of, new slants on, the understanding of reality.

There have been attempts to understand artistic activity from this point of view (Beres, 1957), but they have been confined almost entirely to narrative content, the story-telling component of a work of art. How unconscious fantasy may affect the abstractive process of formal construction as the artist applies it to his immediate physical surroundings also deserves study. For instance, Graetz (1964) suggests that the formal compositional solutions worked out by Van Gogh have such personal symbolic significance. Affective resonances with a fantasy may motivate formal innovations—transformations of color, texture, depth, and pattern—that give to the viewer a freshened awareness of a reality hitherto obscured by his own pragmatic schemata.[10]

---

[10] The role of unconscious fantasy in inspiration also deserves further attention (see Kris, 1939, for a related suggestion). Inspiration as far as work is concerned usually occurs through exceptional preoccupation with reality, involving a heightened sensual awareness, an enhanced receptiveness, and insight. For example, the apparent vitality of a suddenly perceived form "inspires" the painter to see it and to abstract it from its recessive status in

The fact that a cognitive transformation may originate in unconscious fantasy neither validates nor invalidates the insight into reality that may result from fantasy-induced behavior. The peculiarly personal character of cognitive products issuing from such fantasies may be the special stamp that distinguishes the creative from the merely inventive; personal creation from ornament making; mere craft from symbolic rediscovery of an unknown facet in the familiar and banal.

Peripheral Ideation in Intentional Thought

How intentional, veridically oriented thinking maintains itself in the face of activated but irrelevant ideational systems and, conversely, the conditions under which such peripheral ideation can intrude upon intentional thinking have become subjects of considerable interest at New York University's Research Center for Mental Health.

Pre-Freudian psychology and even many theories that followed Freud have simply assumed that, when a motive or intention to make contact with reality is operative, other possible motivational trends are silent and uninfluential. Freud brought to light another principle—that an ideational system can exercise motivational attributes without being consciously accessible, that such ideas in imbalance can affect action and thought. His formulation raises the question of how it is possible for intentional behavior, in the face of multiple influences from without and within, to fulfill its objectives adequately and effectively.

I have not said much about intentional trains of thought in this chapter but have spoken mainly of nonintentional, peremptory ideation. Orientation toward an objective, perceptual maneuvers, cognition, action homeostatically locked into the objective, and terminal action dictated by criteria of adequacy—these are

---

reality. The degree to which such formal insights have their source in displacement-induced experiences of intensified involvement, fostered by unconscious fantasy, seems a legitimate problem for study. The different ways of arousing experiences of novelty suggested earlier in the chapter seem to be good starting points.

the essential features of an intentional train of thought. Intentional thought is guided by projections of outcome. Sensorimotor events are coordinated with anticipated outcome in a manner analogous to that in which meaning precedes and guides words into sentences, thus becoming particularized. The measure of integrity and adaptiveness of an intentional thought is the degree of aptness of behavioral events to the initiating imbalances created by intention. This effectiveness of an intentional sequence of thought depends upon its *relative autonomy* from, on the one hand, other trains of thought having other objectives, and, on the other hand, intrusive stimulation, exteroceptive and enteroceptive, that may provoke primings and activations incompatible with or irrelevant to it.

How is this relative autonomy of intentional thought maintained, and how is it subverted? How do simultaneously active, nonintentional trains of thought intersect with this sequence and invade conscious thought and action?

To the clinician such intersections and intrusions are apparent enough in the therapeutic situation. There are, of course, slips of the tongue, such as spoonerisms and other parapraxes. They are preemptions of a response channel—a sharp interruption of the dominant, intended train of thought. As we know, such intrusions are often interpretable in terms of other thought tendencies and objectives. But there are other, more subtle ways in which the autonomy of intended thought is reduced. A patient may be describing an incident on his job—the intentional train of thought, the only one that he would be willing to acknowledge— and trying to show how he mastered the situation. His words, syntax, voice quality, and gestures are geared to this objective alone. He seems to be telling about one thing, following one line of thought. Gradually one comes to sense in his choice of words and imagery, and perhaps even in his gestures, a *surplus* meaning. If one knows the patient well, one can read an unexpressed, unintentional idea that is making itself known through the intended train of thought but not disrupting it. It may be congruent with the conscious thought, perhaps even stirred by it, or itself a provoking agent of it.

I offer an example of an unintended message conveyed through metaphor in the course of a conscious train of thought. A patient was talking about her dissatisfactions in her teaching job and especially with "grabby older women," the principal of her school in particular, and about how troublesome it was for her to conceal from her aggressive colleagues that she was in analysis. "One person asked me the other week why I am going downtown. Finally I said, 'If you must know, I'm gonna piss in a bottle and see about my kidneys.'" Wish is father to unintended thought here; her cover story constitutes a metaphor for her competitive vendettas with men and older women. The patient is aware of pursuing only one message; she is stating another as well. Both intended and unintended ideomotor systems are woven into the fabric of the spoken communication.

In certain conditions, intention may be even more drastically commandeered and its secondary autonomy almost completely lost in what would ordinarily be peripheral ideation. In such instances, the urgencies of the unintended prevail; thought and action seem to be impelled rather than willed; actions and spoken words may subvert what one intends to say or do. Autonomy in either case seems to be minimal.

Peripheral ideomotor systems thus jeopardize the efficiency of intentional trains of thought. If the measure of autonomy is the effectiveness of intentional thought, the activity of other trains of thought can shake autonomy. As Hartmann (1939, 1950, 1952), Rapaport (1957b), and Gill and Brenman (1959) have put it, autonomy is only relative. Just as with intentional thought, peripherally activated ideational systems also involve relationships with objects. The arousal of a repressed train of thought, like the arousal of an intentional train of thought, produces a state of readiness for or receptiveness to a certain range of objects in the stimulus field. And, although we speak of peripherally activated ideas, we recognize that they also involve partial motor excitations. In these respects, peripheral ideas constitute a continuous source of intrusion upon intentional sequences.

The question of how unintended, peremptory ideas intrude upon thought can be approached by asking how they are ordinarily *held in check* through supportive processes of intentional thought. A thirsty person still considers differences between the picture of an ice-cream soda and the real thing; in an experiment the thirsty subject is generally capable of judging the size of a stimulus without giving way to the desire to drink it. Intentional thought is ordinarily not easily deflected. Elsewhere I have discussed in more detail the conditions that help to sustain this relative autonomy of intentional thought (this volume, Chapters 7, 9, 10, and 13). Such supportive components include *awareness and attentional processes,* including *postural and orienting sets; error-correcting motor and sensory feedbacks;* and *stabilized strategies of cognitive control.* Together they help to establish a background of activity and reference standards that sustain direction in terms of projected outcome. Impairment of these processes tends to produce a condition of inhibitory failure, creating an opportunity for peripherally active ideas to occupy response channels.

For the experimenter, the critical questions concern the conditions of task, stimulation, and organism that produce a reduction in this autonomy of intentional thinking. One of our approaches is to undermine or by-pass various supports of intentional thought and to look for evidence of peripheral ideation in the thinking and behavior that follow upon their removal.

I shall briefly describe three experimental attempts to specify the activity of concurrent trains of thought and to illustrate the grades of intrusion just described. They involve manipulations of awareness and attention, which are among the important supports of effective intentional thinking. The experimental manipulations promote inattention to stimuli, or they induce difficulty in focusing attention during intentional response, or a combination of the two. I have to omit a considerable number of equally relevant studies from our laboratory and elsewhere, but I must at least mention Luborsky's work (Luborsky, Blinder & Mackworth, 1963; Luborsky & Blinder, 1964).

A study by Eagle, Wolitzky, and Klein (1966) illustrates the biasing of intentional thought by primed peripheral associations induced by an incidental background stimulus. Subjects were shown a picture containing two forms, one perceptually dominant (a tree) and one perceptually recessive (the outline of a duck shaped by the branches of the tree). The question was whether a hidden stimulus of this kind (the duck) can bias the imaginal behavior of a person who is responding to the focal percept (the tree). The experimental picture was shown in three one-second exposures to separate groups. To other groups a control picture, showing only the tree, modified so as to eliminate the outlined duck, was shown. All subjects were given the same task —to conjure up an image of a scene from nature and to draw it as best they could. The graphic products as well as verbal descriptions of the imagery were assessed with respect to the frequency with which duck-related contents (determined in advance of the experiment through association tasks on other subjects) appeared in the imagery protocols.

A significantly higher proportion of subjects gave duck-related associations following the experimental picture than following the control stimulus. The issue of response probability is, of course, crucial, that is, whether subjects will as a matter of course give many duck-related responses when they are asked to image a nature scene. Therefore the data were compared with those of other subjects who produced images under the same instruction but without any stimulus at all. Neither control group (the one that saw only the tree and the one that received no stimulus) produced duck-related associations with the frequency provoked by the experimental picture.

Although the intentional focus upon a nature scene does not, therefore, seem to account for the significant increase in duck associations, we cannot infer that the response intention had no part in making the duck stimulus *effective*. In our view, the instruction and intention did contribute to the stimulus potency of the hidden duck by priming its associates. Because of their congruence with the subjects' intention, the primed duck associates were then easily assimilable to the imaged scene. The instruction enabled the otherwise weak activations of a peripheral stimulus to have some biasing effect. This experiment illustrates, then, a type of peripheral intrusion: When both an intentional response and peripheral activations are congruent in theme and when the task, in this case imagery, allows multiple options of response, the setting is favorable to intrusion into intentional thought of unattended elements of a background stimulus.

An experiment by Spence and Gordon (1967) highlights still another condition of such intrusion: when a peripheral train of thought acquires *affective* potency. This study began with the question whether a stimulus of a very low level of detectability can effectively bias intentional response because of the affective intensity of a peripheral train of thought that is concurrently active. The study made use of the well-known clinical observation that love, feeding, and the mother's breast are symbolic equivalents, persisting from early childhood, that may be invoked in fantasies occasioned by severe jolts to self-esteem. Rejection can thus promote a craving for food in some people. The hypothesis was that, if such people were made to feel rejected, they would behave as if deprived of food even to the extent of reactivating the infantile context of feeding, and that their responses to a subliminal food stimulus would show this sensitization. Feelings of rejection were effectively induced (as well as a good deal of guilt in the experimenters) by contriving to make it seem that certain subjects were deemed by their peers to be unattractive and undesirable as possible friends. That the situation provoked what was intended is indicated by an increase in hunger ratings among the rejected people (an effect that was even greater among subjects who were known to score high on a scale of orality). This situation was immediately followed by the experimental task. Rejected and unrejected subjects were shown a list of thirty words for immediate recall. The words were of three kinds: associates of the word "milk" that also connoted the infantile feeding situation, like "suck," "warm," "mother," "sleep"; more ordinary popular associates of "milk," with less obvious links to the infantile oral theme, like "dairy," "cream," "bread"; and a group of control words. Immediately prior to the memory task, the critical stimulus—"milk"—was exposed at a subliminal intensity to half the rejected and to half the unrejected subjects.

Only the main findings can be cited. First, although rejection did not significantly affect the total amount of recall, it did produce a significant increase in the recall of infantile oral words. Second, the increase in recalled infantile words was especially significant in rejected subjects who were exposed to the subliminal stimulus "milk." The results are suggestive on the point that a background train of thought—in this case having to do with rejection and feeding and involving the activation of a wish—can prepare the way for a related subliminal stimulus, and bias the selective activity of intentional thought—the remembering of words—in directions consonant with the peripherally aroused infantile wish.

Another study (Klein & Barr, manuscript) suggests still another condition conducive to intrusions of peripherally active associations into intentional thought: the impairment of sustained attentional focus such that incidental stimuli acquire an effectiveness that they would not ordinarily have. Subjects under the influence of LSD-25 were shown a line drawing of a face described as that of a "South American native" and asked to describe his personality. In one group, the face was called by the name "Takete," in the other "Uloomu." Both words are known to evoke reliable and distinct physiognomic stereotypes (Hochberg & Brooks, 1954). Would these physiognomic connotations of the words rub off on personality descriptions of the face? In a second procedure immediately following the first task, each word alone was responded to *directly* by the subjects.

Both drug and placebo subjects were responsive to the physiognomic connotations of the words alone, as expected, but the words were contrasted much more sharply and with much less variability by the placebo subjects than by the drug subjects; LSD subjects had trouble separating "Takete" and "Uloomu" qualities in their descriptions. The results were quite different, however, when the words were paired with the face. The LSD group responded much more readily to the physiognomic meanings of "Takete" and "Uloomu" in describing the face; placebo subjects were much less responsive. In addition, the placebo subjects showed greater variability than did LSD subjects in their descriptions of the face. This greater variability seemed to arise from the placebo subjects' tendency to anchor personality descriptions to one or another facial feature; the qualities inferred from these features overrode any influence from the incidental names. Such a systematic rationale seemed less evident in the drug subjects' descriptions. Putting together the contrasting findings from the direct and indirect exposures of the words—on the one hand, the more distinct responsiveness to the words by placebo subjects in the direct condition and their minimal responsiveness to the words in the incidental condition and, on the other hand, the less contrasted responsiveness to the words by drug subjects in the direct condition and greater responsiveness to the words in the incidental condition—we have a basis for saying that impaired attentiveness induced by the drug accounts for the subjects' behavior. The very difficulty in concentration that caused variability and reduced contrast in *direct* response to the words made for *increased* responsiveness to the physiognomic qualities of the words in the incidental condition.

I have chosen in this chapter to retread some old ground and some assumptions more familiar perhaps to the clinician than to the experimenter on cognition. I directed myself first to a basic problem of motivation, its direction and impetus, and tried to locate these properties within the structure of knowledge-inducing activity of a motivated train of thought. Second, I considered the "force" of trains of thought that are usually concealed by the more disciplined, self-corrective supports of intentional behavior, in particular that of repressed tendencies to action, trying to show in what ways a repressed train of thought is motivational, even creative, in its influence. Finally, I offered examples of changes induced by peripheral ideation upon intentional, reality-oriented thinking, showing how peripheral trains of thought may serve as encoding foci even while behavior is answering the requirements of intentional anticipations and objectives.

For most of these considerations, the course I followed was

made hazardous by the paucity of experimental data. My reference points have had to be mainly clinical, based somewhat on my own experience but mostly on that of others. Furthermore, phenomena of repression and unconscious fantasy are not often well described even in the clinical situation, and they are described in ways that defy translation to viable laboratory prototypes. Yet there is in the clinical situation still unmined gold for an experimental psychology of cognition. Bringing phenomena of repression and of unconscious fantasy into the laboratory is an objective that every clinical researcher should have in mind to help accomplish, even those who work exclusively with clinical data. The reason is not the trivial one of laboratory prestige, but the fact that the stimulus conditions for repression and unconscious fantasy have great practical and theoretical importance. We do not know what these conditions are; only situations favorable to the manipulation of variables will tell us. I am aware, of course, that I have offered no clear model, only more problems.

PART SIX

A PERSONAL POSTSCRIPT

Chapter 15

Credo for a "Clinical Psychologist"

If public display of my values as a clinical psychologist deserves more than casual notice, it is because I believe a good many of my colleagues share them. Still, a few facts of autobiography are unavoidable, if only to emphasize that my identity as a clinical psychologist—how I think clinical psychology is represented in my work life and how I think clinical psychology ought to be shaped in the future—is probably more a reflection of my professional history than of values won from clinical psychology itself. My conviction rests on the fact that clinical psychology is not really a well-structured specialty. It has neither the tradition, systematized knowledge, nor defined objectives that are bequeathed to a neophyte physician by a 2,000-year-old medical tradition, nor the intangibles of pride and superego that surround the rite of the Hippocratic oath. This being so, I may as well state the main outlines of my professional pedigree.

My beginnings in clinical psychology date from a four-year stint at the Menninger Clinic, from which I emerged with a strong inclination to look at things psychoanalytically. Before that, however, I did absorb a powerful eclectic orientation at Columbia and was indoctrinated in the experimental approach by R. S. Wood-

worth, John Volkmann, and Gardner Murphy; my doctoral dissertation was on sensory factors in the perception of motion and
was in part an arid expression of reverence for a great teacher,
the biophysicist Selig Hecht. Not counting the latency period of
my professional development (four years of aviation psychology
in World War II, until salvation by the Menningers), my professional life has combined these two emphases—some would prefer
to say that it has shown contamination of one by the other. I have
come to depend upon my understanding of psychoanalytic ideas
and of therapeutic experience to feed an undimmed passion for
investigation, mainly through experimentation; research is the
core of my work life as a clinical psychologist. My favorite
subject was from the beginning, and still is, perception. I no
longer do diagnostic work, though I respect it. I do, and intend
always to do, psychotherapy in one form or another. I consider
classroom teaching a rather irritating necessity; personal contact
with students, life's blood.

So, when I speak of my personal values as a clinical psychologist, you are hearing from one who happens to be simultaneously
a member of the American Psychological Association's Division 12
(the clinical division) and Division 8 (the personality division)
and—of all things—the Psychonomic Society. [1]

I say it is only fair to tell you all this because it is harder and
harder these days to define clinical psychology or to speak of the
typical clinical psychologist. That was not the case when I started
out in 1946, with a not-so-fresh Ph.D. and four years of the Air
Force behind me, in a $125-a-month internship at the Menninger
Clinic. Although clinical psychology was not then as clearly pro-
fessionalized as it is now, it was easier to say what clinical
psychologists were doing and where they were. The clinical psychologist worked mostly in a clinic or in a hospital. His duties
were mainly intelligence testing and diagnosis. Here and there he
also did psychotherapy, usually in state hospitals, where he was
often the only one interested in it. Having low status—as did

---

[1] A society dedicated to fostering the experimental approach in psychology.

psychotherapy itself—he posed no threat to medical authority who saw little harm in his dabblings as long as his diagnostic reports were in on time.

The picture is far more complex now. The image of the clinical psychologist with his kit of tests is going, if not already gone. Even the diagnostic function itself has been completely disowned by some clinical psychologists, particularly those who grew up with Carl Rogers; for the rest of us it has evolved into a highly sophisticated notion of personality assessment. Many psychologists even regard the word "patient" with distaste; it is rather too medical, you see, for those clinical psychologists who are preoccupied with throwing off the shackles of medical parenthood. So they prefer to say "client," a designation that sticks in my own craw because of its connotations of business and the law. Today therapy is surely the dominant defining activity of the clinical psychologist. Even in that sphere, however, the picture is no longer clear-cut. Notions of the therapeutic function have loosened and broadened, so that it is much less easy to distinguish explicit therapeutic aims of the traditional fifty-minute hour from the less explicit ones of guidance, counseling, and school psychology, which are becoming increasingly popular habitats for clinical psychologists. It is not at all uncommon, at the same time, to find that many clinical psychologists never treat or test anybody, directly or indirectly. They are teaching or engaging in research in universities and hospitals, in industry, in schools, and in government agencies.

Nor is the clinical psychologist easily identified by his research interests any more. There are many, of course, whose research directly confronts the therapeutic process and the data of therapy, but my guess is that there are many more whose research does not, and whose subject matter is in the more conventional realms of perception, learning processes, group phenomena, and the like. You will find clinical psychologists hovering over rats and monkeys in Skinner boxes and in stereotaxic instruments of the physiology laboratories. Blurring the lines even more is the interesting trend for a good many "clinical phenomena," once the exclusive preserve of the psychiatrist and clinical psychologist, to crop up in the work of people who wouldn't be caught dead alongside the professional clinical psychologist. These days even Skinnerians are apt to talk quite knowledgeably about schizophrenia. And what Harry Harlow has to say about maternal deprivation and Donald Hebb about social isolation and fear is as important for clinical psychologists as are Erik Erikson's views on these matters. You will not find Harlow's name, nor Hebb's, on rosters of clinical psychologists.

Times have certainly changed.

Now I do not indulge myself in this historical reflection to inspire respect for my age or seniority, nor to complain about the blurring of lines, nor to lay bare clinical psychology's octopal designs on the rest of psychology. The blurring of distinctions is a good thing: There is my first value. I find it not at all disturbing that clinical psychology is less clearly defined in its functions than it previously was. I believe, with my teacher David Rapaport, that the professionalization of clinical psychology, with its trappings of certification and pseudo certitude, licensing examinations, and all the rest of the paraphernalia by which vested economic interests are served by professional ones, was and still is dubious evidence of maturity. Do not infer from the existence of specialty boards, examinations, and "entrance requirements" nor from the fact that clinical psychologists make more money than do many other psychologists that great strides in knowledge have been made for which all this professional respectability is a just reward. Much of this professionalization is riding the crest of a wave of social need created by World War II. I am personally as pleased as anybody at the material gains that have come of it to psychologists generally. But insofar as this professionalization courts the image of the practicing physician who has separated himself from the physiologist and feels no commitment to investigation, insofar as it has encouraged private practice at the price of dulling the curiosity that motivates inquiry and of muting the obligation to share doubts with colleagues, professionalization has been a bad thing. That is my second value.

Of course, a similar congealing of professional vested interest has occurred in other parts of psychology too. Take the gradual emergence of the "experimental psychologist" as a professional expert whose status in a separate calling is being legitimized by lucrative offers from engineering and missiles corporations. I cannot see any advantages, except in promoting idiotic considerations of prestige that are causing the world enough trouble as it is, to be won from dividing psychologists by preferences for particular research strategies. And that is all experimenting is—a strategy of observation, by no means the only strategy and not always the most desirable one. Surely method is not more important than phenomena, yet something of this outlook is encouraged by the tendency of some psychologists to distinguish themselves from their colleagues according to a particular methodological preference or expertise. It is impossible to assess the price paid in quality of observation and theory that may be traced to overcommitment to experimentation, or to say how much it has contributed to a rigid brand of antiseptic superego that seems to say that one ought *not* to look unless by experiment. The costs are perhaps most visible in the area of learning theory, a field that has over the years existed in unwholesome isolation from the complex atmosphere of nature's own experiments in learning—the schoolroom. (A hopeful reversal of this trend is just now taking place.) Again, do not mistake me. I am not condemning experimentation. My jeremiads have to do only with the appearance in psychology of cleavages produced less by organic considerations of psychology's subject matter than by considerations of professional advantage, prestige, defensive postures, and competitive vendettas.

Well then, if "clinical psychology" no longer precisely describes what clinical psychologists actually do, is there nothing in the term to provide some clue for its diverse functions? Does the designation carry no implications of professional identity and values? Here consultation with Webster's Dictionary may help. We find that "clinical" is embedded in the history of medicine and is linked generally with connotations of "the bedridden person and bedside." After this, the term has a variety of specific meanings. It denotes a teaching function, of examining and treating patients in the presence of students. It has to do with medical study or practice "based on active treatment or observation of a patient as distinguished from experimental or laboratory study." And it implies a purely scientific, dispassionate interest in the phenomena observed at the bedside, as "she regarded his death with *clinical* detachment." Never mind the ecclesiastical usage that is also given.

Note that not all these meanings have to do with therapy and diagnosis. Note especially "dispassionate interest"; observation, investigation, and teaching are prominently involved. I take issue only with the dictionary's rather sharp separation of clinical and experimental, on the grounds that, if the objectives of "observation" and "understanding" are underscored, actual practice might require that the phenomena be studied under conditions of *controlled* observation, and that is often experiment. Whether the actual scene is a laboratory or a bedside is a small matter. After all, the psychotherapeutic situation and the psychoanalytic couch are themselves detached from the life context of the patient's suffering. At any rate, the moral I draw from this dictionary inventory is that to identify "clinical" with "therapeutic" is a rather arbitrary narrowing of the term's meaning.

This point is, I think, important if we are to discover the real root of the clinician's activities. This root, I submit, is a primary acquaintance and concern with, and even identification with, phenomena of mental suffering, with the travails and miscarriages of adjustment—the realm that used to be called "psychopathology." This fact irrevocably binds the interests of clinical psychologists, whatever their theoretical persuasion. It is the starting point of the clinical psychologist's training. From it diverge the various stems of clinical psychology, whether they involve an interest in psychosis, or a compensatory overemphasis on the healthy, or an interest in the play of children. Certainly the clinical trainee is likely to see more suffering in the raw than are other psychologists. From the start, especially if the start is in a hospital, the emergencies he encounters are life-and-death matters, not merely "interesting psychological issues." Norman Cameron has put it well: "The fears . . . [the clinician] deals with are very real, the sorrows are deep and lasting sorrows, and the defeats are often final and irrevocable. They are not the consequences of put-up jobs which can be accurately timed and prearranged, as laboratory situations are" (1937, p. 440). The *essential* training of the clinical psychologist is experience with *nature's experiments* and their outcomes.

As a result of this indoctrination in aberration and anguish, the clinical psychologist has an opportunity to develop "the easy tolerance of the naturalist for variability and unreliability in his material that would be out of place in laboratory procedure. . . . his interpretations are apt to show scientific judgment that is tempered a little with human kindness. His view of man, as a result of all this, is less clean-cut and broader" (Cameron, 1937, pp. 440–441), but it perhaps does fuller justice to his social habitat, to human hopes and yearnings and aborted potentialities, however much it may lose in precision.

But there is another by-product of the clinician's journey into aberration to which I would draw attention. It is an outlook on human behavior, an orientation toward data, a point of view or selective bias of observation that is most vividly perceptible in the acts of diagnosis and therapy, but in research too. It may characterize the outlook of other psychologists as well, but so intimately does it seem to me linked to the clinical enterprise that it deserves to be called the *clinical attitude* (this volume, Chapter 4).

It consists of an automatic inclination to give priority in the observation of behavior to questions of Why? and What is it for? over those of How does it work? and What is its process? It favors attention to an individual's purposive trends, directions, and meanings—conscious and unconscious—and their links to behavior. Individuality, along with purpose and direction, engage the clinician mainly, more than do properties of specific functions like perception or memory, except as these functions are viewed from an organismic perspective. Questions of purpose or function are, of course, familiar in biology. Clinical psychologists are similarly inclined, I think, to become interested in the mechanisms of behavior or phenomena only after they have achieved some opinion about the behavior's function, its utility in the organism's adjustive pattern. This emphasis on function or adjustive significance is clear in the character of the clinician's descriptive concepts. Many psychoanalytic concepts are of this nature. Repression, for instance, describes a kind of accomplishment. The process itself is obscure, but the term is nonetheless useful clinically.

Now I have perhaps created the impression that I consider this functionalist bias of the clinical attitude superior to other points of view. I really have no such promotional intent. The functionalist bias, like all biases, can breed blindness or fallacy. Its overzealous application may lead us to forget that the question What is the function? is only a prelude to How? Describing the direction of behavior is but one way of comprehending behavior, one phase of the process of explanation. David Krech and I once stated the matter as follows: "Some behavior theories have failed to ask the 'why' question and thereby have lost the organism; some personality theories have failed to answer in terms of 'how' and 'what' and have thereby lost theory—explanatory theory" (Klein & Krech, 1951, p. 11). Furthermore, the clinical attitude can produce investigative scotomata for the lawfulness of phenomena whose adaptive significance is not immediately apparent. Personally, I consider it the purest kind of scientific curiosity, which I admire the more perhaps because I am myself incapable of it, to be interested in a phenomenon simply because it is there, without the hecklings of an inner voice that insistently asks how much the interest will pay off in curing people. It is very hard to convince clinical students that serious regard for the learning process of a cockroach requires no other justification than that it presents a God-given regularity. It does take something of a wrench away from the clinical attitude to enjoy, without guilt or immediate promise of improving the human condition, a leisurely stroll through the world of animals and men in the manner of the great naturalist Uexküll (1934).

Yet, on balance, I believe that the clinical attitude is useful for research, so much so that I wish that training were more committed than is now the case to nourishing it through more intensive, firsthand contact with the phenomena of mental aberration. It cannot be doubted that the clinical attitude has contributed a large number of questions that might not otherwise have been asked and has brought many phenomena into the foreground that might otherwise have taken longer to attract systematic interest. Phobias and fears, dreams and fantasies, twisted hates and loves, deprivation and depression, phenomena of defense and regression—all have come to the psychologist's attention via the clinic and have been brought into the foreground by the clinician's concern about their meanings within the adjustive economy of a person's life.

I have said that the clinical attitude pervades all the clinician's functions, that it can apply equally to his *research* and to his *therapeutic* efforts. Here is perhaps an appropriate place to pause over the question of the relative status of these two functions within the clinical psychologist's identity and values.

Somewhere along the line, most clinical psychologists encounter problems of preserving a compatible marriage between the two. The issue is perhaps more poignant for the clinical psychologist than for the psychiatrist because lingering echoes of his graduate training remind him now and again that his Ph.D. is after all a research degree. Friction can come from different sources. That different talents and different objectives are involved in the two is suggested by the common opinion that clinicians can be good researchers and perhaps good supervisors of therapy yet not particularly good therapists. The opposite may happen more often—good therapists may not be good researchers. Nevertheless I doubt that the two roles are incompatible; besides, little can be done about deficits of talent on either side.

Another source of trouble, more correctable, arises whenever the clinician's research curiosity is attracted by the events of therapy itself. It may tempt him to interventions guided more by investigative opportunism than by therapeutic necessity. He then has to face the reality that what is good for research may not be good for therapy and vice versa. But the promptings of research curiosity are not easily stilled.

I am not especially impressed with the opinion that therapy

is itself a form of research, for this view confuses objectives and stretches the word "research" beyond its sensible meaning of scientific investigation. To do research means to court doubt and to manipulate conditions in the interest of controlling variation alone—surely not a happy context for the conduct of therapy. The therapist may doubt the efficiency of what he does, and why he does it, in advance of the therapy hour; he may be depressed at his accomplishments after it; but *during* it he cannot operate from a perspective of basic doubt about the theory and premises of his technique. He must work intuitively and artfully; the theory, experience, and knowledge that carry him must have free rein in the hour. Insofar as he *conducts* therapy this way, he is not *testing* hypotheses; his manipulations have not an experimenter's objective but the objective of being "good for the patient."

To be sure, *reflection* upon the therapeutic hour has generated many important hypotheses and propositions for investigative enterprise. But on the crucial matter of *controlling variables* there can be no equivocation: During therapy, manipulation of variables is justifiable only by therapeutic intent, not by research for its own sake.

Having said this much, I feel there is no contradiction in asserting that a commitment to research ought to be preeminent in the value hierarchy of the clinical psychologist. The primary aim of the clinical psychologist ought to be what it is for all psychologists—the perception and formulation of lawful patterns and of the determining conditions of this lawfulness. I do not believe that the preeminence of this commitment to research need make him a worse therapist, any more than the "desire to cure" necessarily makes him a better one. As between a "desire to cure" and a desire to nourish one's research intentions as motives for engaging in therapy, I am not at all convinced that the former is the more salutary, however more altruistic it may seem at first look. If the conduct of therapy ought not to be distracted by the research intention, neither should it be distracted by the "compulsion to cure," a condition that can lead to passionate and harmful overinvolvement, intolerance of therapeutic failure, and a narrowing of the therapist's responsiveness to only those patients who show signs of being helped or cured. Patients who in our present state of ignorance offer little hope of cure have little to sustain the therapist who looks only for this to justify himself. I should like to close my emphasis on the matter with a quotation from a man after whom young clinicians might profitably fashion their professional identities:

. . . I can throw a little light, for anyone who may be interested, on my own motives. After forty-one years of medical activity, my self-knowledge tells me that I have never really been a doctor in the proper sense. I became a doctor through being compelled to deviate from my original purpose; and the triumph of my life lies in my having, after a long and roundabout journey, found my way back to my earliest path. . . . In my youth I felt an overpowering need to understand something of the riddles of the world in which we live and perhaps even to contribute something to their solution. The most hopeful means of achieving this end seemed to be to enrol myself in the medical faculty; but even after that I experimented—unsuccessfully—with zoology and chemistry, till at last . . . I settled down to physiology . . . I scarcely think, however, that my lack of a genuine medical temperament has done much damage to my patients. For it is not greatly to the advantage of patients if their doctor's therapeutic interest has too marked an emotional emphasis. They are best helped if he carries out his task coolly and keeping as closely as possible to the rules.

The speaker was Sigmund Freud (1927, pp. 253–254).

I have drawn, I admit, a rather complex, perhaps even bewildering, sketch of a clinical psychologist: a fellow who feels no need to call himself a "clinical psychologist" yet is closely identified with the clinical attitude; who dislikes being called "a therapist" because his main calling is that of looking for lawfulness rather than curing people, yet who insists on doing psychotherapy; who prefers working in a clinical setting but at the same time considers the academic tradition of investigation and psychology's link to biological science preeminent in his professional identity; a fellow who believes too that what is good about clinical psychology—its orientation to suffering—should ideally be part of the working equipment of every psychologist, and that what is good about experimental psychology—its concern for controlled observation and for understanding the conditions of the occurrence of phenomena—should be part of the conscience of all clinical psychologists. Where all psychologists should join, he believes, is in the naturalist's love of phenomena and of their investigation.

My hope is that what now may seem a confusing pattern of mixed loyalties, identifications, ambivalences, and paradoxes will become tomorrow's accepted standard of coherent identity.

Bibliography

Adams, J. K. 1957. Laboratory Studies of Behavior Without Awareness. *Psychol. Bull.*, 54: 383–405.

Allers, R. & J. Teler. 1924. On the Utilization of Unnoticed Impressions in Associations. *Psychol. Issues*, Monogr. 7: 121–150. New York: International Universities Press, 1960.

Allport, F. H. 1954. The Structuring of Events: Outline of a General Theory with Applications to Psychology. *Psychol. Rev.*, 61: 281–303.

———. 1955. *Theories of Perception and the Concept of Structure.* New York: Wiley.

Allport, G. W. 1935. Attitudes. In *The Nature of Personality: Selected Papers.* Cambridge, Mass.: Addison-Wesley, 1950, pp. 1–47.

———. 1937. *Personality.* New York: Holt.

———. 1961. *Pattern and Growth in Personality.* New York: Holt.

Ames, A., Jr. 1946–1947. Nature and Origin of Perception: Preliminary Laboratory Manual for Use with Demonstration Disclosing Phenomena Which Increase Our Understanding of the Nature of Perception. Hanover, N. H.: Institute for Associated Research, mimeographed.

Angyal, A. 1941. *Foundations for a Science of Personality.* New York: Commonwealth Fund.

———. 1948. The Holistic Approach in Psychiatry. *Amer. J. Psychiat.*, 105: 178–182.

Anokhin, P. K. 1961. Features of the Afferent Apparatus of the Conditioned Reflex and Their Importance for Psychology. In N. O'Connor, ed., *Recent Soviet Psychology.* New York: Liveright.

Ansbacher, H. 1937. Perception of Number as Affected by Monetary Value of the Objects. *Arch. Psychol.*, No. 215.

Arlow, J. A. 1959. The Structure of the *Déjà Vu* Experience. *J. Amer. Psychoanal. Assn.*, 7: 611–631.

———. 1960. Fantasy Systems in Twins. *Psychoanal. Quart.*, 29: 175–199.

———. 1961. Ego Psychology and the Study of Mythology. *J. Amer. Psychoanal. Assn.*, 9: 371–393.

———. 1963. Conflict, Regression, and Symptom Formation. *Int. J. Psycho-Anal.*, 44: 12–22.

Arnheim, R. 1949. The Gestalt Theory of Expression. *Psychol. Rev.*, 56: 156–171.

Asch, S. E. 1952. *Social Psychology.* New York: Prentice-Hall.

Ashby, W. R. 1947. The Nervous System as Physical Machine: With Special Reference to the Origin of Adaptive Behavior. *Mind*, 56: 44–59.

Bach, S. & G. S. Klein. 1957. Conscious Effects of Prolonged Subliminal Exposures of Words. *Amer. Psychologist*, 12: 397.

Bartlett, F. C. 1932. *Remembering: A Study in Experimental and Social Psychology.* Cambridge, Eng.: Cambridge University Press.

Bartley, S. H. 1946. Vision. In E. H. Spiegel, ed., *Progress in Neurology and Psychiatry.* New York: Grune & Stratton.

Békésy, G. von & W. A. Rosenblith. 1951. The Mechanical Properties of the Ear. In S. S. Stevens, ed., *Handbook of Experimental Psychology.* New York: Wiley, pp. 1075–1115.

Benfari, R. 1966a. The Scanning Control Principle and Its Relationship to Affect Manipulation. *Percept. Motor Skills*, 22: 203–216.

———. 1966b. Defense and Control: Further Indications. *Percept. Motor Skills*, 22: 736–738.

Berdach, E. & P. Bakan. 1967. Body Position and the Free Recall of Early Memories. *Psychotherapy: Theory, Research and Practice*, 4: 101–102.

Beres, D. 1957. Communication in Psychoanalysis and in the Creative Process: A Parallel. *J. Amer. Psychoanal. Assn.*, 5: 408–423.

———. 1962. The Unconscious Fantasy. *Psychoanal. Quart.*, 31: 309–328.

Bertalanffy, L. von. 1950. The Theory of Open Systems. *Science*, 111: 23–29.

———. 1952. *Problems of Life: An Evaluation of Modern Biological Thought.* London: Watts.

———. 1955. An Essay on the Relativity of Categories. *Phil. Sci.*, 22: 243–263.

Bettelheim, B. 1967. *The Empty Fortress.* New York: Free Press.

Bexton, W. H., W. Heron & T. H. Scott. 1954. Effects of Decreased Variation in the Sensory Environment. *Canad. J. Psychol.*, 8: 70–76.

Bibring, E. 1943. The Conception of the Repetition Compulsion. *Psychoanal. Quart.*, 12: 486–519.

Binet, A. 1896. *Alterations of Personality*. New York: Appleton.

Boardman, W. K. 1957. Utilization of Word Structure in Prerecognition Responses. *J. Pers.*, 25: 672–685.

Bokert, E. 1967. The Effects of Thirst and a Related Verbal Stimulus on Dream Reports. Unpublished doctoral dissertation, New York University.

Boring, E. G. 1952. The Gibsonian Visual Field. *Psychol. Rev.*, 59: 246–247.

———. 1953. The Role of Theory in Experimental Psychology. *Amer. J. Psychol.*, 66: 169–184.

Breger, L. 1967. The Function of Dreams. *J. Abnorm. Psychol. Monogr.*, 72(5, Whole No. 641).

Breuer, J. & S. Freud. 1893. On the Psychical Mechanism of Hysterical Phenomena: Preliminary Communication. In *Standard Edition*, 2: 1–18. London: Hogarth, 1955.

———. 1893–1895. Studies on Hysteria. In *Standard Edition*, 2. London: Hogarth, 1955.

Bricker, P. D. & A. Chapanis. 1953. Do Incorrectly Perceived Tachistoscopic Stimuli Convey Some Information? *Psychol. Rev.*, 60: 181–188.

Broadbent, D. E. 1958. *Perception and Communication*. New York: Pergamon.

Brown, E. L. 1961. Human Performance and Behavior During Zero Gravity. In E. T. Benedikt, ed., *Weightlessness: Physical Phenomena and Biological Effects*. New York: Plenum, pp. 156–170.

Bruner, J. S. 1957a. On Perceptual Readiness. *Psychol. Rev.*, 64: 123–152.

———. 1957b. Going Beyond the Information Given. In Bruner *et al.*, *Contemporary Approaches to Cognition*. Cambridge, Mass.: Harvard University Press, pp. 41–69.

———. 1966. On Coping and Defending. *Toward a Theory of Instruction*. Cambridge, Mass.: Belknap, pp. 129–148.

Bruner, J. S. & C. C. Goodman. 1947. Value and Need as Organizing Factors in Perception. *J. Abnorm. Soc. Psychol.*, 42: 33–44.

Bruner, J. S. & G. S. Klein. 1960. The Functions of Perceiving: New Look Retrospect. In S. Wapner & B. Kaplan, eds., *Perspectives in Psychological Theory*. New York: International Universities Press, pp. 61–77.

Bruner, J. S. & L. Postman. 1948. Symbolic Value as an Organizing Factor in Perception. *J. Soc. Psychol.*, 27: 203–208.

Bruner, J. S. & J. S. Rodrigues, Jr. 1953. Some Determinants of Apparent Size. *J. Abnorm. Soc. Psychol.*, 48: 17–24.

Brunswik, E. 1934. *Wahrnehmung und Gegenstandswelt*. Vienna: Deuticke.

———. 1947. *Systematic and Representative Design of Psychological Experiments*. Berkeley: University of California Press.

———. 1952. The Conceptual Framework of Psychology. *International Encyclopedia of Unified Science*, Vol. 1, No. 10. Chicago: University of Chicago Press.

———. 1956. *Perception and the Representative Design of Psychological Experiments*, 2nd ed. Berkeley: University of California Press.

Brunswik, E. & J. Kamiya. 1953. Ecological Cue-Validation of "Proximity" and of Other Gestalt Factors. *Amer. J. Psychol.*, 66: 20–32.

Burlingham, D. T. 1952. *Twins: A Study of Three Pairs of Identical Twins*. New York: International Universities Press.

Cameron, N. 1937. Experimental Psychology and Medicine. *Psychol. Rec.*, 1: 437–445.

Cantril, H. 1947. *Understanding Man's Social Behavior: Preliminary Notes*. Princeton: Public Opinion Research.

Carter, L. F. & K. Schooler. 1949. Value, Need, and Other Factors in Perception. *Psychol. Rev.*, 56: 200–207.

Cherry, C. 1957. *On Human Communication*. New York: Wiley.

Colby, K. M. 1955. *Energy and Structure in Psychoanalysis*. New York: Ronald.

Dahl, H. 1965. Observations on a "Natural Experiment": Helen Keller. *J. Amer. Psychoanal. Assn.*, 13: 533–550.

Dement, W. 1960. The Effect of Dream Deprivation. *Science*, 131: 1705–1707.

Dement, W. & N. Kleitman. 1957a. The Relation of Eye Movements During Sleep to Dream Activity: An Objective Method for the Study of Dreaming. *J. Exp. Psychol.*, 53: 339–346.

———. 1957b. Cyclic Variations in EEG During Sleep and Their Relation to Eye Movements, Body Motility, and Dreaming. *EEG Clin. Neurophysiol.*, 9: 673–690.

Dement, W. & E. A. Wolpert. 1958. The Relation of Eye Movements, Body Motility, and External Stimuli to Dream Content. *J. Exp. Psychol.*, 55: 543–553.

Deutsch, J. A. 1960. *The Structural Basis of Behavior*. Chicago: University of Chicago Press.

Diamond, S., R. S. Balvin & F. R. Diamond. 1963. *Inhibition and Choice*. New York: Harper.

Diven, K. 1937. Certain Determinants in the Conditioning of Anxiety Reactions. *J. Psychol.*, 3: 291–308.

Dixon, N. F. 1956. Symbolic Associations Following Subliminal Stimulation. *Int. J. Psycho-Anal.*, 37: 159–170.

Eagle, M. 1959. The Effects of Subliminal Stimuli of Aggressive Content upon Conscious Cognition. *J. Pers.*, 27: 578–600.

———. 1962. Personality Correlates of Sensitivity to Subliminal Stimulation. *J. Nerv. Ment. Dis.*, 134: 1–17.

Eagle, M., D. Wolitzky & G. S. Klein. 1966. Imagery: Effect of a Concealed Figure in a Stimulus. *Science*, 151: 837–839.

Eccles, J. C. 1964. *The Physiology of Synapses.* Berlin: Springer.

Ehrenreich, G. A. 1960. Headache, Necrophilia, and Murder: A Brief Hypnotherapeutic Investigation of a Single Case. *Bull. Menninger Clin.*, 24: 273–287.

Ehrenzweig, A. 1953. *The Psychoanalysis of Artistic Vision and Hearing.* New York: Julian Press.

Engel, G. L. 1962. Anxiety and Depression-Withdrawal: The Primary Affects of Unpleasure. *Int. J. Psycho-Anal.*, 43: 89–97.

Eriksen, C. W. 1960. Discrimination and Learning Without Awareness: A Methodological Survey and Evaluation. *Psychol. Rev.*, 67: 279–300.

Erikson, E. H. 1946–1956. Identity and the Life Cycle: Selected Papers. *Psychol. Issues*, Monogr. 1. New York: International Universities Press, 1959.

———. 1951. *Childhood and Society.* New York: Norton.

———. 1954. The Dream Specimen of Psychoanalysis. *J. Amer. Psychoanal. Assn.*, 2: 5–56.

Federn, E. 1967. How Freudian Are the Freudians? Some Remarks on an Unpublished Letter. *J. Hist. Behav. Sci.*, 3: 269–281.

Fenichel, O. 1945. *The Psychoanalytic Theory of Neurosis.* New York: Norton.

Ferenczi, S. & O. Rank. 1925. *The Development of Psychoanalysis.* New York: Nervous and Mental Disease Publishing Co.

Fisher, C. 1954. Dreams and Perception: The Role of Preconscious and Primary Modes of Perception in Dream Formation. *J. Amer. Psychoanal. Assn.*, 2: 389–445.

———. 1956. Dreams, Images, and Perception: A Study of Unconscious-Preconscious Relationships. *J. Amer. Psychoanal. Assn.*, 4: 5–48.

———. 1957. A Study of the Preliminary Stages of the Construction of Dreams and Images. *J. Amer. Psychoanal. Assn.*, 5: 5–60.

———. 1960. Introduction to "Preconscious Stimulation in Dreams, Associations, and Images: Classical Studies by Otto Pötzl, Rudolf Allers, and Jakob Teler." *Psychol. Issues*, Monogr. 7: 1–40. New York: International Universities Press.

Fisher, C., J. Gross & J. Zuch. 1965. Cycle of Penile Erection Synchronous with Dreaming (REM) Sleep. *Arch. Gen. Psychiat.*, 12: 29–45.

Fisher, C. & I. H. Paul. 1959. The Effect of Subliminal Visual Stimulation on Images and Dreams: A Validation Study. *J. Amer. Psychoanal. Assn.*, 7: 35–83.

Fiss, H. 1966. The Effects of Experimentally Induced Changes in Alertness on Response to Subliminal Stimulation. *J. Pers.*, 34: 577–595.

Fiss, H., F. Goldberg & G. S. Klein. 1963. Effects of Subliminal Stimulation on Imagery and Discrimination. *Percept. Motor Skills*, 17: 31–44.

Fox, M. 1960. Differential Effects of Subliminal and Supraliminal Stimulation. Unpublished doctoral dissertation, New York University.

Frank, J. 1950. Some Aspects of Lobotomy (Prefrontal Leucotomy) under Psychoanalytic Scrutiny. *Psychiatry*, 13: 35–42.

Frenkel-Brunswik, E. 1951. Personality Theory and Perception. In R. R. Blake & G. V. Ramsey, eds., *Perception: An Approach to Personality*. New York: Ronald, pp. 356–419.

Freud, A. 1936. *The Ego and the Mechanisms of Defence.* New York: International Universities Press, 1946.

Freud, S. 1887–1902. *The Origins of Psychoanalysis: Letters to Wilhelm Fliess, Drafts and Notes, 1887–1902.* New York: Basic Books, 1954.

––––––. 1893. On the Psychical Mechanism of Hysterical Phenomena: A Lecture. In *Standard Edition*, 3: 27–39. London: Hogarth, 1962.

––––––. 1894. The Neuro-Psychoses of Defence. In *Standard Edition*, 3: 43–68. London: Hogarth, 1962.

––––––. 1895. Project for a Scientific Psychology. In Freud, *The Origins of Psychoanalysis: Letters to Wilhelm Fliess, Drafts and Notes, 1887–1902.* New York: Basic Books, 1954, pp. 347–445.

––––––. 1900. The Interpretation of Dreams. In *Standard Edition*, 4, 5. London: Hogarth, 1953.

––––––. 1901. The Psychopathology of Everyday Life. In *Standard Edition*, 6. London: Hogarth, 1960.

––––––. 1905a. Three Essays on the Theory of Sexuality. In *Standard Edition*, 7: 130–243. London: Hogarth, 1953.

––––––. 1905b. Fragment of an Analysis of a Case of Hysteria. In *Standard Edition*, 7: 7–122. London: Hogarth, 1953.

––––––. 1905c. Jokes and Their Relation to the Unconscious. In *Standard Edition*, 8. London: Hogarth, 1960.

––––––. 1909. Notes upon a Case of Obsessional Neurosis. In *Standard Edition*, 10: 155–318. London: Hogarth, 1955.

––––––. 1911. Formulations on the Two Principles of Mental Functioning. In *Standard Edition*, 12: 218–226. London: Hogarth, 1958.

––––––. 1912. Recommendations to Physicians Practising Psycho-Analysis. In *Standard Edition*, 12: 109–120. London: Hogarth, 1958.

––––––. 1915a. Repression. In *Standard Edition*, 14: 146–158. London: Hogarth, 1957.

––––––. 1915b. The Unconscious. In *Standard Edition*, 14: 166–215. London: Hogarth, 1957.

―――. 1916–1917. Introductory Lectures on Psychoanalysis, Part III. In *Standard Edition*, 16: 243–463. London: Hogarth, 1963.

―――. 1917. A Metapsychological Supplement to the Theory of Dreams. In *Standard Edition*, 14: 222–235. London: Hogarth, 1957.

―――. 1919a. The "Uncanny." In *Standard Edition*, 17: 217–252. London: Hogarth, 1955.

―――. 1919b. "A Child Is Being Beaten": A Contribution to the Study of the Origin of Sexual Perversions. In *Standard Edition*, 17: 177–204. London: Hogarth, 1955.

―――. 1920. Beyond the Pleasure Principle. In *Standard Edition*, 18: 7–64. London: Hogarth, 1955.

―――. 1923. The Ego and the Id. In *Standard Edition*, 19: 12–66. London: Hogarth, 1961.

―――. 1924. The Economic Problem of Masochism. In *Standard Edition*, 19: 159–170. London: Hogarth, 1961.

―――. 1925. A Note upon the "Mystic Writing-Pad." In *Standard Edition*, 19: 227–232. London: Hogarth, 1961.

―――. 1926. Inhibitions, Symptoms and Anxiety. In *Standard Edition*, 20: 87–172. London: Hogarth, 1959.

―――. 1927. Postscript to "The Question of Lay Analysis." In *Standard Edition*, 20: 251–258. London: Hogarth, 1959.

―――. 1933. New Introductory Lectures on Psycho-Analysis. In *Standard Edition*, 22: 5–182. London: Hogarth, 1964.

―――. 1936. A Disturbance of Memory on the Acropolis. In *Standard Edition*, 22: 239–248. London: Hogarth, 1964.

Friedman, N. 1967. *The Social Nature of Psychological Research: The Psychological Experiment as a Social Interaction*. New York: Basic Books.

Gardner, R. W. 1953. Cognitive Styles in Categorizing Behavior. *J. Pers.*, 22: 214–233.

―――. 1962. Cognitive Controls and Adaptation: Research and Measurement. In S. J. Messick & J. Ross, eds., *Measurement in Personality and Cognition*. New York: Wiley, pp. 183–198.

―――. 1964a. The Development of Cognitive Structures. In C. Scheerer, ed., *Cognition: Theory, Research, Promise*. New York: Harper, pp. 147–171.

―――. 1964b. The Menninger Foundation Study of Twins and Their Parents. Paper presented to American Psychological Association, Los Angeles, September.

―――. 1965. Genetics and Personality Theory. In S. G. Vandenberg, ed., *Methods and Goals in Human Behavior Genetics*. New York: Academic Press, pp. 223–229.

Gardner, R. W., P. S. Holzman, G. S. Klein, H. B. Linton & D. P. Spence.

1959. Cognitive Control: A Study of Individual Consistencies in Cognitive Behavior. *Psychol. Issues*, Monogr. 4. New York: International Universities Press.

Gardner, R. W., D. N. Jackson & S. J. Messick. 1960. Personality Organization in Cognitive Controls and Intellectual Abilities. *Psychol. Issues*, Monogr. 8. New York: International Universities Press.

Gardner, R. W. & L. J. Lohrenz. 1960. Leveling-Sharpening and Serial Reproduction of a Story. *Bull. Menninger Clin.*, 24: 295–304.

Gardner, R. W. & R. I. Long. 1962. Control, Defence and Centration Effect: A Study of Scanning Behaviour. *Brit. J. Psychol.*, 53: 129–140.

Gardner, R. W. & A. Moriarty. 1968. *Personality Development at Preadolescence: Explorations of Structure Formation.* Seattle: University of Washington Press.

Gerard, R. W. 1956. Imagination in Science. Address to the Associates of the Bank Street College of Education Conference, New York.

Gerathewohl, S. J. 1962. Effect of Gravity-Free State. In K. E. Schaeffer, ed., *Environmental Effects on Consciousness.* New York: Macmillan, pp. 73–85.

Ghiselen, B., ed. 1952. *The Creative Process: A Symposium.* New York: New American Library, 1955.

Gibson, J. J. 1950a. *The Perception of the Visual World.* Boston: Houghton Mifflin.

———. 1950b. The Perception of Visual Surfaces. *Amer. J. Psychol.*, 63: 367–384.

———. 1951. Theories of Perception. In W. Dennis *et al.*, *Current Trends in Psychological Theory.* Pittsburgh: University of Pittsburgh Press, pp. 85–110.

———. 1953. Social Perception and the Psychology of Perceptual Learning. In M. Sherif & M. O. Wilson, eds., *Group Relations at the Crossroads.* New York: Harper, pp. 120–138.

———. 1954. Ordinal Stimulation and the Possibility of a Global Psychophysics. Paper presented at the Fourteenth International Congress of Psychology, Montreal.

———. 1959. Perception as a Function of Stimulation. In S. Koch, ed., *Psychology: A Study of a Science.* New York: McGraw-Hill, pp. 456–501.

———. 1964. Introduction to "The Formation and Transformation of the Perceptual World." *Psychol. Issues*, Monogr. 12: 5–13. New York: International Universities Press.

———. 1966. The Problem of Temporal Order in Stimulation and Perception. *J. Psychol.*, 62: 141–149.

Gill, M. M. 1959. The Present State of Psychoanalytic Theory. *J. Abnorm. Soc. Psychol.*, 58: 1–8.

———. 1967. The Primary Process. In R. R. Holt, ed., *Motives and*

Thought: Psychoanalytic Essays in Honor of David Rapaport. *Psychol. Issues,* Monogr. 18/19: 260–298. New York: International Universities Press.

Gill, M. M. & M. Brenman. 1959. *Hypnosis and Related States.* New York: International Universities Press.

Gill, M. M., J. Simon, G. Fink, N. A. Endicott & I. H. Paul. 1968. Studies in Audio-Recorded Psychoanalysis. I. General Considerations. *J. Amer. Psychoanal. Assn.,* 16: 230–244.

Glover, E. 1925. Notes on Oral Character Formation. In *On the Early Development of Mind,* Vol. 1. New York: International Universities Press, 1956, pp. 25–46.

Goldberger, L. 1961. Reactions to Perceptual Isolation and Rorschach Manifestations of the Primary Process. *J. Proj. Tech.,* 25: 287–303.

———. 1962. The Isolation Situation and Personality. In G. Nielson, ed., *Proceedings of the XIV International Congress of Applied Psychology,* Vol. 2: *Personality Research.* Copenhagen: Munksgaard, pp. 128–143.

———. 1966a. Experimental Isolation: An Overview. *Amer. J. Psychiat.,* 122: 774–782.

———. 1966b. The Interaction of Situational and Organismic Variables in the Effects of Perceptual Isolation. In *Recent Research in Sensory Deprivation.* Symposium at the New York State Psychological Association, May.

Goldberger, L. & R. R. Holt. 1958. Experimental Interference with Reality Contact (Perceptual Isolation): Method and Group Results. *J. Nerv. Ment. Dis.,* 127: 99–112.

———. 1961a. Experimental Interference with Reality Contact: Individual Differences. In P. Solomon *et al.,* eds., *Sensory Deprivation.* Cambridge, Mass.: Harvard University Press, pp. 130–142.

———. 1961b. A Comparison of Isolation Effects and Their Personality Correlates in Two Divergent Samples. *USAF ASD Tech. Rep.,* No. 61–417.

Goldstein, K. 1939. *The Organism.* New York: American Book.

———. 1942. Some Experimental Observations Concerning the Influence of Colors on the Function of the Organism. *Occup. Ther. Rehabil.,* 21: 147–151.

Graetz, H. R. 1964. *The Symbolic Language of Vincent van Gogh.* New York: McGraw-Hill.

Granit, R. 1955. *Receptors and Sensory Perception.* New Haven: Yale University Press.

Gregory, R. L. 1963. Distortion of Visual Space as Inappropriate Constancy Scaling. *Nature,* 199: 678–680.

———. 1966. *Eye and Brain: The Psychology of Seeing.* London: World University Library.

Haber, R. N. & M. H. Erdelyi. 1967. Emergence and Recovery of Initially Unavailable Perceptual Material. *J. Verb. Learn. Verb. Behav.*, 6: 618–628.

Hampshire, S. 1959. *Thought and Action.* London: Chatto & Windus.

Hanfmann, E. 1939. Analysis of the Thinking Disorder in a Case of Schizophrenia. *Arch. Neurol. Psychiat.*, 41: 568–579.

Hanrahan, T. S. & D. Bushnell. 1960. *Space Biology: The Human Factors in Space Flight.* New York: Basic Books.

Harlow, H. F. & G. C. Comstock. 1961. Development of Affectional Patterns in Primates. Paper presented to the New York State Division of the American Psychiatric Association.

Harlow, H. F. & M. K. Harlow. 1961. A Study of Animal Affection. *Nat. Hist.*, 70(10): 48–55.

Hartline, H. K. & F. Ratliff. 1956. Inhibitory Interaction of Receptor Units in the Eye of *Limulus*. *J. Gen. Physiol.*, 40: 357–376.

Hartmann, H. 1939. *Ego Psychology and the Problem of Adaptation.* New York: International Universities Press, 1958.

———. 1948. Comments on the Psychoanalytic Theory of Instinctual Drives. In *Essays on Ego Psychology.* New York: International Universities Press, 1964, pp. 69–89.

———. 1950. Comments on the Psychoanalytic Theory of the Ego. In *Essays on Ego Psychology.* New York: International Universities Press, 1964, pp. 113–141.

———. 1952. The Mutual Influences in the Development of the Ego and Id. In *Essays on Ego Psychology.* New York: International Universities Press, 1964, pp. 155–181.

Hartmann, H., E. Kris & R. M. Loewenstein. 1946. Comments on the Formation of Psychic Structure. *Psychol. Issues*, Monogr. 14: 27–55. New York: International Universities Press, 1964.

Hebb, D. O. 1949. *The Organization of Behavior: A Neuropsychological Theory.* New York: Wiley.

———. 1954. The Problem of Consciousness and Introspection. In J. F. Delafresnaye, ed., *Brain Mechanisms and Consciousness.* Springfield, Ill.: Thomas, pp. 402–417.

———. 1955a. The Mammal and His Environment. *Amer. J. Psychiat.*, 111: 826–831.

———. 1955b. Drives and the C.N.S. (Conceptual Nervous System). *Psychol. Rev.*, 62: 243–254.

———. 1957. Perception and Perceptual Learning. Address to the Eastern Psychological Association, New York, April.

———. 1958. *A Textbook of Psychology.* Philadelphia: Saunders.

Hebb, D. O., E. S. Heath & E. A. Stuart. 1954. Experimental Deafness. *Canad. J. Psychol.*, 8: 152–156.

Heider, F. 1926. Thing and Medium. *Psychol. Issues,* Monogr. 3: 1–34. New York: International Universities Press, 1959.

———. 1930. The Function of the Perceptual System. *Psychol. Issues,* Monogr. 3: 35–52. New York: International Universities Press, 1959.

———. 1944. Social Perception and Phenomenal Causality. *Psychol. Rev.,* 51: 358–374.

Heider, F. & M. Simmel. 1944. An Experimental Study of Apparent Behavior. *Amer. J. Psychol.,* 57: 243–259.

Held, R. & A. V. Hein. 1958. Adaptation of Disarranged Hand-Eye Coordination Contingent upon Re-afferent Stimulation. *Percept. Motor Skills,* 8: 87–90.

Held, R. & M. Schlank. 1959. Adaptation to Disarranged Eye-Hand Coordination in the Distance-Dimension. *Amer. J. Psychol.,* 72: 603–605.

Helmholtz, H. von. 1910. *Treatise on Physiological Optics,* 3rd ed., Vol. 3. Rochester, N.Y.: Optical Society of America, 1924–1925.

Helson, H. 1948. Adaptation-Level as a Basis for a Quantitative Theory of Frames of Reference. *Psychol. Rev.,* 55: 297–313.

———. 1953. Psychiatric Screening of Flying Personnel: Perception and Personality—A Critique of Recent Experimental Literature. *USAF Air University School of Aviation Medicine Project Report* (Project #21-0202-0007, Report #1), July.

———. 1959. Adaptation Level Theory. In S. Koch, ed., *Psychology: A Study of a Science,* Vol. 1. New York: McGraw-Hill, pp. 565–621.

Hernandez-Peón, R., H. Scherrer & M. Jouvet. 1956. Modification of Electric Activity in Cochlear Nucleus During "Attention" in Unanesthetized Cats. *Science,* 123: 331–332.

Herold, C. M. 1941–1942. Critical Analysis of the Elements of Psychic Functions. *Psychoanal. Quart.,* 10: 513–544; 11: 59–82, 187–210.

Heron, P. 1955. Inspiration for the Painter. *New Statesman & Nation,* January 1.

Hilgard, E. 1951. The Role of Learning in Perception. In R. R. Blake & G. V. Ramsey, eds., *Perception: An Approach to Personality.* New York: Ronald, pp. 95–120.

———. 1962. Impulsive Versus Realistic Thinking: An Examination of the Distinction Between Primary and Secondary Processes in Thought. *Psychol. Bull.,* 59: 477–488.

Hochberg, J. E. 1954. Psychophysics and Stereotypy in Social Perception. Paper at the Third Conference in Social Psychology (Emerging Problems in Social Psychology), Norman, Oklahoma, March.

———. 1957. Effects of the Gestalt Revolution: The Cornell Symposium on Perception. *Psychol. Rev.,* 64: 73–84.

Hochberg, J. E. & V. Brooks. 1954. Takete and Uloomu—An Item Analysis of Physiognomic Connotation. New York University, mimeographed.

Hochberg, J. E. & H. Gleitman. 1949. Towards a Reformulation of the Perception-Motivation Dichotomy. *J. Pers.,* 18: 180–191.

Holmes, C. & P. S. Holzman. 1966. Effect of White Noise on Disinhibition of Verbal Expression. *Percept. Motor Skills,* 23: 1039–1042.

Holt, R. R. 1956. Gauging Primary and Secondary Processes in Rorschach Responses. *J. Proj. Tech.,* 20: 14–25.

————. 1960. Cognitive Controls and Primary Processes. *J. Psychol. Res., Madras,* 4: 105–112.

————. 1965a. Ego Autonomy Re-evaluated. *Int. J. Psycho-Anal.,* 46: 151–167.

————. 1965b. A Review of Some of Freud's Biological Assumptions and Their Influence on His Theories. In N. S. Greenfield & W. C. Lewis, eds., *Psychoanalysis and Current Biological Thought.* Madison: University of Wisconsin Press, pp. 93–124.

————. 1967a. The Development of the Primary Process: A Structural View. In Motives and Thought: Psychoanalytic Essays in Honor of David Rapaport. *Psychol. Issues,* Monogr. 18/19: 345–383.

————. 1967b. Beyond Vitalism and Mechanism: Freud's Concept of Psychic Energy. *Science and Psychoanalysis,* 11: 1–41. New York: Grune & Stratton.

Holt, R. R. & L. Goldberger. 1959. Personological Correlates of Reactions to Perceptual Isolation. *USAF WADC Tech. Rep.,* No. 59–735.

Holt, R. R. & J. Havel. 1960. A Method for Assessing Primary and Secondary Process in the Rorschach. In M. A. Rickers-Ovsiankina, ed., *Rorschach Psychology.* New York: Wiley, pp. 263–315.

Holzman, P. S. 1954. The Relation of Assimilation Tendencies in Visual, Auditory, and Kinesthetic Time-Error to Cognitive Attitudes of Leveling and Sharpening. *J. Pers.,* 22: 375–394.

————. 1957. Focussing: A Style of Reality Contact. *Amer. Psychologist,* 12: 388.

————.1966. Scanning: A Principle of Reality Contact. *Percept. Motor Skills,* 23: 835–844.

Holzman, P. S. & R. W. Gardner. 1959. Leveling and Repression. *J. Abnorm. Soc. Psychol.,* 59: 151–155.

Holzman, P. S. & G. S. Klein. 1954. Cognitive System-Principles of Leveling and Sharpening: Individual Differences in Assimilation Effects in Visual Time-Error. *J. Psychol.,* 37: 105–122.

————. 1956. Intersensory and Visual Field Forces in Size Estimation. *Percept. Motor Skills,* 6: 37–41.

Holzman, P. S. & C. Rousey. 1966. The Voice as a Percept. *J. Pers. Soc. Psychol.,* 4: 79–86.

Holzman, P. S., C. Rousey & C. Snyder. 1966. On Listening to One's Own

Voice: Effects on Psychophysiological Responses and Free Associations. *J. Pers. Soc. Psychol.*, 4: 432–441.

Home, H. J. 1966. The Concept of Mind. *Int. J. Psycho-Anal.*, 47: 42–49.

Isaacs, S. 1948. The Nature and Function of Phantasy. In J. Riviere, ed., *Developments in Psycho-Analysis*. London: Hogarth, 1952, pp. 67–121.

Isakower, O. 1939. On the Exceptional Position of the Auditory Sphere. *Int. J. Psycho-Anal.*, 20: 340–348.

Israel, N. R. 1966. Individual Differences in GSR Orienting Response and Cognitive Control. *J. Exp. Res. Pers.*, 1: 244–248.

———. 1968. Cognitive Control and Patterns of Autonomic Response. Paper presented to Eastern Psychological Association, Washington, D.C., April.

Jacob, P. 1954. *The Behavior Cycle*. Ann Arbor: Edwards.

James, W. 1890. *The Principles of Psychology*, 2 vols. New York: Holt.

Jenkin, N. 1957. Affective Processes in Perception. *Psychol. Bull.*, 54: 100–127.

Jensen, A. R. 1965. Scoring the Stroop Test. *Acta Psychol.*, 24: 398–408.

Jensen, A. R. & W. D. Rohwer, Jr. 1966. The Stroop Color-Word Test: A Review. *Acta Psychol.*, 25: 36–93.

Johansson, G., I. Dureman & H. Sälde. 1955. Motion Perception and Personality, I. *Acta Psychol.*, 11: 289–296.

Johnson, H. & C. W. Eriksen. 1961. Preconscious Perception: A Reexamination of the Poetzl Phenomenon. *J. Abnorm. Soc. Psychol.*, 62: 479–503.

Jones, E. 1953. *The Life and Work of Sigmund Freud*, Vol. 1. New York: Basic Books.

Jouvet, M. 1961. Telencephalic and Rhombencephalic Sleep in the Cat. In G. E. W. Wolstenholme & M. O'Connor, eds., *The Nature of Sleep*. Boston: Little Brown, pp. 188–206.

Katz, D. 1948. *Gestalt Psychology*, rev. ed. New York: Ronald, 1950.

Kaufman, I. C. 1960. Some Ethological Studies of Social Relationships and Conflict Situations. *J. Amer. Psychoanal. Assn.*, 8: 671–685.

Klein, G. S. 1949. Adaptive Properties of Sensory Functioning. *Bull. Menninger Clin.*, 13: 16–23.

Klein, G. S. & H. L. Barr. Manuscript. Effects of LSD-25 upon Incidental and Focal Responsiveness to Physiognomic Properties of Words.

Klein, G. S., H. L. Barr & D. L. Wolitzky. 1967. Personality. *Ann. Rev. Psychol.*, 18: 467–560.

Klein, G. S., R. W. Gardner & H. J. Schlesinger. 1962. Tolerance for Unrealistic Experiences: A Study of the Generality of a Cognitive Control. *Brit. J. Psychol.*, 53: 41–55.

Klein, G. S. & R. R. Holt. 1960. Problems and Issues in Current Studies of Peripheral Activation. In J. G. Peatman & E. L. Hartley, eds.,

Festschrift for Gardner Murphy. New York: Harper, pp. 75–93.
Klein, G. S. & P. S. Holzman. 1950. The "Schematizing Process": Perceptual Attitudes and Personality Qualities in Sensitivity to Change. *Amer. Psychologist,* 5: 312.
Klein, G. S. & D. Krech. 1951. The Problem of Personality and Its Theory. *J. Pers.,* 20: 1–23.
———. 1952. Cortical Conductivity in the Brain-Injured. *J. Pers.,* 21: 118–148.
Klein, G. S. & H. J. Schlesinger. 1949. Where Is the Perceiver in Perceptual Theory? *J. Pers.,* 18: 32–47.
———. 1951. Perceptual Attitudes Toward Instability. I: Prediction of Apparent Movement Experiences from Rorschach Responses. *J. Pers.* 19: 289–302. Also in M. H. Sherman, ed., *A Rorschach Reader.* New York: International Universities Press, 1960, pp. 288–301.
Klein, G. S., H. J. Schlesinger & D. M. Meister. 1951. The Effect of Personal Values on Perception: An Experimental Critique. *Psychol. Rev.,* 58: 96–112.
Klein. G. S., D. P. Spence, R. R. Holt & S. Gourevitch. 1958. Cognition Without Awareness: Subliminal Influences upon Conscious Thought. *J. Aborm. Soc. Psychol.,* 57: 255–266.
Klein, G. S. & D. L. Wolitzky. 1970. Vocal Isolation: The Effects of Occluding Auditory Feedback from One's Own Voice. *J. Abnorm. Psychol.,* 75: 50–56.
Klüver, H. 1930. Fragmentary Eidetic Imagery. *Psychol. Rev.,* 37: 441–458.
Knapp, P. H., ed. 1963. *Expression of the Emotions in Man.* New York: International Universities Press.
Koffka, K. & M. Harrower. 1932. Colour and Organization. *Smith Coll. Stud. Psychol.,* 3: 177–303.
Kohler, I. 1951. The Formation and Transformation of the Perceptual World. *Psychol. Issues,* Monogr. 12: 19–133. New York: International Universities Press, 1964.
———. 1953. Rehabituation in Perception. *Psychol. Issues,* Monogr. 12: 135–164. New York: International Universities Press, 1964.
———. 1956. Die Methode des Brillenversuchs in der Wahrnehmungspsychologie mit Bemerkungen zur Lehre von der Adaptation. *Z. Exp. Angew. Psychol.,* 3: 381–417.
Köhler, W. 1947. *Gestalt Psychology,* rev. ed. New York: Liveright.
Köhler, W. & H. Wallach. 1944. Figural After-Effects. *Proc. Amer. Phil. Soc.,* 88: 269–357.
Kouwer, B. J. 1949. *Colors and Their Character.* The Hague: Nijhoff.
Krauss, R. 1930. Über Graphischen Ausdruck. *Beihefte Z. Angew. Psychol.,* 14(Whole No. 48).

Krech, D. 1949. Notes Toward a Psychological Theory. *J. Pers.*, 18: 66–87.

———. 1951. Cognition and Motivation in Psychological Theory. In W. Dennis *et al., Current Trends in Psychological Theory.* Pittsburgh: University of Pittsburgh Press, pp. 111–139.

Kris, E. 1939. On Inspiration. *Psychoanalytic Explorations in Art.* New York: International Universities Press, 1952, pp. 291–302.

———. 1950. On Preconscious Mental Processes. *Psychoanalytic Explorations in Art.* New York: International Universities Press, 1952, pp. 303–318.

———. 1956. The Recovery of Childhood Memories in Psychoanalysis. *Psychoanal. Study Child,* 11: 54–88. New York: International Universities Press.

Kubie, L. S. 1943. The Use of Induced Hypnagogic Reveries in the Recovery of Repressed Amnesic Data. *Bull. Menninger Clin.,* 7: 172–182.

———. 1945. The Value of Induced Dissociated States in the Therapeutic Process. *Proc. Roy. Soc. Med.,* 38: 681–683.

———. 1947. The Fallacious Use of Quantitative Concepts of Dynamic Psychology. *Psychoanal. Quart.,* 16: 507–518.

———. 1954. Psychiatric and Psychoanalytic Considerations of the Problem of Consciousness. In J. F. Delafresnaye, ed., *Brain Mechanisms and Consciousness.* Springfield, Ill.: Thomas, pp. 421, 444–469.

Kubie, L. S. & S. Margolin. 1942. A Physiological Method for the Induction of States of Partial Sleep, and Securing Free Association and Early Memories in Such States. *Trans. Amer. Neurol. Assn.,* 68: 136–139.

Lacey, J. I. 1959. Psychophysiological Approaches to the Evaluation of Psychotherapeutic Process and Outcome. In *Research in Psychotherapy.* Washington, D.C.: American Psychological Association, pp. 160–208.

Lacey, J. I., J. Kagan, B. C. Lacey & H. A. Moss. 1963. The Visceral Level: Situational Determinants and Behavioral Correlates of Autonomic Response Patterns. In P. Knapp, ed., *Expression of the Emotions in Man.* New York: International Universities Press, pp. 161–196.

Lacey, J. I. & R. L. Smith. 1954. Conditioning and Generalization of Unconscious Anxiety. *Science,* 120: 1045–1052.

Lambert, W. W., R. L. Solomon & P. D. Watson. 1949. Reinforcement and Extinction as Factors in Size Estimation. *J. Exper. Psychol.,* 37: 637–641.

Lapkin, B. 1960. The Relation of Primary Process Thinking to the Recovery of Subliminal Material. Unpublished doctoral dissertation, New York University.

Lashley, K. S. 1949. Persistent Problems in the Evolution of Mind. In F. A. Beach, D. O. Hebb, C. T. Morgan & H. W. Nissen, eds., *The Neuropsychology of Lashley*. New York: McGraw-Hill, 1960, pp. 455–477.

———. 1951. The Problem of Serial Order in Behavior. In F. A. Beach, D. O. Hebb, C. T. Morgan & H. W. Nissen, eds., *The Neuropsychology of Lashley*. New York: McGraw-Hill, 1960, pp. 506–528.

———. 1954. Dynamic Processes in Perception. In J. F. Delafresnaye, ed., *Brain Mechanisms and Consciousness*. Springfield, Ill.: Thomas, pp. 422–443.

———. 1958. Cerebral Organization and Behavior. In F. A. Beach, D. O. Hebb, C. T. Morgan & H. W. Nissen, eds., *The Neuropsychology of Lashley*. New York: McGraw-Hill, 1960, pp. 529–543.

Lauenstein, O. 1932. Ansatz zu einer physiologischen Theorie des Vergleiches und der Zeitfehler. *Psychol. Forsch.*, 17: 130–178.

Lazarus, R. S. & R. A. McCleary. 1951. Autonomic Discrimination Without Awareness: A Study of Subception. *Psychol. Rev.*, 58: 113–122.

Levine, R., I. Chein & G. Murphy. 1942. The Relation of the Intensity of a Need to the Amount of Perceptual Distortion: A Preliminary Report. *J. Psychol.*, 13: 283–293.

Lewin, K. 1946. Behavior and Development as a Function of the Total Situation. In L. Carmichael, ed., *Manual of Child Psychology*. New York: Wiley, pp. 791–844.

Lewy, E. & D. Rapaport. 1944. The Psychoanalytic Concept of Memory and Its Relation to Recent Memory Theories. In *Collected Papers of David Rapaport*. New York: Basic Books, 1967, pp. 136–159.

Lifton, R. J. 1956. "Thought Reform" of Western Civilians in Chinese Communist Prisons. *Psychiatry*, 19: 173–195.

———. 1961. *Thought Reform and the Psychology of Totalism*. New York: Norton.

Linton, H. B. & R. J. Langs. 1962. Subjective Reactions to Lysergic Acid Diethelamide (LSD-25): Measured by a Questionnaire. *Arch. Gen. Psychiat.*, 6: 352–368.

———. 1964. Empirical Dimensions of the LSD-25 Reaction. *Arch. Gen. Psychiat.*, 10: 469–485.

Lipin, T. 1963. The Repetition Compulsion and "Maturational" Drive-Representatives. *Int. J. Psycho-Anal.*, 44: 389–406.

Lippmann, P. 1961. Effects of Hypnotically Activated Drives upon Response to Masked Visual Stimuli. Unpublished doctoral dissertation, New York University.

Loewenstein, R. M. 1956. Some Remarks on the Role of Speech in Psycho-Analytic Technique. *Int. J. Psycho-Anal.*, 37: 460–467.

Loomis, H. K. & S. Moskowitz. 1958. Cognitive Style and Stimulus Ambiguity. *J. Pers.* 26: 349–364.

Lovinger, R. J. 1969. Process and Adaptive Aspects of Leveling-Sharpening. Unpublished doctoral dissertation, New York University.

Luborsky, L. 1967. Momentary Forgetting During Psychotherapy and Psychoanalysis: A Theory and a Research Method. In R. R. Holt, ed., Motives and Thought: Psychoanalytic Essays in Honor of David Rapaport. *Psychol. Issues*, Monogr. 18/19: 177–217. New York: International Universities Press.

Luborsky, L. & B. Blinder. 1964. Eye Fixation and the Contents of Recall and Images as a Function of Heart Rate. *Percept. Motor Skills*, 18: 421–436.

Luborsky, L., B. Blinder & N. Mackworth. 1963. Eye Fixation and Recall of Pictures as a Function of GSR Responsivity. *Percept. Motor Skills*, 16: 469–483.

Luborsky, L. & H. Shevrin. 1956. Dreams and Day-Residues: A Study of the Poetzl Observation. *Bull. Menninger Clin.*, 20: 135–148.

————. 1962. Forgetting of Tachistoscopic Exposures as a Function of Repression. *Percept. Motor Skills*, 14: 189–190.

Luchins, A. S. 1951. An Evaluation of Some Current Criticisms of Gestalt Psychological Work on Perception. *Psychol. Rev.*, 58: 69–95.

Lundholm, H. 1921. The Affective Tone of Lines. *Psychol. Rev.*, 28: 43–60.

Luria, A. R. 1961. *The Role of Speech in the Regulation of Normal and Abnormal Behaviour*. New York: Pergamon.

McConnell, J. V., R. L. Cutler & E. B. McNeil. 1958. Subliminal Stimulation: An Overview. *Amer. Psychologist*, 13: 229–242.

MacCorquodale, K. & P. E. Meehl. 1948. On a Distinction Between Hypothetical Constructs and Intervening Variables. *Psychol. Rev.*, 55: 95–107.

McCulloch, W. S. 1948. A Recapitulation of the Theory, with a Forecast of Several Extensions. *Ann. N.Y. Acad. Sci.*, 50: 259–274.

Mackworth, J. D. 1963. The Relation Between the Visual Image and Post-Perceptual Immediate Memory. *J. Verb. Learn. Verb. Behav.*, 2: 75–85.

Mahl, G. F. 1961. Sensory Factors in the Control of Expressive Behavior: An Experimental Study of the Function of Auditory Self-Stimulation and Visual Feedback in the Dynamics of Vocal and Gestural Behavior in the Interview Situation. *Acta Psychol.*, 19: 497–498.

Malmo, R. B., C. Shagass, D. J. Bélanger & A. A. Smith. 1951. Motor Control in Psychiatric Patients Under Experimental Stress. *J. Abnorm. Soc. Psychol.*, 46: 539–547.

Maslow, A. H. 1943. Dynamics of Personality Organization, I. *Psychol. Rev.*, 50: 514–539.

Mausner, B. & A. Siegal. 1950. The Effect of Variation in "Value" on

Perceptual Thresholds. *J. Abnorm. Soc. Psychol.*, 45: 760–763.

Menninger, K. A. 1958. *The Theory of Psychoanalytic Technique.* New York: Basic Books.

Michotte, A. 1946. *The Perception of Causality.* New York: Basic Books, 1963.

———. 1950. The Emotions Regarded as Functional Connections. In M. L. Reymert, ed., *Feelings and Emotions: The Mooseheart Symposium.* New York: McGraw-Hill, pp. 114–126.

———. 1951. La Perception de la Fonction "Outil." In G. Ekman, T. Husén, G. Johansson & C. I. Sandström, eds., *Essays in Psychology Dedicated to David Katz.* Uppsala: Almqvist & Wiksells, pp. 193–312.

Miller, G. A. 1951. *Language and Communication.* New York: McGraw-Hill.

Miller, J. G. 1939. Discrimination Without Awareness. *Amer. J. Psychol.*, 52: 562–578.

———. 1951. Unconscious Processes and Perception. In R. R. Blake & G. V. Ramsey, eds., *Perception: An Approach to Personality.* New York: Ronald, pp. 258–282.

Miller, S. C. 1962. Ego-Autonomy in Sensory Deprivation, Isolation, and Stress. *Int. J. Psycho-Anal.*, 43: 1–20.

Murphy, G. 1947. *Personality: A Biosocial Approach to Origins and Structure.* New York: Harper.

———. 1956. Affect and Perceptual Learning. *Psychol. Rev.*, 63: 1–15.

Murray, H. A. 1938. *Explorations in Personality.* New York: Oxford.

———. 1951. Toward a Classification of Interactions. In T. Parsons & E. A. Shils, eds., *Toward a General Theory of Action.* Cambridge, Mass.: Harvard University Press, pp. 434–464.

Niederland, W. G. 1964. Ego Function and the Recovery of Early Memories. In W. G. Niederland, rep., Scientific Proceedings—Panel Reports: Memory and Repression. *J. Amer. Psychoanal. Assn.* (1965), 13: 619–633.

Olden, C. 1941. About the Fascinating Effect of the Narcissistic Personality. *Amer. Imago*, 2: 347–355.

Omwake, E. G. & A. J. Solnit. 1961. "It Isn't Fair": The Treatment of a Blind Child. *Psychoanal. Study Child*, 16: 352–404. New York: International Universities Press.

Osgood, C. E. 1957. A Behavioristic Analysis of Perception and Language as Cognitive Phenomena. In J. S. Bruner *et al.*, *Contemporary Approaches to Cognition.* Cambridge, Mass.: Harvard University Press, pp. 75–118.

Ostow, M. 1963. Familiarity and Strangeness. *Israel Ann. Psychiat. Relat. Discipl.*, 1: 31–42.

Ostwald, P. F. 1960. Human Sounds. In D. A. Barbara, ed., *Psychological and Psychiatric Aspects of Speech and Hearing.* Springfield, Ill.: Thomas, pp. 110–137.

Oswald, I. 1962. *Sleeping and Waking.* New York: American Elsevier.

Paul, I. H. 1959. Studies in Remembering. *Psychol. Issues,* Monogr. 2. New York: International Universities Press.

———. 1967. The Concept of Schema in Memory Theory. In R. R. Holt, ed., Motives and Thought: Psychoanalytic Essays in Honor of David Rapaport. *Psychol. Issues,* Monogr. 18/19: 218–258. New York: International Universities Press.

———. Manuscript. The Personality Correlates of a Remembering Style.

Paul, I. H. & C. Fisher. 1959. Subliminal Visual Stimulation: A Study of Its Influence on Subsequent Images and Dreams. *J. Nerv. Ment. Dis.,* 129: 315–340.

Penfield, W. & T. Rasmussen. 1950. *The Cerebral Cortex of Man.* New York: Macmillan.

Piaget, J. 1936. *The Origins of Intelligence in Children,* 2nd ed. New York: International Universities Press, 1952.

———. 1941. *The Child's Conception of Number.* London: Routledge, 1952.

Pieron, H. 1955. Les Données Psychophysiologiques de Base. In A. Michotte *et al., La Perception.* Paris: Presses Universitaires, pp. 7–15.

Pine, F. 1960. Incidental Stimulation: A Study of Preconscious Transformations. *J. Abnorm. Soc. Psychol.,* 60: 68–75.

———. 1961. Incidental Versus Focal Presentation of Drive Related Stimuli. *J. Abnorm. Soc. Psychol.,* 62: 482–490.

———. 1964. The Bearing of Psychoanalytic Theory on Selected Issues in Research on Marginal Stimuli. *J. Nerv. Ment. Dis.,* 138: 205–222.

Polanyi, M. 1958. *Personal Knowledge: Towards a Post-Critical Philosophy.* London: Oxford.

———. 1966. *The Tacit Dimension.* Garden City, N.Y.: Doubleday.

Postman, L. 1964. Short-Term Memory and Incidental Learning. In A. W. Melton, ed., *Categories of Human Learning.* New York: Academic Press, pp. 145–201.

Postman, L. & J. S. Bruner. 1952. Hypothesis and the Principle of Closure: The Effect of Frequency and Recency. *J. Psychol.,* 33: 113–125.

Pötzl, O. 1917. The Relationship Between Experimentally Induced Dream Images and Indirect Vision. *Psychol. Issues,* Monogr. 7: 41–120. New York: International Universities Press, 1960.

Pribram, K. 1965. Freud's Project: An Open, Biologically Based Model for Psychoanalysis. In N. S. Greenfield & W. C. Lewis, eds., *Psychoanalysis and Current Biological Thought*. Madison: University of Wisconsin Press, pp. 81–92.

Proshansky, H. & G. Murphy. 1942. The Effects of Reward and Punishment on Perception. *J. Psychol.*, 13: 295–305.

Purdy, D. M. 1935. The Structure of the Visual World. I: Space-Perception and the Perception of Wholes. *Psychol. Rev.*, 42: 399–424.

Pustell, T. E. 1957. The Experimental Induction of Perceptual Vigilance and Defense. *J. Pers.*, 25: 425–438.

Rapaport, D. 1942. *Emotions and Memory*, 2nd (unaltered) ed. New York: International Universities Press, 1950.

———. 1950a. Review of *Cybernetics*, by N. Wiener. In *Collected Papers*. New York: Basic Books, 1967, pp. 329–333.

———. 1950b. On the Psychoanalytic Theory of Thinking. In *Collected Papers*. New York: Basic Books, 1967, pp. 313–328.

———, ed. 1951a. *Organization and Pathology of Thought*. New York: Columbia University Press.

———. 1951b. States of Consciousness: A Psychopathological and Psychodynamic View. In *Collected Papers*. New York: Basic Books, 1967, pp. 385–404.

———. 1951c. The Autonomy of the Ego. In *Collected Papers*. New York: Basic Books, 1967, pp. 357–367.

———. 1952. Projective Techniques and the Theory of Thinking. In *Collected Papers*. New York: Basic Books, 1967, pp. 461–469.

———. 1953. On the Psychoanalytic Theory of Affects. In *Collected Papers*. New York: Basic Books, 1967, pp. 476–512.

———. 1956. The Psychoanalytic Theory of Consciousness and the Study of Dreams. Lecture to the Detroit Psychoanalytic Society, January.

———. 1957a. Cognitive Structures. In *Collected Papers*. New York: Basic Books, 1967, pp. 631–664.

———. 1957b. The Theory of Ego Autonomy: A Generalization. *Collected Papers*. New York: Basic Books, 1967, pp. 722–744.

———. 1958. A Historical Survey of Psychoanalytic Ego Psychology. In *Collected Papers*. New York: Basic Books, 1967, pp. 745–757.

———. 1959a. The Structure of Psychoanalytic Theory: A Systematizing Attempt. *Psychol. Issues*, Monogr. 6. New York: International Universities Press, 1960.

———. 1959b. The Theory of Attention Cathexis: An Economic and Structural Attempt at the Explanation of Cognitive Processes. In *Collected Papers*. New York: Basic Books, 1967, pp. 778–794.

———. 1960. On the Psychoanalytic Theory of Motivation. In *Collected Papers*. New York: Basic Books, 1967, pp. 853–915.

Rapaport, D. & M. M. Gill. 1959. The Points of View and Assumptions of

Metapsychology. In Rapaport, *Collected Papers*. New York: Basic Books, 1967, pp. 795–811.

Rapaport, D., M. M. Gill & R. Schafer. 1945–1946. *Diagnostic Psychological Testing*, 2 vols. Chicago: Year-Book Publishers.

Razran, G. 1955. Conditioning and Perception. *Psychol. Rev.*, 62: 83–95.

Rechtschaffen, A. & D. Foulkes. 1965. Effect of Visual Stimuli on Dream Content. *Percept. Motor Skills*, 20: 1149–1160.

Rechtschaffen, A., P. Hauri & M. Zeitlin. 1966. Auditory Awakening Thresholds in REM and NREM Sleep Stages. *Percept. Motor Skills*, 22: 927–942.

Reich, W. 1949. *Character-Analysis*, 3rd ed. New York: Orgone Institute Press.

Riesen, A. H. 1958. Plasticity of Behavior: Psychological Aspects. In H. F. Harlow & C. N. Woolsey, eds., *Biological and Biochemical Bases of Behavior*. Madison: University of Wisconsin Press, pp. 425–450.

———. 1960. Effects of Stimulus Deprivation on the Development and Atrophy of the Visual Sensory System. *Amer. J. Orthopsychiat.*, 30: 23–36.

Rosenthal, R. 1966. *Experimenter Effects in Behavioral Research*. New York: Appleton.

Rosett, H. L., H. Robbins & W. S. Watson. 1967. Standardization and Construct Validity of the Physiognomic Cue Test. *Percept. Motor Skills*, 24: 403–420.

———. 1968. Physiognomic Perception as a Cognitive Control Principle. *Percept. Motor Skills*, 26: 707–719.

Rubinfine, D. L. 1967. Notes on a Theory of Reconstruction. *Brit. J. Med. Psychol.*, 40: 195–206.

Rubinstein, B. B. 1965. Psychoanalytic Theory and the Mind-Body Problem. In N. S. Greenfield & W. C. Lewis, eds., *Psychoanalysis and Current Biological Thought*. Madison: University of Wisconsin Press, pp. 35–56.

———. 1967. Explanation and Mere Description: A Metascientific Examination of Certain Aspects of the Psychoanalytic Theory of Motivation. In R. R. Holt, ed., Motives and Thought: Psychoanalytic Essays in Honor of David Rapaport. *Psychol. Issues*, Monogr. 18/19: 20–77. New York: International Universities Press.

Rubinstein, D. 1952. Physiognomic Perception. Unpublished master's thesis, University of Kansas.

Rycroft, C. 1966. Introduction: Causes and Meaning. In *Psychoanalysis Observed*. London: Constable, pp. 7–22.

Sandler, J., *et al.* 1962. The Classification of Superego Material in the Hampstead Index. *Psychoanal. Study Child*, 17: 107–127. New York: International Universities Press.

Sandler, J. & H. Nagera. 1963. Aspects of the Metapsychology of Fantasy. *Psychoanal. Study Child*, 18: 159–194. New York: International Universities Press.

Sandler, J. & B. Rosenblatt. 1962. The Concept of the Representational World. *Psychoanal. Study Child*, 17: 128–145. New York: International Universities Press.

Schafer, R. 1948. *The Clinical Application of Psychological Tests*. New York: International Universities Press.

———. 1954. *Psychoanalytic Interpretation in Rorschach Testing*. New York: Grune & Stratton.

———. 1958. Regression in the Service of the Ego: The Relevance of a Psychoanalytic Concept for Personality Assessment. In G. Lindzey, ed., *Assessment of Human Motives*. New York: Rinehart, pp. 119–148.

Schafer, R. & G. Murphy. 1943. The Role of Autism in a Visual Figure-Ground Relationship. *J. Exp. Psychol.*, 32: 335–343.

Scheerer, M. & J. Lyons. 1957. Line Drawings and Matching Responses to Words. *J. Pers.*, 25: 251–273.

Schilder, P. 1924. *Medical Psychology*. New York: International Universities Press, 1953.

Schlesinger, H. J. 1954. Cognitive Attitudes in Relation to Susceptibility to Interference. *J. Pers.*, 22: 354–374.

———. 1964. The Place of Forgetting in Memory Functioning. In W. G. Niederland, rep., Scientific Proceedings—Panel Reports: Memory and Repression. *J. Amer. Psychoanal. Assn.* (1965), 13: 619–633.

Schur, M. 1960. Phylogenesis and Ontogenesis of Affect- and Structure-Formation and the Phenomenon of Repetition Compulsion. *Int. J. Psych-Anal.*, 41: 275–287.

———. 1966. *The Id and the Regulatory Principles of Mental Functioning*. New York: International Universities Press.

Schwartz, F. & R. O. Rouse. 1961. The Activation and Recovery of Associations. *Psychol. Issues*, Monogr. 9. New York: International Universities Press.

Schwartz, F. & P. H. Schiller. 1967. Rapaport's Theory of Attention Cathexis. *Bull. Menninger Clin.*, 31: 3–17.

———. 1970. A Psychoanalytic Model of Attention and Learning. *Psychol. Issues*, Monogr. 23. New York: International Universities Press.

Sears, R. R. 1936. Functional Abnormalities of Memory with Special Reference to Amnesia. *Psychol. Bull.*, 33: 229–274.

Segal, S. J. 1967. Patterns of Response to Thirst in an Imaging Task (Perky Technique) as a Function of Cognitive Style. Paper presented to Eastern Psychological Association, Boston, April.

Segal, S. J. & M. Glicksman. 1967. Relaxation and the Perky Effect: The

Influence of Body Position on Judgments of Imagery. *Amer. J. Psychol.*, 80: 257–262.

Shakow, D. 1960. The Recorded Psychoanalytic Interview as an Objective Approach to Research in Psychoanalysis. *Psychoanal. Quart.*, 29: 82–97.

Sherif, M. 1936. *The Psychology of Social Norms.* New York: Harper.

Shevrin, H. & L. Luborsky. 1958. The Measurement of Preconscious Perception in Dreams and Images: An Investigation of the Poetzl Phenomenon. *J. Abnorm. Soc. Psychol.*, 56: 285–294.

Shevrin, H. & D. E. Fritzler. 1968a. Visual Evoked Response Correlates of Unconscious Mental Processes. *Science*, 161: 295–298.

———. 1968b. Brain Response Correlates of Repressiveness. *Psychol. Rep.*, 23: 887–892.

Shevrin, H., W. H. Smith & D. E. Fritzler. 1969. Repressiveness as a Factor in the Subliminal Activation of Brain and Verbal Responses. *J. Nerv. Ment. Dis.*, 149: 261–269.

Silverman, A. J., S. I. Cohen, B. M. Schmavonian & G. Greenberg. 1961. Psychophysiological Investigations in Sensory Deprivation: The Body-Field Dimension. *Psychosomat. Med.*, 23: 48–61.

Silverman, J. 1964a. Perceptual Control of Stimulus Intensity in Paranoid and Nonparanoid Schizophrenia. *J. Nerv. Ment. Dis.*, 139: 545–549.

———. 1964b. Scanning-Control Mechanism and "Cognitive Filtering" in Paranoid and Non-Paranoid Schizophrenia. *J. Consult. Psychol.*, 28: 385–393.

———. 1964c. The Problem of Attention in Research and Theory in Schizophrenia. *Psychol. Rev.*, 71: 352–379.

———. 1967. Variations in Cognitive Control and Psychophysiological Defense in the Schizophrenias. *Psychosomat. Med.*, 29: 225–251.

Silverman, L. H. 1966. A Technique for the Study of Psychodynamic Relationships: The Effects of Subliminally Presented Aggressive Stimuli on the Production of Pathological Thinking in a Schizophrenic Population. *J. Consult. Psychol.*, 30: 103–111.

Silverman, L. H. & S. E. Silverman. 1967. The Effects of Subliminally Presented Drive Stimuli on the Cognitive Functioning of Schizophrenics. *J. Project. Tech.*, 31: 78–85.

Silverman, L. H. & R. H. Spiro. 1967. A Further Investigation of the Effects of Subliminal Aggressive Stimulation on the Ego Functioning of Schizophrenics. *J. Consult. Psychol.*, 31: 225–232.

———. 1968. The Effects of Subliminal, Supraliminal and Vocalized Aggression on the Ego Functioning of Schizophrenics. *J. Nerv. Ment. Dis.*, 146: 50–61.

Singer, J. L. 1966. *Daydreaming: An Introduction to the Experimental Study of Inner Experience.* New York: Random House.

Skinner, B. F. 1957. *Verbal Behavior*. New York: Appleton.

———. 1963. Behaviorism at Fifty. *Science*, 140: 951–958.

Smith, G. J. W. 1952. *Interpretations of Behavior Sequences*. Lund, Swe.: Gleerup.

Smith, G. J. W. & G. S. Klein. 1953. Cognitive Controls in Serial Behavior Patterns. *J. Pers.*, 22: 188–213.

Smith, G. J. W., D. P. Spence & G. S. Klein. 1959. Subliminal Effects of Verbal Stimuli. *J. Abnorm. Soc. Psychol.*, 59: 167–176.

Smith, K. U. 1962. *Delayed Sensory Feedback and Behavior*. Philadelphia: Saunders.

Smith, K. U. & W. M. Smith. 1962. *Perception and Motion: An Analysis of Space-Structured Behavior*. Philadelphia: Saunders.

Smith, M. B. 1952. Social Psychology and Group Processes. *Ann. Rev. Psychol.*, 3: 175–204.

Smith, W. M., J. W. McCrary & K. U. Smith. 1960. Delayed Visual Feedback and Behavior. *Science*, 132: 1013–1014.

Solomon, P., *et al.*, eds. 1961. *Sensory Deprivation*. Cambridge, Mass.: Harvard University Press.

Spence, D. P. 1961a. An Experimental Test of Schema Interaction. *J. Abnorm. Soc. Psychol.*, 62: 611–615.

———. 1961b. The Multiple Effects of Subliminal Stimuli. *J. Pers.*, 29: 40–53.

———. 1967. Subliminal Perception and Perceptual Defense: Two Sides of a Single Problem. *Behav. Sci.*, 12: 183–193.

Spence, D. P. & C. M. Gordon. 1967. Activation and Measurement of an Early Oral Fantasy: An Exploratory Study. *J. Amer. Psychoanal. Assn.*, 15: 99–129.

Sperling, G. 1963. A Model for Visual Memory Tasks. *Human Factors*, 5: 19–31.

Stein, M. H. 1965. States of Consciousness in the Analytic Situation. In M. Schur, ed., *Drives, Affects, Behavior*, Vol. 2. New York: International Universities Press, pp. 60–86.

Stone, L. 1961. *The Psychoanalytic Situation*. New York: International Universities Press.

Storch, A. 1924. *The Primitive Archaic Forms of Inner Experience and Thought in Schizophrenia*. New York: Nervous and Mental Disease Publishing Co.

Strachey, J., *et al.* 1962. The Emergence of Freud's Fundamental Hypotheses [Appendix to "The Neuro-Psychoses of Defence"]. In *Standard Edition*, 3: 62–68. London: Hogarth.

Stratton, G. M. 1897. Vision Without Inversion of the Retinal Image. *Psychol. Rev.*, 4: 341–360, 463–481.

Straus, E. W. 1952. The Upright Posture. *Psychiat. Quart.*, 26: 529–561.

Stroop, J. R. 1935. Studies of Interference in Serial Verbal Reactions. *J. Exper. Psychol.*, 18: 643–662.

Stross, L. & H. Shevrin. 1968. Thought Organization in Hypnosis and the Waking State: The Effects of Subliminal Stimulation in Different States of Consciousness. *J. Nerv. Ment. Dis.*, 147: 272–288.

Tajfel, H. 1957. Value and the Perceptual Judgment of Magnitude. *Psychol. Rev.*, 64: 192–204.

Thurstone, L. L. 1944. *A Factorial Study of Perception.* Chicago: University of Chicago Press.

Tolman, E. C. 1948. Cognitive Maps in Rats and Man. *Psychol. Rev.*, 55: 189–208.

———. 1949. The Nature and Functioning of Wants. *Psychol. Rev.*, 56: 357–369.

———. 1951. A Psychological Model. In T. Parsons & E. A. Shils, eds., *Toward a General Theory of Action.* Cambridge, Mass.: Harvard University Press, pp. 276–361.

Tomkins, S. S. 1962. *Affects, Imagery, Consciousness.* New York: Springer.

Troland, L. 1932. *The Principles of Psychophysiology.* Vol. 3: *Cerebration and Action.* New York: Van Nostrand.

Tyler, L. E. 1956. *The Psychology of Human Differences,* 2nd ed. New York: Appleton.

Uexküll, J. von. 1934. A Stroll Through the Worlds of Animals and Men. In C. H. Schiller, ed., trans., *Instinctive Behavior.* New York: International Universities Press, 1957, pp. 5–80.

Urbantschitsch, V. 1907. *Über Subjektive Optische Anschauungsbilder.* Vienna: Deuticke.

Vinacke, W. E. 1962. Motivation as a Complex Problem. In M. R. Jones, ed., *Nebraska Symposium on Motivation 1962.* Lincoln: University of Nebraska Press, pp. 1–46.

Voor, J. H. 1956. Subliminal Perception and Subception. *J. Psychol.*, 41: 437–458.

Waelder, R. 1960. *Basic Theory of Psychoanalysis.* New York: International Universities Press.

Wallach, H. 1949. Some Considerations Concerning the Relation Between Perception and Cognition. *J. Pers.*, 18: 6–13.

———. 1955. Memory Effects in Perception. Symposium on Recent Trends in Perception Theory. *Acta Psychol.*, 11: 180.

Wallach, H. & P. Austin. 1954. Recognition and the Localization of Visual Traces. *Amer. J. Psychol.*, 67: 338–340.

Waugh, N. C. & D. A. Norman. 1965. Primary Memory. *Psychol. Rev.*, 72: 89–104.

Werner, H. 1940. *Comparative Psychology of Mental Development,* rev. ed. New York: International Universities Press, 1957.

————. 1945. Motion and Motion Perception: A Study on Vicarious Functioning. *J. Psychol.*, 19: 317–327.

Werner, H. & B. Kaplan. 1957. Symbolic Mediation and Organization of Thought: An Experimental Approach by Means of the Line Schematization Technique. *J. Psychol.*, 43: 3–25.

Werner, H. & B. D. Thuma. 1942. A Deficiency in the Perception of Apparent Motion in Children with Brain Injury. *Amer. J. Psychol.*, 55: 58–67.

Werner, H. & S. Wapner. 1949. Sensory-Tonic Field Theory of Perception. *J. Pers.*, 18: 88–107.

Wertheimer, M. (1923), Laws of Organization in Perceptual Forms. In *A Source Book of Gestalt Psychology*, ed. W. D. Ellis. New York: Humanities Press, 1950, pp. 71–88.

White, R. W. 1963. Ego and Reality in Psychoanalytic Theory: A Proposal Regarding Independent Ego Energies. *Psychol. Issues*, Monogr. 11. New York: International Universities Press.

Wiener, N. 1948. *Cybernetics*. New York: Wiley.

Witkin, H. A. 1949. Perception of Body Position and of the Position of the Visual Field. *Psychol. Monogr.* 63 (7, Whole No. 302).

————. 1950. Individual Differences in Ease of Perception of Embedded Figures. *J. Pers.*, 19: 1–15.

————. 1965. Psychological Differentiation and Forms of Pathology. *J. Abnorm. Psychol.*, 70: 317–336.

Witkin, H. A., et al. 1954. *Personality Through Perception: An Experimental and Clinical Study*. New York: Harper.

Wolitzky, D. L. 1967a. Effect of Food Deprivation on Perception-Cognition: A Comment. *Psychol. Bull.*, 68: 342–344.

————. 1967b. Cognitive Control and Cognitive Dissonance. *J. Pers. Soc. Psychol.*, 5: 486–490.

Woodworth, R. S. 1918. *Dynamic Psychology*. New York: Columbia University Press.

————. 1937. Situation- and Goal-Set. *Amer. J. Psychol.*, 50: 130–140.

————. 1947. Reënforcement of Perception. *Amer. J. Psychol.*, 60: 119–124.

Woodworth, R. S. & H. Schlosberg. 1954. *Experimental Psychology*, rev. ed. New York: Holt.

Wright, H. F. 1937. The Influence of Barriers upon Strength of Motivation. *Contr. Psychol. Theory*, 1(Whole No. 3).

Zangwill, O. L. 1937. A Study of the Significance of Attitude in Recognition. *Brit. J. Psychol.*, 28: 12–17.

————. 1960. Speech. In *Handbook of Physiology, Section I: Neurophysiology*, Vol. 3, ed. J. Field, H. W. Magoun & V. E. Hall. Washington, D.C.: American Physiological Society, pp. 1709–1722.

Zaporozhets, A. V. 1954. Development of Voluntary Movements. In

Communications at the XIV International Congress of Psychology. Montreal, Academy of Pedagogical Sciences of RSFSR, pp. 68–76.

Zetzel, E. R. 1964. Repression of Traumatic Experience and the Learning Process. In W. G. Niederland, rep., Scientific Proceedings—Panel Reports: Memory and Repression. *J. Amer. Psychoanal. Assn.* (1965), 13: 619–633.

Zietz, K. & H. Werner. 1927. Über die Dynamische Struktur der Bewegung. *Z. Psychol.*, 105: 226–249.

Zubek, J. P. & L. Wilgosh. 1963. Prolonged Immobilization of the Body: Changes in Performance and in the Electroencephalogram. *Science.* 140: 306–308.

Index

Osgood, C. E., 221
Ostow, M., 366
Ostwald, P. F., 328
Oswald, I., 339

Part-to-whole relations, looseness and firmness in, 75, 79
Paul, I. H., 103, 229, 241, 242, 247, 250, 266, 271–273, 293, 308, 360
Penfield, W., 304, 359
Perception, 40, 45, 62, 123, 128, 161, 195, 212–213, 248–250, 282, 303; active nature of, 72; artistic, 81–83, 90, 217–218, 254–255, 403; attribution in, 76–79; and background stimuli, 323; and behavior, 4, 56–57, 98; of brain-injured, 68, 151; of change and nonchange, 67; and conception, 81–83, 216–219, 225, 226; constancy in, 70, 77–78; distorted, 40–42, 45, 46, 71, 106–107, 109, 110, 215, 221; in dreams, 249; effectiveness and reality-attunedness of, 7, 11, 12, 41, 42, 45–48, 61, 92, 101, 112, 130, 160, 207–208, 215–221, 250, 257, 259; experience of, 66–67, 69, 71, 73–74, 76, 79, 85, 250; functionalist view of, 5, 8, 48–49, 112, 131–133, 160; laboratory experiments in, 56–61, 83, 84, 92–101, 103–106, 108, 112, 114, 215, 248–249, 251–252; laws of, 258–259; learning theory of, 49; memory effects in, 52; and motivation, 3–5, 7–11, 13, 37, 39–46, 51–58, 62, 68, 71, 78, 98–99, 105–114, 165–167, 213–214, 257, 360–364; New Look in, 6–8, 39–40; novelty in, 80–83, 397, 404; and personality, 4, 5, 8–10, 38, 42, 44, 61, 71, 110–112, 129–133, 141–142, 167, 201; preconscious, 91, 262; and psychoanalysis, 37, 236; psychophysical approach to, 3, 10, 41, 49–55, 70, 112; recognition in, 81; versus registration, 251; as response, 114; salience in, 53, 63, 64, 70, 73–79, 81–83, 96, 99; schematic versus literal, 51–54; selectivity in, 10–11,

53–55, 64, 70–71, 73, 74, 79, 112, 215–219; and social psychology, 38–39; spatial, 103. *See also* Cognition; Defense, perceptual; Discrimination, perceptual; Individual differences; Intraindividual consistencies; Registration; Stimuli
Perceptual attitudes, 133–139, 141–146, 158–161, 166; and defense, 155–157; sensory-tonic events in, 146, 151. *See also* Cognitive controls
Perceptual development, 218–219
Perceptual system, adaptive properties of, 132–133, 135–138, 143–144
Personality, 231, 349; abnormal and normal in, 120–121, 126; constancy of, 32–33, 42, 44; equilibrium of, 131–132, 138; and perception, 4, 5, 8, 38, 42, 44, 61, 110–112, 129–133; research in, 117–127; theory of, 9, 10, 38, 130–132. *See also* Individual differences; Intraindividual consistencies
Perspective, 78
Phi-phenomenon. *See* Apparent movement
Physiognomic experience, 65, 151–155, 160, 223, 410–411
Piaget, J., 78, 208, 228, 231, 361, 386
Pieron, H., 217
Pine, F., 244, 266, 274, 293, 301, 360
Polanyi, M., 76, 341
Postman, L., 129, 166, 167, 173, 174, 177, 302
Posture, 12, 94, 101–105, 109, 254, 293, 340
Pötzl, O., 42, 44, 240, 241, 243, 266, 273, 292
Poussin, N., 90
Pribram, K., 35
Primary process, 6, 12, 15, 24, 27–28, 171, 173, 214, 227–228, 238, 247, 249, 252, 253, 257, 260, 282, 285, 288, 325–327, 342, 344, 352; mechanisms of, 283, 284, 289–291
Projection, 51, 103, 110
Proshansky, H., 37
Psychoanalysis, 14–20, 91, 103, 119, 155–157, 170–172, 198, 199, 203, 227,

464 / Index